Studies in European Economic Law and Regulation

Volume 13

AF865534

This series is devoted to the analysis of European Economic Law. The series' scope covers a broad range of topics within economics law including, but not limited to, the relationship between EU law and WTO law; free movement under EU law and its impact on fundamental rights; antitrust law; trade law; unfair competition law; financial market law; consumer law; food law; and health law. These subjects are approached both from doctrinal and interdisciplinary perspectives.

The series accepts monographs focusing on a specific topic, as well as edited collections of articles covering a specific theme or collections of articles. All contributions are subject to rigorous double-blind peer-review.

More information about this series at http://www.springer.com/series/11710

Karin Fløistad

The EEA Agreement in a Revised EU Framework for Welfare Services

Springer

Karin Fløistad
Independent Appeals Board for Competition
Cases in Norway, EEA Competition Authority
Simonsen Vogt Wiig Lawfirm
Oslo, Norway

ISSN 2214-2037 ISSN 2214-2045 (electronic)
Studies in European Economic Law and Regulation
ISBN 978-3-030-06961-2 ISBN 978-3-319-95043-3 (eBook)
https://doi.org/10.1007/978-3-319-95043-3

Softcover re-print of the Hardcover 1st edition 2018

This Springer imprint is published by the registered company Springer Nature Switzerland AG
The registered company address is: Gewerbestrasse 11, 6330 Cham, Switzerland

Preface

How are the Contracting Parties to the European Economic Area (EEA) Agreement affected by the revised European Union (EU) constitutional framework for welfare services? This is the key question analysed in this book. The term welfare services means a broad range of services wholly or partly financed through public funds such as public healthcare and educational services (Part I), various social services (Part II) and public utilities such as transport and public broadcasting (Part III). This book demonstrates how the EU/EFTA institutions applying EEA law have attempted a homogenous development of the EEA integration process despite the EU's altered constitutional framework, and how these attempts create both substantive (legal doctrine) and institutional problems. The author engages in the debate from the point of view of the EU Treaty revisions reflecting concern for the social dimension of the market integration process. The findings indicate that although these Treaty revisions have not been reflected in amendments to the EEA agreement, a more advanced understanding of the concept of market integration has also emerged in the EEA integration process. These findings add a new element to the supranational character of the EEA Agreement. Despite the inherent challenge posed by European solidarity to sovereign national welfare provision, the EEA Agreement moves into the welfare sphere, giving unprecedented powers in particular to the EFTA institutions. This book analyses the controversial and disputed consequences for the EU Member States of the EEA Agreement to enlarge the geographical area of application for the provisions on welfare services. The urgent need for better transparency of the process is the recurring theme. The EFTA States are not only associated with the EU Member States; they are adapted and arguably almost assimilated into the internal market through the decision making of the EU/EFTA institutions applying the EEA Agreement. The book demonstrates the complexities involved and calls for political decision making on the part of the Contracting Parties to the EEA Agreement.

The origin of this project stems from long before the Brexit referendum in the United Kingdom in June 2016. Since then, all EU external relations agreements have gained renewed interest in particular in regard to their inspiration for the creation of a new form of agreement between the EU and the UK after the UK has left the Union. The EEA Agreement provides the closest model of integration for non-Member States into the internal market. As such the EEA Agreement is more relevant than ever and certainly high on the agenda both politically and judicially in the Brexit debate. This book sheds light on important aspects of this model of integration in particular with the aim of increasing the understanding of key principles of homogeneity and dynamism.

Oslo, Norway
May 2018

Karin Fløistad

Acknowledgements

I have been fortunate to benefit from generous support and insights provided by a number of people in writing this book which is based on my doctoral thesis from the European University Institute in Florence. First of all, my gratitude belongs to my supervisor Professor Marise Cremona for her unwavering trust, encouragement and wonderful guidance. I have much appreciated our discussions, and I am indebted to her support throughout the years of writing. She has provided invaluable ideas and perspectives on how to shape the analysis and on how to articulate the arguments.

At the European University Institute, a great number of other professors, fellow PhD researchers and participants at seminars, conferences, workshops and working groups have contributed with helpful remarks and fruitful discussions. My greatest tribute should be paid to this unique institution always providing an inspiring academic context for excellent research.

The Centre of European Law at the University of Oslo has also provided generous support in finishing this project. My thanks go to the professors, assistant professors and doctoral researchers at the centre. Inger M. Hemre, the chief librarian, was a great help in finalising the thesis and provided efficient assistance and access to sought-after material day and night.

I would also like to sincerely thank Professor Halvard Haukeland Fredriksen at the University of Bergen who offered valuable comments and constructive feedback in particular on issues concerning general EEA law as well as on free movement of persons in the EEA.

My gratitude must also be extended to my wonderful colleagues both from my former job at the Attorney General's office and from my present job at the law firm Simonsen Vogt Wiig AS. Thank you for your patience and continued assistance.

These acknowledgments would not be complete without thanking my family.

Contents

Chapter 1
Introduction

1.1 Aim and Research Question

How are the Contracting Parties to the European Economic Area (EEA) Agreement affected by the revised European Union (EU) constitutional framework for welfare services? This is the key question analysed in this book. The academic discussion on welfare services in the EU has become rich over the years. However, to date the debate has almost entirely left out the development of EEA law in this field. The present contribution aims to fill this lacuna regarding both impact of EEA law on European Free Trade Association (EFTA)[1] states and on EU Member States as Contracting Parties to the EEA Agreement.[2] A recurring theme is the urgent need for better transparency of the EEA integration process in the field of welfare services and a call for political decision making on the part of the Contracting Parties to the Agreement in this sensitive area.

Here, the term welfare services refers to a broad range of services wholly or partly financed through public funds, such as public healthcare and educational services, various social services and public utilities such as transport and public broadcasting.[3] The research question is asked in the context of the evolution of the EU

---

[1] EFTA is the European Free Trade Association countries. The EFTA States that are members of the EEA Agreement include Iceland, Liechtenstein and Norway. Switzerland is a member of the EFTA but it is not party to the EEA Agreement. For the sake of simplicity the term EFTA States will be used for Iceland, Liechtenstein and Norway.

[2] This subject was briefly touched upon by Henrik Bull in his contribution on the enlarged EEA after the accession of former Eastern European states in Bull (2006).

[3] See the distinction between core welfare services and the outer ring of the welfare services in Damjanovic and De Witte (2009), p. 54 with further references. Core welfare services include public health services, public education, various social services and housing services and the outer ring of the welfare services include public utilities such as infrastructure, transport, energy and public broadcasting.

K. Fløistad, *The EEA Agreement in a Revised EU Framework for Welfare Services*, Studies in European Economic Law and Regulation 13,
https://doi.org/10.1007/978-3-319-95043-3_1

project from an economic community to a union built on a wider system of protection of values.[4] The wider system of protection of values includes some degree of general social protection for European citizens, the balancing of welfare concerns in state aid review and a move to develop a form of European solidarity.

Each EU Member State and EFTA State has independently of the EU and of the EEA Agreement established models for financing and delivering welfare services to its population. These models are different, but they are all based on the principle of universal access and reflect values of community and solidarity. Hence, the provision of welfare services in both the EU Member States and in the EFTA States is organised along national boundaries. The task to set aside public funds for the provision of welfare services and hence also to decide how to spend them is traditionally considered the primary responsibility of each state and is commonly recognised to belong to the category of core state functions.[5] This position is increasingly challenged by the European integration process both in the EU and in the EEA legal orders. The legal framework underpinning the challenge is, nevertheless, different.

In contrast to the revised constitutional framework in the EU legal order introducing new primary law in the Treaty of Maastricht (1993), followed by the Treaties of Amsterdam and Nice (1999, 2001) and finally culminating with the Treaty of Lisbon (2009), the EEA legal order does not include corresponding provisions. The EEA legal order is premised on the legal framework for the original economic community (based on the Treaty of Rome and the single European Act) with the in-principle limited economic objective of extending the market to include the three EFTA States through the four freedoms and the competition rules. The provisions of the main part of the EEA Agreement have not been altered either to encompass a wider system of protection of values or to ensure general citizenship-like social rights or to develop a principle of solidarity between the Contracting Parties.

However, within the scope of the EEA Agreement, the principles of dynamism and homogeneity aim at achieving substantive parity with the developments in the EU legal order. National welfare provision is affected both by the four freedoms, in particular the right to free movement of persons and services, and the competition rules, in particular the prohibition of state aid. Thus, welfare provision is not outside the scope of the EEA Agreement. The principles of dynamism and homogeneity apply, however, according to the wording of the EEA Agreement to the interpretation and application 'of the provisions of this Agreement, insofar as they are identical in substance to corresponding rules of the Treaty'.[6]

[4] Now Article 1 TEU.

[5] Together with taxation powers and matters of justice and security, see i.a. Communication from the EFTA Surveillance Authority, The Notion on State Aid No 3/17/COL, 18.01.17, see Sect. 2.2 on public powers and generally on the concept of economic activity and undertaking. The Authority's communication parallels the communication from the Commission, Commission Notice on the notion of State aid as referred to in Article 107(1) of the Treaty on the Functioning of the European Union, 2016/C 262/01.

[6] Article 6 EEA Agreement.

The principles of dynamism and homogeneity in the EEA integration process were never seen to include a power for the EU/EFTA institutions applying EEA law to remedy the lack of parallel legal provisions. In other words, a limit to this principle was always perceived to lie here. This understanding was also expressed by the EFTA Court in early case law like Cases E-1/01 Einarsson and E-1/02 Post-doc[7] and is very much in line with the general understanding of the role of courts and the role of surveillance authorities. The institutions act within the agreed framework of the provisions and do not create new treaty provisions.[8]

The EEA integration process has, despite its character of being based on an international agreement, developed certain characteristics of a supranational entity. This can be seen in particular in the field of state liability.[9] The same dynamic is clear from the EFTA institutions' pragmatic approach to principles developed by the Court of Justice of the European Union (CJEU)[10] and the paralleling of soft law in state aid supervision.[11] Hence, the nature of the EEA Agreement has changed significantly as a result of accepting relevant case law from the European courts and administrative practices from the European Commission as legal sources for further developing the EEA integration process. Examples include important court-made principles such as the principle of fundamental rights protection,[12] access to justice and effective judicial protection[13] as well as a number of policy decisions in the field of state aid involving research, development and innovation, environmental protection, regional development and infrastructure to be included in the EEA.[14]

---

[7] Both of which are commented on later in Part II.

[8] This position may be contrasted with a statement made by the president of the EFTA Court, Baudenbacher (2013): 'The EEA joint Committee has no competence to change the main part of the EEA Agreement no matter whether the TFEU or the text reference for the EEA Agreement has been amended. The only institutions which may—by way of case-law—'amend' the main part of the EEA Agreement are the EEA Courts: the ECJ, the General Court and the EFTA Court'. For a similar perspective as the author see various contributions from Dr. Pal Wenneras, the last one being in the recent Arnesen et al. (2018), pp. 209–248. See also the Case of Jabbi, E-28/15 analysed later in Part II.

[9] Fredriksen (2013a).

[10] On this, see Arnesen et al. (2018) and Burri and Pirker (2013), pp. 207–229; see also Hreinsson (2014), pp. 349–391.

[11] The European Commission has developed an extensive body of soft law, i.e. Guidelines, Communications and Notices for assessing compatibility of national measures with the prohibition of state aid. Corresponding soft law is applied by the EFTA Surveillance Authority in the EEA.

[12] Referred to by the EFTA Court in a number of cases, see i.a. E-8/97 TV 1000 Sweden v Norway, paragraph 26; E-2/02 Bellona v EFTA Surveillance, paragraph 37; E-2/03 Public Prosecutor v Ásgeirsson Authority, paragraph 23; E-12/10 The Surveillance Authority v Iceland, paragraph 6; E-15/10, Posten Norge AS v EFTA Surveillance Authority, paragraphs 85–86; E-4/11 Arnulf Clauder, paragraph 49; E-28/15 Jabbi. See for an analysis of the legal significance of the EU Charter of Fundamental Rights in the EEA, Fredriksen (2013b), pp. 371–399.

[13] See Case E-15/10 Posten Norge v ESA, paragraph 86; see also EFTA Court (2012); see also the analysis of Case E-3/11 Sigmarsson by Gudmundsdóttir (2012), pp. 2019–2038.

[14] See http://www.eftasurv.int/state-aid/legal-framework/state-aid-guidelines/ Other court-made principles generally seen as part of EEA law are the administrative principle of proportionality and protection of legitimate expectations.

This development of the EEA integration process is to some extent controversial and debated, but the overall picture is one of almost surprising acceptance from all parties involved.[15]

This book intends to engage in this debate from the point of view not primarily of court-developed principles from the CJEU but of the Treaty revisions that reflect the social concerns of the market integration process. The significance of taking this starting point is first of all that this dimension has not been systematically analysed before. However, more importantly, taking this starting point will eventually enable a conclusion that will say something more about the nature of the principles of homogeneity and dynamism and ultimately about the EEA integration process.

The thesis is situated in the context of empirical research. The method may be described as traditional analytical legal positivism. This methodology entails studying and presenting a coherent analysis of the relevant legal sources and material based on the view of the EEA legal order as a dynamic system of law. However, the thesis operates against the rich literature in particular in two fields of theoretical doctrines. First, the discussion in this thesis is informed by the doctrine of the rule of law and theories of democracy.[16] Tension here relates to acceptable legal methodology, the fine distinction between interpretation and creating new rules and the legitimacy of the legal institutions to make largely political choices. This theoretical doctrine also includes the debate surrounding sovereignty and obligations on states in international agreements.[17] The theoretical ground on which this thesis stands may be characterised as a classical approach where the rule of law is seen to impose restraints on the institutions applying the law, in particular by imposing legal limits on law-making power. A crucial matter is the designation of the institution(s) with the final say over interpretation and the power allocation when decisions have political implications. The thesis aims at being informed by the rule of law regarding the issue of restricting the application of discretion. The founding of the EEA was based on the EFTA States choice not to become members of the EU. The theoretical stance in this thesis is informed by this original political choice of the EFTA States and will therefore take a relatively traditional view of the relationship between international treaty obligations and domestic law while recognising the hybrid character of the EEA.

Second, modes of integration provide an important theoretical framework. This doctrine discusses the sophisticated and advanced concept of market integration no longer separated from socially oriented objectives but rather trying to align the

---

[15] Fredriksen and Franklin (2015), pp. 629–684.

[16] A recent contribution to the rule of law doctrine is Palombella and Walker (2009). This book originates based on an idea to identify a common thread and build a bridge between old and new ideas associated with the rule of law. See also the contribution regarding the EU as a supranational institution taking on a greater range of tasks whose effective performance involves the distribution of politically salient resources and reduces the capacity of the states themselves to perform these tasks, Follesdal and Hix (2006), pp. 533–562.

[17] On legal methodology and the EEA Agreement in the context of international agreements, see Arnesen and Stenvik (2015).

economic and the social dimensions.[18] Hence, this theory discusses the right balance between market- or economic-based integration and social concerns relevant for all the areas discussed in-depth in the various chapters of the thesis. This thesis does not take a normative stance regarding the right balance to align social and economic oriented objectives. Most importantly, the thesis does not take a stance regarding the right way forward for European integration (including the EEA integration process) regarding social issues. However, given that the field under examination includes underlying conflicts between economic policy and social protection the thesis takes a critical stance towards conflicts being resolved judicially or administratively. Based on a rule of law viewpoint this thesis argues for political decision making and clarity of rules to better address the complexities involved.

1.2 The Economic Aim of Creating the Internal Market and Welfare Services

From the very start, the EEA Agreement has to some extent influenced the provision of welfare services. The provision of welfare services touches in different ways on the core European *economic* aim to establish and maintain an internal market. First, the mobility of economically active persons depends on whether welfare services (typically social benefits) are provided on equal terms. Equal terms include the proper safeguarding of acquired welfare rights from the home state for EU/EEA migrants including their families and the treatment of nationals and EU/EEA migrants including their families alike in the host state. Second, the task of controlling state aid also applies to the provision of publicly financed welfare services. The control of state aid is an important means of ensuring that equal conditions of competition within the EEA are not distorted by the actions of states. With the adoption of the EEA Agreement, similar state aid rules to those existing in the EU legal order became applicable to the EFTA States with the EFTA Surveillance Authority responsible for the control of the EEA state aid rules when aid is granted by the EFTA States. For EU Member States the adoption of the EEA Agreement extended the application of the state aid rules to include the territories of the three EFTA States. The Commission is responsible for the control of the EEA state aid rules when aid is granted by the EU Member States.

The early recognition of the importance of the provision of welfare services for the internal market led to two sets of provisions in the Treaty of Rome reflecting the two different ways in which welfare services were addressed. The provision on

[18] Often referred to in the context of defining solidarity is Stjernø (2005). Stjernø defines solidarity as 'the preparedness to share resources by personal contribution to those in struggle or in need and through taxation and redistribution organized by the state', see Hervey (2011), p. 186. The perspective of vulnerability to market principles of complex welfare services based on solidarity is a perspective included in most of the literature on the EU and the national health care systems, see i.a. Hancher and Sauter (2012), Mossialos et al. (2010) and Hatzopoulos (2005), pp. 111–168.

social security to ensure worker mobility and the title of social policy dealt with labour law and gender issues, whereas the provision of public services was dealt with under the Treaty chapter on the rules on competition and were called services of general economic interest (SGEI) and state monopolies. However, given the sensitivity of the matter, the European economic project dealt with the provision of welfare services only insofar as necessary to make the project work.[19]

In the Rome Treaty, the necessity of including social policy seemed to arise essentially in order to ensure equal treatment of EU migrant workers for work-related benefits based on the view that social guarantees are of the essence for the very exercise of free movement of workers. Accordingly, the only explicit legislative competence was inserted among the free movement of workers provision through Article 51 European Economic Community (EEC) Treaty (now Article 48 Treaty on the Functioning of the European Union (TFEU)) paralleled in Article 29 EEA.[20] However, consistent with the European Court's approach in other fields, the CJEU applied the legislation on rights for moving workers in an expansive manner by continuously extending both the personal and substantive scope of these provisions.[21] The CJEU construed the term worker as broadly as possible to include basically any economically active person[22] and applied the principles on cross-border access to virtually all welfare benefits,[23] whereas they were originally assumed only to cover work-related benefits. Nevertheless, an important limitation remained in the Court's practice until the late 1990s. The impact on national welfare provision was limited to *economic* activity in the sense that the welfare rights based on EU law were limited to the economically active movers and their family members.[24]

As to the SGEI, Article 90 EEC Treaty (now Article 106 TFEU) paralleled in Article 59 EEA laid down that the competition and free movement rules were only to apply fully insofar as this application would not obstruct the performance, in law

[19] Damjanovic and De Witte (2009), p. 57.

[20] Regulation 3/58 of the Council 25 September 1958 concerning social security for migrant workers was put in place almost immediately but became of true practical relevance in its adapted version of Regulation 1408/71 on the application of social security schemes to employed persons, to self-employed persons and to members of their families moving within the community which followed shortly after the adoption of Regulation 1612/68 on freedom of movement of workers. Both are later replaced—Regulation 1408/71 by Regulation and 883/2004 and Regulation 1612/68 by Directive 2004/38 and Regulation 492/2011.

[21] See A. P. Van der Mei for a comprehensive analysis of the case law under previous Regulation 1408/71, Van der Mei (2003), See also Giubboni (2007), pp. 360–379; Spaventa (2007).

[22] For early case law regarding the broad definition of a worker; the nature of work, see Case Joined Cases 115 and 116/81 Adoui [2982] ECR 1665, the employment relationship, see Joined cases 389/87 and 390/87 Echternach [1982] ECR 723, the context of work, see Case 196/87 Steymann [1988] ECR 6159 and for part-time, see Case 53/81 Levin [1982] ECR 1035, for a recent case on the term worker, see Case C-46/12 L.N., EU:C:2013:97 discussed in Sect. 4.2.2.

[23] The concept covers all rights or benefits 'whether or not linked to a contract of employment', Case 207/78 Even [1979] ECR 2019, paragraph 22, Case C-249/83 Hoeckx [1985] ECR 973, paragraph 20.

[24] Damjanovic and De Witte (2009), p. 63.

or in fact, of the special general interest task inherent in these services.[25] Achieving this general interest task was, until the late 1980s, perceived as leaving the organisation and provision of these services within the full control of the Member States. Hence, state monopolies were accepted and, to some extent, seen to be both necessary and efficient in order to deliver the entrusted public service responsibility. However, in the late 1980s and 1990s, the process of liberalisation fundamentally changed the former structure of state monopolies for the provision of public services.[26] This change was consistent with the dominant economic theory at the time favouring privatisation and de-monopolisation.[27] The improvement of the efficiency of the provision of SGEI by means of liberalising certain sectors was related to the creation and the maintenance of the internal market. The discretionary powers for the Commission were limited to economic market-oriented public services, and the prohibition of state aid in the Treaty of Rome was limited to the preventive control system targeted at addressing distortions of competition.

1.3 Moving from Economic Community to Union: Significance for State Welfare Services Provision

The project to move the primarily economic community to a union has extended the impact of European integration on the national provision of welfare services to go beyond economic activity. While the core European economic aim remains important, additional European aims have emerged, in particular through various primary law changes in the EU legal order. Further welfare integration measures introducing greater cross-European homogeneity represent an ongoing debate in the EU.[28] This

---

[25] See the early Commission's Communications on SGEI; 1996, COM (96)443, COM 2001/C17/04 and 2007, COM(2007)725 as well as the 2003 Green Paper, COM (2003)270 and the 2004 White Paper, COM(2004)374, the recent SGEI package consist of the following documents (all paralleled in the EEA); Commission Notice on the notion of State aid as referred to in Article 107(1) of the Treaty on the Functioning of the European Union, 2016/C 262/01, 2012/21/EU: Commission Decision of 20 December 2011 on the application of Article 106(2) of the Treaty on the Functioning of the European Union to State aid in the form of public service compensation granted to certain undertakings entrusted with the operation of services of general economic interest, Communication from the Commission—European Union framework for State aid in the form of public service compensation (2011), Commission Regulation (EU) No 360/2012 of 25 April 2012 on the application of Articles 107 and 108 of the Treaty on the Functioning of the European Union to de minimis aid granted to undertakings providing services of general economic interest.

[26] In sectors like telecom, energy and transport, liberalisation is an on-going project including also increasingly sectors of communal welfare services.

[27] An economic theory which may still be characterised as dominant.

[28] The on-going debate in the EU legal order on the possible need to create greater cross-European homogeneity in the national organisational structures of the welfare state is outside the topic of this book, see for recent studies De Witte (2015), Sauter (2014) and Damjanovic (2013), pp. 1685–1718. For earlier studies see i.a. the discussion in projects on the EU and welfare published in Neergaard et al. (2009, 2010, 2013), Ross and Borgmann-Prebil (2010) and Cremona (2011).

thesis is, however, limited to the legal effects on the provision of national welfare services of the already-introduced legal changes in European integration process based on a wider system of protection of values.

Three central observations are made regarding the more concrete legal impact on the provision of welfare services caused by the revised EU constitutional framework.

First, the EU legal order, in particular through the case law from the CJEU, has extended free movement rights for patients and students based on their status as services recipients to impact more substantially with Member States' provision of publicly funded healthcare and educational services.

Second, the EU legal order, particularly through the case law from the CJEU, has developed to include non-economically active moving Union citizens into the group of beneficiaries of social rights both in the home and in the host state.[29] Limited cross-European solidarity implies that Member States are no longer sovereign to decide on access to welfare benefits for non-nationals.

Third, in the EU legal order, in particular through the decisional practice of the Commission, the scope of the competences to conduct a state aid review has continuously increased to also include almost all social services, significantly increasing the policymaking role of the Commission.[30] Interpreting the state aid review process to include a wide scope of activities in the field of providing welfare services increases EU institutional powers at the expense of EU Member States' own competence to organise their welfare systems. The state aid review entails a detailed and complicated assessment of compatibility where the EU institutions need to balance various policy objectives, including welfare concerns.[31]

The concrete legal impact on the provision of welfare services included in the three observations from the institutional practices—both case law and administrative practice—has in various ways been endorsed by the Member States in amendments to the Treaties and in a number of secondary legislation adopted to this effect, not least through the Citizens Directive legislating large parts of the case law on Union citizenship. This endorsement constitutes precisely the backdrop for the research question asked in this thesis on how the revised constitutional framework affects the Contracting Parties in the EEA.

---

[29] The case law is mostly based on an interpretation of the concept of Union citizenship, see Articles 20–25 TFEU and a vast amount of literature on Union citizenship.

[30] The limit of application of competition law to economic activity has not prevented the Commission to intervene in matters of social housing, public broadcasting and various other welfare services, see the 2011 package (revising the 2005-package) on the Commission's general policy support for SGEI and the Broadcasting guidelines from 2009 (replacing the guidelines from 2001), See also the interpretation by the Commission of changes in primary law, i.a. Treaty of Amsterdam, Protocol on the Systems of Public Broadcasting in the Member States (1997) now protocol 29 annexed to the TFEU and Protocol on Services of General Interest, OJ 2007, C 306/158.

[31] For an example of the so-called 'micro-management' of public service media, see the case analysis of Commission practices in the state aid review of public broadcasters in Donders (2015), pp. 68–87. See also the controversy on the Commission's and the Court's intervention in state housing policy, Reynolds (2015), pp. 259–280.

1.4 The EEA Agreement

1.4.1 Scope and Limits to the Dynamic Nature

The EEA Agreement is a special form of association created for states wanting close economic relations with the EU without becoming members of the Union. The Agreement's essential ambition is to strengthen and intensify trade and economic relations between the Contracting Parties. The overall aim of the Agreement is to include the EFTA States in large parts of the internal market while excluding selected areas of cooperation of the EU treaties. The Agreement is restricted to nationals of the EU and EFTA States leaving legislation concerning third-country nationals (TCNs) in principal outside. Furthermore, the Agreement does not cover important parts of the internal market leaving in principal tax harmonisation, the establishment of a customs union and common trade policy also outside the scope.[32] The Agreement applies only to a limited degree to fisheries and agriculture given that the EU Common Fisheries and Agricultural Policies are not part of the Agreement.[33] Finally, the Economic and Monetary Union, the Common Foreign and Security Policy and Justice and Home affairs are not part of the Agreement (Norway and Iceland participate in Schengen but this is an international cooperation outside the scope of the EEA Agreement and hence without the EFTA institutions such as the Authority and the Court playing a role).

The overall aim of the EEA Agreement is to extend the free movement of persons, goods, services and capital to the EFTA States: Iceland, Liechtenstein and Norway to provide for equal conditions of competition and to abolish discrimination on grounds of nationality. The dynamic nature of the Agreement is the mechanism to achieve this overall aim in a constantly evolving internal market.[34] Hence, a basic principle in the EEA Agreement is that it shall be dynamic in the sense that it shall develop in step with changes in EU law that lie within the scope of the EEA Agreement. The dynamic nature is meant to ensure a homogenous development

[32] The extent to which these exempted areas are still affected by EEA law is outside the topic of this book. For instance on the conformity of national tax rules the EFTA Court has handed down four significant cases, see Rust (2014), pp. 459–471.

[33] See also Article 8(3) EEA regarding products exempted from the Agreement. This provision regarding the scope of the Agreement was central in a recent case on agricultural products where the EFTA Surveillance Authority argued for a quite wide reaching application of the Agreement compared to earlier practices, compare Case E-4/04 Pedicel with Case E-1/16 Synnøve Finden, The Court did not agree with the Authority.

[34] Most literature on EEA law has praised the achievements of both the EFTA Court and the CJEU to ensure homogeneity in both of these aspects. For a recent contribution see Arnesen et al. (2018). See also several chapters in EFTA Court (2014); Skouris (2014), p. 5; Norberg (2014), p. 483; Barnard (2014), p. 168, and several analysis by Fredriksen such as Fredriksen and Franklin (2015), pp. 629–684 and for an earlier analysis see Fredriksen (2010a), pp. 731–760 with further references.

between EEA law and the internal market law of the EU.[35] Homogenous development includes both legislative homogeneity and homogeneous interpretation of EEA law and those provisions of EU law that are substantially reproduced in the EEA Agreement.[36] The continued substantial reproduction of provisions is ensured by decisions of the EEA Joint Committee[37] that incorporate novel EU legislation of relevance to the EEA into the Agreement.[38] New legal acts have been added continuously through amendments of the annexes and the protocols of the Agreement since the entry into force on 1 January 1994.[39] Formally, each change of the Agreement through the decisions in the Joint Committee is a new international legal obligation between the Contracting Parties.[40] The EEA Joint Committee is thus the *legislative* organ of the EEA. It is, however, not empowered to make new EEA-specific secondary legislation but only to copy and adjust existing EU secondary legislation.[41] This delimitation of applying this procedure is laid down in Article 102 EEA referring to new legislative acts 'governed by this Agreement'. The outer limits of what is 'governed by' the EEA Agreement are not always clear and hence this political question is decided by the representatives of the Contracting Parties in the EEA Joint Committee with a procedure regarding national constitutional requirements in Article 103 EEA.[42]

As far as legislative homogeneity between the EU and the EEA is concerned, the dynamic nature of the EEA Agreement does not include the main part of the Agreement (i.e. the part where (some) primary EU law is reproduced in the EEA).[43] Under Article 98 EEA, the EEA Joint Committee may only amend the annexes and

[35] The Agreement itself explicitly excludes part of the EU internal market from the association such as agriculture and fisheries see Article 8(3) EEA. It is self-evident that areas excluded from the Agreement are also excluded from the dynamic mechanism.

[36] References to the homogeneity objective can be found in recitals 4, 5 and 14 of the Preamble to the EEA Agreement and Articles 1(1), 6, 102, 105 and 106 EEA, see also the Agreement between the EFTA States on the establishment of a Surveillance Authority and a Court of Justice, OJ L 344, 31.1.1994 (the Surveillance and Court Agreement (SCA)) Article 3.

[37] The EEA Joint Committee is responsible for managing the EEA Agreement. Both the EU side and the EFTA side are represented in the Committee and each block speaks with one voice, see the rules of procedures adopted by Decision No 1/94 on 8 February 1994. The Committee meets on a monthly basis.

[38] Articles 93, 94 and 102 EEA.

[39] See for an overview of this in Europautvalget [2012] NOU 2012:2 Utenfor og innenfor, p. 108.

[40] See the procedure laid down in Article 102 EEA regarding new EU acts 'governed by this Agreement'.

[41] Sejersted (1997), p. 48.

[42] After the legislation has been incorporated into the EEA Agreement through a decision by the EEA Joint Committee it must be incorporated into national legislation, see Article 7 EEA. Decisions of the EEA Joint Committee incorporating legislation cannot be directly challenged before the EFTA Court nor can the EFTA Court decide on the validity of such decisions or of the acts incorporated, see however the EFTA Court's decision in CIBA, Case E-6/01, CIBA and others.

[43] There is however no primary and secondary law in the EEA at least structurally in the Agreement, it is all part of one international agreement, see for a more detailed analysis Fredriksen (2014), pp. 95–113, see for more on this point footnote 102.

some protocols, which means that only, in EU terms, secondary legislation is continually updated. The substantive provisions of the main part of the EEA Agreement, negotiated as they were in 1990–1992, still mirror the corresponding provisions of EU primary law as it stood at that time.[44] Thus, the subsequent amendments to EU primary law accomplished through the Treaties of Maastricht, Amsterdam, Nice and Lisbon are not reflected in the main part of the EEA Agreement and not included in the annexes or the protocols.[45] Thus, the dynamic nature of the agreement to ensure legislative homogeneity does not include EU primary law changes. This phenomenon in EEA law has been described as the widening gap between the EU Treaties and the EEA Agreement.[46] The widening gap includes the revised constitutional framework for the provision of welfare services in the EU legal order which is at centre stage in this project. First and foremost the widening gap challenges the Agreement's basic aim to secure a joint and parallel development of the legal orders of the EU and the EFTA States in areas covered by the Agreement.

1.4.2 Homogeneity as a Fundamental (Constitutional) Principle of the EEA

Homogeneity across the EEA is to be achieved in a particular institutional setting. The institutional setting consists of an EU-pillar and an EFTA-pillar with a set of EEA institutions bridging the two-pillar system.[47] This setting essentially prevents the transfer of legislative- and judicial powers to supranational institutions and ensures that decisions adopted by the EU institutions are not directly applicable to the EFTA States.

The unique two-pillar institutional construction reconciles the aim of economic integration with the aim of preserving sovereignty albeit creating a complex legal regime. In conjunction with the EEA Agreement, the EFTA States signed an agreement on the establishment of a surveillance authority and a court of justice (SCA) to ensure in the EFTA pillar that states fulfil their obligations and respect EEA law.

[44] Illustrative of this point is the wording in the unchanged article 6 EEA referring to homogenous interpretation between the provisions of the EEA Agreement and the corresponding rules of the *Treaty establishing the European Economic Community* and the *Treaty establishing the European Coal and Steel Community.*

[45] In Part III it will be demonstrated how a protocol being primary law of the EU to some extent has entered the Agreement through a reference in the annexes.

[46] An analysis of the widening gap in the EEA after the Lisbon Treaty can be found in Fredriksen (2012), pp. 868–886.

[47] The already mentioned EEA Joint Committee encompasses surveillance of the implementation of the EEA Agreement, the settlement of disputes and most importantly the incorporation of new EU legislative acts into the Agreement. Other EEA institutions include the EEA Council, and the Joint Parliamentary Committee with consultative functions.

In the EU pillar, the European Commission and the CJEU similarly ensure that the EU Member States fulfil their obligations and respect EEA law.

Academics and practitioners of EEA law almost unanimously pronounce their support for the strength of the homogeneity principle for the successful functioning of the EEA Agreement.[48] Catherine Barnard has characterised this principle as having constitutional significance for the interpretation of EEA law.[49] It is, of course, possible to envisage a different development of the EEA (both historically and in the future) whereby the principle of homogeneity is attributed less importance than the current consensus indicates. The EFTA Court, the European Courts, the EFTA Surveillance Authority and the European Commission could all have built on the provisions in the EEA Agreement more independently of their EU counterparts to resolve questions in individual cases.[50] In other words, the legal interpretation in individual cases could be more or less harmonised with the views of the European Courts and the Commission in identical EU law cases. To the extent that discrepancies between EEA and EU law emerged with a more independent approach, concrete solutions would have to be found to resolve, i.a. questions of reciprocity.[51] Thus, it is possible to envisage a more independent development of EEA law being less subordinated or loyal to the legal solutions found in EU law albeit at cost of homogeneity.

With some very limited exceptions,[52] this is, nevertheless, not what has happened in practice, as is well illustrated by the L'Oréal case.[53] Furthermore, even if there are mixed signals, a more independent approach seems to have limited support from the Contracting Parties of the EEA.[54] All institutions responsible for the interpretation of the Agreement have expressed their effort to rely on the great weight of the

---

[48] A recent contribution to this is Skouris (2014), p. 5, see also S. Norberg in the same publication in The EEA Surveillance Mechanism in EFTA Court on p. 483 stating that '[The principle of homogeneity] explains the genesis of the EEA Agreement and guarantees its continued existence'. For a different view based on one decision by the EFTA Court see Case E-16/11 EFTA Surveillance Authority v Iceland (Icesave) which has been analysed in the literature as opening up to questioning the earlier emphasis by the Court of similarities between EEA and EU law, see Chalmers (2014), pp. 408–416.

[49] Barnard (2014), p. 168.

[50] Or in their general Communications which are an important part of the decisional practice in state aid law.

[51] Reciprocity is the idea that the EEA not only ensures equal rights for citizens and undertakings from EFTA States in the EU but equally ensures citizens and undertakings from the EU equal treatment in the EFTA States.

[52] Examples from the CJEU include the string of tax cases commented upon by Fredriksen (2012), pp. 874–875. See also the comment by Zimmer (2010), pp. 1–4. These examples represent, however, a limited and specific area of which a solution in practical terms seems to already have been found in Iceland and Norway being parties to the OECD/Council of Europe convention on mutual administrative assistance in tax matters, see Lyal (2014), p. 735.

[53] Cases E-9/07 and E-10/07 L'Oréal, Fredriksen (2010b), pp. 481–499; Magnússon (2011), pp. 507–534; van Stiphout (2009), pp. 7–18; Rognstad (2001), pp. 435–464.

[54] As pointed to by Tarjei Bekkedal less homogenous interpretation may be more controversial politically, see Bekkedal (2008), pp. 146–147.

homogeneity principle and to always strive for homogenous interpretation of EU and EEA law. As already referred to, it has been argued convincingly by academics that this approach has been essential to the success of the Agreement. This author concurs with the broad consensus of the overall importance attributed to the principle of homogeneity and joins the view that the principle of homogeneity has been important for the survival and for the well-functioning of the EEA Agreement.

Taking this as a starting point, however, the question arises of how to reconcile the importance of the homogeneity principle with the lack of substantial reproduction of EU primary law changes in the EEA. The starting point in the next section, is the perspective offered by law on treaties. This perspective is included as one of many reference points for the analysis.

1.4.3 Law on Treaties: National Legal Autonomy

From the point of departure of international law on treaties, it is clear that contracting parties to an international agreement must agree in order for additional legal provisions to be included in an agreement. Clearly, there is therefore, according to standard international law, a requirement of mutual agreement before new provisions can be made part of the EEA Agreement. The revised constitutional framework of the EU is based on a series of Treaty changes made through decisions taken by EU Member States. The EU Member States constitute one of the pillars created to establish the EEA Agreement. The other pillar—the EFTA side—has not played a part in the series of Treaty revisions in the EU. Hence, to make these Treaty revisions applicable in the EEA would amount to only one of the Contracting Parties to the EEA Agreement—the EU side to amend the EEA Agreement. As long as not both the EU and the EFTA side have agreed to include the revised constitutional framework into the EEA Agreement, the provisions are not as such part of the Agreement. Clearly, when the provisions are not part of the Agreement, they are not judicially binding EEA law and cannot in principle be applied by the EU/EFTA institutions when applying EEA law. The institutions are limited in their function to apply only the provisions that have been made part of the EEA Agreement. Therefore, based again on law on treaties as a reference point, the institutions cannot apply the revised constitutional framework in the EU when they apply EEA law.

A different starting point would undoubtedly deviate from the fundamental position of every state to be legally autonomous in its relation with other states and international organisations as demonstrated in the Vienna Convention on the Law of Treaties. If the revised constitutional framework of the EU was made part of the EEA without the EFTA States' consent, this would be equal to the EU deciding EFTA States' international legal obligations singlehandedly and effectively removing national legal autonomy for the EFTA States.

Hence, the Norwegian Government only stated the obvious in the intervention made in Case E-26/13 Gunnarsson referred to in paragraph 48 of the decision, saying that 'the legal basis for this is Article 21(1) TFEU, which has no equivalent in the EEA Agreement. [...] Union Citizenship falls outside the material scope of the annexes to the EEA Agreement'.[55]

However, anyone familiar with EEA law is aware of the complicated hybrid of the EEA Agreement placing itself somewhere in between an ordinary international treaty and the supranational system of the EU legal order. This hybrid structure also means that there is a much more complicated answer to the question of how to meet the challenge of the explained legal phenomenon of the EEA Agreement than the answer provided by applying international treaty law.[56] The aim of the next section is to help set the stage for the more detailed discussion in the subsequent chapters starting with the EU based on new aims and values.

1.5 The EU Based on New Aims and Values: An Overview of Primary Law Changes After the Signing of the EEA Agreement 1 May 1992

1.5.1 The Treaty of Maastricht

The Treaty of Maastricht entered into force 1 November 1993 and changed the name of the EEC removing the term 'economic' from the European Community (EC). This change had at least symbolic importance.

Thus, with the Maastricht Treaty, the development of a social dimension became more important. The character of the system began to change in new directions, which also may be derived already from the formulation of Article 2 EC and the insertion of new activities in Article 3 EC.[57]

---

[55] Reply to questions by the Court from the Kingdom of Norway, 9 April 2014. The same position is clear from Case E-28/15, Jabbi see also Case E-12/10 EFTA Surveillance Authority v Iceland. However, in the last case the Icelandic Government referred to several Articles in the Charter of Fundamental Rights for their defence, see Report for the Hearing, paragraph 92 even if the Charter as such has not been made part of EEA law.

[56] Nils Wahl has analysed the legal significance of the Charter of Fundamental Rights in the EEA taking the same starting point for the analysis, namely to state that formally the provisions simply do not exist in the EEA. Then he engages in a debate on how the courts influence each other's case law in the field of fundamental rights, see Wahl (2014), pp. 281–298.

[57] See in particular subparagraphs (i)–(t): (i) a policy in the social sphere comprising a European Social Fund; (j) the strengthening of economic and social cohesion; (k) a policy in the sphere of the environment; (l) the strengthening of the competitiveness of Community industry; (m) the promotion of research and technological development; (n) encouragement for the establishment and development of trans-European networks; (o) a contribution to the attainment of a high level of health protection; (p) a contribution to education and training of quality and to the flowering of the cultures of the Member States; (q) a policy in the sphere of development co-operation; (r) the association of the overseas countries and territories in order to increase trade and promote jointly economic and social development; (s) a contribution to the strengthening of consumer protection; (t) measures in the spheres of energy, civil protection and tourism.'

To complete the picture, it is also appropriate to mention the objectives of the EU enshrined in the Treaty of the European Union (TEU) from Maastricht in Article B emphasising the following:

> The Union shall set itself the following objectives:
>
> [...]
>
> – to promote economic and social progress which is balanced and sustainable, in particular through the creation of an area without internal frontiers, through the strengthening of economic and social cohesion [...].

Furthermore, the concept of Citizenship of the Union was introduced in Maastricht through Articles 8 and 8A (now Articles 20–25 TFEU). As will be demonstrated later, these provisions have introduced into the catalogue of EU-based rights, rights of access to social welfare far beyond the economically active citizens. The Maastricht Treaty also included provisions on social policy (now titles X and XI TFEU), education (now title XII TFEU), culture (now title XIII TFEU) and public health (now title XIV TFEU) into the primary law of the EU.[58] The legal significance of the new provisions regarding education and public health is analysed in Part I. The provisions on Union citizenship are analysed in Part II and the provisions on culture are included in Part III.

1.5.2 *The Treaty of Amsterdam*

The social dimension concerning aims and values is further underscored with the Treaty of Amsterdam, which entered into force 1 May 1999. For instance, it may be mentioned that in the preamble of the TEU, it is stated that the Contracting Parties are

> DETERMINED to promote economic and social progress for their peoples [...].

Other important changes in primary law relevant for welfare services are the insertion of Article 16 EC (now in a revised version as Article 14 TFEU) on the value of public services and a new protocol on public service broadcasting (now Protocol 29 annexed to the TFEU on the system of public broadcasting in the Member States). These provisions are analysed in Part III.

[58] The EEA Agreement has elements from the Maastricht Treaty included in the main part of the Agreement given the parallel time period of negotiations. The free movement of capital provision in Article 40 EEA provides an example.

1.5.3 *The Treaty of Nice*

The Treaty of Nice entered into force 1 February 2003 and included the proclamation of the Charter of Fundamental Rights.[59] The Charter was actively used by the EU institutions even if it was not legally binding until the adoption of the Treaty of Lisbon. Relevant Charter provisions in the social field are pointed to in various chapters, such as the right to education in Article 14 and access to preventive healthcare enshrined in Article 35 (Part I), Article 7 on the right to family life (Part II) and Article 36 on SGEI (Part III).

1.5.4 *The Treaty of Lisbon*

The EU took one more step in this general direction of new aims and values with the Treaty of Lisbon, which entered into force 1 December 2009. Regarding values, the new Article 2 of the TEU emphasises that:

> The Union is founded on the values of respect for human dignity, freedom, democracy, equality, the rule of law and respect for human rights, including the rights of persons belonging to minorities. These values are common to the Member States in a society in which pluralism, non-discrimination, tolerance, justice, solidarity and equality between women and men prevail.

The reference to a society in which, among other things, solidarity prevails is an important statement. In this context, note should also be taken of Article 3(4) where the Union

> [...] shall respect its rich cultural and linguistic diversity, and shall ensure that Europe's cultural heritage is safeguarded and enhanced.

Reference should also be made to the new Article 4(2) TEU on the respect for national identities.

It seems particularly significant from the Treaty of Lisbon that the 'social market economy' will play an explicit role. Article 3(3) TEU expressly states that the objective of the Union is to work for a 'social market economy'. The context in which this is found, namely Article 3(3) TEU, is cited in its entirety:

> The Union shall establish an internal market. It shall work for the sustainable development of Europe based on balanced economic growth and price stability, a highly competitive social market economy, aiming at full employment and social progress, and a high level of protection and improvement of the quality of the environment. It shall promote scientific and technological advance. It shall

[59] Charter of Fundamental Rights of the European Union (2000/C 364/01), there is voluminous academic literature on the Charter in the EU legal order. On the Charter in the EEA legal order see Wahl (2014), pp. 281–298; Fredriksen (2013), pp. 371–399.

combat social exclusion and discrimination, and shall promote social justice and protection, equality between women and men, solidarity between generations and protection of the rights of the child. It shall promote economic, social and territorial cohesion, and solidarity among Member States. It shall respect its rich cultural and linguistic diversity, and shall ensure that Europe's cultural heritage is safeguarded and enhanced.

This expression of a social market economy can be contrasted to the previous Article 3(1)(g) in the EC Treaty stating that the activities of the Community shall include

> [...] a system ensuring that competition in the internal market is not distorted [...].

This economic aim of undistorted competition is now found in a protocol rather than in a Treaty provision. Protocol 27 to the Lisbon Treaty has the following content:

> THE HIGH CONTRACTING PARTIES,
>
> CONSIDERING that the internal market as set out in Article 3 of the Treaty on European Union includes a system ensuring that competition is not distorted.

Normally, especially due to Article 51 TEU,[60] in EU law, significant interpretational weight is attributed to a protocol to a Treaty. Protocols are legally equivalent to that of Treaty provisions. It has been argued, however, that it is questionable how much weight Protocol 27 should be given in the present situation.[61] It is argued that somehow the situation where a Treaty provision is moved to a protocol seems different from a situation where a provision is first expressed in a protocol. Even if it may not be correct to claim that the aim of undistorted competition should be viewed as less important to the aim of a social market economy, there has been a significant change. The emphasis is clearly on the importance of the social aspects of the market. So far, it may be concluded that regarding aims and values, important developments have taken place when viewed solely from the amendments of primary law.

The new status of Union citizenship introduced in the Maastricht Treaty is a key primary law change referred to in all three Parts of the book and a premise for the analysis in Part II. The provision on the value of SGEI introduced in the Amsterdam Treaty is most significant for the analysis of state aid competence in Part III. As will be demonstrated already in Part I the inclusion of the provisions on healthcare and education have also had significant impact on the evolving EU law for the provision of welfare services.

---

[60] Article 51 TEU has the following wording: 'The Protocols and Annexes to the Treaties shall form an integral part thereof'.

[61] Neergaard (2009), p. 193.

1.6 Relevance, Identifying and Contributing to Closing the Knowledge Gap

The literature thus far has mostly dealt with the principle of homogeneity in the context of diverging case law between the two Courts—the CJEU and the EFTA Court.[62] The contribution in this book is aimed at supplementing this literature by analysing the principle of homogeneity in a situation where the substantive EU Treaty provisions are not reproduced in the EEA. Thus, the contribution aims at describing and discussing techniques and methodologies observed and applied by the EU/EFTA institutions when interpreting the EEA Agreement to address this legal phenomenon, limited for reasons of space, to the provision of welfare services.

The scepticism of applying primary law changes in the EU on the EEA Agreement was expressed early on:

> In my view, to hold that the EFTA states are under an obligation to let their obligations be influenced by revisions of the treaties between the Member States of the European Union would certainly give new meaning to the concept of supranationality. This would amount to a situation where the EFTA states were legally bound to development caused by treaties concluded by foreign states.[63]

Niels Fenger discusses the possibility of applying the homogeneity principle to remedy the widening gap. Even if he concludes that there are limitations, he states the following:

> The very objective behind the EEA's establishment of common rules and equal competition will be eroded if treaty amendments in the EU influencing provisions corresponding to those in the EEA Agreement do not have an effect on the interpretation of the EEA Agreement. From a homogeneity perspective, a dynamic interpretation of the EEA is therefore equally desirable in cases where the corresponding provisions in the EC Treaty have been amended since the conclusion of the Agreement in 1992.[64]

A more principled approach is expressed by Halvard Haukeland Fredriksen regarding the Charter of Fundamental Rights where Fredriksen distinguishes between situations where the new legal provision(s) constitute an interpretative factor for a particular legal outcome and situations where the new legal provision(s) is in itself the legal basis for a particular legal outcome.[65]

Fredriksen is of the opinion that the sovereignty of the EFTA States must prevail in cases where it is not possible to interpret EEA law in parallel with EU law without basing the interpretation on EU law provisions that have not been made part of

[62] See for instance the L'Oréal saga referred to above in Sect. 1.4.2.

[63] Graver (2002), p. 88.

[64] Fenger (2006), p. 134.

[65] See the distinction between sections 4 (p. 378) and 5 (p. 385) in Fredriksen (2013), pp. 371–399.

the EEA Agreement.[66] He adds, however, that this position is merely a starting point that may not always provide guidance to solve concrete cases.

To contribute to moving forward in understanding this phenomenon of EEA law, the book offers within one sector a systematic study of institutional practice. Essentially, there are two possible outcomes of the study. The outcome that is expected from a simple application of the international law on treaties is that the institutions applying EEA law continue the role of applying the provisions in the EEA Agreement and disregard provisions (at least when these provisions constitute in themselves the legal basis for a right with a corresponding obligation) included in the EU integration process but not made part of the EEA Agreement. The other possible outcome is that the EEA integration process continues to develop in parallel with the EU integration process despite the lack of the same legal provisions. In so far as there is evidence of the latter development, an aim of the book is to identify different legal techniques applied by the institutions and discuss possible implications.

1.7 Scope and Limitations

The intention is to answer the broader question by conducting an analysis of the case law and the administrative decisional practice of the EU/EFTA institutions applying EEA law. The book will not even try to provide a systematic analysis of the political will of the Contracting Parties. The will of the Contracting Parties will be referred to when appropriate, but the main focus is always on the EU/EFTA institutions applying the Agreement. It should be noted that conflicting signals are given from the Contracting Parties on how to reconcile the conflicting concerns and this point is returned to in particular in the concluding section.[67]

Including also the administrative decisional practice means that examples where the cases have never reached the Courts are also adequately presented. This was particularly important in the field of educational services where the discussion will illustrate that the EFTA State did not object to the principal argumentation by the EFTA Surveillance Authority and consequently changed national law according to the understanding of the administrative authority. Likewise, administrative

[66] Fredriksen and Mathiesen (2014), pp. 256–258.

[67] On the one side, the Contracting Parties have made statements like the later analysed Joint Declaration to the incorporation of the Citizens Directive into the EEA Agreement making it clear that Union citizenship has no equivalent in the EEA Agreement and similar statements have been made from Government lawyers in the litigation in the EFTA Court, see i.a. Case E-26/13 Gunnarsson and the Case of E-28/15 Jabbi. On the other side, the Contracting Parties have relied on EU primary law which has not been made part of the EEA Agreement in their defence in litigation in the EFTA Court, see i.a. Case E-1/02 EFTA Surveillance Authority v Norway regarding Article 141(4) EC, paragraph 28 and Case E-12/10 EFTA Surveillance Authority v Iceland regarding Articles 31 and 34 of the Charter of Fundamental Rights, see the Report for the hearing, paragraph 92. This point will be returned to in the concluding Chap. 15.

decisional practice is an important factor in the state aid review analysis given the broad competences of the surveillance authorities in this field. Furthermore, the inclusion of decisional practice of the EFTA Surveillance Authority demonstrates how the case law from in particular the EFTA Court subsequently is relied on and applied more generally by the Authority in its on-going supervisory role controlling EFTA State compliance with EEA law.

The view of the European Commission is demonstrated rather consistently in a number of oral and written observations in various cases regarding the interpretation of EEA law both in the CJEU and in the EFTA Court, most recently made clear in a submission to the EFTA Court in Case E-28/15 Jabbi.[68] The written submissions by the Commission are referred to in a number of cases throughout the book.

The scope of this contribution is also limited to one sector, welfare services. The book will, however, take a broad view of the notion of welfare services to include both what is commonly referred to as 'core' welfare and an 'outer ring' of welfare services commonly referred to as services of general interest (SGI).[69]

The reasons why the provision of welfare services is chosen as the subject matter to illustrate a broader phenomenon in EEA law are twofold.

First, in the welfare field, the impact of the changes in primary law is clearly visible. From the case law of the European courts, it is possible to observe directly in the reasoning, as well as by concrete references in the judgments, that the outcomes rely and build on the existence of the primary law provision. In Fredriksen's terminology, this would include cases where the new legal provision constitutes an interpretative factor for a particular legal outcome and a situation where the new legal provision in itself is the legal basis for a particular legal outcome. This is most clearly spelt out in the case law on the Union citizenship provisions, but elements of the same reasoning are visible in the free movement of services case law as well as in the changes concerning services of general interest (SGI). For healthcare, it is the structure of EU law distinguishing between primary and secondary law that is most striking.

Second, welfare concerns and European solidarity are quite plainly different from economic market concerns. Both the development in the direction of protecting the free movement of non-economically active citizens (as well as rights in the field of cross-border health and educational services) and the influence more at the EU level on the provision of SGI can be clearly distinguished from the economic logic of 'pure' internal market law.

Welfare integration is therefore a particularly suited case study to illustrate the consequences of the legal phenomenon at centre stage in this project. In the context of the broader question asked in this book, there is, however, ample room for extending the analysis to include other areas. Specifically, it would be relevant to undertake the same analysis on this legal phenomenon of the widening gap in areas such

[68] See further Sect. 8.3.

[69] Leibfried and Starke (2008), p. 176; Damjanovic and De Witte (2009), p. 53.

as, for example, environmental law,[70] energy security law[71] and consumer law.[72] Later projects to include these areas as well would certainly increase the knowledge of how the phenomenon in the EEA is dealt with by relevant actors. All the mentioned areas of law have moved the EU integration process beyond market integration in economic terms. Being closely related to welfare services, the justification for excluding labour law will be elaborated further.[73]

Labour market regulation includes institutional arrangements for the social partners and equality policies. In this book, labour market regulation and equality policies will not be included in the concept of welfare services. In the areas of labour law and equality policies, the EU is empowered with far-reaching competences of which it has also made extensive use by adopting a wide range of secondary legislation. Thus, it is less clear to what extent primary law not paralleled in the main part of the EEA Agreement is essential for rights and duties within the field of labour law, and it is therefore less illuminating for the purposes of the present research question.[74] Furthermore, labour law and equality policies differ fundamentally from redistributive and regulatory welfare policy. The latter typically require some sort of funding, and in this respect, they differ from employment and equality policies.

---

[70] In this sector primary law changes like Article 191 TFEU is relevant, see Articles 73–75 EEA.

[71] In this sector primary law changes like Article 194 TFEU is relevant.

[72] In this sector primary law changes like Article 169 TFEU is relevant, see Article 72 EEA.

[73] Labour law provisions are included in Title X on Social policy in the TFEU, see Articles 151–161 TFEU, confer Chapter V EEA, Articles 66–71 EEA.

[74] Having said this, more generally, it should nevertheless be pointed out that the EFTA Court in Case E-10/14 Deveci was confronted with the question of the position of Article 16 of the Charter of fundamental Rights in the EEA. The case concerned the interpretation of Article 3 of Directive 2001/23/EC on safeguarding employees' rights in case of transfers of undertakings. The question in the case was essentially whether the transferee was bound by collective agreements entered into by the transferor and the conditions thereof. Regarding the interpretation of a similar conflict in Case C-426/11 Alemo-Herron the CJEU expressed its opinion to be that the dynamic clause 'adversely affect the very essence' of the freedom to conduct business. Hence, the CJEU had interpreted the provision in the Directive in conformity with Article 16 of the Charter of Fundamental Rights in its decision in Alemo-Herron. Article 16 of the Charter does not only protect 'the freedom to operate a business but also the freedom to conduct a business, the freedom to enterprise and the freedom to contract', confer Explanations relating to the Charter, 2007/C 303/02. Hence, this is a different right than rights according to the ECHR as interpreted by the ECHR in Strasbourg. The EFTA Court referred to the Alemo-Herron decision when limiting the time period upon which the transferee was bound by the collective agreement entered into by the transferor, see paragraph 63. Given that the CJEU relied on Article 16 of the Charter to reach its interpretative result in Alemo-Herron, it may be argued that the EFTA Court gave effect to this provision also in the EEA. The EFTA Court sees the need to make it explicit in paragraph 64 that the Court does not need to address the question of the position of Article 16 in the EEA. The reasoning is that the EEA Agreement has linked the markets of the EFTA States to the single market and the actors of a market are undertakings. The freedom to conduct a business lies therefore, according to the EFTA Court, at the heart of the EEA Agreement and must be recognised in accordance with EEA law and national law and practices. It is difficult to understand the statement made by the EFTA Court other than an implicit recognition of Article 16 of the Charter also in the EEA. The CJEU did not simply refer to the fundamental freedoms but relied expressly on the provision to reach its interpretative result.

1.8 Materials, Methodology and Terminology

For the purpose of this book, it was necessary to collect a significant amount of material not previously made public. This included in particular material from the EFTA Surveillance Authority as well as material from the EFTA Court case documents. A complete list of documents, some of which were only made available upon request or only available through actual presence in the EFTA Court, is included. This material is on-file with the author. Otherwise, the analysis builds on public documents all included in the bibliography.

The book analyses the development of the EEA Agreement through the complex relationship in EU law between primary and secondary law.[75] Three different areas of welfare services are examined in this perspective. In the examination of these three areas, the analysis must separate the situation where the revised primary law provision applies in EU law to interpret secondary legislation that has been incorporated into the EEA Agreement from situations where the revised primary law is the primary source for rights and obligations.[76] It is the second situation that is the most problematic if no proper amendments to the Agreement have been made. In particular, the existing literature has pointed to the concerns of applying the homogeneity principle to include applying primary law provisions not paralleled in the EEA in cases where this would limit individual rights.[77]

The material analysed in this book include the fields of social assistance, social security schemes, social housing as well as public healthcare, public education and public service broadcasting. Basic services in the sectors of communications, energy and transport are commented upon when appropriate, but these services are largely liberalised and regulated by secondary legislation. In the main part of the EEA Agreement, welfare services are dealt with rather differently and under two different headings depending on whether they are considered SGEI. SGEI are dealt with under the chapter regarding rules on competition in part IV. They are regarded as special economic activities, but SGEI are in principle part of the EEA project, and in this, they differ from other welfare services. Other welfare services are considered essentially outside the scope of the Agreement constituting non-economic activity.

Other welfare services are dealt with under the heading of social policy in part V, but the chapter is limited to labour law and gender issues. Hence, the main part of the EEA Agreement does not foresee institutions that apply EEA law to engage in social policy matters. Welfare services are only dealt with insofar as it is necessary

---

[75] A recent article on the complicated relationship between primary and secondary law in the EU in the field of free movement rights for the non-economically active persons can be found in Syrpis (2015), pp. 461–488. In the EEA this relationship is complicated further by the in principle lack of hierarchy between norms in the main part of the Agreement and the annexes.

[76] See this distinction made for the Charter provisions by Fredriksen (2013), pp. 371–399, Nils Fenger applies a similar distinction in his article on the limits of homogeneity. Fenger (2006), pp. 131–154.

[77] Fenger (2006), pp. 131–154.

to make the EEA project work. Based on the view that social guarantees constitute essential prerequisites for the very exercise of the free movement of workers, social policy rights are inserted among the free movement of workers provisions in part III, Article 29 EEA.[78] The purpose of this is to ensure that national states' social security schemes do not inhibit labour mobility.

The title on social policy itself appears more like a confirmation of the national states' own responsibilities in this area. Public healthcare and public education are not mentioned and seem therefore to be considered by the Contracting Parties to be within the exclusive responsibility of the national states.[79]

1.9 Parts and Chapters

The book is organised in three main parts. The analysis distinguishes between publicly funded healthcare and educational services (essentially patients' and students' rights) (Part I), social rights for non-economically active moving persons (Union citizenship rights) (Part II) and the application of state aid rules to public welfare services (focusing on public service broadcasting) (Part III). Each part contributes something different to the overall research question. Hence, the three parts are not only piling evidence on top of each other to demonstrate a homogeneous development but systematise and explain the phenomenon and articulate different angles to the overall question of the project. The services section (Part I on public healthcare and education) is based on the assessment that this development (in particular in healthcare) was to some extent more expected than the two next case studies. By more expected, it is meant that it was less clear that the legal basis for the development was different in the EEA Agreement. Hence, the paralleling of the EU legal order of patients' right to cross-border healthcare seems more obvious than later developments. The Union citizenship section (Part II on social welfare benefits) developed from a legal basis in the EU legal order initially not clearly different from the legal basis in the EEA legal order. Subsequent developments in the EU legal order were based on legal provisions not paralleled in the EEA, making the homogenous development in the EEA less challenging. The section on the exercise of state aid competence (Part III on welfare services) is partly without the same legal basis in the EEA, and this is made explicit also by the institutions, including how they will decide cases in the fields where no parallel provisions exist in the EEA legal order.

Each part includes both a description of how the EU legal order has developed based on the relevant primary law revisions and an analysis of how the EEA legal order has developed accordingly. The analysis of the development in the EEA legal

---

[78] This is explored in detail in Part II.

[79] Health is mentioned in the preamble section 10 where the Contracting parties are 'DETERMINED to take, in the further development of rules, a high level of protection concerning health, safety and the environment as a basis'.

order is based on relevant case law and decisional practice from the institutions. In all of the three parts, the analysis includes both case law from the EFTA Court and decisional practice of the EFTA Surveillance Authority. The material of case law from the CJEU and statements from the Commission on EEA law specifically is limited and therefore not present for all sectors analysed.

Part I on free movement rights for patients and students as service recipients starts out by describing the evolution of EU law to reach further into the realms of publicly financed healthcare and educational services in the Member States. In the section on healthcare services, it is demonstrated how this evolution differed from the objectives set by secondary law[80] and to what extent the hierarchical relationship between primary and secondary law in the EU preconditioned the evolution. Next, the case law and decisional practice regarding the impact of EEA law in the health sector are analysed. The analysis demonstrates how the EFTA Court parallels the reasoning of the CJEU regardless of the limitations set by the (secondary) legislation included in the annex of the EEA Agreement and the lack of a hierarchical relationship between the main part of the EEA Agreement and the annex. Further, it is demonstrated how the EFTA Surveillance Authority builds on this case law from the EFTA Court in its decisional practice. In the section on educational services, it is demonstrated how the revised primary law provisions increased the obligations on Member States in this sector, in particular in recent case law from the CJEU regarding rights for own citizens (home state obligations). Next, the decisional practice of the EFTA Surveillance Authority in the field of publicly financed educational services including obligations on own citizens is analysed. The analysis demonstrates how the EFTA Surveillance Authority has paralleled the reasoning of the CJEU and even refers to the case law directly, regardless of the lack of paralleling in the EEA of the legal bases upon which the CJEU has relied.

Part II on social rights for non-economically active moving persons starts out by describing the evolution of EU law from being limited to economically active movers to including (albeit with only limited residence rights in the host state) some categories of non-economically active persons[81] aiming at abandoning the differentiation of economically active and non-economically active persons through the creation of Union citizenship. The analysis of the institutional practice in the EEA is complex due to the inclusion of the Citizens Directive[82] and the coordination regime for social security benefits[83] in the EEA Agreement. Hence, before moving into the analysis of the institutional practice, a section of this chapter concentrates on analysing the secondary legislation and the added value of primary law in the EU legal order. The Icelandic Government's initial view in the negotiations on including the Citizens Directive in the EEA Agreement was that the provisions both on social

---

[80] In particular Article 22 of Regulation 1408/71 (later replaced by Article 20 Regulation (EC) No 2004/883).

[81] Such as students, pensioners, persons with sufficient means.

[82] Directive 38/2004/EC, see Part II.

[83] Regulation (EC)No 2004/883, see Part II.

policy and on immigration policy overstepped the legal boundaries of the EEA.[84] The provisions of the Citizens Directive were nevertheless incorporated in the EEA Agreement without any changes or modifications as to their substantive content.[85] However, when the Citizens Directive was incorporated into the EEA Agreement, a Joint Declaration from the Contracting Parties emphasised that Union citizenship and immigration policy are not part of the EEA Agreement.[86] This Declaration is the starting point for the analysis of EEA law. Next, the case law from the EFTA Court and the CJEU and the decisional practice of the EFTA Surveillance Authority regarding the impact of EEA law on non-economically active movers is analysed, separating between cases in the field of the Citizens Directive and cases in the field of the coordination regime for social welfare benefits. The analysis demonstrates how the EFTA Court, the CJEU and the EFTA Surveillance Authority have paralleled the free movement rights of the non-economically active in the EEA legal order regardless of the lack of the same legal provisions that constitute the legal bases for these rights in the EU legal order.

Part III on applying state aid provisions to publicly financed welfare services starts out by describing how the provisions of public services moved from being in the periphery of the EU legal order to taking centre stage after the liberalisation and de-monopolisation processes beginning in the late 1980s. The changing role of the Commission as the authority controlling state aid measures in the EU legal order is compared to the role of the EFTA Surveillance Authority controlling state aid measures from EFTA States in the EEA legal order.

The position in the EU's constitutional framework of competition and state aid law and policy has shifted significantly as a result of the revision processes in the amending treaties. The revised constitutional framework in the EU is now more favourable to public services, but that does not mean that they are freely governed at the national level without impact from EU law. Perhaps paradoxically, by securing guarantees for public services at the EU level in the constitutional texts, the Member States have also outlined and legitimised the increased application of EU law to public services.

In the analysis of the institutional practice, a distinction is made between legal tools in primary law to protect Member States' welfare provisions from competition and state aid law and primary law as part of the legal basis to increase the scope of review by the state aid authorities. A case study in the field of public service broadcasting illuminates the increase in scope and the balancing of welfare concerns in state aid review. Public service broadcasting is a service defined precisely by the

[84] Jonsdottir (2013), pp. 97, 103.

[85] The usual adaptations such as substituting the words 'Union citizen(s)' with the words 'national(s) of EC Member States and EFTA States' were naturally included in the incorporating decision, confer Decision annex VIII 1(c).

[86] Joint declaration, Decision by the EEA Committee No 158/2007 (OJ 2008L 124, p. 20, and EEA Supplement No 26, 8.5.2008, p. 17).

fact that it will not be provided by the market.[87] The state aid scrutiny in the decisional practice of the Commission has evolved from respecting Member States' autonomy in the field to a kind of 'micro-management' of public service media with detailed appropriate measures required to find national measures compatible with EU law.[88] Next, the decisional practice of the EFTA Surveillance Authority is analysed, including both the paralleling of the Commission's state aid guidelines as well as the paralleling of the 'micro-management' in the decisional practice. The analysis demonstrates how the EFTA Court and the EFTA Surveillance Authority have paralleled the reasoning of the CJEU and the Commission regardless of the lack of a parallel revised constitutional framework for public services in the EEA.

The relevant law is stated as of January 2018.

References

Arnesen F, Stenvik A (2015) Internasjonalisering og juridisk metode. Særlig om EØS rettens betydning i norsk rett. Universitetsforlaget, Oslo

Arnesen F, Fredriksen HH, Graver HP, Mestad O, Vedder C (eds) (2018) Agreement on the European economic area, a commentary. C.H. Beck/Hart/Nomos/Universitetsforlaget, München/Oxford/Baden-Baden/Oslo

Barnard C (2014) Reciprocity, homogeneity and loyal cooperation: dealing with recalcitrant National Courts? In: EFTA Court (ed) The EEA and the EFTA Court – decentred integration. Hart, Oxford, pp 151–169

Baudenbacher C (2013) The EFTA Court and Court of Justice of the European Union: coming in parts but winning together in Court of Justice of the European Union, the Court of Justice and the construction of Europe: analyses and perspectives on sixty years of case law. Springer, Berlin

Bekkedal T (2008) Frihet, likhet og fellesskap. Fagbokforlaget, Bergen, pp 146–147

Bull H (2006) Market freedoms: challenges to social security and welfare policy. In: Müller-Graff PC, Selvig E (eds) The European Economic Area enlarged. Berlin Verlag, Berlin, pp 69–95

Burri T, Pirker B (2013) Constitutionalization by association? The doubtful case of the European Economic Area. Yearb Eur Law 32:207–229

Chalmers D (2014) Icesave-limited homogeneity and unlimited judicial interpretation. In: EFTA Court (ed) The EEA and the EFTA Court – decentred integration. Hart, Oxford, pp 408–416

Cremona M (2011) Market integration and public services in the European Union. Oxford University Press, Oxford

Damjanovic D (2013) The EU market rules as social market rules: why the EU can be a social market economy. Common Mark Law Rev 50:1685–1718

Damjanovic D, De Witte B (2009) Welfare integration through EU law: the overall picture in the light of the Lisbon treaty. In: Neergaard U, Nielsen R, Roseberry LM (eds) Integrating welfare functions into EU law – from Rome to Lisbon. DJØF Publishing, Copenhagen, pp 53–96

[87] See i.a. Guidelines for the application of state aid rules to Public Service Broadcasting [2009] http://www.eftasurv.int/media/state-aid-guidelines/Part-IV%2D%2D-The-application-of-the-state-aid-rules-to-public-service-broadcasting.pdf and the three models discussed by Schweitzer in Schweitzer (2011), p. 43.

[88] See in particular for an analysis of the Commission decisional practice, Donders (2015), pp. 68–87.

De Witte F (2015) Justice in the EU: the emergence of transnational solidarity. Oxford University Press, Oxford

Donders K (2015) State aid to public service media: European Commission decisional practice before and after the 2009 broadcasting communication. Eur State Aid Law Q 14:68–87

EFTA Court (ed) (2012) Judicial protection in the European Economic Area. German Law Publishers, Frankfurt

EFTA Court (ed) (2014) The EEA and the EFTA Court decentred integration. Hart Publishing, Oxford

Fenger N (2006) Limits to a dynamic homogeneity between EC law and EEA law. In: Fenger N, Hagel Sørensen K, Vesterdorf B (eds) Festskrift Claus Gulman. Karnov Group, Copenhagen, pp 131–154

Follesdal A, Hix S (2006) Why there is a democratic deficit in the EU: a reply to Majone and Moravcsik. J Common Mark Stud 44:533–562

Fredriksen HH (2010a) The EFTA Court 15 years on. Int Comp Law Q 59(3):731–760

Fredriksen HH (2010b) One market, two courts: legal pluralism vs. homogeneity in the European Economic Area. Nordic J Int Law 79:481–499

Fredriksen HH (2012) Bridging the widening gap between the EU treaties and the agreement on the European Economic Area. Eur Law J 18(6):868–886

Fredriksen HH (2013) Betydningen av EUs pakt om grunnleggende rettigheter for EØS-retten. Jussens Venner 48:371–399

Fredriksen HH (2013a) Offentligrettslig erstatningsansvar ved brudd på EØS-avtalen, PhD ved Universitet i Bergen

Fredriksen HH (2013b) Betydningen av EUs pakt om grunnleggende rettigheter for EØS-retten. Jussens Venner 48:371–399

Fredriksen HH (2014) EEA main agreement and secondary EU law incorporated into the annexes and protocols. In: Baudenbacher C (ed) The handbook of EEA law. Springer, Berlin, pp 95–113

Fredriksen HH, Franklin CNK (2015) Of pragmatism and principles: the EEA agreement 20 years on. Common Mark Law Rev 52:629–684

Fredriksen HH, Mathiesen (2014) EØS-rett, 2nd edn. Fagbokforlaget, Bergen, pp 256–258

Giubboni S (2007) Free movement of persons and European solidarity. Eur Law J 13:360–379

Graver HP (2002) Mission impossible: supranationality and national legal autonomy in the EEA agreement. Eur Foreign Aff Rev 7:73–90

Gudmundsdóttir D (2012) Case E-3/11 Sigmarsson v. the Central Bank of Iceland. Common Mark Law Rev 49:2019–2038

Hancher L, Sauter W (2012) EU competition and internal market law in the healthcare sector. Oxford University Press, Oxford

Hatzopoulos VG (2005) Health law and policy: the impact of the EU. In: De Burca G (ed) EU law and the welfare state. Oxford University Press, Oxford, pp 111–168

Hervey T (2011) If only it were so simple: public health services and EU law. In: Cremona M (ed) Market integration and public services in the European Union. Oxford University Press, Oxford, pp 179–250

Hreinsson P (2014) General principles and prohibition of discrimination on grounds of nationality. In: Baudenbacher C (ed) The handbook of EEA law. Springer, Berlin, pp 349–391

Jonsdottir J (2013) Europeanization and the European Economic Area. Routledge, Abingdon, p 97

Leibfried S, Starke P (2008) Transforming the 'cordon sanitaire': the liberalization of public services and the restructuring of European welfare states. Soc Econ Rev 6:175–198

Lyal R (2014) Tax law. In: Baudenbacher C (ed) The handbook of EEA law. Springer, Berlin, pp 721–748

Magnússon S (2011) Judicial homogeneity in the European Economic Area and the authority of the EFTA Court. Some remarks on an article by Halvard Haukeland Fredriksen. Nordic J Int Law 80:507–534

Mossialos E, Permanand G, Baeten R, Hervey T (eds) (2010) Health systems governance in Europe: the role of EU law and policy. Cambridge University Press, Cambridge

Neergaard U (2009) Services of general (economic) interest: what aims and values count? In: Neergaard U, Nielsen R, Roseberry LM (eds) Integrating welfare functions into EU law – from Rome to Lisbon. DJØF Publishing, Copenhagen, pp 191–224

Neergaard U, Nielsen R, Roseberry LM (2009) Integrating welfare functions into EU law – from Rome to Lisbon. DJØF Publishing, Copenhagen

Neergaard U, Nielsen R, Roseberry LM (2010) The role of courts in developing a European social model – theoretical and methodological perspectives. DJØF Publishing, Copenhagen

Neergaard U, Szyszczak E, van de Gronden JW, Krajewski M (eds) (2013) Social services of general interest in the EU. Asser Press, The Hague

Norberg S (2014) The EEA surveillance mechanism. In: EFTA Court (ed) The EEA and the EFTA Court – decentred integration. Hart, Oxford, pp 481–498

Palombella G, Walker N (2009) Relocating the rule of law. Hart Publishing, Oxford

Reynolds S (2015) Housing policy as a restriction of free movement and member states' discretion to design programmes of social protection: Libert. Common Mark Law Rev 52:259–280

Rognstad OA (2001) EF-domstolen og EFTA domstolens praksis som rettskilder ved tolkning av EØS avtalen. Tidsskrift for Rettsvitenskap 2001:435–464

Ross M, Borgmann-Prebil Y (2010) Promoting solidarity in the European Union. Oxford University Press, Oxford

Rust A (2014) To tax or not to tax: reflection on the case law of the EFTA Court. In: EFTA Court (ed) The EEA and the EFTA Court – decentred integration. Hart, Oxford, pp 459–471

Sauter W (2014) Public services in EU law. Cambridge University Press, Cambridge

Schweitzer H (2011) Services of general economic interest: European law's impact of the role of markets and of member states. In: Cremona M (ed) Market integration and public services in the European Union. Oxford University Press, Oxford, pp 11–62

Sejersted F (1997) Between sovereignty and supranationalism in the EEA context – on the legal dynamics of the EEA agreement. In: Müller-Graff PC, Selvig E (eds) The European Economic Area. Berlin Verlag, Berlin, pp 43–73

Skouris V (2014) The role of the Court of Justice of the European Union in the development of the EEA single market. In: EFTA Court (ed) The EEA and the EFTA Court – decentred integration. Hart, Oxford, p 5

Spaventa E (2007) Free movement of persons in the European Union, barriers to movement in their constitutional context. Kluwer Law International, Alphen aan den Rijn

Stjernø S (2005) Solidarity in Europe. Cambridge University Press, Cambridge

Syrpis P (2015) The relationship between primary and secondary law in the EU. Common Mark Law Rev 52:461–488

Van der Mei AP (2003) Free movement of persons within the European Community cross-border access to public benefits. Hart, Oxford

van Stiphout T (2009) The L'Oréal cases – some thoughts on the role of the EFTA Court in the EEA legal framework: because it is worth it! Jus & News 1(7):7–18

Wahl N (2014) Unchartered waters: reflection on the legal significance of the charter under EEA law and judicial cross-fertilization in the field of fundamental rights. In: EFTA Court (ed) The EEA and the EFTA Court – decentred integration. Hart, Oxford, pp 281–298

Zimmer F (2010) ECJ settles dispute over Italian withholding tax, raises new concerns about EEA agreement. Worldwide Tax Daily 11(5):1–4

Miscellaneous

NOU 2012:2 Utenfor og Innenfor Norges avtaler med EU (Europautredningen)

Part I
The EEA Integration Process and Free Movement of Services: Patients' and Students' Mobility in Publicly Financed Systems of Healthcare and Education

Chapter 2
Free Movement of Services and Article 56 TFEU and Article 36 EEA

2.1 Aim and Background

From the very start, the EEA Agreement has ensured free movement rights in the market for healthcare and education within the EEA. Some healthcare goods (pharmaceuticals, medical devices) are traded goods, and healthcare and educational services (medical treatment, insurance, privately financed schools) use market models and structures for their provision albeit in highly regulated markets. The exercise of freedom of movement for services in the EEA is enshrined in Article 36 EEA paralleling Article 56 TFEU.[1] However, health and educational services, financed through public funds and mainly delivered through benefits in kind, were initially conceived as distinct and separate from areas of free movement of services and market integration. The inclusion of the EFTA States into the internal market, including the right to free movement of services, was a matter for EEA decision making, whereas social matters, such as publicly financed healthcare and educational services, were to be left within the scope of national competences.

Hence, the main part of the EEA Agreement only mentions healthcare in the preamble as a value meant to be protected in the development of the law. Education is mentioned as an area of closer cooperation outside the four freedoms in Articles 1(2)(f) and 78 EEA. Systems of health and educational services, mainly financed through public funds and delivered through benefits in kind, seem therefore to have been considered by the Contracting Parties to be the responsibility of the national states in line with the delimitation regarding social matters in the Rome Treaty.

In the EU legal order, the inclusion of health protection and the importance of education as aims and values in EU law were introduced in the Maastricht Treaty in

[1] Similarly, the EEA Agreement ensures the right of mutual recognition of professional qualifications, including in the field of health care and education, recognised across the EEA, see i.a. Case E-1/11 Dr. A on the refusal of the Norwegian Registration Authority to grant a medical doctor trained in Bulgaria a license to practice as a medical doctor in Norway.

K. Fløistad, *The EEA Agreement in a Revised EU Framework for Welfare Services*, Studies in European Economic Law and Regulation 13,
https://doi.org/10.1007/978-3-319-95043-3_2

Articles 126, 127 and 129 EC along with other new aims and values.[2] Articles 126 and 127 on education were continued in Articles 149 and 150 EC after the Amsterdam Treaty and are now in their current form Articles 165 and 166 TFEU after the Lisbon Treaty. Article 129 EC on health was continued in Article 152 EC and is now in its current form Article 168 TFEU. Furthermore, the right of access to preventive healthcare is enshrined in Article 35 and the right to education in Article 14 of the Charter of Fundamental Rights.[3] The Member States have continually emphasised their primary responsibility to provide healthcare and educational services in the mentioned Treaty provisions. The CJEU has confirmed this position, stating frequently that 'the organisation and delivery of healthcare services is the responsibility of the Member States'.[4] Furthermore, the CJEU has continually referred to the responsibility of the Member States for the content of teaching and the organisation of education systems and their cultural and linguistic diversity.[5] In Humbel, the CJEU held that, by establishing and maintaining a system of public education, the state did not intend to involve itself in remunerated activities but was carrying out its task in 'the social, cultural and educational fields' towards its population.[6] This position was later also confirmed in cases like C-109/92 Wirth[7] and C-76/05 Schwarz in the field of education.[8] In regard to social security systems, the CJEU found in Cases C-159 and 160/91 Poucet and Pistre[9] that these systems were not subject to the Treaty rules on competition, a position later confirmed in Case C-70/95 Sodemare where, in the view of the Court, the state retains the powers to organise its social security system.[10] Similarly, for publicly financed health services, the Advocate General recognised in Geraets-Smits and Peerbooms the need for Member States to retain control over social welfare expenditure and that financial equilibrium was essential to the public interest.[11]

---

[2] Such as the value of culture enshrined in Article 128 TFEU, see Part III and new aims and values commented upon in the introduction Sect. 1.5.

[3] Charter of Fundamental Rights of the European Union (2000/C 364/01), made legally binding through the Lisbon Treaty.

[4] Joined Cases C-159/91 and 160/91 Poucet and Pistre v AGF and Cancava [1993] ECR I-637, paragraph 6, Case C-70/95 Sodemare v Regione Lombardia [1997] ECR I-3395, paragraph 27. In a more recent Court decision the lack of EU competence in the health sector was an important argument in favour of not finding any violation of the state aid prohibition in the Irish financing system for a SGEI in the field of health insurance, case T-289/03 BUPA v Commission [2008] ECR II-81, see Part III.

[5] Case C-76/05 Schwarz [2007] ECR I-6849, paragraph 50.

[6] Case 263/86 Humbel [1988] ECR I-5365, paragraph 18.

[7] Case C-109/92 Wirth [1993] ECR I-6447.

[8] Case C-76/05 Schwarz [2007] ECR I-6849, see in particular paragraph 39, see further analysis of the CJEU case law in Sect. 4.2.2 below.

[9] See for an analysis of this case in Part III.

[10] Case C-70/95 Sodemar [1997] ECR I-3395, paragraph 32.

[11] Opinion of the Advocate General Ruiz-Jarabo Colomer in case C-157/99 Geraets-Smits and Peerbooms [2001] ECR I-5473.

Significant academic analysis demonstrates, however, that the relationship between EU and national law in the public healthcare and educational sectors is not simple but rather complex and still unfolding.[12] For the purpose of this book, the evolving EU law regarding healthcare and educational services along with the free movement rights for patients and students are of interest as an area to compare the EEA integration process with the EU integration process for the following three reasons.

First, free movement rights for service providers and service recipients in the fields of healthcare and education are examples of the integration process moving beyond the economic dimension. Second, in the EU integration process, free movement rights in these fields have emanated (partly) from the revised primary law provisions. Furthermore, it is argued here that the distinction between primary and secondary law was a significant part of the justification for the development in the case law in the EU legal order. The EEA Agreement has not paralleled the revised primary law provisions relevant in the fields of healthcare and education, and in principle, the Agreement does not distinguish between primary and secondary law.[13] More precisely, the EEA Agreement includes neither provisions corresponding to the present Articles 165, 166 and 168 TFEU, Articles 14 and 35 in the Charter of Fundamental Rights nor provisions corresponding to the Union citizenship provisions in Articles 20 and 21 TFEU. Third, the EFTA institutions have rendered decisions that, in various ways, have had to reconcile the lack of a hierarchal relationship between provisions in the EEA Agreement as well as the lack of equivalent primary law provisions in these fields with the principles of dynamism and homogeneity in the EEA Agreement.

2.2 Organisational Choices

Scholars have seen the early case law from the CJEU on patients' rights as a predecessor of the later Union citizenship case law even if the Court developed its reasoning based on the free movement of services provision.[14] The CJEU case law in the field of education has been based on a combination of the provisions on free

[12] Hervey (2011b), pp. 179–250; Hatzopoulos (2005), pp. 111–168; de Witte (2013), pp. 203–216; Dougan (2008), pp. 723–738.

[13] This difference between EU and EEA law stems from the fact that the EEA Agreement is an international treaty and hence the main part and the annexes are all part of the international agreement in principle at the same level as binding legal provisions, see Fenger (2006), p. 137. There is academic discussion on the extent to which the EEA Agreement parallels the EU legal order on this point, see a recent contribution Fredriksen (2014), pp. 95–113, see also the previous chapter Introduction, Chap. 1, footnote 43.

[14] See for example Dougan and Spaventa (2003), pp. 703, 705.

movement of services and free movement rights for Union citizens, with the latter gradually becoming more dominant.[15]

Free movement rights for Union citizens based on Articles 20 and 21 TFEU is the main focus of Part II. In this Part I, the focus is on the application of the right to free movement of services as enshrined in Article 56 TFEU and the parallel provision of Article 36 EEA, in particular on the rights of non-economically active service recipients such as patients and students. Article 56 TFEU embraces the perspectives of both the service provider and the service receiver, whereas Articles 20 and 21 TFEU are only concerned with the perspective of the citizen as an individual, thus leaving aside the specific consideration for the rights of the provider of the service as a market actor.

Given that the rights of patients and students in the EU legal order is based on a combination of Articles 56 on free movement of services and 20 and 21 TFEU on free movement of Union citizens, a choice must be made as to the organisation of the analysis. That is, it must be decided whether to include patients' and students' rights as Union citizens in this chapter on free movement of services or to leave this to the general chapters on free movement rights for non-economically active moving citizens (Part II). The choice made is to include not only the rights of patients and students as service recipients but also their rights as patients and students based on their status as Union citizens in this Part I. This means that Part II will analyse free movement rights for the non-economically active in the EEA integration process more generally,[16] whereas Part I will be limited to the category of patients and students, and the starting point is the rights granted to these categories of service recipients as a consequence of the Treaty provision on free movement of services.

This choice better illuminates the EEA perspective of the analysis, given that in the EEA integration process, the legal basis in the fields of healthcare and education (at least formally) is limited to the free movement of services provision.[17] The organisational choice is also based on the need to look at the EEA integration process in the healthcare and educational sectors in their entirety. The CJEU refers in a number of cases in these sectors, regardless of whether the case is mainly about free

[15] See the following statement in paragraph 23 in the recent decision in case C-359/13 Martens: 'In that respect, it must be stated that, although the Member States are competent, under Article 165(1) TFEU, as regards the content of teaching and the organisation of their respective education systems, they must exercise that competence in compliance with EU law and, in particular, in compliance with the Treaty provisions on the freedom to move and reside within the territory of the Member States, as conferred by Article 21(1) TFEU on every citizen of the Union (judgments Joined Cases C-11/06 and 12/06 Morgan and Bucher [2007] ECR I-9161, paragraph 24, and Prinz and Seeberger, EU:C:2013:524, paragraph 26 and the case-law cited'.

[16] Some of the rights analysed in the next chapter may be relevant for patients and students such as social security benefits and tax rights. However, the perspective in the next chapter is not concerned with the rights of free movers in their capacity of being patients or students which is the topic for the present chapter.

[17] Note that students may derive rights as family members of an economically active person from Articles 45 and 49 TFEU and secondary legislation. These legal bases are paralleled in Articles 28 and 31 EEA, see Sects. 4.2 and 4.3.

movement of services or about free movement of persons, to the general Treaty provisions on healthcare and education. This also underlines the need to do this analysis and comparison without considering the distinction between patients and student having rights both as service recipients and as Union citizens in the EU legal order.

The question is whether the EEA integration process, despite the legal differences, nevertheless, develops in step with the EU integration process in the fields of publicly financed healthcare and education services. Before moving into the developments in the EU legal order and subsequently the EEA legal order in both sectors, this first introductory section will point to general characteristics of public healthcare and educational systems and the sensitivity of introducing market mechanisms to these essentially closed-in solidaristic systems of delivering a particular type of service to the population. These are concerns that may be advocated both in the EU and in the EEA integration process. However, they seem particularly relevant in the context of the main question in the book. Given the importance of the public health and educational sectors for the society as well as their character of involving sensitive political decisions on how to prioritise limited public funds, the commitment by states to involve European institutions in this decision making arguably must be clearly laid down in the legal framework to legitimise the intervention by these institutions into domestic systems.

2.3 The Sensitive Character of (Largely) Publicly Financed Health and Educational Systems

2.3.1 Closed-in Solidaristic Systems of Providing Healthcare and Educational Services

Each EU Member State and EFTA State has, independently of the EU and of the EEA Agreement, established a singular model for financing and delivering healthcare and educational services to its population. These models are widely different. However, despite the diversity of systems, they all have principles in common, principles that distinguish them from models in other continents, such as, for example, North America.

Publicly financed healthcare services and educational systems reflect values of community, solidarity and substantive equality.[18] Notwithstanding the significant differences between systems in the different EU Member States and the EFTA States, they all converge on operating based on the principle of universal access to

[18] See for an analysis of healthcare services as a positive right and a critical approach to the CJEU's case law where the author thinks individualism in respect of national health resources is more likely to generate unequal access to care, Newdick (2006), p. 1665.

healthcare and education irrespective of the ability of the patient or the student to pay, and thus, all the systems operate on the basis of solidarity.

All the public healthcare and educational systems, as part of their welfare systems, embody solidarity in the sense of being based on taxation and organised by the state. The ability to secure a fair allocation of the healthcare and educational resources of the state presupposes a closed system of rights holders who contribute collectively to the financing of the system. Solidarity implies that everyone is included in the system. There is mandatory affiliation in the sense that no one may opt out of the system and mandatory acceptance in the sense that national health and educational systems may not exclude some categories of persons. In terms of funding of the systems, solidarity implies income-related contributions independent of the extent to which the contributing patient or student uses or will use the system. Solidarity consequently implies cross-subsidisation between healthy and unhealthy, clever and not so clever, rich and poor, and across different age groups. In the context of healthcare systems,[19] solidarity also implies that as coverage is based on the medical needs of the patient; all patients are treated equally, regardless of their contributions to the system.[20]

These solidarity features of national public healthcare and educational systems in the EU Member States and the EFTA States underpin their public nature. They are not simply organised on the basis of private activity within regulated markets (although they may include such activity); they also involve public institutions, such as public hospitals, schools and universities, taxation and mandatory social institutions. The solidarity features also underpin the national nature of the systems and the allocation decisions made nationally on how to distribute limited public funds to provide these services to the population.

Within finite budgets, decisions on healthcare and educational rights in systems based on social welfare cannot be made without regard to the impact on others. In making allocation decisions, the states need to take 'opportunity costs' into account.[21] This concept is concerned both with the cost of the treatment or education and the alternative ways in which that sum could benefit others.

2.3.2 *Market Elements in Healthcare and Educational Systems*

The market allocates goods and services in society in accordance with willingness to pay for those goods or services to encourage the efficient production of goods or provision of services at the lowest possible cost. It also encourages consumer choice, through ensuring open access to a market of competing suppliers. Principles of solidarity imply a fundamentally different perspective to that of competition law

[19] See Palm (2002), pp. 196–197.

[20] Hervey (2011a), p. 186.

[21] Newdick (2006), p. 1650.

and reliance on the market.[22] For instance, providing healthcare on a basis of equal access according to medical need may be achieved by restricting the power of individual consumers to buy healthcare services on a market in accordance with their ability to pay.[23] Mandatory participation is an important part of the financing of the systems. Consequently, solidarity may lead to the opposite result of that stemming from an open competitive market approach.

Nothing in EU or EEA law prevents EU Member States or EFTA States from organising their public healthcare and educational systems on the basis of solidarity. However, if or when a state chooses to bring 'market elements' into its healthcare and educational system, then, in principle, EU or EEA free movement and competition law will apply.[24] The application of EEA free movement of services law depends on whether there is an activity characterised as a service. The concept of a service has, however, as will be demonstrated, evolved significantly over time.

Health and educational services mainly financed through public funds and delivered through benefits in kind are not the typical traded goods, and in some sense, access to them is considered a fundamental right. Consequently, they are based on a complex system of cross-subsidies. Policies developed to sustain the principle of solidarity with its complex system of cross-subsidies may be vulnerable to market principles.[25] The CJEU has, however, treated healthcare services, even when provided in the framework of a social security scheme, as tradable services within the meaning of the Treaty and applied both competition law and free movement law to national healthcare systems. The CJEU has been more reluctant in the field of education, although it has not excluded the possibility. The law on the free movement of Union citizens has been applied to publicly funded educational services. This extension of the scope of welfare integration in the EU and the subsequent developments of EEA law is the topic for discussion in Chaps. 3 and 4.

2.4 Structure

Part I is organised in two main chapters with the addition of a concluding section in Chap. 5 which provides reflections on the EEA integration process extending into the publicly financed provision of healthcare—and educational services. The two sectors of healthcare and education are looked at separately in the following analysis. Chapter 3 looks at the health sector, and Chap. 4 looks at the educational sector.

---

[22] Often referred to in the context of defining solidarity is Stjernø (2005). Stjernø define solidarity as 'the preparedness to share resources by personal contribution to those in struggle or in need and through taxation and redistribution organized by the state', see Hervey (2011b), p. 186.

[23] Hervey (2011b), p. 188.

[24] See Prosser (2005, 2010).

[25] This perspective is included in most of the literature on the EU and the national health care systems, see i.a. Hancher and Sauter (2012), Mossialos et al. (2010), Hatzopoulos (2005), pp. 111–168; Hervey (2011b), pp. 179–250.

In order to facilitate the analysis, it is necessary within both chapters first to describe the evolving development in EU law impacting on the national systems respectively, including in particular the various territorial limitations on the financing of patients and students. Both sections therefore separate the analysis between the developments in the EU legal order and the subsequent developments in the EEA legal order. The EEA integration process in the health sector is mainly analysed based on case law from the EFTA Court.[26] The EEA integration process in the educational field is analysed in terms of the decisional practice of the EFTA Surveillance Authority, given that the EFTA Court has not decided a relevant case on student financing rights in a cross-border situation. However, there are several references in the educational sector to the developments that have taken place in the healthcare sector and it will be demonstrated that the two are closely related. The case law in the healthcare sector is also relied on for developments in the state aid law analysed in Part III.

Compared to the next chapters in Part II, which deal exclusively with the rights of Union citizens, the application of the homogeneity principle to create equal rights for this initial group of rights holders in the EU legal order also in the EEA was facilitated by the existence of (some) parallel provisions in the EEA Agreement at the primary law level, namely the right to free movement of services. Hence, the paralleling of rights both for the service providers and for the service recipients (such as patients and students) in the EEA integration process may, at first sight, be interpreted as a straightforward application of the core of the homogeneity principle. It will be demonstrated in the following analysis that this, in fact, was not a straightforward exercise, in particular due to the lack of the same legal basis in terms of revised primary law provisions as well as the difference between the primary/secondary law distinction and last but not least the significant impact of the healthcare case law in other areas of welfare services.

References

de Witte F (2013) Who funds the mobile student? Shedding some light on the normative assumptions underlying EU free movement law. Common Mark Law Rev 50:203–216

Dougan M (2008) Cross-border educational mobility and the exportation of student financial assistance. Eur Law Rev 33(5):723–738

Dougan M, Spaventa E (2003) Educating Rudy and the (non-)English patient: a double-bill on residency rights under Article 18 EC, 28. Eur Law Rev 28:699–671

Fenger N (2006) Limits to a dynamic homogeneity between EC law and EEA law. In: Fenger N, Hagel Sørensen K, Vesterdorf B (eds) Festskrift Claus Gulman. Karnov Group, Copenhagen, pp 131–154

Fredriksen HH (2014) EEA main agreement and secondary EU law incorporated into the annexes and protocols. In: Baudenbacher C (ed) The handbook of EEA law. Springer, Berlin, pp 95–113

---

[26] A recent letter of formal notice regarding the organisation of the right to health care services abroad in the Norwegian legislation from the EFTA Surveillance Authority is also made part of the analysis, see Sect. 3.2.4.

Hancher L, Sauter W (2012) EU competition and internal market law in the healthcare sector. Oxford University Press, Oxford

Hatzopoulos VG (2005) Health law and policy: the impact of the EU. In: De Burca G (ed) EU law and the welfare state. Oxford University Press, Oxford, pp 111–168

Hervey TK (2011a) Public health services and EU law. In: Cremona M (ed) Market integration and public services in the European Union. Oxford University Press, Oxford, pp 179–250

Hervey T (2011b) If only it were so simple: public health services and EU law. In: Cremona M (ed) Market integration and public services in the European Union. Oxford University Press, Oxford, pp 179–250

Mossialos E, Permanand G, Baeten R, Hervey T (eds) (2010) Health systems governance in Europe: the role of EU law and policy. Cambridge University Press, Cambridge

Newdick C (2006) Citizenship, free movement and health care cementing individual rights by corroding social solidarity. Common Mark Law Rev 43:1645–1668

Palm W (2002) Voluntary health insurance and EU insurance directives: between solidarity and the market. In: McKee M et al (eds) The impact of EU law on health care systems. Peter Lang, Bruxelles, pp 196–197

Prosser T (2005) The limits of competition law: markets and public services. Oxford Scholarship online, Oxford

Prosser T (2010) EU competition law and public services. In: Mossialos E, Permanand G, Baeten R, Hervey T (eds) Health systems governance in Europe: the role of EU law and policy. Cambridge University Press, Cambridge

Stjernø S (2005) Solidarity in Europe. Cambridge University Press, Cambridge

Chapter 3
The Provision of Healthcare Services: Free Movement Rights for Patients

3.1 The EU Legal Order

3.1.1 The Case Law from the CJEU on Healthcare Services

The CJEU clarified already in the Luisi and Carbone cases[1] that healthcare services are not automatically excluded from the ambit of 'economic fundamental freedoms' of the EU. The Court recognised not only that cross-border provision of health services is governed by now Article 56 TFEU but also that recipients of such services have equivalent rights to providers thereof. The Court's early position was reiterated in Grogan.[2] However, neither of the cases provided details or further clarifications on the issue.

It is important to distinguish the application of EU law to the situation where medical services are paid for by the patient either directly or indirectly via a private healthcare scheme of which the patient is a member from the situation where medical services are covered by public health schemes (benefits-in-kind systems funded through general taxation). The situation examined by the Court in the Luisi and Carbone case concerned the possibility for a citizen to go to another Member State to receive medical services for which he was prepared to pay from his own resources. It was in this context that the Court made the breakthrough decision and held that the freedom to provide services also included the freedom to receive services—a fundamental precondition for later case law.

The situation is clearly different where medical services to be received in another Member State are to be paid for by a public health scheme.

[1] Joined Cases 286/82 and 26/83 Luisi & Carbone [1984] ECR 377, paragraph 16.

[2] Case C-159/90 Society for the protection of unborn children Ireland [1991] ECR I-4685.

K. Fløistad, *The EEA Agreement in a Revised EU Framework for Welfare Services*, Studies in European Economic Law and Regulation 13,
https://doi.org/10.1007/978-3-319-95043-3_3

With its judgments in the Kohll[3] and Decker cases,[4] the CJEU for the first time also qualified healthcare services provided within a social/public insurance system as economic services to the patients that come within the scope of the free movement of services provision. The cases date back to the year 1998 and they were therefore decided after the signing of the EEA Agreement. In the cases, the Court followed Advocate General Tesauro and made it clear that Article 56 TFEU does apply to health services even when they are provided in the context of a social security scheme. Kohll concerned medical treatment by a dentist acting alone, and thus, it was not until the Vanbraekel and Peerbooms cases that the Court made the significant step to also include treatment offered in a hospital infrastructure as a service in the meaning of Article 56 TFEU.

In Vanbraekel[5] and Geraets-Smits and Peerbooms[6] from 2001, the CJEU clarified and extended the applicability of internal market principles to cover the way that healthcare services are provided and, therefore, indirectly, the way national social policies are given shape.

The Vanbraekel case concerned a Belgian woman trying to obtain reimbursement from her social security fund for treatment received in a French hospital. She had complied with the conditions of then Articles 22(1) and 29 of the Regulation 1408/71[7] concerning prior authorisation. However, in the case under discussion, benefits provided for by the French (host) legislation were lower than those offered by the Belgian fund for the same treatment administered within Belgium. Therefore, the question arose as to whether the rule in Regulation 1408/71 entitled beneficiaries to recover the higher benefits stipulated by the legislation of their home state or whether the refund was limited to the level stipulated for by the host state legislation.

In the Peerbooms case, the very requirement of prior authorisation was challenged under the Treaty rules on services. Under the Dutch social security system, patients are treated for free by care providers (mostly national) who have concluded an agreement with the social security fund. Authorisation to be treated by a care provider with whom no agreement had been concluded was only given by the fund if two conditions were met: The treatment for which authorisation was required should be considered (a) normal in the professional circles concerned, and (b) it should be necessary—in terms of both time and quality—for the particular patient.[8]

It is interesting to note that in both cases, the two opinions of the Advocate Generals and many of the intervening Governments contended that the Treaty rules on services did not apply precisely, because healthcare services provided in the

---

[3] Case C-158/96 Kohll [1998] ECR I-1931.

[4] Case C-120/95 Decker [1998] ECR I-01831.

[5] Case C-368/98 Vanbraekel [2001] ECR I-5363.

[6] Case C-157/99 Geraets-Smits and Peerbooms [2001] ECR I-5473.

[7] Now Regulation 883/2004 on coordination of social security systems, referred to at point 1 of chapter I of annex VI to the EEA Agreement, see Article 20. See for a more detailed account of the coordination regime in Part II, in particular Sect. 5.3.3 and Chap. 8.

[8] Case C-157/99 Geraets-Smits and Peerbooms [2001] ECR I-5473, paragraphs 23 and 24.

context of social security schemes do not fall within the ambit of Article 56 TFEU for lack of remuneration.

The cases were distinguished prima facie from the judgments in Decker and Kohll because of the difference between, on the one hand, social security systems where patients are treated for 'free' by care providers chosen by the social security fund and, on the other hand, systems where the patients go to the practitioner of choice and are then entitled to a refund. For healthcare benefits offered in kind, both Advocate Generals concluded that there was no element of remuneration that they found to be a condition for the applicability of the free movement of services provision.

The reasoning by the Advocate Generals that led to the conclusion that healthcare services offered free to patients did not qualify as 'services' also relied on the Court's judgment in Humbel.[9] This case is also dealt with in more detail in Chap. 4 on educational services as well as in Part III regarding state aid to educational facilities.[10] In Humbel, the Court held that national education systems stand outside the scope of the free movement of services provision and that the eventual payment of registration fees did not constitute remuneration. Regarding healthcare offered in hospitals, it was emphasised that such services form an integral part of the national health systems, since they are set up and run by the state and financed through public funds.[11]

The Court, on the other hand, stated that the medical activities fell within the scope of the Treaty and there was no need to distinguish between care provided in a hospital environment and care provided outside such environment. In the justification, the CJEU has arguably stretched the notion of remuneration to cover payments that bear only indirect relation to the service provided. The decision may, however, have been partly motivated by the difficulty of distinguishing between the Member States depending on the national choices as to the model for financing and delivering healthcare to the population. In other words, the Court may have felt compelled to introduce the same or similar protection under EU law for patients regardless of whether they were covered by a national system adhering to a public[12] or to a private/market oriented[13] organisation of treatment. The CJEU seems to have perceived healthcare as a personal entitlement, unconnected to the patient's relationship with a specific national social security scheme.

In the later Müller-Faure case[14] decided in 2003, a refund was asked for by an institution operating a benefits-in-kind scheme. The general direction of increasingly

[9] Case 263/86 Humbel [1988] ECR I-5365.

[10] Section 11.3.2.

[11] Opinion of Advocate General Saggio in Case C-368/98 Vanbraekel [2001] ECR I-5363, paragraphs 20–21, see also Advocate General Ruiz-Jarabo Colomer in Case C-157/99 Geraets-Smits and Peerbooms [2001] ECR I-5473, paragraphs 44–46.

[12] Like the NHS system in the UK, see for a recent analysis by de Mars (2014), pp. 770–789.

[13] Like the Dutch system where the Government is more oriented towards regulating than operating the deliverer of the healthcare services.

[14] Case C-385/99 Müller-Faure [2003] ECR I-4509.

including national healthcare provision into the scope of EU law seems to have been extended to also apply to healthcare services provided through a tax-based system operating a benefits-in-kind system. Implicitly, the Court has confirmed that this position also applies in principle where the cross-border service of healthcare is received by a patient who is insured under a national healthcare system financed largely by public taxation provided that the patient has received a cross-border service.[15] However, in the Watts[16] and the subsequent Stamatelaki[17] cases, the Court was not required to answer the specific question of whether hospital treatment provided by a national health system funded largely by taxation constitutes a service in the sense of Article 56 TFEU, given that in the cases, the patients had themselves directly remunerated the hospital. The Watts case demonstrates, however, that states are required to have a mechanism by which costs of healthcare received in another Member State are to be calculated to help facilitate cross-border enjoyment of services for patients. This mechanism must be based on objective non-discriminatory criteria known in advance again demonstrating the degree of intervention by EU law into domestic systems of welfare provision.[18]

In the case of Elchinov,[19] the CJEU found the national rule that excluded, in all cases, payment for hospital treatment given in another Member State without prior authorisation incompatible with the free movement of services provision and Regulation 1408/71 Article 22.[20] In the case at hand, the patient could not for medical reasons wait for the authorisation procedure to be completed before Mr. Elchinov had the operation.[21] The case concerned a resident of Bulgaria who had received hospital treatment in Germany but was refused reimbursement of costs from the Bulgarian healthcare scheme. The treatment in question was an advanced therapy that was not yet available in Bulgaria and the legal question was whether it could be classified under the heading of types of treatment covered by the Bulgarian legislation.[22] The CJEU required the national court to interpret the national rule that defined which types of treatment were reimbursable based on objective and non-discriminatory criteria.[23] Furthermore, authorisation must be given if the alternative treatment (in the resident state) is not equally effective provided that the treatment abroad is covered by the national legislation.[24]

---

[15] Hervey (2011), pp. 222–223.

[16] Case C-372/04 Watts [2006] ECR I-4325.

[17] Case C-444/05 Stamatelaki [2007] ECR I-3185.

[18] See also the case of Inizan, Case C-56/01 Inizian [2003] ECR I-12403.

[19] Case C-173/09 Elchinov [2010] ECR I-8889, see also Case C-512/08 Commission v. France [2010] ECR I-8833 where the Court rejected both of the Commission claims against the French system of reimbursement of costs for medical expenses.

[20] Replaced by Regulation 883/2004 Article 20.

[21] Paragraphs 45–50.

[22] Paragraphs 56–62.

[23] Paragraphs 68–72.

[24] Paragraphs 63–67.

As demonstrated above, the reasoning of the CJEU in the cases is built on arguments relating to the rights of the service provider and the service recipient. The outcome of the case law is the creation of the new right to effective and speedy medical treatment to patients—an outcome that brings the EU closer to its citizens. Now, Union citizens are entitled to benefit from high-quality healthcare in their home state, but if this cannot be achieved, they can seek medical treatment in another Member State for which the home state will be liable. The emergence of this new right for Union citizens to seek healthcare in another Member State represents significant challenges for national public health systems.

> There is no doubt that the new right, even in its imperfect form, provides a tangible right for EU citizens. They will neither have to wait indefinitely to obtain medical treatment nor have to accept substandard treatment in their Member State of insurance.[25]

In Stamatelaki, the Advocate General pointed to the general right of citizens to healthcare.[26] Specifically, Article 35 of the Charter of Fundamental Rights was highlighted by the Advocate General, who also stated, 'being a fundamental asset, health cannot be considered solely in terms of social expenditure and latent economic difficulties'.[27] The reference to the Charter-protected rights illuminates how different provisions work together in the formulation of the legal reasoning. Kaczorowska has argued convincingly on the political importance of Article 35 and claimed that its significance to inspire the CJEU to develop and embroider a new right to effective and speedy medical treatment should not be underestimated.[28]

3.1.2 Primary and Secondary Law in the EU Legal Order in the Field of Public Healthcare Services

In order to better understand the significance of the case law developments from the CJEU regarding healthcare services in an EEA context it is necessary to first explain the situation of patient's free movement rights according to the secondary legislation. The significance of applying the primary law provision of free movement of services as well as the reliance on the distinction between primary/secondary law in the EU will then subsequently be explained in an EEA context. Before moving into the substance it should also be clarified that the case law by the CJEU in the healthcare sector has proven important as a reference point for the scope of EU law into the provision of publicly financed educational services (see Chap. 4) and for the scope of application of the state aid provision (see Part III).

[25] Kaczorowska (2006), p. 370.

[26] Advocate General Ruiz-Jarabo Colomer' s opinion in Case C-444/05 Stamatelaki [2007] ECR I-3185, paragraph 40.

[27] Advocate General Ruiz-Jarabo Colomer' s opinion in Case C-444/05 Stamatelaki [2007] ECR I-3185C-444/05, paragraph 40.

[28] Kaczorowska (2006), pp. 345–346.

The Citizens Directive 2004/38

The Citizens Directive 2004/38[29] has been analysed in the context of the sustainability of public health systems in the area of non-economically active citizens' right to move freely. In particular, the question of whether the United Kingdom National Health Service (NHS) can rely on concepts of 'unreasonable burden' or 'real link' tests to restrict non-economically active Union citizens' access to the NHS has been discussed in the literature.[30] The free movement rights of non-economically active persons are analysed generally in Part II. For the purpose of the case study of free movement of healthcare services and patients' free movement rights, it suffices to analyse the coordination system for social security, since neither the CJEU nor the EFTA Court or the Surveillance Authority has applied the Citizens Directive in this field for rights under the EEA Agreement.

The Coordination Regime for Social Security Benefits and Free Movement of Services

Under Regulation 1408/71,[31] access to cross-border healthcare provision financed by the home state social security/public insurance system was to be provided only in very special cases: first, when the condition of urgency of the treatment was met, and second, when a prior authorisation from the patient's competent social security/public insurance institution had been given.[32]

The initial rationale of Regulation 1408/71 was far from offering to patients a choice as to the most efficient healthcare service provider but rather to take away impediments in the area of social security in order to facilitate free movement of workers and self-employed persons.[33] The main elements of coordination are non-discrimination through aggregating periods of insurance, work or residence, payment of benefits and determining the legislation applicable. The Regulation limits its ambit to the coordination of the basic national rules in the field of social and welfare benefits.[34] The Regulation follows the principle confirmed time and again

---

[29] Directive 2004/38 was incorporated into the EEA Agreement through an amendment of annexes V and VIII, and the Directive entered into force in the EEA on 1 March 2009, see decision by the EEA Committee No 158/2007 OJ 2008L 124, p. 20, and EEA Supplement No 26 8.5.2008, p. 17. The Citizens Directive in the EEA is analysed extensively in Part II, see Sect. 5.3.2 and Chap. 7.

[30] de Mars (2014), pp. 770–789.

[31] Incorporated in the EEA Agreement in annex VI Social Security and later replaced by Regulation 883/2004. The revised Regulation was incorporated in the EEA Agreement in annex VI Social Security. The coordination regime in the EEA is analysed extensively in Part II, see Sect. 5.3.3 and Chap. 8.

[32] See article 22 of Regulation 1408/71, the equivalent provision in Regulation 883/2004 is worded slightly different, see below in Sect. 3.2.4.

[33] For an analysis of to what extent Regulation 883/2004 changed the scope of persons covered, see Pennings (2005), pp. 241–260.

[34] See First recital of the Regulation.

by the Court that social security systems remain a domain reserved for Member States' competence. It therefore does not touch the core of the national rules but only establishes some degree of coordination, whereby fundamentally different systems may work together in order to secure minimal social and healthcare benefits.

Given that the Regulation only performed coordination on Member States' social security and healthcare and did not achieve (or aim to achieve) any substantial degree of harmonisation, the CJEU in several instances interpreted the Regulation in an extensive manner so as to cover gaps not directly covered under the provisions of the Regulation.[35] The activist approach by the Court led the Council to amend the Regulation on several occasions, thus reversing and restricting previous judicial interpretations. This, in turn, led the Court in its later case law to base its judgments directly on the Treaty provisions on free movement, which are beyond the reach of the legislator.[36] Recently, the case law from the Court has been partly codified in the Patients' Rights Directive.[37] For the present analysis, the purpose is to analyse the increased rights of patients justified by an interpretation of the primary law and the subsequent evolution of the same rights in the EEA legal order. Hence, the following analysis will comment on the relationship between the previous secondary legislation as adopted in Regulation 1408/71 and primary law.[38]

An EU citizen may thus be entitled to move to another Member State to receive healthcare services either under the specific provisions of previous Regulation 1408/71 or as a recipient of services in the sense of Article 56 and the case law. The rights under the Regulation are to be seen as *lex specialis* in relation to the Treaty provision, not in the sense of allowing derogation but in the sense of being a more specific application of a general rule. The former Regulation 1408/71 sets the minimal coordinating standards, enhancing the various healthcare systems to work together in view of the realisation of the objectives of free movement.[39] However, according to the CJEU, the Regulation may not work to the detriment of the effects stemming from the direct application of the above Treaty provisions.

Without invalidating Regulation 1408/71, the CJEU interpreted it in such a way as to eliminate its alleged restrictive effects. The CJEU used a technique whereby it stated that the existence of the Regulation does not preclude the application of the

[35] See as an example, Case C-117/77 Pierik [1978] ECR 825, see for an account of the history of social security coordination by Raptopoulou (2015), pp. 15–26.

[36] For a comprehensive analysis of the history and background of social security coordination, see Van der Mei (2003), see Part II for a more detailed analysis in the context of non-economically active Union citizens.

[37] The legal basis for the Patients' Rights Directive or Directive 2011/24 is not only Article 114 TFEU but also Article 168 TFEU making it less obvious that all parts of the Directive are of EEA relevance The Directive was nevertheless incorporated in its entirety into the EEA Agreement by Joint Committee Decision No 153/2014 and entered into force on 1 August 2015, see the act referred to in point 2 of annex X to the EEA Agreement.

[38] This is the Regulation in force when the EFTA Court handed down is principal decision in Joined Cases E-11/07 and E-1/08 Rindal and Slinning, see Sect. 3.2.

[39] For a more detailed account, see Hatzopoulos (2002), p. 696.

Treaty rules and then went on to construe the two in a complimentary way.[40] The alternative would be to treat Regulation 1408/71 as the only occasion in which social security funds may be called upon to reimburse expenses incurred in another Member State. In more concrete terms, a possible interpretation of EU law requirements regarding public funding for the receipt of healthcare services in another Member State could be, except for in emergencies, to obtain an authorisation by the competent fund in the home state. This is the procedure envisaged in Article 22 in Regulation 1408/71, which could be seen as a specific application of the general Treaty rules on free movement in terms of the reimbursement of health expenditures.

A starting point when interpreting the secondary legislation as provisions seen as a specific application of the general Treaty rules on free movement is to interpret them to not only regulate when reimbursement must be made (minimum requirements) but also set the conditions of when reimbursement must be made according to EU law (maximum requirements). In other words, prior to the case law, Member States could have relied on the compatibility of a national requirement of prior authorisation before medical services received in other Member States had to be reimbursed. Put differently, the Regulation could have been interpreted as the only occasion in which social security funds may be called upon to reimburse expenses for healthcare services received in other Member States.[41] This was, however, not the way forward chosen by the Court. The interpretation by the CJEU, relying on primary law, arguably undermined the very importance of the Regulation. It has even been stated that the Court reduced the importance of the relevant Regulation provisions, 'since it deprived them of any clear content'.[42]

When the Court chose another approach, namely to apply the Treaty provisions in a complimentary way, thereby effectively undermining the limits inherent in the secondary legislation, the explanation seemed to be (partly) the hierarchal relationship between Treaty provisions on the one hand and Regulations (and Directives) on the other hand.[43] Treaty provisions are primary law and as such may lead to the conclusion that it deprives the Regulation of its allegedly restrictive effects. Hence, the Court developed a system whereby patients could receive funding for healthcare received in other Member States without prior authorisation. Ignoring the requirement of prior authorisation in the Regulation led to the possibility of patients going

---

[40] See as an example Case C-56/01 Inizian [2003] ECR I-12403.

[41] In a previous case on pension rights, case C-100/78 Rossi [1979] ECR 831 the CJEU found that the answer could not be determined based on the Regulation dealing with social security for migrant workers, the Court chose to interpret the Regulation in light of the aims pursued by the provisions of the Treaty. Hence, in this case the Regulation and the Treaty provision were not applied cumulatively. In the healthcare cases the Court has opted for the cumulative approach.

[42] Hatzopoulos (2002), p. 697.

[43] See for a similar approach regarding the hierarchal relationship between the provisions in Hatzopoulos (2002), p. 696 with references to commentators who take a different position, see Chap. 1 in footnote 64.

directly to their practitioner of choice in any Member State and then asking for a refund from their national home state fund.[44]

As is demonstrated by the case law from the CJEU, it was not until long after the EEA Agreement had been agreed that the Court made it clear that a patient could rely on the Treaty provisions alone to include healthcare provided for free in a hospital as a service, thereby bringing it within the scope of the EU fundamental freedoms (and therefor also within the scope of the EEA fundamental freedoms). Consequently, this facilitated the top-up of the reimbursement provided for by the Regulation.

Furthermore, the EU constitutional framework for health regulation had changed since the signing of the EEA Agreement, including healthcare protection in EU law through the present Articles 168 TFEU and 35 in the Charter of Fundamental Rights. Furthermore, the EU constitutional framework includes the status of Union citizenship, Articles 20 and 21 TFEU.

In an EEA context, an objection to a parallel application of the development in the healthcare sector is the lack of a hierarchical structure in addition to the much more limited scope of the Agreement not including any parallel provisions to present Articles 168 TFEU and 35 in the Charter of Fundamental Rights nor any Union citizenship provisions. Thus, the freedom of movement of services is at the outset on an equal footing with the Regulation—there is no hierarchy, and the Agreement includes no general health protection provisions. Given this starting point, it was much less evident to interpret the right to receive reimbursement for healthcare beyond the *lex specialis* provision in Article 22 in Regulation 1408/71 based on the free movement of services provision in an EEA context. In other words, in the EEA, there is support for understanding and interpreting Regulation 1408/71 as the only occasion in which the social security funds may be called upon to reimburse expenses in other EEA states.

The central tenet of the CJEU's approach in the healthcare case law is the economic nature of medical services. It is for this reason that they are held to be within the scope of the free movement of services provision.[45] Through the choice of the CJEU to deliver the judgments in an economic rather than welfare language, the paralleling of the Court's interpretation may seem more obvious in an EEA context. After all, the legal basis of free movement of services is paralleled in the EEA legal order. The case law by the CJEU has, however, met extensive criticism in the academic analysis primarily based on the impact of focusing on individual rights and applying the economic terminology of services rather than properly assessing systemic considerations of welfare provision.[46] In short, the case law may have benefitted the legal position of some individuals, but in doing so, it has also entered into the complex consequences of patient mobility and the organisation of social security systems. As commented upon in the introduction solidaristic systems may be undermined by excessive movements of patients. The financial implication of

[44] For a comparison of differences and points in common in the two options for the patients, the Regulation or the provision of free movement of services, see Hatzopoulos (2005), pp. 142–145.

[45] For an analysis of healthcare as an economic service, see Koutrakos (2005), pp. 105–130.

[46] Examples include Hervey (2011), pp. 179–250; Hatzopoulos (2002), pp. 683–729.

judicially driven market integration for healthcare service provision is an aspect that elevates the case law to have broader consequences than the language of economic services may imply. Hence, even if the legal basis of free movement of services is paralleled in the EEA and the economic language fits the rhetoric in the decisions from the CJEU of the market integration objective of the Agreement, the subject matter goes far beyond this limited objective.

These points were never discussed when the EFTA Court for the first time addressed the issue of reimbursement rights for costs of receiving cross-border health services in the case of Slinning and Rindal.[47] On the contrary, the EFTA Court seemed to have rephrased the question from the national court so as to avoid the principal question of any possible differences between the EU and the EEA legal order in the healthcare sector. In later sections, it will be demonstrated that the institutions applying the EEA Agreement continued down the same path for other aspects of welfare integration but this time without the parallel provisions in the Agreement. The area of public healthcare may have been an important first step of welfare integration in the EEA hidden in the language of healthcare being limited to an economic service.

The potential consequences for the EU Member States and their social security systems should also be noted. Paralleling the EU legal order in the field of healthcare to be included in the EEA Agreement also means extending the territories upon which the EU Member States may be required to reimburse patients' treatment. In other words, patients from EU Member States may also seek medical treatment in the three EFTA States and claim reimbursement from the social security systems in their home state provided the interpretation by the EFTA Court is accepted in the EU legal order.[48]

3.2 The EEA Legal Order: Including Publicly Funded Patient Mobility in the EEA—Cases E-11/07 and E-1/08 and Case No 72376

3.2.1 Introduction

The EFTA Court Cases E-11/07 and E-1/08[49] concerned two preliminary references from Norwegian domestic courts regarding requests for reimbursement of medical expenses incurred by treatment in another EEA state. The EFTA Surveillance Authority Case No 72376 concerns access to hospital treatment in other EEA states.

---

[47] Joined Cases E-11/07 and E-1/08, Olga Rindal and Therese Slinning v Staten v/Dispensasjons— og klagenemnda for bidrag til behandling i utlandet.

[48] This potential effect on the EU Member States of EEA law obligations is explained further in Sects. 7.2.9.2 and 7.3.4.

[49] Decided 19 December 2008.

3.2.2 EFTA Court: The Facts of the Two Cases

One of the plaintiffs, Olga Rindal, was diagnosed with whiplash after having suffered an automobile accident in 1987. In spite of different forms of treatment, including surgery in May 1999, her pain did not go away. In 2000, the final specialist report concluded that further surgical treatment was not indicated. Therefore, no further surgery was offered to Ms. Rindal. Later, Ms. Rindal was referred by her doctor to a private clinic in Germany, where she received surgical treatment. The operations consisted of fixation of the neck and stabilisation of the lower back through the use of titanium plates. According to Ms. Rindal, both operations improved her state of health. Her claim for reimbursement was rejected by the Norwegian national administrative authority.

The Board of Appeals stated, inter alia, that while immobilisation of the neck was an operation that was also performed to a relatively large degree in Norway, it was not performed on the basis of Ms. Rindal's indications. With regard to the neck operation, the administrative authority stated, in particular, that there was scant documentation and that the method could not be considered the norm in international medical circles applied in relation to the indications that Ms. Rindal had.

The other plaintiff, Therese Slinning, sustained a serious brain injury in a traffic accident in March 2002. Early on, it was presumed that she would not survive, and therefore, in the beginning, it was not considered appropriate to offer her rehabilitation at a specialised hospital. Ms. Slinning lived mostly in a nursing home mainly equipped for elderly people. Ms. Slinning underwent treatment at Hammel Neurocenter in Denmark, and at the time of the treatment, the rehabilitation arrangement at Hammel was not on offer in Norway.

According to the written observations of the Government of Denmark, all patients in Denmark have a right to be referred to this rehabilitation service, provided that they meet the indication criteria. Efforts were made to establish several elements of the Danish treatment as test treatment in Norway. Ms. Slinning's application for coverage of her expenses at Hammel Neurocenter was rejected by the Norwegian administrative authority.

The administrative authority based its decision on two sets of grounds. First, it stated that there was adequate treatment for Ms. Slinning available in Norway, even though it considered the treatment offered at Hammel Neurocenter to be more comprehensive and intensive than that offered at Norwegian hospitals. The Board found that the treatment available in Norway ought, as a main rule, to be utilised even if a possibly more advanced treatment had been developed abroad. Second, the treatment at Hammel was considered to be experimental/test treatment and not scientifically documented. The right to treatment abroad did not encompass experimental or test treatment.

Based on the facts of the two cases, it seemed as if neither Ms. Rindal nor Ms. Slinning had received particularly successful treatments by the national healthcare system. The facts do point in the direction that, to a certain extent, the national healthcare had failed in improving their medical situation, something that had been achieved by the treatment abroad. The medical conditions, including the alternative treatments, in the two cases were, however, extremely complicated and open to a difference of medical opinion. The plaintiffs' arguments were largely based on the understanding that given the national right to healthcare and the perceived need for them to go abroad to receive this healthcare, they should not be left with the responsibility of covering the costs. The overall principal question was therefore if EEA law provided any protection in the situation where the medical treatment abroad provided more sufficient treatment of a particular medical condition compared to the national medical healthcare.

3.2.3 *The Opinion of the EFTA Court in Cases E-11/07 and E-1/08*

The relationship between the Regulation and the main part of the EEA Agreement.

The questions from the national courts were based both on Article 22 Regulation 1408/71 and on Article 36 EEA on the freedom to provide services. A first observation to note is the fact that the Court did not apply the Regulation. The Court stated that it only found it appropriate to assess the issues under Articles 36 and 37 EEA.[50] The EFTA Court stated that:

> as the Regulation entails coordination rather than harmonisation of social security systems, Article 22 would allow an EEA State to deny prior authorisation to receive treatment abroad which according to international medicine must be considered experimental or test treatment, in cases where Article 36 EEA, in accordance with the Court's findings below, would allow the State to refuse coverage of expenses for such treatment.[51]

Thus, the Court builds its reasoning on an understanding of the Regulation and the right to free movement giving parallel rights and obligations. This is not a correct interpretation. Article 22 can, in certain situations, give patients further rights than what is covered by the freedom to provide/receive services. An example of this would be the situation where the host state provides more advanced treatment than the home state. The principle of equal treatment ensures that the worker must be offered the treatment right at his or her place of residence and this may have to be financed by the home state. Free movement of services, however, does not compel the home state to expand its offered medical services beyond the national scope. Furthermore, the amount of reimbursement, according to Article 22, may be topped up by host state tariffs, whereas according to the freedom of services rules, it can never exceed tariffs in the home state even if the patient has paid more. This means that even if the Court found that Articles 36 and 37 were not violated by the administrative decisions, they should have proceeded to assess whether Article 22 of the Regulation would give the patients such rights.

---

[50] Paragraph 41.

[51] Paragraph 41.

To complicate matters further, it is also true that in other situations, the fundamental freedom of movement of services can extend patients' rights compared to the Regulation. Regulation 1408/71 paragraph 22 concerns the reimbursement of health expenses but is limited in terms of personal scope of the Regulation as well as the requirement of prior authorisation. In case law, the CJEU has ignored the limits in the Regulation by acknowledging healthcare as a service falling under Article 56 TFEU where both providers and recipients have rights.

It is possible that the EFTA Court's reasoning on this point relates to the sensitivity of applying Articles 36 and 37 EEA in the case. It will be recalled that this was quite controversial in the EU legal order. By 'pretending' that these rights also follow from the Regulation, the threshold for the EFTA Court is lowered. Yet, it must have been clear to the EFTA Court that the Regulation was not applicable in the situations at hand. The plaintiffs were not migrating workers or family members of migrating workers. The case concerned two Norwegian nationals seeking reimbursement from the Norwegian social security fund. The only cross-border element in the case was related to the service provider being established in another EEA state. Furthermore, neither of the patients had acquired any prior authorisation. However, through applying the fundamental freedom of movement of services in the same manner as the CJEU (including the understanding that recipients are protected), the EFTA Court was in a position to reach an outcome of securing patient's rights also in the EEA. However, this protection of service providers and service recipients only stems from the primary law provisions in EU law and in parallel Articles 36 and 37 EEA and not from the harmonised Regulation even if the EFTA Court tried to indicate otherwise.

The above demonstrates that there were no alternatives for the EFTA Court but to rely on Articles 36 and 37 EEA given that, based on the facts, the Regulation was not applicable in the case. Through its decision, the Court included the protection of health service recipients' rights to go abroad to receive services and potentially claim reimbursement from the national social security fund. This observation begs the question of why the EFTA Court did not discuss the principal extension of EEA law, namely to provide welfare protection under EEA law ensuring non-economically active own nationals' reimbursement rights against national welfare funds. It was evident from the wording of the Regulation that this type of claim was never envisaged under the harmonised legislation, which had been incorporated into the EEA Agreement to protect the free movement of workers (the economically active). Thus, when the EFTA Court applied Articles 36 and 37 EEA to the facts of the case, this in itself represented a significant extension of scope of the EEA Agreement. There is, however, no evidence in the case of the Court taking a principal view on this question or indeed highlighting the alternative choices that could be made. On the contrary, the Court seems to have avoided the questions hiding behind a cryptic statement that the result would also follow from the Regulation.[52]

---

[52] See the cited paragraph 41.

Furthermore, the EFTA Court's reliance on the Regulation and the free movement provision to essentially give rights and obligations in parallel is consistent with the Court avoiding to clarify a more legal technical difference between the EU and the EEA. The analysis of the case law from the CJEU has demonstrated the 'necessity' for the reasoning in the CJEU case law of the distinction between primary and secondary law to reach the result. At the outset, Regulation 1408/71 Article 22 did provide a detailed harmonised legislative measure on the extent of the right to recover expenses from the home state for medical treatment abroad. From the wording of the harmonised legislation, a possible interpretation would be that this provision also represented the limits of such cover of expenses from the home state. However, as demonstrated above, the CJEU developed the principle in the Treaty on the right to receive services to go beyond the Regulation. In this line of argument, an important element of the CJEU reasoning was the need to rely on the Treaty obligation to be primary law in the EU. Without a similar distinction in EEA law between primary and secondary law, the same type of interpretation seems at least questionable and again should have been addressed by the Court in such a principal and novel decision.

3.2.4 The EFTA Surveillance Authority: Case No 72376

The EFTA Surveillance Authority Case No 72376 concerns an alleged breach of Article 20 of Regulation 883/2004[53] and/or Article 36 EEA in the system in place in Norway concerning access to hospital treatment in other EEA states (so-called in-patient treatment).[54] The conditions inherent in the national system are relevant for anyone who is insured under the national insurance scheme, primarily Norwegian nationals. Provided the patient in general is entitled to healthcare, the system foresees two alternative situations in which patients can be entitled to treatment abroad.

The first only becomes active following the expiry of the time limit set pursuant to Section 2-1b(2) of the national Patients' Rights Act, entitling the patient to treatment abroad or with a private service provider on specific conditions. The second concerns the right to medical treatment abroad if there are no adequate medical services in the realm, provided certain conditions are met, in particular regarding acceptable methods. However, the right to treatment abroad is limited generally to situations where the necessary competence in Norway is lacking:

[53] Former Article 22 of Regulation 1408/71 was worded slightly differently than Article 20 of Regulation 883/2004. Article 20(2) of Regulation 883/2004 which incorporates case law from the Court provides that authorisation 'shall be accorded where the treatment in question is among the benefits provided for by the legislation in the Member State where the person concerned resides and where he cannot be given such treatment within a time-limit which is medically justifiable, taking into account his current state of health and the probable cause of the illness'.

[54] See letter of formal notice to Norway 14 May 2014, Case No. 72376, see also supplementary letter 3 February 2016 of formal notice to Norway concerning criteria for access to in-patient treatment in other EEA states from Norway.

> A basic requirement for contributions to treatment abroad has been a lack of medical competence in Norwegian hospitals. If treatment can be performed properly in Norway according to accepted methods, the Social Security Administration has not been allowed to pay contributions to the treatment abroad. This limitation will be continued under the present legislation. The general rule is that one should utilize the treatment found in Norway, even though a possibly more advanced treatment may have been developed abroad. This applies even if the patient wants treatment performed at a foreign institution for a method that is not used in Norway.[55]

The letter of formal notice concerns both substantive and procedural requirements in EEA law on the field of national health regulation. The Authority's opinion on the requirements of EEA law based on the free movement of services provision is stated in point 3.3 on page 10 and is based on the case law of the CJEU and the EFTA Court:

> a national social security administration cannot refuse under Article 36 EEA a request for reimbursement for in-patient treatment abroad, which is covered by its own system, when effective treatment cannot, at all or within a medically justifiable time limit, be provided to the patient under its national healthcare system.

This understanding of the Authority is based on a reference to the Rindal and Slinning cases dealt with in Sects. 3.2.2 and 3.2.3 above. The Authority also finds support for this understanding in Case C-173/09 Elchinov; see Sect. 3.1.1 above.

This is not the place for an in-depth discussion of EU/EEA law requirements on national health systems based on the provisions that are paralleled in the EEA Agreement, namely the provision of free movement of services and the coordination regime in the secondary legislation.[56] It will suffice to point out the same distinction that was made above regarding the cases of Rindal and Slinning. There is a difference between the requirements on national law, which can be based on the free movement of services provision, and the coordination regime. It is not surprising that the Authority follows the interpretation by the EFTA Court in the Rindal and Slinning cases.[57]

The points to address in this context are the Authority's claims against both the substantive and the procedural requirements that must be met regarding the authorisation/reimbursement procedure.[58] In its argumentation to support the understanding

---

[55] Rundskriv IS 12/2004 om lov om pasientrettigheter Section 2-1b(5), translated by the Authority unofficially on page 5 in the Reasoned opinion.

[56] See for a recent case analysis of Elchinov, C-173/09 and Commission v. France, C-512/08 concerning cross-border access to health care, Van der Mei (2011), pp. 1297–1311.

[57] In principle, EEA law does not require national systems to extend the treatments paid for by public funds. This is a political decision within the competences of the state and its prerogative of deciding how to organise their social security systems. Neither the Letter of formal notice nor the response by the Norwegian Ministry of Health and Care services (15 August 2015) mention the French case where the CJEU dismisses the Commission objections to the French system of reimbursement of costs for medical expenses, see Case C-512/08 Commission v. France See further on a recent interpretation by the Court in this field, Case C-268/13 regarding the Romanian system of reimbursement of costs for medical expenses, see also case C-255/09 regarding the Portuguese system which the CJEU did not find compatible with EU law obligations.

[58] See page 10 of the Reasoned opinion.

that the Norwegian system is incompatible with EEA law obligations, the Authority relies on an understanding of EEA law to always require the administrative procedure to take into account the specific circumstances of the patient's medical condition.[59] The Authority concludes that the national system does not adequately ensure on a case-by-case assessment whether equally effective treatment can be provided to the individual patient within a medically justifiable deadline.[60] The Authority illustrates the point by going through a number of decisions rejecting applications for funding and the reference in the decisions by the national health authority to the existence of Norwegian medical competence in the field.[61]

Two points can be made regarding the position of the Authority. First, the letter of formal notice seems to extend significantly the protection of patients requiring not only treatment within specific deadlines but also treatment with a specific quality and efficiency. States have limited funds at their disposal for the provision of healthcare services. Requiring reimbursement based on criteria of quality and efficiency endorses 'a race to the top' for the provision of healthcare services in the EEA.[62] This may seem to be an admirable aim viewed from the individual patient, but in practice, it places a serious restriction on states' ability to distribute the funds available to them in a way that reflects national healthcare provision.

The patients find themselves in a cross-border situation precisely because they seek treatment abroad.[63] The Authority's interpretation of the EEA Agreement is not directed at ensuring these patients equal rights to the patients who have never exercised their right to free movement. In fact, the patients seeking refund for treatment abroad are ensured an increased protection as compared to internal patients (static citizens). To this end, the question that must be addressed is whether the EEA Agreement without the legal framework regarding health protection enshrined in Article 168 TFEU and the patient's rights in Article 35 of the Charter, as well as the protection of Union citizens in Articles 20 and 21 TFEU, requires the community of citizens contributing to financing the national health services to bear the extra cost related to one patient's choice to have the treatment performed in a different Member State.

Second, the letter of formal notice seems to extend significantly the requirements of making individual assessments of each patient in terms of reimbursement. In the EU legal order, the detailed requirements of an individually based assessment taking the circumstances of each claimant into account specifically in the administrative decision is particularly highlighted and developed in the CJEU decisions on

---

[59] See page 13 of the Reasoned opinion.

[60] See page 16 of the Reasoned opinion.

[61] See pages 17–21 of the Reasoned opinion.

[62] The expression is used in connection with healthcare services in Lynskey (2011), p. 9.

[63] Relying on EEA law to protect patients, in particular own nationals who wish to receive refund for medical treatment abroad from their home state's social security fund seems to be more focused on protecting the individual patient than securing the free movement of services. These patients are not service recipients based on an already existing cross-border situation for instance situations where treatment is needed when the patient is already abroad for other purposes like tourism.

Union citizens' rights starting with the Baumbast decision.[64] This is elaborated on in more detail in Part II, in particular in Sect. 9.5 analysing the right to child support benefits. Case No 72376 is ongoing, and for the purpose of this analysis, it is sufficient to point to the case as an illustration of the extent to which the EFTA Surveillance Authority based on the case law from the CJEU and the EFTA Court interprets EEA law to in detail require adaptations of national social security systems in an EFTA State. Some reflections on the general consequences of the EEA integration process paralleling the EU integration process in the field of healthcare services and free movement rights of patients are provided after the next chapter (Chap. 4) on the EEA integration process and the provision of educational services (see Chap. 5).

References

de Mars S (2014) Economically inactive EU migrants and the United Kingdom's National Health Service: unreasonable burdens without real links? Eur Law Rev 39(6):770–789

Hatzopoulos VG (2002) Killing national health and insurance systems but healing patients? The European market for health care services after the judgments of the ECJ in Vanbraekel and Peerbooms. Common Mark Law Rev 39:683–729

Hatzopoulos VG (2005) Health law and policy: the impact of the EU. In: Burca GD (ed) EU law and the welfare state. Oxford University Press, Oxford, pp 111–168

Hervey T (2011) If only it were so simple: public health services and EU law. In: Cremona M (ed) Market integration and public services in the European Union. Oxford University Press, Oxford, pp 179–250

Kaczorowska A (2006) A review of the creation by the European Court of Justice of the right to effective and speedy medical treatment and its outcomes. Eur Law J 12(3):345–370

Koutrakos P (2005) Healthcare as an economic service under EC law. In: Dougan M, Spaventa E (eds) Social welfare and EU law. Hart, Oxford, pp 105–130

O Lynskey (2011) Revising the role of national courts in judicial dialogue in the EU; Elchinov, a missed opportunity? Eur Law Rep 01/2011, p 9

Pennings F (2005) Inclusion and exclusion of persons and benefits in the new co-ordination regulation. In: Spaventa E, Dougan M (eds) Social welfare and EU law. Hart, Oxford, pp 241–260

Raptopoulou KK (2015) EU law and healthcare services, normative approaches to public health systems. Wolters Kluwer, Alphen aan den Rijn, pp 15–26

Van der Mei AP (2003) Free movement of persons within the European Community cross-border access to public benefits. Hart, Oxford

Van der Mei AP (2011) Case 512/08, Commission v. France and case C-173/09, Georgi Ivanov Elchinov v. Natsionalna zdravnoosiguritelna kasa. Common Mark Law Rev 48:1297–1311

Miscellaneous

Rundskriv IS 12/2004 om lov om pasientrettigheter Section 2-1b(5), translated by the Authority unofficially on page 5 in the Reasoned opinion

---

[64] Case C-413/99 Baumbast v Secretary of State [2002] ECR I-7091.

Chapter 4
The Provision of Educational Services: Free Movement Rights for Students

4.1 Introduction

4.1.1 Financing Education: Member States Competence

Education involves costs for at least the state providing the education and the student (if financially independent) or those on whom the student is financially dependent. As a matter of EU law, Member States remain competent to decide whether or not to fund higher education and, if so, to what extent. Furthermore, EU law does not, in principle, have an impact on Member State's decision to make funding available for studies pursued at higher education institutions established outside its territory or the conditions it attaches to such finance.[1]

However, as continually confirmed by the CJEU, the Member States must exercise their competence in the educational field in compliance with EU law, i.e. certain national rules may violate the right to free movement of services and the situation of certain applicants for the funding may be covered by Union citizenship law. Such service providers and service recipients as well as such applicants may therefore derive rights under EU law including in relation to their Member State of origin. Thus, in the exercise of the Member States' competence in the field of education, they must comply with EU law.[2]

Since the primary law changes made in the Maastricht Treaty, the EU shall contribute to the development of quality education by encouraging cooperation between Member States and if necessary by supporting and supplementing their action.[3]

---

[1] Opinion of Advocate General Sharpston, Case C-359/13 B. Martens EU:C:2014:2240, paragraph 36.

[2] Opinion of Advocate General Sharpston, Case C-359/13 B. Martens EU:C:2014:2240, paragraph 37.

[3] See present Articles 165 and 166 TFEU.

K. Fløistad, *The EEA Agreement in a Revised EU Framework for Welfare Services*, Studies in European Economic Law and Regulation 13,
https://doi.org/10.1007/978-3-319-95043-3_4

Increasingly, the CJEU relies on a combination of the general Treaty provisions on education enshrined in Articles 165 and 166 TFEU and the status of Union citizenship as the legal bases to require Member States to make changes in their financing systems in cross-border study situations.[4] To this end, the EU integration process includes various rights for service providers and individuals with corresponding obligations on states in the field of education.

Hence, this field provides another suited case study for the overall objective of this book given the reliance in the EU integration process in the educational field on primary law provisions not paralleled in the EEA Agreement. Furthermore, the decisional practice of the EFTA Surveillance Authority demonstrates in various ways how the Authority has reconciled the lack of equivalent primary law provisions in this field with the principles of dynamism and homogeneity in the EEA Agreement.

The following section describes and analyses the EEA integration process in the field of educational services. Both the situation where a migrant student has an individual right to financial assistance to pursue higher education in the host state and the situation where a migrant student has the right to export student benefits abroad from the home state are of interest in an EEA context.

4.1.2 Methodology: The Interaction Between Primary and Secondary EU Law

The relationship between primary and secondary law in the EU legal order is complex.[5] An analysis of the legal effects of the Treaty provisions of education and Union citizenship must take into account the interaction of these provisions with the secondary legislation adopted to ensure the right to freedom of movement, residence and equal treatment for Union citizens.[6] This interaction takes different forms in the case law. As demonstrated in the legal literature, there are inconsistencies in the approach by the CJEU.[7]

It is important to point out first that neither the free movement of workers Regulation nor the Citizens Directive effectively displace primary law—so-called

[4] Case C-224/98 D'Hoop [2002] ECR I-6191, paragraph 32, Case C-147/03 Commission v. Austria [2005] ECR I-5969, paragraph 44, Joined Cases C-11/06 and 12/06 Morgan and Bucher [2007] ECR I-9161, paragraph 27, Joined Cases C-523/11 and C-585/11 Prinz and Seeberger, EU:C:2013:524, paragraph 26, Case C-359/13 B. Martens EU:C:2015:118, paragraph 27, Case C-220/12, Thiele, EU:C:2013:683, paragraph 48.

[5] A recent contribution is Syrpis (2015), pp. 461–488 with further references.

[6] The two most important pieces of the current harmonising legislation in the field of rights for student financing in cross-border situations are the free movement of workers Regulation No 492/2011 and the Citizens Directive 2004/38.

[7] Syrpis (2015), p. 462.

total harmonisation measures.[8] In the field of education, it is intended that primary and secondary law will coexist.

In the situation of coexistence, the common approach for the Court where the facts of the case fall within the scope of secondary legislation is to first examine the case with regard to the provisions in this legislation interpreted in light of primary law.[9] Thereafter, if appropriate, the questions referred to the Court will be examined with regard to the Treaty provisions themselves. Regarding the applicability of different primary law provisions, the CJEU will first examine Articles 45, 49 and 56 TFEU depending on whether the case concerns a worker, the freedom of establishment or a provider/recipient of services, respectively. Only when these provisions regarding forms of economic activity are not applicable or insufficient will the Court apply Article 21(1) TFEU on Union citizenship.[10] Yet, even where a case is decided on the basis of Articles 45, 49 and 56 TFEU, the CJEU may consider citizenship-type principles, i.e. universal rights independent of economic activity.[11] General provisions such as in the field of education are traditionally supporting arguments and referred to in conjunction with another legal provision, typically the status of Union citizenship.

In order to properly take into account the complexity of the different approaches by the CJEU, the following analysis of the decisional practice of the EFTA Surveillance Authority is based on describing first how the CJEU has reasoned on specific questions. The aim of the chosen approach is to make the legal basis for the conclusions drawn regarding the EEA integration process as clear as possible.

The subsequent analysis of the decisional practice of the EFTA Surveillance Authority will demonstrate that in the EEA legal order, the Authority is relying on the free movement of services provision to require the EFTA States to change their financing systems in the educational field, in particular own nationals' rights against their home state. It is argued that the application of the free movement of services provision in the EEA by the Authority has no parallel in the case law from the CJEU. The legal basis in the EU integration process for own nationals' rights against the home state in the educational field has been primarily based on a combination of the general provisions in the field of education (now Articles 165 and 166 TFEU) and the student's status of being a Union citizen (now Article 20–21 TFEU).

[8] In the situation of free movement, residence and equal treatment for Union citizens, it is intended that primary and secondary law will coexist and in that sense the secondary law is not total harmonisation measures, see the same terminology in Syrpis (2015), pp. 461–488.

[9] Case C-341/05 Laval [2007] ECR I-11767, paragraph 61, see also same methodology in the EFTA Court in Case E-2/11 STX, paragraph 35, Case C-46/12 L. N. EU:C:2013:97, paragraph 35.

[10] Cases C-100/01 Olazabal [2002] ECR I-10981, C-392/05 Alevizos [2007] ECR I-3505 paragraph 80, C-152/05 Germany [2008] ECR I-39, paragraph 18.

[11] Cases C-60/00 Carpenter [2002] ECR I-6279, C-291/05 Eind [2007] ECR I-10719, C-228/07 Jørn Petersen v Arbeitsmarktservice [2008] ECR I-6989, Joined Cases C-502/01 & C-31/02 Gaumain Cerri and Barth [2004] ECR I-6483.

4.1.3 Structure

The analysis is divided into two main parts. Section 4.2 is mainly focused on the case law from the CJEU in the EU legal order. It is demonstrated that the right for service providers, service recipients and applicants of various support mechanisms in student financing go beyond limitations inherent in harmonisation measures (secondary law). In other words, it is demonstrated and explained how the CJEU has applied in particular the Treaty provisions on Union citizenship in order to set aside national limitations on various support mechanisms in student financing despite the fact that the national limitations are seemingly compatible with secondary law. Hence, primary law constitutes a significant legal basis in the educational field with rights for non-economically active citizens and corresponding obligations on states. This demonstration is important given the complexity of EEA law where harmonising measures (secondary law) are continually updated and included in the annexes, whereas no similar process exists for changes in EU primary law.

The next main part, Sect. 4.3, focuses on the decisional practice of the EFTA Surveillance Authority. The EEA integration process in the field of education is analysed in light of the importance of primary law in the EU legal order for these rights. The findings indicate a parallel development in the EEA integration process in the field of requiring changes in national law for various support mechanisms in student financing as compared to the EU even without the paralleling in the EEA Agreement of the general provisions on education in Articles 165 and 166 TFEU and the Union citizenship provisions in Articles 20 and 21 TFEU.

4.2 The EU Legal Order

4.2.1 Primary and Secondary Law in the EU Legal Order in the Field of Education

Access to Financial Assistance in the Case of the Economically Active Citizen

In the case of migrant workers (including the self-employed), the basic principle that an active contribution to the economic life of the Member State justifies the assimilation of the migrant worker and the protected family members to be included in the system of public services and benefits also applies to financial assistance in the field of education. The worker may derive educational rights from Article 45 TFEU[12] and the harmonised secondary legislation[13] in two main situations: first,

[12] Paralleled in Article 28 EEA.

[13] In particular. Regulation 492/2011 on freedom of movement of workers, see Article 7(2) and Directive 2004/38, see Articles 7(1), 24(1), 7(3)(d), both of which are included in the annexes of the EEA Agreement, see annexes V and VIII.

when the claimant simultaneously works and studies, and secondly, when the claimant works and subsequently undertakes studies. The protected family members may derive educational rights under Regulation 492/2011 on the freedom of movement of workers as well as rights under the Citizens Directive 2004/38.

It is not uncommon for students to remain dependent on family members (typically parents) during all or part of their studies. In that case, obtaining study finance may alleviate the financial burden otherwise borne by those family members. It is settled law that assistance granted for maintenance and education in order to pursue university studies evidenced by a professional qualification, including for children of migrant workers, is a social advantage within the meaning of Article 7(2) of Regulation 492/2011 but only insofar as the migrant worker continues to support his or her child. There is a complicated relationship between the rights of students as family members of an economically active Union citizen and the rights of students as independent Union citizens. In the EEA legal order, the legal provisions regarding the first category of rights holders, namely the student as a dependent family member of a worker, are fully paralleled in the EEA Agreement.[14] Regarding the second category of rights holders, the provisions in the secondary legislation are included in the Agreement but without the person having the status of Union citizenship enshrined in primary law. This situation calls for some further explanation regarding the situation for the student as an independent non-economically active citizen, hence the situation of students not having rights as family members.

Access to Financial Assistance in the Case of the Non-economically Active Citizen

The secondary legislation regarding students dealt with the right of residence for students first in Directive 93/96, later repealed by the Citizens Directive 2004/38. The right of residence in the secondary legislation is conditioned on the student having sufficient resources not to become a burden on the social assistance system of the host state during the period of residence. Article 3 in the previous Directive 93/96 stated clearly that the right of residence for students did not establish an entitlement to the payment of maintenance grants by the host state. Directive 2004/38 lays down the principle that the right to equal treatment in the host state does not include the right to maintenance grants.[15] Furthermore, in the Citizens Directive, it is made clear that students are also under the obligation of having

[14] This is regulated by the right to free movement of workers as enshrined in Articles 45 TFEU and 28 EEA and secondary law made part of the annexes of the EEA Agreement, Regulation No 492/2011 on freedom of movement of workers, Directive 2004/38 on the right of citizens of the Union and Regulation 883/2004 on coordination of social security benefits.

[15] See Article 24(2).

sufficient resources and sickness insurance for a right of residence for longer than 3 months to apply.[16]

The basic conditions under which migrant students must exercise their right of residency are contained in Articles 7(1)(c), 14(2) and 14(3) in Directive 2004/38 read together with recitals 10 and 16. Free movement rights have been extended to benefit students enrolled for the principal purpose of following not only vocational training courses but any educational course of study. Article 8 of the Citizens Directive limits the Member States' discretion as to the level of sufficient resources that such individuals must demonstrate for the purpose of completing the administrative formalities associated with residency.

When it comes to equal treatment, Article 24 of the Citizens Directive deals with the various forms of financial assistance that may be offered by Member States. As regards registration/tuition fees, the prohibition against discrimination on grounds of nationality under Article 18 TFEU will continue to apply with full force. The express exclusion of maintenance grants from the scope of equal treatment remains in place, at least prior to acquisition of the new right of permanent residence.[17] Finally, Article 24(2) states that the host state shall not be obliged to confer upon Union citizens—including migrant students—entitlement to social assistance benefits during their first 3 months of residence nor is the host state obliged to grant maintenance aid for studies, including vocational training, consisting of student grants or student loans.[18]

The coordination regime of social security benefits in Regulation 883/2004[19] does not apply to most standard forms of student financial assistance; maintenance grants and loans do not fall within the material scope of the coordination system as defined in Article 3.[20] Nor do general subsistence benefits that may sometimes be claimed by students (see the case of Grzelczyk[21]) and nor does social assistance in the narrow sense of discretionary, means tested public support. See also Article 3(5) of Regulation 883/2004 clarifying that the Regulation does not apply to social assistance and Article 70 on special non-contributory cash benefits that shall be provided exclusively in the Member State in which the persons concerned reside (in other words, the benefit is excluded from the obligation to export from the competent state, see Article 7).

The limitations in the legal framework on the right to financial assistance in the situation of migrant students as independent Union citizens laid down by the EU legislature seems quite clear.

[16] Note that exceptions are made for the retention of worker status in connection with vocational studies, see Article 7 and for family members enrolled in educational establishments, see Article 12.

[17] See Article 16 of the Directive on the creation of a new category of right holders with a right to permanent residence.

[18] Unless the claimant is economically active or entitled to be treated as such or a family member.

[19] The Regulation is included in the annexes of the EEA Agreement, see Part II.

[20] See previously Article 4 in Regulation 1408/71.

[21] See Part II.

A student does not have rights under EU law as a worker or a self-employed person, i.e. a student is considered a non-economically active person. The right to free movement in the sense of taking up studies in other EU Member States is guaranteed in secondary legislation. This right has implications, for instance, regarding the prohibition on states to charge fees or have entrance requirements applying exclusively to foreign students or non nationals.[22] The secondary legislation, however, does not guarantee migrant students equal treatment for financial assistance to pursue education, for instance, at foreign universities.[23] Neither a right to export financial support from the home state nor the right to receive financial assistance on equal terms as nationals in the host state is covered by the secondary legislation.

However, the changes in primary law contained two sets of reforms that were to provide the basis for significant developments, as well as inspiring strong policy arguments in favour of a revised approach to equal treatment for migrant students regarding maintenance assistance within the host state, and to challenge territorial restrictions in the home state limiting the export of financial assistance to students.

One set of reforms was the introduction of new legal bases for EU action in the sphere of education and vocational training. The Maastricht Treaty added to the EU's objectives under Article 3 EC 'a contribution to education and training of quality' and introduced Article 149 EC conferring upon the EU explicit responsibilities in the field of education policy and concerning vocational training currently contained in Articles 165 and 166 TFEU. The Amsterdam Treaty did not substantially amend the provisions but streamlined their respective legislative procedures and introduced a new preamble noting the determination of the Contracting Parties to promote the development of the highest possible level of knowledge for their peoples through a wide access to education and through its continuous updating.[24] Articles 165 and 166 TFEU confer upon the EU merely complementary competences in order to supplement and support Member State activities and do not include power to adopt measures for the harmonisation of national laws.

However, Articles 165 and 166 TFEU did permit the EU institutions to move on from its previous constitutional uncertainties over competence and to instead commence upon a more elevated debate about the substantive content of its educational and training policies.[25,26] The provisions are also referred to by the CJEU, in particular in its latest case law on students' rights, as supporting the relatively broad intervention in national limitations on student mobility.[27] The next section analyses the case law from the CJEU with particular focus on how the relevant primary law

[22] Case 293/83 Gravier [1985] ECR 593, see below.

[23] Art 24 (2) in Directive 2004/38.

[24] See Dougan (2005), p. 949 with further references in Chap. 1, footnote 25.

[25] Dougan (2005), p. 950.

[26] In particular, steps have been taken within the framework of the Lisbon process to address many of the obstacles previously identified in the Commission's 1996 Green Paper, based upon strategic objectives such as the democratisation of mobility within the EU, the promotion of appropriate forms of funding, and improving the conditions for mobility.

[27] See case law analysis below.

reforms first introduced by the Maastricht Treaty have provided a legal basis for the CJEU itself to take the initiative and revisit those aspects of its own case law that hampered greater educational mobility.[28]

4.2.2 The Case Law from the CJEU on Educational Services

The CJEU has challenged national systems in the field of education by making use of two distinct legal tools; the barriers to movement principle as a vehicle of challenging territorial limitations of the home state and the right to equal treatment as a vehicle of overcoming the nationality limitations of the host state. It seems necessary to start the analysis with the case law that brought education within the ambit of the Treaty. In the following, it is necessary to distinguish between students' rights to equal treatment in the sense of tuition fees and vocational training and the national financial support mechanisms for students.

When it came to EU nationals falling outside the realm of the economically active and their protected family members, and thus falling into the category of migrant students per se, the Court in Gravier[29] and Blaizot[30] held that, having regard to provisions in secondary legislation and to various initiatives undertaken by the Council, access to and participation in vocational training fell within the scope of the Treaty. This was enough for the Court to establish a right to equal treatment as regards access to vocational training under the non-discrimination provision (now Article 18 TFEU[31]); prohibiting discrimination against foreign students as regards registration/tuition fees as well as the imposition of quotas on the numbers of foreign students entitled to attend national educational establishments and discriminatory requirements relating to the secondary education diplomas required for entry into higher education.[32]

In the Gravier case, the CJEU found that access to vocational training (a 4-year course at an art academy) fell within the ambit of the Treaty so that a registration fee that was only charged to foreign students was found to be in breach of the principle of non-discrimination on grounds of nationality under now Article 18 TFEU.[33] The decision supported a right of free movement of students to pursue their education in another Member State on a non-discriminatory basis. This right has proved controversial, since cross-border mobility implies the existence of a real market to which all Member States contribute equally. This implication has proved mistaken, particularly with regard to university education, a problem later reflected in the case

[28] See also the analysis by Jørgensen (2009), pp. 1567–1590.

[29] Case 293/83 Gravier [1985] ECR 593.

[30] Case 24/86 Blaizot [1988] ECR 379.

[31] Then Article 12 EC, paralleled in Article 4 in the EEA Agreement.

[32] See case C-65/03 Commission v. Belgium [2004] ECR I-6427.

[33] Case 293/83 Gravier [1985] ECR 593.

law.[34] The CJEU decision on equal treatment regarding requirements for admission to a course of education was later dealt with in the secondary legislation and included in the EEA Agreement.[35] However, the question of rights of payment for the education in another Member State of migrant students, whether from the home or the host state, is an entirely different matter and has proved controversial.

In Gravier, the Court adopted a broad approach to material scope disputes; if an issue fell within the content of some provisions of the Treaty, it automatically fell within the material scope of the Treaty even if there was no direct connection between that trigger provision and the pending claim to equal treatment. Indeed, maintenance grants and other forms of social assistance to students could fall within the content of provisions, such as Article 7(2) of Regulation 492/2011 concerning migrant workers. However, this piece of legislation is entirely unconnected to the purpose of challenging discrimination by the host state against a non-economically active migrant students under Article 18 TFEU. Later case law has, however, limited this potentially broad implication of Gravier.

Regarding student financing, the Court decided in the Lair and Brown cases[36] that, at that stage in the development of EU law, migrant students did not enjoy any right to equal treatment also as regards assistance offered by the Member State to its own nationals (for example) in the form of maintenance or training grants. In particular, the Court believed that such assistance fell outside the material scope of the Treaty for the purposes of delimiting the potential reach of the non-discrimination provision (now Article 18 TFEU), being, on the one hand, a matter of educational policy, which is not as such among the spheres entrusted to the EU and, on the other hand, a matter of social policy, which falls within the competence of the Member States insofar as it is not covered by specific provisions of the Treaty.

The cases of Humbel[37] and Wirth[38] both concerned the question of whether services provided by certain public educational institutions could be considered services 'normally provided for remuneration' and therefore as falling within the provision of freedom of movement of services. Economic activity is usually defined as any activity consisting in offering goods and services on a given market. The essential characteristic of goods and services offered on a market is that they are normally provided for remuneration. The analysis in Part III regarding state aid to public services will revisit this case law on education from the CJEU in light of the application of state aid law to the educational sector.[39]

---

[34] See Case C-147/03 Commission v. Austria [2005] ECR I-5969.

[35] The previous directive on residence rights of students Directive 93/96, replaced later by the Citizens Directive 2004/38, see part II.

[36] Case 39/86 Lair [1988] ECR 3161, Case 197/86 Brown [1988] ECR 3205, see also Case C-357/89 Raulin [1992] ECR I-1027.

[37] Case 263/86 Humbel [1988] ECR 5365.

[38] Case C-109/92 Wirth [1993] ECR I-6447.

[39] The EFTA Court refers to the Humbel case in its assessment of whether the kindergarten sector in Norway is a service rendered with the essential characteristic of remuneration, see Sects. 12.3.2 and 13.6.2 on the question of compatible state aid to the Norwegian kindergarten sector.

From the judgments in Humbel and Wirth, it can be concluded that institutions, of whichever level, that form part of the national education system and that are essentially funded by the state are not to be regarded as providers of a service. In running these establishments, the state is not pursuing gainful activity. It is thus not providing a service on a market. Rather, the CJEU found that the state, in establishing and maintaining these systems, was 'fulfilling its duties towards its own population in the social, cultural and educational fields'.[40]

As demonstrated the Court in the Lair and Brown cases decided that maintenance assistance to students fell outside the scope of the Treaty. However, the Court in Grzelczyk seemed prepared to revisit its previous position, taking into account subsequent developments in the state of European integration within the field of education, in particular, the adoption of Directive 93/96 (now Directive 2004/38) obliging Member States to grant a right of residence to students under certain conditions, together with the introduction by the Maastricht Treaty of the new title on education and vocational training (now Articles 165 and 166 TFEU), and the creation of the generalised right to free movement as a fundamental conception of Union citizenship (now Articles 20 and 21 TFEU).[41] The Court held in Grzelczyk that nothing in the Treaty text suggested that students were to be deprived of the rights that are conferred upon migrant Union citizens ensuring claimants' rights to social assistant benefits.[42] In Bidar[43] handed down 4 years later the Court further clarified that financial assistance to cover student's maintenance cost now falls within the scope of EU law. At issue in the case was the compatibility with EU law of the refusal of the UK to grant to a French university student a subsidised loan to cover his maintenance costs, due to the fact that he was not 'settled' in the UK. The reasoning of the Court provides a useful illustration of the development of the law due to the revised primary law provisions.

On the question of scope of EU law based on the limitations held in the earlier cases of Lair and Brown the CJEU made the following pronouncement;

> 38. In those judgments the Court considered that such assistance was, on the one hand, a matter of education policy, which was not as such included in the spheres entrusted to the Community institutions, and, on the other, a matter of social policy, which fell within the competence of the Member States in so far as it was not covered by specific provisions of the EEC Treaty.

[40] Cases 263/86 Humbel [1988] ECR 5365, paragraph 18, C-109/92 Wirth [1993] ECR I-6447 paragraphs 16–19. The Court thus held that, 'by establishing and maintaining such a system of public education, financed as a general rule by the public budget and not by pupils or their parents, the State did not intend to involve itself in remunerated activities, but was carrying out its task in the social, cultural and educational fields towards its population'.

[41] Case C-184/99 Grzelczyk [2001] ECR I-6193, see also Advocate General Jacobs Opinion of 20 January 2005 in Case C-147/03 Commission v. Austria [2005] ECR I-5969, see for more on this case for the development of the rights of the non-economically active Union citizens in Part II.

[42] Case C-184/99 Grzelczyk [2001] ECR I-619, paragraph 35, see also Case C-209/03 Bidar v London Borough of Ealing [2005] ECR I-211, paragraph 34.

[43] Case C-209/03 Bidar [2005] ECR I-5969.

The Court then continued;

> 39. However, since judgment was given in Lair and Brown, the Treaty on European Union has introduced citizenship of the Union into the EC Treaty and added to Title VIII (now Title XI) of Part Three a Chapter 3 devoted inter alia to education and vocational training (Grzelczyk, paragraph 35).
>
> 40. Thus Article 149(1) EC gives the Community the task of contributing to the development of quality education by encouraging cooperation between Member States and, if necessary, by supporting and supplementing their action, while fully respecting the responsibility of those States for the content of teaching and the organisation of education systems and their cultural and linguistic diversity.
>
> 41. Under paragraphs 2 and 4 of that article, the Council may adopt incentive measures, excluding any harmonisation of the laws and regulations of the Member States, and recommendations aimed in particular at encouraging the mobility of students and teachers (see D'Hoop, paragraph 32).

The conclusion by the Court based on the revised primary law (even if it was qualified in paragraphs 56 and 57) was for student benefits to fall within the scope of EU law;

> In view of those developments since the judgments in Lair and Brown, it must be considered that the situation of a citizen of the Union who is lawfully resident in another Member State falls within the scope of application of the Treaty within the meaning of the first paragraph of Article 12 EC for the purposes of obtaining assistance for students, whether in the form of a subsidised loan or a grant, intended to cover his maintenance costs.[44]

The Grzelczyk and Bidar cases concerned rights against the host state for students. In D'Hoop, the CJEU incorporated into the case law on Union citizenship the well-established principle that domestic measures that create obstacles to economic mobility by own nationals are caught by the Treaty, based upon disincentives to move from rather than remain within the home state.[45] As the Court held in D'Hoop, this approach is particularly important within the context of the free movement of Union citizens for educational purposes, having regard to the EU's objective of contributing to education of quality as set out in Article 3 EC (now Article 6(e) TFEU) and to the EU's responsibility for encouraging greater mobility for students and teachers under then Article 149 EC (now Article 165 TFEU).[46]

---

[44] Paragraph 41.

[45] Case C-224/98 D'Hoop [2002] ECR I-6191, see Iliopoulou and Toner (2003), p. 389.

[46] Case C-224/98 D'Hoop [2002] ECR I-6191, paragraph 32. D'Hoop itself concerned Belgian rules on access to special unemployment benefits for young people leaving full time education in search of their first job, where the qualifying criteria contained in the applicable social security legislation effectively penalised own nationals who had exercised their rights under Article 21 TFEU by completing their secondary education in another Member State, then returned to Belgium to undertake their university studies, as compared to the treatment of own nationals who had opted to remain within the domestic territory for the entire duration of their education. However, the same principle of non-discriminatory barriers to/unequal treatment on the grounds of movement could readily apply also to a refusal by the home state to provide financial support to own nationals who choose to exercise their rights under Article 21 TFEU so as to follow their university studies in another Member State, as compared to the treatment (in terms of assistance with tuition fees and

Before examining in more detail migrant students' independent rights as Union citizens, the analysis of the evolving EU law in the field of education based on the free movement of services provision will be continued. As indicated in the introduction, this has been the legal basis for decisional practice of the EFTA Surveillance Authority in the context of the EEA Agreement.

After the decisions in Humbel and Wirth, the question arose as to the compatibility under German income tax law of the possibility that existed of offsetting against taxable income the fees paid for private schooling, albeit limited to fees paid to educational institutions established in Germany. In Case C-76/05 Schwarz,[47] the limitation in German law was challenged by the parents who had opted to send their children to a private school in Scotland. Based on the system in the German income tax legislation, the Commission began infringement proceedings against Germany in Case C-318/05.[48] A fundamental point in the two cases was whether Article 56 TFEU could apply given the argument that the character of education is not a service provided for remuneration.[49]

In the same time period as the Schwarz case and the infringement proceedings against Germany by the Commission, the German educational funding system was also challenged in the joined cases of Morgan and Bucher.[50] This case concerned the compatibility of a number of criteria in German law on the award of education and training grants to students wishing to attend education or training establishments abroad. The scrutiny included conditions of a so-called continuation proviso, which required completion first of at least 1 year in Germany of the same studies that would then be pursued abroad as well as a permanent residence criterion applying to students living close to the German borders.[51]

In all cases against the German educational financing system, the CJEU found a restriction on free movement and was unpersuaded by the state arguments submitted as justifications. It was recognised that competence for the content and organisation of educational systems (and indeed matters of direct taxation) lies with the Member States.[52] The compatibility assessment was nevertheless based on the view that these competences must be exercised in compliance with EU law. Article 56 TFEU proscribes 'the application of any national rules which have the effect of making the provision of services between Member States more difficult than the

towards the costs of maintenance) provided to own nationals who decide to stay at home for their university education.

[47] Case C-76/05 Schwarz [2007] ECR I-6849.

[48] Case C-318/05 Commission v. Germany [2007] ECR I-6957.

[49] Confer above, the cases of Humbel and Wirth.

[50] Joined Cases C-11/06 and 12/06 Morgan and Bucher [2007] ECR I-9161.

[51] See for an analysis of the cases, Dougan (2008), pp. 723–738.

[52] Case C-76/05 Schwarz [2007] ECR I-6849, paragraph 69, Case C-318/05 Commission v. Germany [2007] ECR I-6957, paragraphs 85 and 86, Joined Cases C-11/06 and 12/06 Morgan and Bucher [2007] ECR I-9161, paragraph 24.

provision of services within a Member State'.[53] The legal framework governing the relation between an EU citizen and the home state has as its basic principle that Member States may not penalise their own nationals for having exercised their right to free movement by providing less favourable treatment than that afforded to own nationals who chose to remain at home.[54] In Schwarz and Commission v. Germany, the contested provisions were found to contravene both Articles 56 and 21 TFEU, and in Morgan and Bucher, the provision in Article 21 TFEU was found to have been violated. In support of the Court's reasoning in Schwarz and Commission v. Germany, numerous references are made to comparable developments relating to health services.[55] In the cases, the Court referred to the role of the EU in the educational sector as laid down in Articles 165 and 166 TFEU.[56]

Later, the Dutch law that made the exportability of student grants conditional on a criterion of prior residence, the so-called three-out-of-six-years rule, was challenged in Case C-542/09 Commission v. Netherlands.[57] The Commission disputed the rule only to the extent that it applied to dependent children of migrant workers, hence limiting the legal bases to Article 7(2) of Regulation 492/11 and Article 45 TFEU. The Dutch Government disputed the discriminatory character of the rule, arguing that residence provided an objective difference as well as defending any difference in treatment being justified by both the need to prevent an unreasonable burden on its welfare system and for it to be able to target the students who 'deserve' to export student grants.[58] The argument was based on the view that the 'deserving' students were the ones who would have studied in the Netherlands in the absence of the right to export their student grants and who are likely to return to the Netherlands upon completion of their degree. The arguments are based on reciprocity stressing the rights of students based on previous residence and the assumption that the support is based on the student returning and then contributing to the Dutch society.

The decision by the Court was based on a distinction between the rights of a student as a dependent family member (hence, rights of the economically active, often a parent) and the independent rights of a student as a Union citizen (hence, rights of the non-economically active). The recognition by the Court in rulings like Bidar[59] and Förster[60] to allow Member States to limit eligibility for social

[53] Case C-76/05 Schwarz [2007] ECR I-6849, paragraph 61, Case C-318/05 Commission v. Germany [2007] ECR I-6957, paragraph 81.

[54] For a more in depth analysis of the Morgan and Bucher cases regarding home state obligations, see M. Dougan' s case analysis (2008), pp. 723–738.

[55] Case C-76/05 Schwarz [2007] ECR I-6849, paragraphs 45–46, Case C-318/05 Commission v. Germany [2007] ECR I-6957, paragraphs 73–76.

[56] Case C-147/03 Commission v. Austria [2005] ECR I-5969, paragraph 44, Joined Cases C-11/06 and 12/06 Morgan and Bucher [2007] ECR I-9161, paragraph 27.

[57] Case C-542/09 Netherlands v Commission EU:C:2012:346. For a broad analysis of the case, see de Witte (2013), pp. 203–216.

[58] Case C-542/09 Netherlands v Commission EU:C:2012:346, paragraph 26.

[59] Case C-209/03 Bidar v London Borough of Ealing [2005] ECR I-211.

[60] Case C-158/07 Förster [2008] ECR I-08507.

entitlements to those migrants who can demonstrate 'a sufficient degree of integration'[61] may only be applied to non-economically active migrants. Hence, a similar requirement cannot be applied to economically active migrants, given that these persons have established a sufficient degree of integration in the host state by virtue of their participation in that state's employment market.[62] In other words, migrant workers cannot impose an unreasonable burden on the welfare state. In conclusion, the Court found that the current Dutch residence requirement could not be applied to students who were dependent family members of a migrant worker.

Given the limited scope of the infringement proceedings by the Commission in the case, only challenging the residence criterion applying to dependent children of workers, the next case on the legality of the Dutch residence criterion was awaited with great interest. In Case C-359/13 Martens,[63] the legality of the three-out-of-six-years rule was challenged regarding the rights of a Dutch national who had exercised her right to free movement and who was rejected financial support for pursuing studies in an overseas country based on the lack of fulfilling the residence requirements. Advocate General Sharpston went to great length to make it possible based on the facts to decide the Martens case based on the rights of dependents of the economically active.[64] However, the Court took no notice of the possibility that Martens could be covered by the rights of her father as a dependent family member of a worker who had exercised his right to free movement. The Court decided the case entirely based on the understanding that Martens was a Union citizen with free movement rights according to the Treaty provisions.[65]

What is particularly interesting here is the Court's reference in connection with the status of Union citizenship to the Treaty provision in Article 165(1) TFEU elevating education to a protected aim and value of the Union.[66] This reference is made to underline that even if Member States are competent as regards the content of teaching and the organisation of their respective education systems, they must exercise that competence in compliance with EU law. This reference provides an example of how a Treaty provision designed mainly to protect Member States' autonomy in a specific field may also contribute to the EU exercising its powers to influence national choices and, in particular, national practices.

Furthermore, the Court points to the Treaty articles in the field of education, which is spelt out by Article 6(e) TFEU and the second indent of Article 165(2) TFEU, namely, inter alia, encouraging the mobility of students and teachers.[67]

---

[61] Case C-158/07 Förster [2008] ECR I-08507, paragraphs 60–62.

[62] Case C-542/09 Netherlands v Commission EU:C:2012:346, paragraph 66.

[63] Case C-359/13 Martens, EU:C:2015:118.

[64] Opinion of Advocate General Sharpston in Case C-359/13 Martens EU:C:2014:2240, paragraphs 36–97.

[65] Case C-359/13, Martens, EU:C:2015:118, paragraphs 20 and 21.

[66] Case C-359/13 Martens, EU:C:2015:118, paragraph 23.

[67] Case C-359/13 Martens, EU:C:2015:118, paragraph 27.

These provisions on the aim and value of education in combination with the right of free movement as a Union citizen conferred by Article 21(1) are, according to the Court, not fully effective if a national of a Member State could be dissuaded from using the right by obstacles resulting from a stay in another Member State. In other words, legislation in the state of origin that penalises the mere fact of a student (as a Union citizen) having exercised the right to free movement is incompatible with the Treaty provisions.[68] This is a clear statement by the Court on education as an aim and value of the Union as well as the right to exercise free movement rights for the non-economically active.

With references to previous decisions on migrant students' independent rights, the Court recognised that both the integration of students and the desire to verify the existence of a connecting link between the society of the Member State providing a benefit and the recipient can constitute objective considerations of public interest that are capable of justifying the conditions. The Court referred to cases decided regarding the German financial assistance for students in Prinz and Seeberger and Thiele (see below). The Court, furthermore, referred to its previous decision regarding the application of the same rule to the economically active in Case C-542/09 and argued that the residence requirement was too exclusive, because it did not make it possible to take account of other factors that may connect such a student to the Member State providing the benefit, such as the nationality of the student, his or her schooling, family, employment or language skills or the existence of other social and economic factors.[69]

In three previous cases to Martens regarding residence requirements for student financing in Germany, the Court concluded in all cases that the national residence requirements violated the free movement rights of Union citizens enshrined in Articles 20 and 21 TFEU. The joined Cases C-523/11 and C-585/11 Prinz and Seeberger[70] concerned the incompatibility of the German rule that made the award of an education grant subject to a 3-year residence requirement. The case of C-220/12 Thiele[71] concerned the incompatibility of the German rule that made the award of an education grant for studies pursued in another Member State subject to the sole condition of having fulfilled the establishment of a permanent residence requirement on the territory.

The Court has, in this context, held that Member States that make available education or training grants for studies in another Member State must ensure that the detailed rules for the award of those grants do not create an unjustified restriction of the right to move and reside within the territory of Member States laid down in Article 21 TFEU.[72] A condition requiring uninterrupted residence during a defined

[68] Case C-359/13 Martens EU:C:2015:118, paragraph 26.

[69] Case C-542/09 Netherlands v Commission EU:C:2012:346, paragraphs 39–42.

[70] Joined Cases C-523/11 and C-585/11 Prinz and Seeberger, EU:C:2013:524.

[71] Case C-220/12, Thiele, EU:C:2013:683.

[72] Case C-220/12 Thiele EU:C:2013:683, paragraph 25, Joined Cases C-523/11 and C-585/11 Prinz and Seeberger, EU:C:2013:524, paragraph 30 and case law cited.

period has been held to be such a restriction; it is likely to dissuade nationals from exercising their right to freedom of movement and residence in another Member State, because if they do so, they are likely to lose the right to the education or the training grant.[73]

The cases were all decided based on the Treaty citizenship provisions,[74] and the Court referred to the general Treaty provisions on education as supporting arguments.[75] Similarly, the residence requirement was assessed based on the status of Union citizenship,[76] and the Court referred to the general Treaty provisions on education as supporting arguments.[77] Accordingly, in recent years, a significant number of decisions from the CJEU have recognised that the free movement right of the non-economically active Union citizen includes a right against the home state for various financial benefits in the field of education.[78]

Finally, a case regarding the distinction between an economically active worker and a non-economically active student will be discussed. In the case of C-46/12 L.N., the CJEU assessed the compatibility of Danish residence requirements for the grant of maintenance aid to students.[79] The question in the case was whether Mr. N was to be considered as a worker according to Article 45 TFEU or as a non-economically active student. As a worker, Mr. N could not be denied the maintenance grant, whereas the Danish residence requirement was compatible with the Citizens Directive in terms of students.[80] The facts of the case pointed clearly in the direction that Mr. N entered Denmark with the intention of studying.

The Danish and the Norwegian Governments argued to the effect that the intention of Mr. N when he entered Danish territory, which was to follow a course of study, precluded him from having the status of 'worker' within the meaning of Article 45 TFEU. The Governments were presumably motivated by the possibility to circumvent national limitations on rights to financial support in the host state of migrating students by taking up part-time employment in the summer in anticipation of courses starting in the fall.

The CJEU began its reasoning in the case with numerous references to the rights of Union citizens, the fundamental status of Union citizenship and its Union citizenship case law.[81] This line of reasoning almost seemed to indicate that the Court

[73] Case C-220/12 Thiele EU:C:2013:683, paragraphs 27 and 28, Joined Cases C-523/11 and C-585/11 Prinz and Seeberger, EU:C:2013:524, paragraph 31 and 32.

[74] Case C-220/12 Thiele EU:C:2013:683, paragraph 23 and Joined Cases C-523/11 and C-585/11 Prinz and Seeberger, EU:C:2013:524, paragraph 24.

[75] Case C-220/12 Thiele EU:C:2013:683, paragraph 24 and Joined Cases C-523/11 and C-585/11 Prinz and Seeberger, EU:C:2013:524, paragraph 26.

[76] Case C-220/12 Thiele EU:C:2013:683, paragraph 19.

[77] Case C-220/12 Thiele EU:C:2013:683, paragraph 21.

[78] See for a more general analysis on the right to free movement of the non-economically active Union citizen in Part II.

[79] Case C-46/12 L.N., EU:C:2013:97.

[80] See Articles 7(1(c) and 24(2) of the Citizens Directive.

[81] Case C-46/12 L.N., EU:C:2013:97, paragraphs 25, 27–30.

disagreed with the limitation in the Citizens Directive whereby Union citizens can be denied equal treatment, in particular in regard to student maintenance grants.[82] In paragraph 38, the Court refutes the argument that entering the territory of Denmark with the principal intention of following a course of study precludes Mr. N from having the status of worker. The Court then leaves it to the national court to assess the employment activities of Mr. N but underlines that low level of remuneration, low productivity, or the fact that the person works only a small number of hours per week do not preclude that person from being recognised as covered by the autonomous meaning specific to EU law of a worker.[83]

The case law review demonstrates how EU law based on various primary law provisions limits Member States' freedom in the educational sector. The scope of intervention varies depending on the content and structure of the national law being scrutinised as well as the factual situation of the claimant. Increasingly, the tendency seems to be towards treating the student as a Union citizen having independent rights, in particular in the situation of rights against the home state. The case of L.N. demonstrates that the Court does not sympathise with the Member States trying to protect their financing systems in the educational sector from migrant students.

4.3 The EEA Legal Order

4.3.1 The EFTA Surveillance Authority and Access to Financial Assistance from the Norwegian State Educational Loan Fund: Case No 69199

In a Reasoned opinion delivered by the EFTA Surveillance Authority 2 July 2014, the conditions for financial assistance from the Norwegian State Educational Loan Fund are claimed to be incompatible with Norway's obligations under the EEA Agreement. In particular, the Authority alleges that the residence requirement that states that in order to qualify for educational support for studies pursued outside Norway, applicants must have resided in Norway consecutively for at least two out of the last 5 years prior to the start of their studies (the two-out-of-five-years rule) is incompatible with EEA law obligations.[84] The Authority relies on the case law from the CJEU, in particular Cases C-542/09 Commission v. Netherlands and C-20/12 Giersch, in its argumentation.[85]

[82] See also the formulation in paragraph 32 on the Member States not *being obliged* to grant the financial support.

[83] Case C-46/12 L.N., EU:C:2013:97, paragraphs 39 and 41.

[84] There are some minor exceptions in national law for instance regarding service in the foreign office but these are described by the Norwegian Government as minor and exceptional, see letter from the Ministry of education and research 1 March 2014.

[85] See Reasoned opinion paragraphs 30–36, 58, 68, 73, 79, 84–89 and numerous references.

In an EEA context, the central issue is the distinction between a student's right as a dependent family member and a student's independent right as a Union citizen. In the first category, the rule protects the economically active. Social benefits, including social benefits to family members, are part of the protection of the migrant worker's right to equal treatment with national workers. This has been interpreted as a rather mechanical rule leading, in various situations, to an outcome where the EEA state cannot apply residence requirements for the right to social benefits on the migrant worker.[86] The migrant worker is considered to have the necessary link to the host state through the economical contribution of being a worker and paying taxes.[87]

When the Commission successfully launched infringement proceedings against the Netherlands for applying the three-out-of-six-years rule on students, the case was limited to the situation of dependent students.[88] Hence, the Dutch rule was only found to violate EU law in that particular situation. Later case law demonstrated, however, that the Dutch rule was incompatible with EU law in a more general manner, namely when the independent right of free movement for students as Union citizens is affected.[89] This case law is, as demonstrated, entirely based on the primary law changes in the EU, including the provisions on education as well as the existence of Union citizenship and the inherent right of Union citizens to move freely.

The decision to open a case against Norway based on the incompatibility of the two-out-of-five-years residence requirement led to changes in Norwegian domestic law that effectively ensured students would have the same protection in the EEA Agreement as compared to the protection provided by the status of Union citizenship in the EU legal order. The residence requirement was not just lifted for students having rights as family members of a migrant worker (in connection with an economically active person protected under Regulation 492/2011 and Article 28 EEA). The domestic limitation on the right to export financial support for students has been completely amended with the consequence that an unconditional residence requirement no longer applies.[90] This has consequences for all students, not just the rights holders under the scope of protection for the economically active in the EEA Agreement.

There are good reasons for treating students as independent persons when the compatibility of national requirements for financial assistance is assessed. The right to social benefits for a student as a family member of an economically active person is limited to the situation where the worker is still supporting his or her child. Hence,

---

[86] See the case law on the interpretation of the secondary legislation, described in more detail in Part II.

[87] Although for the frontier worker the economic contribution in the form of paying taxes may not always be present given that taxes are usually paid in the state of residence.

[88] Case C-542/09 Netherlands v Commission EU:C:2012:346.

[89] Case C-359/13 Martens EU:C:2015:118.

[90] See Letter from the Ministry of Education and Research to the Authority 17 March 2015 with a reference to the revised Study Financing Regulation for the academic year of 2015–2016, in particular section 33-5.

only in this situation is the social welfare benefit connected to equal treatment of workers. However, to assess compatibility of national limitations for financial assistance to students only for the category of students already receiving financial support from parents does not sit well with the usual reasoning behind student support mechanisms.[91]

Even if there are good substantive arguments for the chosen solution in Norwegian domestic law, it is worth reflecting on the procedure that led to this outcome. The correspondence from the Ministry of Education and Research does not indicate awareness of the difference between Norway's obligations under EEA law regarding the economically active and the non-economically active. On the contrary, the letters refer a number of times to case law from the CJEU based on students' rights as Union citizens without pointing to the difference between the provisions in the EU legal order and the EEA legal order.[92]

Interestingly, the EFTA Surveillance Authority also points to Case C-46/12 L.N. to substantiate the incompatibility of the Norwegian support system.[93] It will be recalled that this case concerned a person who arguably entered the territory of a Member State primarily in order to pursue a course of study. The facts of the case seemed to indicate clearly that Mr. N's intention was to move to Denmark to study and not to seek employment. It will be remembered that the harmonised legislation requires students to have sufficient means and medical insurance to avoid becoming an unreasonable burden of the welfare state in order to exercise their right to free movement.[94] Furthermore, the right to move and reside to study does not give a right to student maintenance grants in the host state.[95]

Mr. N had applied to the Copenhagen Business School before 15 March 2009, which was the deadline for application. He entered Denmark on 6 June 2009. He was full-time employed in an international wholesale firm in the summer for the 3 months starting from 10 June 2009 and ending 10 September 2009 when he began his studies.

The CJEU relied in this case on a combination of the right of the economically active and the rights of the non-economically active person as a Union citizen in order to reach the conclusion that the Danish provision requiring 5 years of continuous residence in Denmark to be eligible for maintenance aid for studies was incompatible with EU law in the situation of the claimant.[96] This case seems to stretch the right to free movement of students and disregard the sometimes legitimate and

---

[91] See for more on this topic, de Witte (2013), pp. 203–216.

[92] Letter 30 March 2007 from Ministry of Education and Research to the Authority referring to Case C-11/06 and 12/06 Morgan and Bucher, letter 25 January 2006 from Ministry of Education and Research to the Authority referring to Case C-138/02 Collins.

[93] Reasoned opinion paragraphs 37, 49–53, 65–67.

[94] Article 7 in the Citizens Directive.

[95] Article 24(2) in the Citizens Directive.

[96] See the references in case C-46/12 L. N. in paragraph 25 to Article 20 (1) TFEU and the status of Union citizenship as well as the references to numerous Union citizenship cases in paragraphs 27–29 such as Martinez Sala, Grzelczyk, D'Hoop and Bidar.

recognised right of states to limit the eligibility of the national support system given the possibility of circumventing national limitations.

Relying on the decision in the case of L.N., the Authority concludes that the objective pursued by an EEA national in applying to enter the territory are of no account as long as the person pursues or wishes to pursue effective and genuine employment activities.[97] In other words, the case law from the CJEU explicitly substantiated by the existence of the status of Union citizenship is effectively reflected in the Authority's reasoning for requiring Norway to change the conditions for access to financial assistance to students.

This view by the Authority becomes even clearer in a different case also regarding financial assistance from the Norwegian State Educational Loan Fund.

4.3.2 The EFTA Surveillance Authority and Access to Financial Assistance from the Norwegian State Educational Loan Fund: Case No 71579

By letter of formal notice on 15 May 2013, the EFTA Surveillance Authority concluded that the Norwegian legislation concerning the award of financial assistance for education was contrary to Articles 36 and 4 EEA.[98] The Norwegian legislation limited the eligibility for financial assistance from the Norwegian State Educational Loan to students pursuing online courses at Norwegian online institutions only. The Authority claimed that some universities must be considered as service providers. According to the Authority, the legislation was contrary to Article 4 EEA as discrimination based on nationality provided that educational training fell within the scope of the EEA Agreement.

The legislation applied equally to all groups, in principle falling within the personal scope of entitlement to financial support for conducting studies. Hence, it applied equally to Norwegian citizens, persons residing legally in Norway as well as EEA nationals with a professional or other special attachment to Norway. The overall purpose of the limitation was to limit financial support to certain educational courses. The Authority took the view that the national limitation was contrary to the rights of service providers established outside of Norway.[99] The approach by the Authority seems to be built on a comparison of this limitation with the same legislation allowing for some form of foreign higher education being included in the entitlement for financial support.[100] The inclusion of some institutions providing courses

[97] See also the later Reasoned opinion, paragraph 53.

[98] Article 4 EEA corresponds to Article 18 TFEU.

[99] Letter of formal notice to Norway concerning access to financial assistance from the Norwegian State Educational Loan Fund 15 May 2013, paragraphs 15 and 40.

[100] Letter of formal notice to Norway concerning access to financial assistance from the Norwegian State Educational Loan Fund 15 May 2013, paragraphs 15, 39 and 87.

abroad in the system of entitlement to financial assistance was, however, conditioned by the requirement of the applicant to live where the institution was located and to attend the classes physically.[101] Given that this condition could not be met for online studies, the eligibility requirement was limited accordingly.

The extent to which the EEA Agreement may require the state to extend the scope of its financial assistance system for students is clearly a complicated matter. In the EU legal order, student financing may be connected to the right of migrant workers, either as a part of the occupational task itself or in the form of social welfare rights to members of the worker's family. In addition, a right to student financing may arise in terms of the right to free movement of the non-economically active person where the student is viewed as an independent Union citizen. Thirdly, incompatibility of national limitations to student financing may arise as a consequence of the right to free movement of services, including the rights of service providers and the rights of service recipients.

It is this last angle that prompted the Authority to open an investigation of the limitations in the Norwegian legislation on the right to financial assistance for online studies at national institutions.

The Authority referred to the case law in the health sector to justify its reasoning.[102] The national limitation was found to be directly discriminatory on grounds of nationality. The restriction was not found to be justified based on legitimate objectives, and in all events, it was not compatible with the proportionality test.[103] The approach by the Authority was never assessed by the EFTA Court, since the Norwegian Government changed the national legislation to comply with the concerns of the Authority and the case was closed.[104]

The approach taken by the Authority in this Reasoned opinion based on the right of service providers/service recipients in the field of financial assistance for educational purposes has no parallel in the approach by the CJEU.[105] In the field of education, the CJEU has found violations of free movement of services law when the national financial systems in the form of tax deductions for school fees created an unjustified restriction on the right to move and reside within the territory of the Member States. The CJEU has not interpreted the right to free movement of services to include an obligation on Member States in the field of education to extend their financial assistance systems to include service providers abroad. On the contrary, to conclude that an EFTA State has to extend the scope of its welfare benefits based on the EEA Agreement stands in contrast to the repeated emphasis of the

[101] In addition, a list of criteria had to be fulfilled for the institution to be listed as recognised for financial support.

[102] Letter of formal notice to Norway concerning access to financial assistance from the Norwegian State Educational Loan Fund 15 May 2013, paragraph 81.

[103] Letter of formal notice to Norway concerning access to financial assistance from the Norwegian State Educational Loan Fund 15 May 2013, paragraphs 84 and 86.

[104] Letters from the EFTA Surveillance Authority to the Norwegian Government 3 and 8 June 2015, case number 71579.

[105] The field of healthcare is different, see section 3.

CJEU on Member States' autonomy to decide exclusively their funding systems of higher education expressed in the following way: 'EU law does not impose any obligation on Member States to provide a system of funding for higher education pursued in a Member State or abroad'.[106]

However, even if the CJEU has been rather reserved in its approach regarding Member States' obligations in the field of education based on the right to free movement of services provision, the Court has undertaken an increasingly more rights-oriented approach in the field of student financing based on the existence of Union citizenship and the right to free movement for the non-economically active.[107] This has been particularly evident in cases regarding own nationals' rights against their home state. As was clear from the review of the case law from the CJEU above, the recent cases on student financing have been decided based exclusively on the Union citizenship status of the claimant and, as a supporting argument, the Union's general provisions in the field of education to reach the conclusion that own nationals have rights to student financing against their home state.

Case No 71579 from the Authority precisely concerns this subject matter. The concern of the Authority is mainly the restriction on free movement rights inherent in a system where the Norwegian student only receives support when the student attends a national institution. The case is parallel to the rights of own nationals against their home state as enshrined in the case law where the legal basis is the right of Union citizens and the EU's role in the field of education. The case law of the CJEU demonstrates that the Court does not find a legal basis in the freedom of movement of services provisions to ensure these rights for students against their home state. The Court has repeatedly stated that it applies first the four freedom provisions, and only when these do not apply will the Court use Union citizenship as the legal basis.[108]

The approach by the EFTA Surveillance Authority means effectively to parallel rights for students in the EU legal order with students' rights in the EEA legal order. The position by the Authority on the application of parallel rights in the EEA in the field of education as that of Union citizens in the EU is, furthermore, made even clearer through explicit references to the case law on Union citizens in its correspondence. In its letter dated 17 June 2015 to the Norwegian Ministry of Education and Research, the Authority requests information on the safeguarding of the changes made in the criteria of Norwegian legislation for educational support to situations similar to joined Cases C-523/11 and 523/11 Prinz and Seeberger and C-359/13 B. Martens.[109] In formulating its request, the Authority makes it clear that the rights bestowed upon Union citizens enshrined in the Treaty provisions on Union

---

[106] Case C-359/13 Martens EU:C:2015:118, paragraph 24.

[107] Most recently in Case C-359/13 Martens EU:C:2015:118.

[108] See the analysis in Syrpis (2015), pp. 461–488 with further references and Advocate General Sharpston's opinion in Case C-359/13 Martens EU:C:2014:2240.

[109] Letter from the Authority 17 June 2015 to the Norwegian Ministry of Education and Research in case number 77396.

citizenship and the general provisions on education must also be ensured under the EEA Agreement. The wording on page 2 is hereby cited:

> Regarding Norwegian nationals who have exercised their free movement rights in another EEA State and their family members:
>
> 5. How the criteria for support under the new rules are compatible with judgments of The Court of Justice of the European Union in Prinz, C-523/11 and C-585/11, and B. Martens, C-359/13, where the Court stated, in essence, with regard to nationals who have exercised their free movement rights in another EEA State that a sufficient degree of integration should be established by taking into account such factors as the nationality of the student, his schooling, family, employment, language skills or the existence of other social and economic factors, as well as the employment of the family members on whom the student depends in the EEA State providing the benefit?
>
> 6. Would the student support be given under the Norwegian rules at issue in an analogous situation as the situation examined in judgment in B. Martens, C-359/13, where a national of an EEA State moves to another EEA State with his family to take up an employment there and, while being resident in that another EEA State, works in his State of nationality as a frontier worker for, in total, two years, and where his daughter who applies for support has not attended school in her State of nationality? Would the support be given if the national of an EEA State has not worked as a frontier worker in his State of nationality after having moved his residence to another EEA State?[110]

With this in mind we move to the next chapter with some reflections on the EEA integration process extending into healthcare and education services.

References

de Witte F (2013) Who funds the mobile student? Shedding some light on the normative assumptions underlying EU free movement law. Common Mark Law Rev 50:203–216

Dougan M (2005) Fees, grants, loans, and dole cheques: who covers the costs of migrant education within the EU? Common Mark Law Rev 42:943–986

Dougan M (2008) Cross-border educational mobility and the exportation of student financial assistance. Eur Law Rev 33(5):723–738

Iliopoulou A, Toner H (2003) A new approach to discrimination against free movers? Eur Law Rev 28:389

Jørgensen S (2009) The right to cross-border education in the European Union. Common Mark Law Rev 46:1567–1590

Syrpis P (2015) The relationship between primary and secondary law in the EU. Common Mark Law Rev 52:461–488

[110] Letter from the Authority 17 June 2015 to the Norwegian Ministry of Education and Research in case number 77396, page 2.

Chapter 5
Some Reflections on the EEA Integration Process Extending Into Healthcare and Educational Services Publicly Financed and Mostly Delivered Through Benefits in Kind

This chapter has analysed the EEA integration process in the field of freedom of movement of patients and students in publicly financed healthcare and educational systems. The overall question was the extent to which the EU/EFTA institutions applying EEA law have paralleled the increased free movement rights for patients and students in the EU legal order. In other words, the question was whether the EEA Agreement also requires the Contracting Parties to provide public funding for patients and students in certain cross-border situations to comply with EEA obligations.

The chapter began with a rough outline of the sensitive character of healthcare and educational services as part of national welfare systems. The starting point for the legal analysis was the free movement of services provision in the case law from the CJEU. This provision supplemented or replaced the secondary legislation. Furthermore, it was demonstrated how the legal basis for the decisions from the CJEU were reinforced by the revised constitutional framework in these sectors.

The analysis of the case law in the EU legal order on healthcare has demonstrated the requirement on Member States to ensure that citizens protected in national health systems benefit from a right to high-quality healthcare in the home state and, if this cannot be achieved, that the patients can seek medical treatment in another Member State for which the home state will be liable. In the context of education, the Court has held that Member States that make available education or training grants for studies in another Member State must ensure that the detailed rules for the granting of those subsidies do not create an unjustified restriction of the right to move and reside. Increasingly, the tendency seems to be towards treating the student as a Union citizen having independent rights, in particular in the situation of rights against the home state.

For the EEA analysis in the healthcare sector, the incorporation of the secondary legislation needed to be addressed, and attention was given to the scope of the former Article 22 in the coordination regime for social security benefits as well as the lack of the primary/secondary law distinction in the EEA Agreement.

K. Fløistad, *The EEA Agreement in a Revised EU Framework for Welfare Services*, Studies in European Economic Law and Regulation 13,
https://doi.org/10.1007/978-3-319-95043-3_5

For students, the limitations through the scope in the Citizens Directive for the right to student financing, in particular in Article 24, were analysed. The analysis of the case law from the EFTA Court and the decisional practice of the Authority all point in the direction of having paralleled the free movement rights for patients and students in publicly financed systems of healthcare and educational services in the EEA.

The new right for citizens insured under national sickness insurance schemes is the right to obtain effective and speedy medical treatment from their own EEA state or, if this is not available, from any other EEA state. The new right for citizens seeking education abroad is a right to export student financing beyond previous national limitations. The manner in which these new rights have been created is surprising if one takes into account that, first, EEA law does not apply to purely domestic situations and, second, that the EEA Agreement contains no revised constitutional framework in the healthcare and educational sectors nor parallel provisions to Articles 20 and 21 on Union citizenship. Finally, it has been demonstrated that no attention was paid to the lack of a clear distinction between primary/secondary law in the EEA Agreement.

The application of EEA law with the inherent competences of the EU and the EFTA institutions set up to ensure compliance and enforcement of EEA law in the fields of healthcare and education undoubtedly has an effect on the regulatory autonomy of the EFTA States in organising their national public health and educational systems. Furthermore, for the EU Member States, this interpretation of EEA law increases the territory upon which Union citizens can seek treatment and claim funding against their home state potentially affecting public welfare budgets. It is clear that the structure of free movement law involves a move from viewing public healthcare and educational services as part of an integrated system of protection towards viewing such services as a system of individually based entitlements anchored in the freedom of choice.

There are different aspects to this application of EEA law on the provision of healthcare and educational services. On the one hand, the rigidity of national systems is challenged and market-oriented reforms enhance free choice and the opening of new markets with subsequent positive effects. All the cases analysed regardless of whether the case originated in the EU or in the EEA legal order demonstrate how rights based on EU/EEA law improved the legal claims of the individual patients. On the other hand, a claim of individual rights may in some instances undermine collective decisions about agreed distribution of public funds and may bring unwanted results for the allocation of limited resources. There is an underlying conflict between economic policy and social protection.

In all the cases analysed, different states submitted observations as to the effect of limiting the application of free movement law in the publicly funded systems of providing healthcare and educational services to the population. As demonstrated, there may be a number of reasons for why states do not want to export state funding to pay for these services. In the field of healthcare, an individual travelling to another EEA state to receive healthcare (perhaps more quickly) may effectively bypass policy choices made for the distribution of public funds within the national public health system. In addition, those able to travel to another EEA state may not be those most in need of healthcare. Thus, applying individual rights to public healthcare services may also have fairness implications.

Furthermore, in the educational sector, a requirement to export student assistance may create undesired financial impacts that are difficult to predict and to this end challenge the financial equilibrium of the national educational budget. In the absence of a formal system for academic quality assurance, it may seem unreasonable to expect states to subsidise foreign university studies over which they have no real supervisory input. States might argue further that the provision of student assistance, specifically for education within the domestic territory, is an important component in the long-term planning and maintenance of an essential public service.[1]

Furthermore, if the claimant has the nationality of an EEA state—but has perhaps never lived there, or at least not resided there for some considerable period of time—the state might justifiably object to a claim for the exportation of financial aid mechanisms for educational purposes. Similarly, it is not intuitive that an EEA national who passes a period of residence in an EEA state—not necessarily even in an economically active capacity—then expects that state to fund his/her education abroad.[2] In addition, concerns may arise for states having invested considerable public resources in the cross-border education of a migrant student when there is little guarantee that the student will ever return to this state and contribute to the national economy.

The EU integration process is undergoing the development of a revised balance and a new structure to incorporate a better understanding of the roles of markets in welfare provisions in the societies. The objective of greater exportability is arguably best viewed as part of a broader process of constructing a European area of higher education and healthcare services that also includes a political commitment to address concerns such as common standards of quality assurance.[3] Within that framework, the objective of facilitating cross-border educational and healthcare mobility through the enhanced portability of financial support is a matter of public policy. Tensions between economic policy and social protection may be better solved politically compared to judicially. To this end, the EEA Agreement lacks the

[1] As for example also Norway did in the analysed cases from the Authority on compatibility of the state funding systems with EEA law.

[2] The coordination regime for social security benefits contains a complex set of provisions to determine the competent state to whose social security legislation the individual will be subject, i.a. for the purposes of applying the aggregation and exportation principles.

[3] For a recent study on normative approaches in public health systems, see Raptopoulou (2015).

necessary legal framework and the clear mandate in the Agreement itself and for the EU/EFTA institutions applying the Agreement to intervene extensively in the sensitive issues involved.

Reference

Raptopoulou KK (2015) EU law and healthcare services, normative approaches to public health systems. Wolters Kluwer, Alphen aan den Rijn

Part II
The EEA Integration Process and Union Citizenship: Social Welfare Rights for Non-economically Active Moving EEA Citizens

Chapter 6
Free Movement of Persons and Articles 45, 48 and 21 TFEU and Articles 28 and 29 EEA

6.1 Aim and Background

From the very start, the EEA Agreement has ensured social welfare benefits to economic actors who migrate within the EEA, on the presumption that equality of access to the social rights in the respective national welfare systems constituted an essential precondition for the exercise of freedom of movement in the EEA. The principle of equal treatment among EEA workers as regards access to employment and conditions of work and employment is enshrined in Article 28 EEA and the right to social security protection in Article 29 EEA.[1] Similarly, the self-employed are protected through Article 31 EEA on freedom of establishment and the free movement of service providers and recipients enshrined in Article 36 EEA.[2] The social welfare protection of 'non-nationals' or 'non-members of the welfare community' was limited in principle to those who participated in market processes through economic activity. In other words, the economic contribution to the finances of the state legitimated the moving EEA citizen's full inclusion into said state's social welfare system.

In the literature on welfare protection in EU law, it is argued that if the EU is to be more than a market, it is necessary to promote solidarity as a value and as a principle.[3] To this end, an important policy objective is a general right to free movement to be enjoyed in a meaningful way by all citizens regardless of their financial and

---

[1] Corresponding provisions in the EU legal order are Articles 45 and 48 TFEU.

[2] Corresponding provisions in the EU legal order are Articles 49 and 56 TFEU.

[3] Ross and Borgmann-Prebil (2010). See for a recent contribution in the field of Union Citizenship, Guild et al. (2010). See also Shaw (2000). There is an argument being made critiquing that the principle of solidarity has suffered a setback or at least has been given too little weight in the present economic situation in Europe by the European Courts, see for instance the critique in Countouris and Freedland (2013), see also Kilpatrick (2014).

K. Fløistad, *The EEA Agreement in a Revised EU Framework for Welfare Services*, Studies in European Economic Law and Regulation 13,
https://doi.org/10.1007/978-3-319-95043-3_6

economic status.[4] Hence, certain fundamental considerations in the move towards a Union favoured the extension of free movement rights beyond the economically active and beyond cross-border requirements. Union citizenship has contributed to reaching this policy objective even if Union citizens from other Member States only may expect 'a certain degree of financial solidarity' in the EU legal order.[5]

The wording of present Article 21 TFEU on the right to free movement for Union citizens is the following:

> Every citizen of the Union shall have the right to move and reside freely within the territory of the Member States, subject to the limitations and conditions laid down in the Treaties and by the measures adopted to give them effect.[6]

Hence, increasingly, the Union citizen is seen as the beneficiary of a right to move and reside across EU territory not only in the sphere of economic activity but to whatever personal end and in whatever capacity seems appropriate.[7] In this context, it is asked why the welfare state in its capacity both as a host state and as a home state should be entitled to restrict a citizen's right to free movement by denying him or her access to national social welfare benefits. Furthermore, supporters of a general right to free movement argue that in order to ensure the effectiveness of this right, the courts should be able to scrutinise any such national restriction so as to ensure that it can be objectively justified by the public interest.

While the free movement rules were originally conceived as instruments to challenge national protectionism and to increase economic efficiency, in the EU legal order, they are increasingly seen to more broadly generate citizen well-being and as instruments to bring the EU closer to its citizens. The CJEU has, as an accessory to the right of free movement in the EU legal order, opened up national social welfare systems for so-called deserving[8] migrants and extended obligations on home states to include citizens who have taken up residence elsewhere.[9]

The Member States have, however, always objected to a right of free movement of persons that would enable individuals in need of social benefits to freely move

---

[4] In EU literature on free movement rights of Third Country Nationals (TCNs) is extensively debated and it is argued that the concept of Union citizenship is inadequate given that it does not include TCNs. This debate will not be part of the EEA analysis given that free movement rights does not in principle include rights for TCNs neither in the main part of the Agreement nor in the annexes, with the exceptions in the Citizens Directive, see Sects. 6.3.2 and 8.3 and the Jabbi-case E-28/15.

[5] Case C-184/99 Grzelczyk [2001] ECR I-6193, paragraph 44, Case C-140/12 Brey EU:C:2013:565, paragraph 72 and for a general analysis Giubboni (2010), pp. 166–197, see for a recent analysis of Union Citizenship, Tryfonidou (2016).

[6] See also Article 20(2) TFEU.

[7] The consequences of the most recent case law from the CJEU limiting this right in specific circumstances will be analysed further in the chapter, see Cases C-333/13 Dano EU:C:2014:2358 and C-67/14 Alimanovic EU:C:2015:5, see also the case on the exporting of child benefits from the UK and Ireland, Case C-308/14, Commission v. UK and Ireland decided 14 June 2016, EU:C:2016:436.

[8] In the case law analysis it will be explained what is meant by the term 'deserving'.

[9] See as an example the recent case law on migrating student's right to export student financing analysed in the previous chapter.

and establish residence in other Member States.[10] The main concern for states is that nationals would move for the purpose of collecting higher benefits. This form of 'social tourism' would affect fundamentally the social welfare systems to the detriment of not only migrants but also the person who has remained within his or her own state (static citizens).[11]

So as not to undermine the national social structures upon which Union citizenship relies, the CJEU has required that Union citizens who apply for welfare entitlements in a host state to be able to reproduce the demands of solidarity that underlie any particular entitlement.[12] Furthermore, the extension of obligations on home states to include citizens who have taken up residence elsewhere is also balanced against national needs.[13] The degree and the actual 'model' of solidarity involved in the various cases thus differ, but the tendency of EU law has for many years been towards a right to general free movement and equal treatment including access to benefits previously denied through the boundaries of national social welfare systems.

The following chapters describe and analyse the EEA integration process in the field of social welfare rights for moving non-economically active EEA citizens. This field is particularly suited as a case study of the overall objective of this book for at least three different reasons. First, free movement rights for non-economically active citizens under EEA law is an example of the integration process moving beyond the economic dimension. It is one thing to allow access to national social welfare benefits and inclusion into the national system of solidarity to citizens of other EEA states who move about the EEA as economically active persons. It is quite another matter to open the national welfare systems to individuals regardless of their participation in the national economic process. On a different level, it is quite another matter to require the national welfare system to open up to individuals who have not demonstrated a deep integration into the host state or who have 'lost' their integration by leaving their home state.

Second, in the EU integration process, free movement rights for non-economically active citizens have emanated (partly) from primary law provisions despite extensive harmonising legislation.[14] Third, the institutions applying EEA law have rendered decisions that, in various ways, have had to reconcile the lack of equivalent

[10] Verschueren (2015), pp. 363–390.

[11] See i.a. the arguments of the Member States in Case C-333/13 Dano EU:C:2014:2358.

[12] De Witte (2012), p. 704 onwards, point IV, de Witte (2011), pp. 86–107.

[13] For example the discussion by the CJEU in Case C-147/03 Commission v. Austria [2005] ECR I-5969 on the sustainability of the Austrian educational scheme, see the previous Chap. 4.

[14] The two most important pieces of the current harmonising legislation in the field of social rights for moving individuals are the Citizens Directive (Directive 2004/38) and the coordination regime for social security benefits (Regulation 883/2004). Both the Citizens Directive and the coordination regime for social security benefits are included in the annexes of the EEA Agreement. The Directive entered into force in the EEA on 1 March 2009 and the Regulation entered into force in the EEA on 1 June 2012.

primary law provisions in this field with the principles of dynamism and homogeneity in the EEA Agreement.[15]

The case study of free movement rights for non-economically active citizens is concentrated primarily on various rights to social welfare benefits (including tax advantages) for moving individuals. The particular situation of patients' and students' rights was analysed in the previous chapters in relation to the free movement of services provision. The freedom of movement, residence and equal treatment of citizens has challenged former national boundaries on rights to social welfare benefits and thereby increased both the scope ratione personae and ratione materiae of EU law. An adjacent right is the right to family reunification, i.e. the derived free movement rights of family members of a Union citizen including TCNs.[16] This adjacent right may have consequences for social welfare rights, but the derived right to free movement of family members is, however, not analysed separately in this Part II given the overall limitation of scope to the welfare sector.[17]

6.2 Organisational Choices: The Interaction Between Primary and Secondary EU Law

It has already been pointed to the complex relationship between primary and secondary law in the EU legal order.[18] An analysis of the legal effect of the Treaty provisions of Union citizenship must take into account the interaction of these provisions with the secondary legislation adopted to ensure the right to freedom of movement, residence and equal treatment for Union citizens. This interaction takes different forms in the case law.[19]

It is important to point out that neither the Citizens Directive nor the coordination regime for social security benefits are secondary legislation that effectively displace primary law—so-called total harmonisation measures. In the situation of free movement, residence and equal treatment for Union citizens, the CJEU has not attached significance to the finding that the legal dispute at issue falls outside the scope of EU

---

[15] This includes the CJEU, the EFTA Court and the EFTA Surveillance Authority. The view of the Commission is clarified in a number of oral and written observations in various cases, see as an example the submission to the EFTA Court in case E-28/15, see Written observations, Brussels, 4 February 2016, paragraph 26.

[16] For a comprehensive analysis of derived rights of family members in EU law, see Guild et al. (2014).

[17] For an analysis of the right to family reunification in the EEA, see M. Grønvik, [2015] Fri bevegelighet for hele familien? Tredjelandsborgeres avledede oppholdsrett etter EU/EØS regelverket https://www.duo.uio.no/bitstream/handle/10852/45475/7/212.pdf.

[18] See Part I.

[19] Syrpis (2015), p. 462. The recent Cases C-333/13 Dano EU:C:2014:2358 and C-67/14 Alimanovic EU:C:2015:5 seem to construe the conditions for free movement in light of the Treaty as more narrow than previous case law on Union citizenship, see below.

secondary legislation. For instance, when the CJEU has found that the Citizens Directive 'does not apply to a situation such as that at issue in the main proceedings'[20] the Court undertakes thereafter an independent assessment based on the primary law provisions.[21]

Where the facts of the case fall within the scope of secondary legislation the CJEU will first examine the case with regard to the provisions in this legislation.[22] Thereafter, if appropriate, the questions referred to the Court will be examined with regard to the Treaty provision itself. Regarding the applicability of different primary law provisions, the CJEU will first examine whether the case concerns a worker, the freedom of establishment or a provider/recipient of services, respectively.[23] Only when these provisions regarding forms of economic activity are not applicable or insufficient will the Court apply the Union citizenship provisions.[24] Yet, even where a case is decided on the basis of Articles 45, 49 and 56 TFEU, the CJEU may consider citizenship-type principles.[25]

At times, the CJEU seems to be determined to disregard specific limitations in the secondary legislation, and the Court bases all the reasoning on the existence of the Treaty provisions without being concerned with the effect, leading to an apparent disregard of legislative choices.[26] Other times, however, the CJEU seems to regard the secondary legislation in the field of free movement, residence and equal treatment as exhaustive, and the Court refrains from applying the Treaty provisions

---

[20] Case C-34/09 Zambrano [2011] ECR I-1177, paragraph 39, see also the later O. and B. case, Case C-456/12, EU:2014:135.

[21] A recent critical comment on the CJEU's approach termed as judicial lawmaking can be found in Horsley (2013), pp. 931–964. Horsley point out that what is required of the Court's lawmaking it to pay sufficient deference to the policy choices of the EU legislature as expressed in secondary EU law. 'The Court should not read these choices as incomplete statements on the scope and intensity of EU law in particular substantive areas', p. 960.

[22] Case C-46/12 L. N. EU:C:2013:9, paragraph 35, Case C-341/05 Laval [2007] ECR I-11767, paragraph 61. The EFTA Court has made statements to the same effect, see Case E-3/12 Jonsson, paragraph 57, see also Case E-2/11 STX, paragraph 35.

[23] Case C-92/01 Stylianakis [2003] ECR I-1291, however, the CJEU has not always been consistent, e.g. Cases C-274/96 Bickel and Franz [1998] ECR I-7637, C-135/99 Elsen [2000] ECR I-10409, see also Dougan and Spaventa (2003), p. 699.

[24] Cases C-100/01 Olazabal [2002] ECR I-10981, C-392/05 Alevizos [2007] ECR I-3505 paragraph 80, C-152/05 Germany [2008] ECR I-39, paragraph 18. For a more recent example in the field of free movement rights for students see Advocate General Sharpston's opinion in Case C-359/13 Martens EU:C:2014:2240 where this approach is clear from the systematic approach to the questions asked by the national court. First, the right to free movement as a dependent family member of an economically active person is assessed and then second, the individual right as a non-economically active Union citizen is examined.

[25] Cases C-60/00 Carpenter [2002] ECR I-6279, C-291/05 Eind [2007] ECR I-10719, C-228/07 Jørn Petersen v Arbeitsmarktservice [2008] ECR I-6989, joined Cases C-502/01 and C-31/02, Gaumain Cerri and Barth [2004] ECR I-6483.

[26] Confer Citizenship cases analysed in this chapter and the observation by Hailbronner (2005), p. 1254 stating that '[t]he Court, however, deviates from secondary Community law without saying so' and p 1255 that '[t]he reasons given for the disregard of secondary Community law are unconvincing'.

as a supplementing legal bases for the claims even if this would seem more consistent with the earlier approach.[27]

In order to properly take into account the complexity of the different approaches by the CJEU, the following analysis of the case law from the EFTA Court and the comparisons made are based on describing first how the CJEU has reasoned on specific questions. The aim of the chosen approach is to make the legal basis for the conclusions drawn regarding the EEA integration process as clear as possible.

6.3 Social Rights in the EEA Agreement

6.3.1 Main Part of the EEA Agreement

The EEA Agreement is, like the EU was, primarily about setting up a regional free market where all factors of production (including labour) can move unrestrained. The aim of the free movement is to achieve the optimal allocation that market forces can guarantee. Except for single clauses like 'equal pay for equal work', the Agreement leaves in principle social security law and labour law to the autonomy of the state.[28] In other words, the EEA Agreement is about neither creating supranational social regulation nor introducing any common social policy.[29]

However, the developments of the European social dimension prior to the conclusion of the EEA Agreement inspired the Agreement in several ways. The European free market project was accompanied by the development and broadening of the European 'social dimension'. This can be exemplified by the Delors' 1985 white paper[30] and later on by the 1992 Maastricht Treaty itself as well as the not legally binding 1989 Community Charter of Fundamental Social Rights of Workers.[31]

Thus, the EEA Agreement itself does make references to the social dimensions in various ways. The seventh recital of the preamble to the EEA Agreement refers to the desire to strengthen the cooperation between the social partners in the EC and the EFTA States. The eleventh recital of the preamble refers to the importance of the

---

[27] Confer Case C 333/13 Dano EU:C:2014:2358.

[28] Labour law has, however, come under dispute in the EEA, in particular, with the decisions by the CJEU in Viking Line and Laval, Cases C-341/05 Laval [2007] ECR I-11767 and C-438/05 Viking Line [2007 ECR I-10779, see for a recent example Case E-14/15 Holship.

[29] Different opinions exist regarding the extent to which the EU legal order is about creating supranational social regulation or about introducing any common social policy, see i.a. the debates leading up to the UK referendum on continued membership of the Union and the Agreement between the EU and the UK anticipating continued membership of the UK in the EU from February 2016.

[30] European Commission, Completing the internal Market, COM (85) 310 final.

[31] On 9 December 1989, the Heads of State or Governments of eleven of the then twelve Member States (the UK signed the Charter in 1998) adopted the text of the Community Charter of Fundamental Social Rights of Workers.

development of the social dimension in the EEA and to the wish to ensure economic and social progress and to promote conditions for full employment, an improved standard of living and improved working conditions within the EEA.

These considerations are further reflected in the main part of the EEA Agreement. Article 1(2)(f) EEA specifically refers to closer cooperation in the field of social policy. Furthermore, Part V, Chapter 1 of the EEA Agreement (Articles 66 to 71) contains provisions on social policy. Article 66 EEA states that the Contracting Parties agree upon the need to promote improved working conditions and an improved standard of living for workers. Article 67 EEA provides that the Contracting Parties shall pay particular attention to encouraging improvements, especially in the working environment, as regards the health and safety of workers. Article 71 EEA provides that the Contracting Parties shall endeavour to promote dialogue between management and labour at the European level. Moreover, Article 78 EEA states that the Contracting Parties shall strengthen and broaden cooperation in the framework of the Community's activities in the field of social policy. In addition, Article 96 EEA makes provision for cooperation between economic and social partners.

Furthermore, the Declaration by the Governments of the EFTA States on the Charter of the Fundamental Social Rights of Workers, annexed to the final act to the EEA Agreement, must be mentioned. In this Declaration, the EFTA States emphasise their commitment to the policy objectives laid down in the Social Charter. In the terms of that Declaration, the EFTA States share the view that an enlarged economic cooperation must be accompanied by progress in the social dimension of integration, to be achieved in full cooperation with the social partners. It is also stated that the EFTA States welcome the strengthened cooperation in the social field with the Community and its Member States established by the EEA Agreement.

As is clear from the inclusion in the EEA Agreement of these provisions and references in the social field, it relates mainly to the social conditions for the economically active and, in particular, for workers. None of these provisions is comparable to the provisions in primary EU law upon which the CJEU has based its requirement on Member States to demonstrate financial solidarity with citizens from other Member States, including the right to social welfare benefits for non-economically active Union citizens.

The annexes of the EEA Agreement, however, include two pieces of secondary legislation relevant for social rights. The next two sections will present the inclusion of this secondary legislation in the EEA Agreement, in particular focusing on the reservations by the Contracting Parties in terms of their application to non-economically active moving EEA citizens. Both the position of the Contracting Parties in Decision No 158/2007 by the EEA Committee and the position of the UK Government in Case C-431/11 UK v. Council indicate that the EU Member States and the EFTA States consider Union citizenship-like rights to be outside the scope of the EEA Agreement. As will be demonstrated later, the EU/EFTA institutions applying EEA law do not seem to share this opinion.

6.3.2 *Incorporating the Citizens Directive in the EEA Agreement, Decision No 158/2007 by the EEA Committee*

The decision to incorporate the Citizens Directive into the EEA Agreement included an unusual Joint Declaration attached to the joint decision from the Contracting Parties, which is discussed in the following section.

The complicated history of the incorporation of the Citizens Directive into the EEA Agreement has already been described and analysed in the literature.[32] In particular, the Icelandic Government's initial view that the provisions on both social policy and immigration policy in the Citizens Directive overstepped the legal boundaries of the EEA has been well documented.[33] The provisions of the Citizens Directive were nevertheless incorporated in the EEA Agreement without any changes or modifications as to their substantive content.[34]

Directive 2004/38 was incorporated into the EEA Agreement through an amendment of the Agreement's annexes V and VIII, and the Directive entered into force in the EEA on 1 March 2009.[35]

When the Directive was included in the EEA Agreement, the Contracting Parties stressed that Union citizenship and immigration policy are not part of EEA law. The preamble to the decision in the EEA Joint Committee incorporating the Directive read as follows:

> THE EEA JOINT COMMITTEE, [...]
>
> (8) The concept of 'Union Citizenship' is not included in the Agreement.
>
> (9) Immigration policy is not part of the Agreement.
>
> [...]
>
> Furthermore, it is stated that the provisions of the Directive shall, for the purposes of the Agreement, be read with the following adaptations:
>
> [...]
>
> (b) The Agreement applies to nationals of the Contracting Parties. However, members of their family within the meaning of the Directive possessing third country nationality shall derive certain rights according to the Directive.

---

[32] Jonsdottir (2013), pp. 96–112.

[33] Jonsdottir (2013), p. 97, 103.

[34] The usual adaptations such as substituting the words 'Union citizen(s)' with the words 'national(s) of EC Member States and EFTA States' were naturally included in the incorporating decision, confer Decision annex VIII 1(c).

[35] Decision by the EEA Committee No 158/2007, OJ 2008L 124, p. 20, and EEA Supplement No 26, 8 May 2008, p. 17.

(c) The words 'Union citizen(s)' shall be replaced by the words 'national(s) of EC Member States and EFTA States.

[…]

The reservations were reinforced by the Contracting Parties in the following Joint Declaration attached to the decision:

> The concept of Union Citizenship as introduced by the Treaty of Maastricht (now Articles 17 seq. EC Treaty) has no equivalent in the EEA Agreement. The incorporation of Directive 2004/38/EC into the EEA Agreement shall be without prejudice to the evaluation of the EEA relevance of future EU legislation as well as future case law of the European Court of Justice based on the concept of Union Citizenship. The EEA Agreement does not provide a legal basis for political rights of EEA nationals. […]

The Citizens Directive is known as the citizens' *rights* directive with the underlying theme of implementing the case law of the CJEU related to the right to move and reside freely conferred on every citizen of the Union through the fundamental status of Union citizenship.[36] Of the 31 recitals of the Directive's preamble, only eight make no explicit reference to Union citizenship. The aim is, according to the preamble, to simplify and strengthen the right to free movement and residence of all Union citizens. The question is how to reconcile the incorporation of the parallel wording of all the provisions providing rights under the Citizens Directive in the EEA Agreement with the statements made in this decision by the Joint Committee.

The Joint Declaration can be interpreted as a signal to the CJEU and the EFTA Court as well as the EFTA Surveillance Authority not to interfere with the welfare policies (or national immigration policies) of the Contracting States under the EEA Agreement in the same manner as the concept of Union citizenship has had an impact on Member States' national welfare policies (and national immigration policies) in the EU.[37] Nothing in the references to this Joint Declaration by the institutions applying EEA law thus far indicate, however, that the Declaration has been interpreted as a legal limitation.

In the first case where the EFTA Court commented on the Joint Declaration[38] regarding a question of interpretation of the Citizens Directive as incorporated into EEA law, the Court made some preliminary remarks indicating that the exclusion of the concept of Union citizenship (and immigration policy) from the EEA Agreement had no material impact on the present case.[39] The interpretation by the CJEU of the

[36] Union citizenship destined to be the fundamental status of nationals of the Member States was first formulated in Case C-184/99 Grzelczyk [2001] ECR I-6193, paragraph 31.

[37] See the analysis of the incorporation process of the Directive into the EEA in Jonsdottir (2013), pp. 96–112.

[38] Case E-15/12 Wahl, paragraphs 72–92.

[39] Case E-15/12 Wahl, paragraph 75. The case concerned the issue of membership of an organisation (Hells Angels) and the denial of entry into Iceland based on a risk assessment. While acknowledging the lack of the concept of Union citizenship in the EEA, the Court seemed less principled in its reasoning compared to earlier decisions such as Case E-1/01, Einarsson, and Case E-2/01 Post doc and more inclined towards an analysis based on a case-by-case approach. In the Einarsson

Joint Declaration in Case C-431/11 UK v. Council is equally clear in emphasising the homogeneity objective rather than to point out any differences due to the lack of Union citizenship provisions in EEA law.[40]

6.3.3 Incorporating the Coordination Regime of Social Security Benefits in the EEA Agreement

The decision by the EEA Joint Committee to incorporate the coordination regime for social security benefits does not contain a similar EEA specific Joint Declaration as the one attached to the decision to incorporate the Citizens Directive.[41] Regulation No 883/2004 and Regulation 987/2009 both, as amended and as adapted to the EEA Agreement Protocol 1 thereto, coordinate the application of social security schemes within the EEA.[42]

The Joint Committee decision to include Regulation 883/2004 in the EEA Agreement was, however, part of the dispute in the EU legal order in Case C-431/11 UK v. Council.[43] The case is one of the rare examples of the CJEU interpreting EEA law specifically. The legal question in the case is directly relevant for the topic of this book, and the decision sheds significant light on the importance of the homogeneity principle in the EEA Agreement from the point of view of the CJEU.[44]

This decision is significant not least because the CJEU has, in its past case law, not refrained from expressing the differences between the EU and the EEA legal order. Thus, historically speaking, the fundamental aim of homogeneity in the EEA Agreement has not prevented the CJEU from putting at times more emphasis on the differences between the two legal orders. In its first decision on the EEA Agreement, the CJEU underlined the fundamental differences between the two legal orders, referring to European unity as a unique concern of the EU legal order going far beyond the economic objective of the EEA legal order.[45] Its emphasis on the different

---

and Postdoc cases the Court rejected any application of revised EU Treaty provisions either directly or by analogy.

[40] See for the analysis of this case Sect. 6.3.3 below.

[41] See the EEA Agreement annex VI Social Security, http://www.efta.int/media/documents/legal-texts/eea/the-eea-agreement/Annexes%20to%20the%20Agreement/annex6.pdf.

[42] Regulation (EC) No 883/2004 of the European Parliament and of the Council of 29 April 2004 on the coordination of social security systems (OJ L 166, 30.4.2004, p. 1.) and Regulation (EC) No 987/2009 of the European Parliament and of the Council of 16 September 2009 laying down the procedure for implementing Regulation (EC) No 883/2004 on the coordination of social security systems (OJ L 284, 30.10.2009, p. 1).

[43] Case C-431/11 United Kingdom v Council EU:C:2013:589, judgment 26 September 2013.

[44] Note, however, that the CJEU reached the same interpretative result in cases involving other association agreements (Switzerland and Turkey) perhaps reducing the significance of the result being EEA specific, see Cases C-656/11 UK v Council and C-81/13 UK v Council.

[45] Opinion 1/91, European Court reports 1991 Page I-06079.

First paragraph second section states the following: '[w]ith regard to the comparison of the objectives of the provisions of the agreement and those of Community law, it must be observed that objectives of the two legal orders was also evident in the line of case law from the CJEU concerning tax deductions.[46]

Furthermore, the CJEU has a long history dating back to the Polydor case[47] of refusing to accept that an interpretation given to provisions of EU law can be automatically applied by analogy to the interpretation of a free trade agreement focusing in particular on the different aims of the treaties.

A different approach from the one described above can, however, be seen in Case C-431/11 concerning the UK's obligations towards moving EEA nationals under Regulation 2004/883. The case involved precisely the rights of moving non-economically active persons in the EEA, and at the heart of the dispute was the possibility of closing in the circle of persons having the status of Union citizenship. The arguments made by the UK and Ireland were based on nationals of the EFTA States being considered as third country nationals (TCNs).

The case of UK v. Council seems, at first glance, like a technical case concerning the choice of the right legal basis on the part of the EU for a decision in the EEA Joint Committee to update the annexes of the EEA Agreement in the field of social welfare benefits. The process of updating the annexes seldom (especially on the EU side) raises problematic issues. The UK and Ireland were, however, concerned that the updated Regulation would give social rights to non-economically active TCNs, given that, in their opinion, nationals of the EFTA States were to be considered as TCNs. An extension of social rights to non-economically active TCNs was, according to the UK, within the content of the reservation the UK had made in the EU policy on immigration. For this reservation right to be invoked also in an EEA context, however, there was a need to change the legal basis for the decision in the Council from Article 48 TFEU to include also Article 79 TFEU. In other words, the attempt by the UK and Ireland was to limit the solidarity in terms of rights to national welfare benefits to Union citizens, leaving EFTA State nationals, in particular non-economically active nationals from the EFTA States outside the circle of beneficiaries.

The dispute was triggered by the extension of the new rules in the coordination regime to the EEA.[48] To that end, the Council had established the position to be taken

---

the agreement is concerned with the application of rules on free trade and competition in economic and commercial relations between the Contracting Parties. In contrast, as far as the Community is concerned, the rules on free trade and competition have developed and form part of the Community legal order, the objectives of which go beyond that of the agreement. Indeed, the EEC Treaty aims to achieve economic integration leading to the establishment of an internal market and economic and monetary union and the objective of all the Community Treaties is to contribute together to making concrete progress towards European unity'.

[46] The string of cases started with Case C-72/09 Rimbaud and continued with Cases C-267/09, C-342/10, C-387/11, C-112/14. The cases all concern the application of Article 40 EEA and the lack of corresponding provisions in the EEA to those of Directive 77/799/EEA (now Directive 2011/16/EU) on mutual assistance between Member States' authorities in the field of direct taxation.

[47] Case 270/80 Polydor [1982] ECR 329.

[48] In this context it should be added that Regulation (EU) No 1231/2010 extending in the EU legal order the application of the coordination regime for social security to nationals of a third country who are not already covered solely on the ground of their nationality never was included in the annexes of the EEA Agreement, see the decision of the EEA Joint Committee 9 July 2014 explic-

by the EU in the EEA Joint Committee having regard to the freedom of movement of workers within the EU internal market enshrined in Article 48 TFEU.[49] The UK, supported by Ireland, challenged the decision, taking the view that regard should be had to the provisions concerning the rights of TCNs in the area of freedom, security and justices, and more precisely Article 79(2) TFEU. The UK argued quite correctly that the practical importance of distinguishing between these provisions was the special rights for the UK and Ireland in the context of Article 79(2)(b) to opt out of legislative acts. In the context of Article 48 TFEU, there is no parallel opt-out and only the possibility of the emergency brake mechanism, which was not relevant in the case.

However, the CJEU did not accept this line of reasoning. In order to reach the conclusion that Article 48 TFEU was the appropriate legal basis, the Court had to 'internalise' the EEA Agreement. This internalisation meant that the Court employed language whereby the EFTA States through the EEA Agreement were almost considered 'one of us', as part of the EU, and therefore not considered part of EU external relations or EU policy regarding TCNs. Only by departing from the ordinary view through characterising the EEA Agreement as semi-internal could the Court achieve the interpretative result desired. Crucially, the citizens of the EFTA States are not put in the same box as TCNs generally, and mobility in the EEA is secured.

Had the Court accepted the view of the UK and Irish Governments, this would have been a serious defeat for the homogeneity principle of the EEA Agreement. The Court relied strongly on the element of reciprocity when it reached its conclusion. It referred repeatedly to the rights of EU citizens in the EFTA countries. Underlying the reasoning and the conclusion was arguably also a sense of solidarity, albeit clearly based on reciprocity. Non-economic EEA individuals are included as members of the EU also in terms of their right to national social welfare benefits provided this same right is extended to EU nationals in the EFTA States. All are, in a sense, members of the same community, a point of view that powerfully reinforced the strength of the homogeneity principle in the EEA as understood by the CJEU.[50]

Regarding the wider implication of the case Rennuy and Elsuwege have concluded that

> the objective to provide for the fullest possible realization of the internal market on the basis of homogeneity arguably puts the contracting EFTA States on par with EU Member States for all areas covered by the EEA Agreement.[51]

Burri and Pirker refer to the concept of 'EEA citizenship'.[52]

---

itly stating that coordination regime applies without this addition in Article 1(b). Hence the Case C-431/11 United Kingdom v Council was only about EFTA States' national s being considered as TCNs.

[49] Council Decision 2011/407/EU of 6 June 2011.

[50] See also the analysis of the case in Rennuy and van Elsuwege (2014), pp. 935–954. The authors conclude on p. 945 that '[N]ationals of the four EFTA States are not to be regarded as third-country nationals as far as the application of the EU's social security rules is concerned. On the contrary, they have the same status as the nationals of EU Member States.'

[51] Rennuy and van Elsuwege (2014), p. 947.

[52] Burri and Pirker (2013), p. 220.

Before moving to the more in-depth analysis of the case law from the EFTA Court and the decisional practice from the EFTA Surveillance Authority, the next section will provide an introduction to the Treaty provisions establishing the concept of Union citizenship and its basis for a model change in EU law going beyond a market/economic-based model of integration to include more general policy integration. The next section will also identify limitations on rights in the secondary legislation and present how these limitations have been challenged by the CJEU based on an interpretation of the primary law provisions.

6.4 Structure

The analysis in Chap. 7 is divided into two main parts in addition to an introduction (Sect. 7.1) and a concluding section (Sect. 7.4). Section 7.3 is mainly focused on the case law from the CJEU in the EU legal order. It is demonstrated that the right for moving citizens to social welfare benefits goes beyond limitations inherent in harmonisation measures (secondary law, analysed in Sect. 7.2). In other words, it is demonstrated and explained how the CJEU has applied the Treaty provisions on Union citizenship (primary law) in order to set aside national limitations on the range of beneficiaries and on the range of welfare services covered despite the fact that the national limitations are seemingly compatible with secondary law. Hence, primary law constitutes a significant legal basis for freedom of movement, residence and equal treatment rights for non-economically active citizens and the corresponding obligations on the states in the EU legal order. This demonstration is important, given the complexity of EEA law where harmonising measures (secondary law) are continually updated and included in the annexes, whereas no similar process exists for changes in EU primary law.

Chapters 8 and 9 both focus on case law from the EFTA Court and decisional practice of the EFTA Surveillance Authority. The EEA integration process in the field of freedom of movement, residence and equal treatment for the non-economically active is analysed in light of the importance of primary law in the EU legal order for these rights. Chapter 8 concerns the field of the Citizens Directive, and Chap. 9 concerns the coordination regime for social security benefits. In both these sections, a distinction is made between rights against the host state and rights against the home state. The reason being that in EEA law, as will be explained in detail,[53] rights against the home state have raised particularly difficult questions. Even though the EEA analysis is primarily based on case law from the EFTA Court, it is supplemented with decisional practice from the EFTA Surveillance Authority when appropriate. Finally, in Chap. 10, some concluding remarks are provided. The findings indicate a parallel development in the field of social welfare rights for moving non-economically active citizens in the EEA even without the existence of the Union citizenship provisions or the revised constitutional framework regarding new aims and values in the EEA Agreement. In the concluding section, the balance

[53] See in particular the analysis of the Case E-26/13 Gunnarsson, Sect. 8.3.

between questions of legal interpretation appropriately decided by the EU/EFTA institutions applying EEA law and more policy-oriented questions are addressed.[54]

References

Burri T, Pirker B (2013) Constitutionalization by Association? The doubtful case of the European Economic Area. Yearb Eur Law 32:207–229

Countouris N, Freedland M (2013) Resocialising Europe in a time of crisis mostly focusing on labour law. Cambridge University Press

de Witte F (2011) The ends of EU citizenship and the means of discrimination. Maastricht J Eur Comp Law 18:86–107

De Witte F (2012) Transnational solidarity and the mediation of Conflicts of Justice, Europe. Eur Law J (ELJ) 18(5):694–710

Dougan M, Spaventa E (2003) Educating Rudy and the (non-)English patient: a double-bill on residency rights under Article 18 EC. Eur Law Rev 28:699–712

Giubboni S (2010) A certain degree of solidarity. In: Ross M, Borgmann-Prebil Y (eds) Promoting solidarity in the European Union. Oxford University Press, pp 166–197

Guild E, Gortázar Rotaeche CJ, Kostakopoulou D (eds) (2010) The reconceptualization of European Union citizenship. Brill Nijhoff, Leiden

Guild E, Peers S, Tomkin J (2014) The EU citizenship directive, a commentary. Oxford University Press

Hailbronner K (2005) Union citizenship and access to social benefits. Common Mark Law Rev 42:1245–1267

Horsley T (2013) Reflections on the role of the Court of Justice as the "motor" of European integration: legal limits to judicial lawmaking. Common Mark Law Rev 50:931–964

Jonsdottir J (2013) Europeanization and the European Economic Area. Routledge, pp 96–112

Kilpatrick C (ed) (2014) Social rights in times of crisis in the Eurozone – the role of fundamental rights challenges. EUI Working Paper 2014/05

Rennuy N, van Elsuwege P (2014) Integration without membership and the dynamic development of EU law: United Kingdom v. Council (EEA). Common Mark Law Rev 51:935–954

Ross M, Borgmann-Prebil Y (2010) Promoting solidarity in the European Union. Oxford University Press

Shaw J (2000) Social law and policy in an evolving European Union. Hart

Syrpis P (2015) The relationship between primary and secondary law in the EU. Common Mark Law Rev 52:461–488

Tryfonidou A (2016) The impact of Union citizenship on the EU's market freedoms. Hart, Oxford

Verschueren H (2015) Preventing 'Benefit Tourism' in the EU: a narrow or broad interpretation of the possibilities offered by the ECJ in Dano? Common Mark Law Rev 52:363–390

Miscellaneous

Legal study on Norway's obligations under the EU Citizenship Directive 2004/38/EC, Advokatfirmaet Simonsen Vogt Wiig AS, 4 January 2016

---

[54] See also more details in Part III in report from the law firm Simonsen Vogt Wiig AS 4 January 2016to the Norwegian administrative authority on immigration (Udi), Legal study on Norway's obligations under the EU Citizenship Directive 2004/38/EC.

Chapter 7
The EU Integration Process and the Right to Free Movement, Residence and Equal Treatment for Union Citizens

7.1 Introducing the Concept of Union Citizenship in the EU Legal Order

Prior to the introduction of Union citizenship by the Treaty of Maastricht, the Treaty-based rights to move and reside were limited to economically active persons, i.e. workers (Article 45 TFEU), the self-employed (Article 49 TFEU) and service providers and recipients (Article 56 TFEU). This is the state of law mirrored in the EEA Agreement, as this Agreement was concluded at a time when the negotiations over the Maastricht Treaty were still pending.

When the Maastricht Treaty introduced the legal concept of citizenship of the Union based on the right to free movement and residence, one possible interpretation of the concept at the time was the existence of a *general* right of free movement, residence and equal treatment for all Union citizens regardless of their economic activity. After all, the right for people to move freely from one state to another is a distinguishing feature of an ever-closer Union. The citizenship rights are, however, according to the wording in the Treaty provision, subject to the limitation whereby they can only be exercised in accordance with the conditions and limits defined by the treaties and the measures adopted thereunder.[1] The understanding of this formulation has, however, undergone a transformation through the interpretation of the concept of Union citizenship by the CJEU and through the evolvement in the secondary legislation, which will be commented on here. At this introductory stage, it suffices to simply point out that the wording of the Treaty provisions themselves creating the novel concept of Union citizenship put limitations on the right of free

[1] Article 20 paragraph 2 TFEU 'These rights shall be exercised in accordance with the conditions and limits defined by the Treaties and by the measures adopted thereunder'. This limitation has not stopped an expansive interpretation by the CJEU as demonstrated in this chapter.

K. Fløistad, *The EEA Agreement in a Revised EU Framework for Welfare Services*, Studies in European Economic Law and Regulation 13,
https://doi.org/10.1007/978-3-319-95043-3_7

movement and residence for Union citizens as well as the right of Union citizens to equal treatment.[2]

For this reason, it was generally perceived, for many years after the introduction of Union citizenship, both in the EU Member States and in the EFTA States, that this status was more symbolic in nature.[3] The practical legal impact of Union citizenship remained largely supplemental and residual to the legal categories into which EU law traditionally divided the nationals of the Member States, such as workers, self-employed, jobseekers, students, family members etc.[4] The capacity of citizenship to supplement and strengthen the rights of free movement, residence and equal treatment laid down in other articles of the Treaty as well as in secondary legislation seemed unlikely for a long time. To this end, the absence of the concept of Union citizenship in the EEA legal order did not appear challenging to the functioning of the EEA Agreement including the fundamental objective of a dynamic and homogeneous interpretation of the provisions on free movement of persons in the EEA.[5]

However, in the last 20 years, the concept of Union citizenship has undergone significant changes. From the case law, it is now possible to identify rights enjoyed by all Union citizens subject to conditions in the following areas:

- Rights of departure, entry and return, including obligations on home states to include citizens who have taken up residence elsewhere
- A right of residence in the host state
- A right to equal treatment, including social welfare rights in the host and home states
- Specific derived rights for family members

It is clear that the Citizens Directive and the coordination regime for social security benefits lay down significant rights for Union citizens and their families in the above areas, but their coverage is far from complete.[6] The CJEU has used the advent of Union citizenship to rethink the case law on free movement of persons.[7] In

[2] A comprehensive overview and summary of Union citizenship can be found in Barnard (2013), pp. 431–496. There is an abundance of literature on Union citizenship, see later references. A recent valuable contribution is Tryfonidou (2016).

[3] See for background information in Dougan and Spaventa (2003), pp. 699–712.

[4] Van der Mei (2003) in chapter 2 on historical context of free movement pf persons which includes EEA nationals under the EEA Agreement, see p. 56.

[5] Article 45 TFEU and Article 28 EEA on free movement of workers, Article 49 TFEU and Article 31 EEA on the right of establishment and Article 56 TFEU, Article 36 EEA on the free movement of services and Article 18 TFEU and Article 4 EEA on the right to equal treatment all give rights relevant for the free movement of persons in the EEA as well as the relevant secondary legislation continually updated and included in the annexes of the EEA Agreement.

[6] A recent commentary of the Citizens Directive is Guild et al. (2014). An older but still quite up to date commentary on substance of the coordination regime for social security benefits is Van der Mei (2003).

[7] The literature analysing the Union citizenship case law is abundant. References will be made to specific pieces of academic analysis in relation to specific questions in the following text. Suffice

particular, the Court has struck down national rules that distinguish between nationals and migrants[8] and between nationals who have migrated and those who have not.[9] The Court has also used citizenship as a justification to disregard the limits of the secondary legislation on migrants' rights.[10] The careful scrutiny of the proportionality of the national rules characterises the case law where Union citizenship entails that the personal circumstances of each individual must be taken into account despite the administrative burden this might entail.[11] Union citizenship is described as the major step forward in the evolution of the right of free movement away from a simple economic right.[12] The CJEU has used Union citizenship as an instrument to overcome the existing basic distinction between economically active and non-economically active Union citizens and create rights for all.[13] In the literature, this has been described as a major condition to 'liberate' the Community from its economic preoccupation and to prepare the way for a community of citizens.[14]

For the present purposes, the creation of a form of European social citizenship is of particular interest.[15] The CJEU has continuously maintained that citizens from other Member States may expect a certain degree of financial solidarity.[16] In this book, no attempt is made to provide for a comprehensive analysis on the case law of Union citizenship and the degree of solidarity required by EU law. The case law is under constant development, and exact limits and boundaries regarding rights based on Union citizenship are far from clear. Instead, the focus here is on the contribution

here to refer to a recent edition of the Common Market Law review including several articles analysing the Court's case law on Union Citizenship, CML Rev (52) 2015.

[8] Case C-456/02 Trojani [2004] ECR I-7573, Dougan (2006), pp. 613–641.

[9] Case C-224/98 D'Hoop [2002] ECR I-6191.

[10] Case C-413/99 Baumbast [2002] ECR I-7091, see also the analysis of the relationship between primary and secondary EU law and the constitutional dimension of the case law on Union citizenship in Dougan (2006), pp. 613–641 and for analysis of this dimension in Dougan (2009a).

[11] Case C-499/06 Nerkowska [2008] ECR I-3993 regarding a Polish residence requirement for the payment of a disability pension, joined Cases C-11/06 and 12/06 Morgan and Bucher [2007] ECR I-9161 on the award of education and training grants for studies in another Member State. This early approach by the Court may have been somewhat modified in the most recent cases where the Court is seen to have taken a retreating step, see Cases C-333/13, EU:C:2014:2358 Dano and C-67/14, EU:C:2015:5 Alimanovic and the recent C-308/14 EU:C:2016:436 on the export of childcare benefits from the UK and Ireland.

[12] Third report from the Commission to the Council and the European Parliament on the application of Directives 93/96, 90/364, 90/365 on the right of residence for students, economically inactive and retired Union citizens, COM(2006)156 final on page 8 and a significant number of references to this change in the literature, i.e. Dougan and Spaventa (2005), Spaventa (2010), pp. 141–168 and Spaventa (2008), pp. 13–45.

[13] Hailbronner (2005), pp. 1245–1267.

[14] Hailbronner (2005), p. 1245.

[15] The political, electoral and diplomatic rights, Articles 20(2)(b-d), 22, 23 and 24 TFEU stemming from Union citizenship are all outside the scope of the EEA Agreement and do not create any specific challenges vis a vis the homogeneity objective in the EEA Agreement.

[16] Case C-184/99 Grzelczyk [2001] ECR I-6193, paragraph 44, Case C-140/12 Brey EU:C:2013:565, paragraph 72.

to the free movement rights, in particular in the area of social welfare benefits of non-economically active Union citizens.[17] This analysis includes rights against the host state and against the home state. It will be shown that the limitations in the secondary legislation both regarding the Citizens Directive and regarding the coordination regime for social security benefits have been modified and sometimes even ignored as a consequence of the rights stemming from the status of Union citizenship in the EU legal order. As a result, national legislation seemingly compatible with the secondary legislation has been found incompatible with primary law.[18] The aim of the selection process regarding EU law is to provide a platform upon which the case law and the decisional practice regarding the EEA Agreement may be assessed.

First, it is necessary to present briefly the evolvement of the secondary legislation culminating into the Citizens Directive. The purpose here is simply to demonstrate how existing limitations regarding in particular non-economically active persons have been continuously upheld in the text in the secondary legislation despite the existence of the concept of Union citizenship in primary law (Sect. 7.2.1). This drafting of the provisions in the secondary legislation has not been decisive for the CJEU, as demonstrated later, which has struck down national legislation seemingly compatible with the Citizens Directive. Second, it is necessary to present briefly the coordination regime of social security benefits to provide the background for the CJEU case law on extended free movement rights based on the status of Union citizenship in the area of social security benefits (Sect. 7.2.2). The case law from the CJEU in the field of the Citizens Directive and in the field of the coordination regime of social security benefits is subsequently presented and analysed in Sect. 7.3.

7.2 Limitations on the Free Movement, Residence and Equal Treatment Rights in Secondary Legislation

7.2.1 Limitations on a General Right to Free Movement, Residence and Equal Treatment: The Citizens Directive

Directive 2004/38/EC codifies and reviews EU instruments dealing with economically active and non-economically active persons separately 'in order to simplify and strengthen the right of free movement and residence of all Union citizens'.[19] Thus, the Citizens Directive repeals a number of directives in force at the time of adoption. Still, case law relating to these replaced directives is of considerable interest when interpreting the Directive.

---

[17] The rights of TCNs are outside the scope of the book with the exception of TCN's derived right as family members under the Citizens Directive and national requirements of sufficient means/ economic activity.

[18] See the case law analysis below.

[19] Directive 38/2004/EC, preamble 3rd recital.

The Citizens Directive gives effect to the rights established by the Treaty to move and reside freely for EU citizens and their (as defined in the Directive) family members. It gives expression to the conditions and limitations on the right to freedom of movement. The Directive also codifies some of the case law of the CJEU on the right to free movement of persons. Further, the Directive adds some new rights, but it does not limit or reduce the already-existing rights enshrined in the replaced acts. The CJEU stated in Case C-127/08 Metock that the Directive 'aims in particular to strengthen the right of free movement and residence of all Union citizens so that Union citizens cannot derive less rights from that directive than from the instruments of secondary legislation which it amends or repeals'.[20] This statement has proven to be of particular importance for the EFTA Court in later case law as will be demonstrated.

The Directive establishes the minimum level of rights that the Member States are obliged to provide for persons falling within its scope (i.e. Union citizens and their family members entering or residing in their territory). Hence, the Member States are not precluded from granting more favourable rights, cf. Article 37.[21] This provision, however, does not imply that national provisions that are more favourable must be 'incorporated into the system introduced by the directive'.[22] It is for each Member State to decide 'whether it will adopt such a system' and 'the conditions and effects of that system'.[23]

The CJEU has ruled that the rights of the Directive should be interpreted broadly, and limitations to them narrowly, so that the rights are not deprived of their full effectiveness another statement proven later to be important in the EEA context.[24] The fundamental right of freedom of movement shall be effective, and in this, the Treaty provisions on Union citizenship have informed the CJEU in its interpretation of the Directive. The CJEU has also ruled that limitations and conditions laid down in secondary legislation must be in accordance with general principles of EU law, particularly the principle of proportionality.[25] Thus, restrictions on the right to move have to be necessary for the protection of the considerations legitimising them.

Under the Directive, rights are strengthened according to the length of residence. Residence of less than 3 months does not confer a right to social welfare benefits; see Article 24(2). Residence of 3 months to 5 years provides a right to equal treatment with some exceptions. After 5 years of legal residence, a right to permanent residence

---

[20] Case C-127/08 Metock [2008] ECR I-6241, paragraph 59.

[21] See also recital 29 in the preamble.

[22] Joined cases C-424/10 and 425/10 Zilokowski and Szeja [2011] ECR I-14035, paragraph 49.

[23] Joined cases C-424/10 and 425/10 Zilokowski and Szeja [2011] ECR I-14035, paragraph 50.

[24] Case C-127/08 Metock [2008] ECR I-6241 paragraphs 84 and 93. In the literature, it is argued that the Grand Chamber recently has reversed the objective of the Directive in Case C-333/13 Dano, see Thym (2015), pp. 17–50. The Court had earlier identified the objective of the Directive to be facilitating the right to move and reside freely whereas in the Dano case Article 7(1)(b) of the Citizens Directive was construed as seeking to prevent non-economically active persons from using the host Member State's welfare system.

[25] Case C-413/99 Baumbast v Secretary of State [2002] ECR I-7091, paragraph 91.

is obtained; see Article 16 and the exception to the right to equal treatment regarding social welfare benefits no longer applies.

The Directive distinguishes between economically active and non-economically active persons. Where a person is considered to be economically active, no further conditions are required for the right to reside. For non-economically active persons, the right to remain for more than 3 months depends on the Union citizen having 'sufficient resources' and comprehensive sickness insurance cover.[26]

Prior to the adoption of the Citizens Directive, the right to move and reside anywhere in the Union was extended beyond the economically active through the rights provided for by the Residence Directives.[27] All the three previous Residence Directives merely provided residence rights for those who could support themselves. This limitation was due to the objective of excluding any risks for the social systems in the Member States stemming from the immigration of persons who might become a burden on the social welfare systems.[28] Article 1 in each of the three Residence Directives stated that the granting of a residence right was only required for nationals of Member States provided that they themselves and the members of their families avoided 'becoming a burden on the social assistance system of the host Member States during their period of residence'.[29]

In principle, the Citizens Directive continued the requirement for non-economically active citizens to have sufficient resources and insurance fully covering the risk of illness for themselves and their family members not to become a burden on the social welfare system of the host state.[30] Although the Directive took up some of the principles and statements of the CJEU in the cases on Union citizenship, the basic distinction between economically and non-economically active citizens, as was included in previously applicable Directives 90/364, 90/365 and 93/96, was not abandoned.[31] In the third report from the Commission to the Council and the European Parliament on the application of the Residence Directives, the then-new Directive 2004/38 is commented upon in the following manner regarding main innovations: 'The Directive (2004/38) maintains the requirement that Union citizens need to exercise an economic activity or, in the case of economically inactive

[26] See Article 7 of the Directive.

[27] Directives 90/364/EEC, 90/365/EEC and 93/96/EEC, OJ 2004 L 158, now replaced by Directive 2004/38.

[28] The scope of Directive 90/364 was general, whereas Directive 90/365 concerned retired people and Directive 93/96 concerned students. All three Residence Directives were included in the annexes of the EEA Agreement upon the adoption of the original Agreement.

[29] Directive 90/365 on retired Union citizens refers to social security instead of social assistance system presumably without any intentional legal difference.

[30] Article 1 of Directive 90/364, Directive 90/365 and Directive 93/96 was recast as Article 8(4) of Directive 2004/38, see also Articles 7 and 24 of the Citizens Directive. The Citizens Directive did, however, create a new category of long-term residents not part of the previous Residence Directives.

[31] See Article 14 (1) and(2) and Article 7 and Article 24.

persons, to dispose of sufficient resources and a comprehensive sickness insurance in order to take up residence in another Member State'.[32]

Thus, in the secondary legislation, the free movement of non-economically active persons is still seen as generally preventing a person not involved in economic life from relying on public funds in the host state. The exception is the new category created of citizens who have resided legally for a continuous period of 5 years in the host Member State to have the right of permanent residence there without being subject to the condition of showing sufficient resources.[33] With permanent residence, the citizen has access to the social welfare benefits on equal footing with nationals.[34]

The three Residence Directives imposed obligations on Member States to grant residence rights to citizens of the Member States provided the conditions were fulfilled. Neither Directive 90/365 nor the other Residence Directives were ever set out to prevent any obstacles to free movement, and they have never been interpreted in that way in the case law from the CJEU. Rather, the Residence Directives, much like the Citizens Directive replacing them, were about prescribing conditions governing the exercise of the right of residence in the host state.[35] It follows directly from the wording in several provisions, which refer to the host state obligations regarding residence rights and the right to equal treatment.[36] Home state obligations to equal treatment by including (own) citizens who have taken up residence elsewhere are not protected by the Citizens Directive.[37]

This general point becomes important for the analysis of the decisions in the EEA legal order, in particular of the Gunnarsson case, E-26/13 (Sect. 8.3) and the Jabbi case, E-28/15 (Sect. 8.3.4). Before moving to the EEA integration process, the next section will comment on the challenge of boundaries in the secondary legislation based on the Treaty provisions on Union citizenship (Sect. 7.3). First, however, the limitations in the coordination regime of social security benefits will be presented (Sect. 7.2.2).

---

[32] Third report from the Commission to the Council and the European Parliament on the application of Directives 93/96, 90/364, 90/365 on the right of residence for students, economically inactive and retired Union citizens, COM(2006)156 final, p. 9.

[33] See Article 16 in the Citizens Directive.

[34] The conditions for expelling a citizen for lack of sufficient resources will not be described here. Suffice to say that there may not always be sufficient grounds for terminating the residence of citizens where they have become temporarily or permanently dependent on social welfare, they must have become 'an unreasonable burden', see the Citizens Directive Article 14.

[35] Chapter II of the Citizens Directive regulates right of exit and entry. The Directive requires the home state to ensure nationals a right to leave the territory. These obligations on home states are, however, limited to not requiring exit visas or equivalent formalities and to issue the necessary identity cards or passports, see Article 4.

[36] See i.a. Chapter III on residence rights, Articles 6, 7 and 16 and generally Article 24 on equal treatment.

[37] See more detailed analysis in the case law analysis.

7.2.2 *Limitations on the Application of the Coordination Regime of Social Security Benefits*

The coordination regime for social security previously through Regulation 1408/71[38] was made part of the EEA Agreement through the inclusion in Point 1 of annex VI at the adoption of the Agreement. By Decision No 76/2011, the EEA Joint Committee made amendments to annex VI to the EEA Agreement by substituting Regulation 1408/71 with Regulation 883/2004.[39] Regulation 883/2004 entered into force in the EEA on 1 June 2012. For the sake of completeness, the inclusion in the EEA Agreement of Regulation 492/2011[40] on freedom of movement of workers, replacing Regulation 1612/68, must also be mentioned.[41] The Joint Committee made amendments to annex V to the EEA Agreement by decision on 30 March 2012, Decision No 52/2012, to include Regulation 492/2011.

The case law from the CJEU on the application of the coordination of social security benefits[42] demonstrates how Union citizenship has set aside limitations in this regime. In essence, the CJEU has built on the right to free movement, including for both the economically active and the non-economically active, to introduce extended obligations on the Member States in the field of exporting social security benefits compared to the obligations in the Regulation itself.[43]

Hence, the reason to include the regime for coordination of social security benefits in this analysis is based on the case law from the CJEU where the status of Union citizenship has served as a basis for complementing and at times extending rights in the field of exporting social security benefits beyond the coordination regime.[44] This case law from the CJEU therefore serves to illuminate

[38] Council Regulation (EEC) No 1408/71 of 14 June 1971 on the application of social security schemes to employed persons, to self-employed persons and to members of their families moving within the Community.

[39] Regulation (EC) No 883/2004 of the European Parliament and of the Council of 29 April 2004 on the coordination of social security systems, OJ L 166, 30.4.2004, 1, corrigendum OJ L 200, 7.6.2004, 1.

[40] Regulation (EU) No 492/2011 of the European Parliament and of the Council of 5 April 2011 on freedom of movement of workers in the Union, replacing Regulation 1612/68.

[41] See for student's rights under this Regulation in Chap. 4.

[42] Regulation (EEC) No 1408/71 of the Council of 14 June 1971 on the application of social security schemes to employed persons and their families moving within the Community. The Regulation has been replaced by Regulation 883/2004, which has also been made part of the EEA Agreement. The case law concerns mainly Regulation 1408/71.

[43] See the section on the case law analysis below. This was the CJEU's position from the Martinez Sala case where the right to social security benefits beyond the scope of the coordination regime was required on Member States based on Union citizenship. See the analysis of the constitutional impact of rulings such as Case C-413/99 Baumbast v Secretary of State [2002] ECR I-7091 and Case C-184/99 Grzelczyk [2001] ECR I-6193 in Dougan (2006), pp. 613–641 and Dougan and Spaventa (2003), pp. 699–712.

[44] A recent decision by the Court in Case C-308/14 EU:C:2016:436 regarding the residence test in the UK for access to child benefits seems, however, more sensitive to Member States arguments of

how Union citizenship has contributed to free movement rights for non-economically active citizens. The question in the analysis of the EFTA Court case law and the EFTA Surveillance Authority's decisional practice in relation to the coordination regime concerns whether a parallel reasoning is applied by these institutions in the EEA Agreement. In other words, the question is whether this case law and decisional practice indicate similar free movement rights for the non-economically active in the EEA to the rights ensured by the CJEU in the EU legal order.

Before entering into the analysis of the case law from the CJEU, it should be pointed out that the relationship between Regulation No 883/2004 and Directive 2004/38 is not clear in the EU legal order. The CJEU has dealt with this relationship in four decisions—Cases C-140/12 Brey, C-333/13 Dano, C-67/14 Alimanovic and C-308/14 UK v Commission. This topic is beyond the scope and purpose of this book. Here, it will suffice to point out that Union citizenship seems to have influenced rights regardless of whether the situation falls under the Directive, the Regulation or a situation where the two pieces of secondary legislation interact.[45]

Regulation 1408/71 was adopted as a social complement to the free movement of workers.[46] Regulation 883/2004 replacing Regulation 1408/71 extended the personal scope of the Regulation beyond workers to include nationals of the Member States.[47] The general purpose of the Regulation is to promote intra-EEA migration by ensuring that someone who moves and settles in another EEA state will not lose his or her social security entitlements. It is the national system that must determine the scope, content and conditions for eligibility of rights. The Regulation is organised through two main principles: The principle of equal treatment applies without exception and sets aside provisions in national legislation that reserve certain coordinated benefits for own nationals or long-term residents. The principle of exportability stipulates that acquired rights are exportable, but unlike the requirement of equal treatment, it is not an absolute principle. Both these principles will be revisited in the case law analysis.

---

the need to protect entitlements to welfare benefits. This opinion concurs with three decisions concerning the relationship between the Regulation and the Citizens Directive, Cases C-140/12 Brey EU:C:2013:565, C-333/13 Dano EU:C:2014:2358 and C-67/14 Alimanovic EU:C:2015:5.

[45] In Case C-140/12 Brey EU:2013:565 the CJEU was required to clarify the meaning of the term social assistance in the Citizens Directive by juxtaposing it with the language and content of the coordination regime of social security benefits.

[46] See also Regulation 492/2011 on freedom of movement of workers.

[47] See for a comparison of Regulation 883/2004 with Regulation 1408/71 in terms of personal and material scope, Pennings (2005), pp. 245–246.

7.3 Challenging Boundaries in the Secondary Legislation Based on the Treaty Provisions on Union Citizenship

7.3.1 Introduction

The legislative choices made in the secondary legislation to protect the boundaries of national social welfare benefits did not prevent the CJEU from rendering a series of judgments based on the provisions on Union citizenship in the Treaty challenging these legislative choices. The CJEU has used Union citizenship as an instrument to overcome the existing basic distinction between economically active and non-economically active Union citizens and create rights for all.[48] To this end, the CJEU introduced a concept of transnational solidarity based on citizenship of the Union. In later case law, the CJEU has taken a retreating step and has to some extent limited its own earlier broad interpretation of Union citizenship rights. The Court has for a time been more sensitive to Member States' concerns regarding possible burdens on national social assistance systems. Both the Dano,[49] Alimanovic cases[50] and the decision by the CJEU in the UK v Commission[51] have led commentators to question the extent of the solidarity principle in the EU legal order.[52] However, as recent as in the Brey decision did the Court emphasise the degree of solidarity expected by the Member States towards Union citizens.[53] Furthermore, the recent case law regarding student rights relies heavily on the status of Union citizenship to find national limitations regarding free movement rights for the non-economically active incompatible with EU law obligations.[54]

Regardless of these adjustments in the case law on the right to social assistance-type benefits for non-nationals, the CJEU has undoubtedly widened the personal and substantive scope of Article 21 TFEU and insisted that, in its application, there be no discrimination on the basis of nationality. The CJEU has thus interpreted Union citizenship as a new individual freedom to be protected by the European constitutional order.[55] Even though Union citizenship is still secondary to national citizenship and the redistributive role of the national welfare state

[48] Hailbronner (2005), p. 1261.

[49] Case C 333/13 Dano EU:C:2014:2358.

[50] Case C-67/14 Alimanovic EU:C:2015:5.

[51] Case C-308/14 UK v Commission, EU:C:2016:436.

[52] An analysis can be found in CML Rev 52 2015, see Shuibhne (2015), pp. 889–938 and Verschueren (2015), pp. 363–390 and Thym (2015), pp. 17–50.

[53] Case C-140/12 Brey EU:C:2013:565, paragraph 72.

[54] In addition, it is unclear to what extent the recent changes in the Court's case law were motivated by the upcoming UK referendum concerning further membership in the Union. Given that the UK has opted to leave the Union, the CJEU may revert to its previous interpretation of Union citizenship.

[55] An analysis of the impact of the case law on Union citizenship and access to social welfare benefits recommending legislative initiatives can be found in Giubboni (2010), pp. 166–197.

remains, in principle, unchallenged, Union citizenship has gradually grown in importance on social entitlements and residence rights. The change is incremental and gradual, but through a series of cases, the emerging consequences of Union citizenship destined to be 'the fundamental status of nationals of the Member States'[56] can be, if not fully so, at least partially observed.[57]

The next sections will review this case law, distinguishing between the case law concerning rights against the host state and rights against the home state, respectively. In addition to this more general overview, the case law from the CJEU will also be referred to in the analysis of the EFTA Court cases and the EFTA Surveillance Authority's decisional practice in Chaps. 8 and 9 to illuminate differences and similarities.

7.3.2 *Union Citizens' Rights Against Their Host State*

The Martinez Sala case[58] was the first instance in which the Court used the provisions on Union citizenship in order to 'circumvent' the specific limitations in secondary law on access to social benefits. In the Sala case, a Spanish national—who after residing and working in Germany for a long time had lost her job and become permanently dependent upon social assistance—claimed childcare allowance. Until this case, certain conditions for the application of then-Regulation 1408/71[59] had been applied in order to determine whether an individual in relying upon the equal treatment clause could be considered a worker/employee. If the individual could not be considered a worker/employee, the citizen could not rely upon the general principle of non-discrimination to grant unlimited equal treatment with regard to social benefits. The Court, departing from its previous case law, decided in Sala that a Union citizen could rely upon the equal treatment clause with respect to all social benefits falling within the scope of application of the Treaty. Therefore, the mere fact of establishing a lawful residence entitled Mrs Sala to claim equal access to a childcare allowance.

[56] The CJEU famously stated this in the leading citizenship case of Grzelczyk, Case C-184/99 [2001] ECR I-6193, paragraph 31 and has repeated the formula constantly in its citizenship jurisprudence. A recent decision where this formula was relied upon in terms of access to welfare benefits was Case C-503/07 Lucy Stewart v Secretary of State for Work and Pensions [2011] ECR I-6497.

[57] E. Spaventa is critical to the possible constitutional impact of Union citizenship. She argues that since the rights, still require a transborder element, the impact of Union citizenship is '[t]he fact that Union citizenship is, or is destined to be the fundamental status of Union citizens appears to be, at present, more a piece of limited rhetoric than a statement of fact'. Spaventa (2010), pp. 141–168.

[58] Case C-85/96 Martinez Sala [1998] ECR I-2691.

[59] This Regulation has been replaced by Regulation (EC) No 883/2004.

A new building block was laid by the ruling in Baumbast.[60] In this case, the Court affirmed that the right to reside within the territory of a Member State was conferred directly on every citizen of the Union, disregarding that Mr Baumbast did not comply with the national requirement to have full medical insurance, a requirement that was fully compliant with the secondary legislation.[61] In a sequence of judgments, the Court considerably expanded its case law. In Grzelczyk[62] and in Bidar,[63] the Court awarded assistance for students in the form of a minimum income under Belgian law and of subsidised loans. In Trojani,[64] the Court decided that a French national residing in Belgium for some time at a campsite and subsequently in a hostel was entitled to the Belgium *minimex,* a kind of social welfare payment. In Collins,[65] the Court decided that an Irish-American dual national was in principle, as a citizen of the Union, entitled to claim a jobseeker's allowance, subject, however, to making it conditional on a residence requirement.

In more recent case law regarding rights against the host state, the CJEU has been less inclined to rely on Union citizenship to ensure social welfare rights. The Dano,[66] Alimanovic[67] cases as well as Case C-308/14 UK v Commission were more directed towards limiting rights to social welfare benefits based on Union citizenship. However, in the case of C-140/12 Brey, the CJEU emphasised the solidarity dimension.[68] The nuancing of earlier case law by Dano, Alimanovic and UK v Commission has also been rather strongly criticised in the literature.[69] Without taking a stance regarding this criticism, it seems fair to describe the abstract principles underlying the requirements on Member States to exercise a certain degree of financial solidarity based on Union citizenship as relatively unclear but nevertheless there. Furthermore, the later shift in emphasis in the case law on social welfare rights has not been paralleled for students, as demonstrated in Chap. 4 where the Court has relied heavily on Union citizenship to ensure rights for the non-economically active (home state obligations). It remains to be seen where the Court will strike the balance.[70] The aim here is simply to analyse the direction of the case

---

[60] Case C-413/99 Baumbast v Secretary of State [2002] ECR I-7091.

[61] See for an analysis of Baumbast in Dougan and Spaventa (2003).

[62] Case C-184/99 Grzelczyk [2001] ECR I-6193.

[63] Case C-209/03 Bidar v London Borough of Ealing [2005] ECR I-2119.

[64] Case C-456/02 Trojani v Centre Public [2004] ECR I-7573.

[65] Case C-138/02 Collins v. Secretary of State for Work and Pensions [2004] ECR I-2703.

[66] Case C-333/13 Dano EU:C:2014:2358.

[67] Case C-67/14 Alimanovic EU:C:2015:5.

[68] Case C-140/12 Brey EU:C:2013:565 paragraph 72. The case law is always evolving and the CJEU is continually deciding cases regarding the free movement rights of persons.

[69] Shuibhne (2015), pp. 889–938.

[70] Some authors also argue for a narrow interpretation of these decisions in order to comply with primary law, an argument in this direction regarding the Dano case is to be found in Verschueren (2015), pp. 363–390, for a critical analysis of the case law, see Shuibhne (2015), pp. 889–938. See also the earlier references to the implications of the UK's future agreement with the EU as perhaps being of relevance for the Court's case law depending of the extent to which the adjustments were motivated on keeping the UK in the Union.

law from the EFTA Court and the decisional practice of the Authority in terms of paralleling rights for the non-economically active and creating this certain degree of financial solidarity also under the EEA Agreement. The aim is not to establish the exact boundaries of EU Member States' and EFTA States' freedom to legislate in the field of social welfare benefits.

7.3.3 Union Citizens' Rights Against Their Home State

The case law on social rights and residence rights based on citizenship of the Union does not only include rights against the host state. In De Cuyper,[71] the Court subjected the national residence requirement in the home state to a proportionality test even though the requirement was (seemingly) in compliance with the right to refuse export in former Regulation 1408/71.[72] Requirements on the home state were further developed in cases like Petersen[73] concerning also the export of an unemployment benefit apparently refused in line with Regulation 1408/71 but not considered proportional under the citizenship review. Other examples of cases concerning rights against the home state are Tas Hagen[74] and Pusa[75] concerning residence requirements and access to veteran benefits and tax advantages, respectively. Further steps have also been taken by the CJEU in terms of students' rights against their home state in cases like D'Hoop[76] and Morgan and Bucher[77] analysed more extensively in Part I in Chap. 4. Another example is the right to export a youth invalidity benefit without any prior or likely future economic activity on the part of the beneficiary, as decided by the Court in Stewart.[78]

According to Regulation 1408/71, the right to export a benefit was conditional on having the status of a worker. However, with the Treaty provisions on citizenship, this condition was set aside by the Court on the grounds that it was sufficient to have the status of citizenship.[79] The revised coordination regime of social security benefits

[71] C-406/04 Gérald De Cuyper v Office national de l'emploi [2006] ECR I-6947.

[72] Regulation 1408/71 Article 10.

[73] Case C-228/07 Jørn Petersen v Arbeitsmarktservice [2008] ECR I-6989.

[74] Case C-192/05 Tas-Hagen and Tas [2006] ECR I-10451.

[75] Case C-224/02 Pusa v Osuuspankkien [2004] ECR I-5763.

[76] Case C-224/98 d'Hoop [2002] ECR I-06191.

[77] Joined Cases C-11/06 and 12/06 Morgan and Bucher [2007] ECR I-9161, see for student's free movement rights in Chap. 4.

[78] Case C-503/07 Lucy Stewart v Secretary of State for Work and Pensions [2011] ECR I-6497.

[79] In Case C-431/11 United Kingdom v Council EU:C:2013:589, see Sect. 6.3.3 above the scope ratio personae of Regulation 883/2004 was in dispute. The UK claimed that Regulation 883/2004 extended the scope of application of the coordination regime to non-economically active persons more generally whereas the Commission argued that the previous Regulation 1408/71 also applied to various categories on non-economically active persons such as family members, pensioners and student.

now includes a wider scope of beneficiaries, but the material scope of the regime is still limited.[80]

For instance, the Gaumain-Cerri and Barth case[81] concerned the compatibility with EU law of rules that made the receipt of some benefits conditional upon residence within the territory of the Member State. Having found that the benefits in question were covered by Regulation 1408/71, thereby falling within the material scope of EU law, the CJEU decided that it was not necessary to investigate whether one of the claimants qualified as a worker falling within the personal scope of either the Regulation or Article 39 EC (now Article 45 TFEU). Instead, the Court found that, according to Article 17 EC (now Article 20 TFEU), the claimants were Union citizens and that this status enabled those 'who find themselves in the same situation to enjoy within the scope of the treaty the same treatment in law, subject to such exceptions as are expressly provided for'. Accordingly, the residence criterion was found to be incompatible with EU law.

7.3.4 Union Citizenship Changing the Methodology of the CJEU's Scrutiny of National Measures

The case law of the CJEU on Union citizenship indicates that, at a national level, it is no longer possible to adopt blanket rules in relation to citizens.[82] Rather, the personal circumstances of the claimant might be relevant in determining the rights.[83] Thus, the national authorities must take into consideration the personal situation of the claimant so that even when the national rule in theory is compatible with EU law, its application to that particular claimant might be contrary to the requirements of proportionality. This *ad hoc* proportionality assessment required by the CJEU concerning the migrant transforms the legislative act of general application into a 'quasi-administrative act' where the authorities always have to exercise discretion in applying the black letter of the law to Union citizens.[84]

This changed methodology occurred first in healthcare cases. These cases concerned mainly the interaction of secondary legislation with the free movement of services. Since Article 56 TFEU is paralleled by Article 36 EEA, the legal situation is different compared to the case law where the Union citizenship provisions are in dispute.[85] Reference is made to Part I Chap. 3 on healthcare. The question in the

---

[80] See on personal and material scope of Regulation 883/2004 and Regulation 987/2009 Sect. 4.2.1 in the chapter on health and educational services.

[81] Joined Cases C-502/01 & C-31/02 Gaumain Cerri and Barth [2004] ECR I-6483.

[82] Spaventa (2010), p. 144.

[83] There is academic discussion regarding the question of whether this principle has been somewhat modified in case law, see CML Rev (52) 2015.

[84] Spaventa (2008), p. 41.

[85] This was also recognised by the EFTA Court in Joined Cases E-11/07 and E-1/08, Olga Rindal and Therese Slinning v Staten v/Dispensasjons - og klagenemnda for bidrag til behandling i utlandet.

initial cases was whether national measures that correctly implemented Article 22 of Regulation 1408/71 were consistent with the free movement of services.[86] Thus, the homogeneous application of the methodology may be anchored in this early case law. However, the citizenship case law has given this novel interpretative technique significant constitutional implication.[87] The principle of proportionality is applied to secondary legislation not to assess the legislation's compatibility with the Treaty, nor as an interpretative aid, but rather to potentially displace the clear wording of the secondary legislation.

The case law on citizenship is characterised by attention towards the individual and towards the individual's particular circumstances. There has been a move away from assessing the national legislation in the abstract; in other words, rather than assessing whether it complies with secondary EU law in general, the concrete facts of the specific case are examined more carefully to determine whether the application of the national law in the case is proportional. The proportionality assessment shifts from the traditional abstract assessment (i.e. the legislation is proportionate or is not proportionate) to a concrete assessment (the legislation applied in this way to this claimant is proportionate or not proportionate). As a result, the application of a piece of domestic legislation might be incompatible with EU law in the case at issue and yet be compatible with EU law in a situation where the circumstances are different.[88,89]

This renewed attention to the individual is the result of an interpretative technique most clearly demonstrated in the case of Baumbast.[90] The national rules at issue in Baumbast implemented correctly the conditions of sufficient resources and comprehensive health insurance as prescribed and defined by previous Directive 90/364. The said directive was compatible with the Treaty, and the case did not concern the exercise of discretion by the Member State. The effect of Union citizenship was nevertheless to require a proportionality assessment of otherwise compatible national requirements. This obliged the authorities to take into account the personal circumstances of the claimants and led to the need to disapply the relevant provisions of national law in relation to those claimants in certain circumstances. It is this 'personalised' assessment of proportionality that brings about a qualitative change in the expansion of judicial review of national rules.[91] Needless to point out,

---

[86] See Case C-157/99, Geraets-Smits and Peerbooms [2001] ECR I-5473 and Case C-385/99 Muller Faure and van Riet [2003] ECR I-4509.

[87] Dougan (2006), p. 613.

[88] Spaventa (2008), p. 42.

[89] This move from abstract to concrete proportionality is not unique to the Union citizenship case law. In the case of Carpenter (Case C-60/00 Carpenter v Secretary of State for the Home Department [2002] ECR I-6279) the issue related to the residence right of a third country spouse in the UK. The Court confines its ruling to the particular facts of the case so that the UK legislation is not declared incompatible with EU law as such. The case concerns fundamental rights as enshrined in the Charter of Fundamental Rights.

[90] Case C-413/99 Baumbast v Secretary of State [2002] ECR I-7091.

[91] Spaventa (2010), pp. 141–168.

this revised methodology further limits the Member States' freedom to legislate and introduces additional requirements for the national legislation and administrative practice to be compatible with EU law. This point became particularly acute in later EFTA Court case law and administrative practices.[92]

The Baumbast case concerns host state requirements. The same approach—namely, the requirement that Member States avoid imposing blanket rules in situations concerning Union citizens—can be found in cases concerning home state requirements. In De Cuyper,[93] the CJEU clarified that even when a prohibition on the exportation of a benefit is consistent with Regulation 1408/71, the Member State must still justify why it is imposing a residence requirement on a claimant. This case law was revisited in the literature after Case C-158/07 Förster[94] where the CJEU allegedly accepted the political compromise in the Citizens Directive (2004/38) by not requiring a concrete factual assessment.[95] Later case law like the Vatsouras case[96] seems, however, to confirm the Baumbast line of case law, giving real effect to the Treaty provisions and the right to move and reside freely conferred by the citizenship provisions. The Dano judgment[97] commented upon earlier presents a shift of emphasis away from assessing the specific circumstances in each individual case. As pointed to earlier, the extent to which this case nuances the earlier case law is yet to be determined.

7.4 Concluding Observations

Michael Dougan has demonstrated how the CJEU's case law has fundamentally changed the conceptual framework for assessing territorial restrictions.[98] The starting point was that the national welfare systems are territorially bound and naturally entitled to restrict the payment of benefits to those residents within the Member State. Regulation 1408/71 later replaced by Regulation 883/2004 merely created certain exceptions to that territoriality principle for the benefit of certain groups of migrant individuals. All three previous Directives[99] on the free movement of non-economically active citizens took great care to provide residence rights merely for those who could support themselves in order to exclude risks for the social systems in the Member States stemming from the immigration of persons who might become a burden on the social assistance systems. The Citizens Directive upheld in principle

[92] See in particular, Sects. 9.4 and 9.5.

[93] Case C-406/04 De Cuyper [2006] ECR I-6947.

[94] Case C-158/07 Förster [2008] ECR I-08507.

[95] Spaventa (2010), pp. 158–165.

[96] Cases C-22/08 and 23/08 Vatsouras and Koupatantze [2009] ECR I-4585.

[97] Case C-333/13 Dano EU:C:2014:2358.

[98] Dougan (2009b), pp. 613–641.

[99] The string of Directives enacted in the early 1990s; Article 1 of Directive 90/364, Directive 90/365, Directive 93/96 (now recast as Article 8 (4) of Directive 2004/38).

the requirement for non-economically active citizens to have sufficient resources and insurance fully covering the risk of illness for themselves and their family members not to become a burden on the social welfare system of the host state. Although the Citizens Directive, as already demonstrated, has taken up some of the principles and statements from the case law of the CJEU, the basic distinction between economically and non-economically active citizens has not been abandoned.[100]

Thus, clearly, the Treaty provisions on Union citizenship have influenced the right to free movement, residence and equal treatment for nationals of EU Member States and their family members both from the host state when they have moved to and resided in another Member State as well as from their home state. The Treaty provisions on Union citizenship have prompted the CJEU over the years to increase both the scope *ratione personae* and *ratione materiae* of the right to free movement, residence and equal treatment beyond the limits posed by the secondary legislation and in other articles in the Treaties.[101] A certain degree of financial solidarity may be expected for citizens from other Member States. Equal access to social benefits may be expected whenever there exists 'a certain degree of integration'.[102] In doing so, the CJEU has increasingly abandoned the distinction between economically active and non-economically active citizens.[103] Rather than confining free movement rights to specific categories of persons, workers are now treated 'as a species of the genus citizen of the Union'.[104]

Of particular interest in an EEA context is the fact that the CJEU is interpreting secondary legislation and Treaty provisions in a particular way based on the Union citizenship provisions in the Treaty. This interpretation has in some cases meant disregarding the provisions in the secondary legislation or interpreting the provisions differently than the wording. Express limitations in the secondary legislation are occasionally disregarded given that the claimant can rely on primary law directly. To this end, political compromises reached in secondary legislation are set aside based on the CJEU's understanding of primary law. This can be seen in relation to both the Citizens Directive and the coordination regime of social security benefits.

The conceptual basis for claims against both the host and the home state is the same. Rules containing a territorial element, such as a residence requirement, affect the right to move of Union citizens as well as the right to choose their place of residence. For this reason, these rules are compatible with the Treaty only insofar as they pursue a legitimate aim in a proportionate way. Thus, it can be argued that, in all those cases, what mattered was discrimination against movers. Those who had moved, or who had returned after having exercised their right to move, were at a disadvantage compared to those who had not moved (static citizens).

---

[100] See Articles 7, 14 (1) and 14(2) and 24.

[101] Such as Article 45 TFEU.

[102] Case C-209/03 Bidar v London Borough of Ealing [2005] ECR I-2119, paragraph 57.

[103] Hailbronner (2007), pp. 317–320. An opposing view can be found in O'Brien (2008), p. 653.

[104] Condinanzi et al. (2008), p. 67.

The next section sets out to explore the case law from the EFTA Court and the decisional practice of the EFTA Surveillance Authority to see if the EU/EFTA institutions applying EEA law are equally determined to abandon the distinction between economically active and non-economically active citizens in the EEA and create a degree of financial solidarity between the Contracting Parties. The two next chapters will separate between cases under the Citizens Directive (Chap. 8) and cases under the coordination regime (Chap. 9) followed by some final reflections (Chap. 10).

References

Barnard C (2013) The substantive law of the EU, 4th edn. Oxford University Press, pp 431–496

Condinanzi M, Land A, Nascimbene B (2008) Citizenship of the Union and free movement of persons. Martinus Nijhoff, The Hague, p 67

Dougan M (2006) The constitutional dimension to the case law on Union citizenship. Eur Law Rev 31(5):613–641

Dougan M (2009a) The spatial restructuring of National Welfare States within the European Union: the contribution of Union citizenship and the relevance of the treaty of Lisbon. In: Neergaard U, Nielsen R, Roseberry LM (eds) Integrating welfare functions into EU law – from Rome to Lisbon. DJØF Publishing

Dougan M (2009b) The spatial restructuring of National Welfare States within the European Union: the contribution of Union citizenship and the relevance of the treaty of Lisbon. Eur Law Rev 31(5):613–641

Dougan M, Spaventa E (2003) Educating Rudy and the (non-)English patient: a double-bill on residency rights under Article 18 EC. Eur Law Rev 28:699–712

Dougan M, Spaventa E (2005) 'Wish You Weren't Here...' New models of social solidarity in the European Union. In: Dougan M, Spaventa E (eds) Social welfare and EU law. Hart, Oxford

Giubboni S (2010) A certain degree of solidarity. In: Ross M, Borgmann-Prebil Y (eds) Promoting solidarity in the European Union. Oxford University Press, pp 166–197

Guild E, Peers S, Tomkin J (2014) The EU citizenship directive, a commentary. Oxford University Press

Hailbronner K (2005) Union citizenship and access to social benefits. Common Mark Law Rev 42:1245–1267

Hailbronner K (2007) Free movement of EU Nationals and Union Citizenship. In: Cholewinski R, Perruchoud R, MacDonald E (eds) International migration law. Developing paradigms and key challenges. T.M.C. Asser Press, The Hague, pp 317–320

O'Brien C (2008) Real links, abstract rights and false alarms: the relationship between the ECJ's "real link" case law and national solidarity. Eur Law Rev 33:653

Pennings F (2005) Inclusion and exclusion of persons and benefits in the new co-ordination regulation. In: Spaventa E, Dougan D (eds) Social welfare and EU law. Hart, Oxford, pp 241–260

Shuibhne NN (2015) Limits rising, duties ascending: the changing legal shape of Union citizenship. Common Mark Law Rev 52:889–938

Spaventa E (2008) Seeing the wood despite the trees? On the scope of union citizenship and its constitutional effects. Common Mark Law Rev 45:13–45

Spaventa E (2010) The constitutional impact of Union citizenship. In: Neergaard U, Nielsen R, Roseberry L (eds) The role of courts in developing a European social model – theoretical and methodological perspectives, DJØF Publishing, pp 141–168

Thym D (2015) The elusive limits of solidarity: residence rights of and social benefits for economically inactive Union citizens. Common Mark Law Rev 52:17–50

Tryfonidou A (2016) The impact of Union citizenship on the EU's market freedoms. Hart, Oxford
Van der Mei AP (2003) Free movement of persons within the European community cross-border access to public benefits. Hart, Oxford
Verschueren H (2015) Preventing 'Benefit Tourism' in the EU: a narrow or broad interpretation of the possibilities offered by the ECJ in Dano? Common Mark Law Rev 52:363–390

Chapter 8
Case Law from the EFTA Court and Decisional Practice of the EFTA Surveillance Authority on the Right to Free Movement, Residence and Equal Treatment Under the Citizens Directive

8.1 Introduction

The case law from the EFTA Court regarding the Citizens Directive includes a case concerning the right of family reunification with an EU national,[1] the right to limit the entry of an EFTA State national based on reasons of public security,[2] the right to equal treatment to avoid obstacles to free movement from the home state of an EFTA State national[3] and the right to family reunification with a TCN.[4] The cases thus far are all preliminary references. Furthermore, the EFTA Surveillance Authority has initiated formal proceedings against Norway for the failure to correctly implement the Citizens Directive.[5]

The analysis will distinguish between rights against the host state, Case E-4/11 Clauder (Sect. 8.2), and rights against the home state, Cases E-26/13 Gunnarsson and E-28/15 Jabbi (Sect. 8.3). Case E-15/12 Wahl concerns entry rights and is therefore analysed more briefly.[6] The decisional practice of the EFTA Surveillance Authority is analysed for Case No 73930 (Sect. 8.4). The analysis of the EEA integration process within the scope of the Citizens Directive is followed by an analysis of the EEA integration process in the field of the coordination regime for social security rights (Chap. 9).

---

[1] Case E-4/11 Clauder.

[2] Case E-15/12 Wahl.

[3] Case E-26/13 Gunnarsson.

[4] Case E-28/15 Jabbi.

[5] Reasoned opinion 8 July 2015, Case No 73930.

[6] A general analysis of the Wahl case can be found in Reding (2013), pp. 199–200, see also Tobler (2013), pp. 246–256.

K. Fløistad, *The EEA Agreement in a Revised EU Framework for Welfare Services*, Studies in European Economic Law and Regulation 13,
https://doi.org/10.1007/978-3-319-95043-3_8

8.2 Rights Against the Host State: Case E-4/11 Clauder

8.2.1 Introduction

The Clauder case was the first preliminary reference to the EFTA Court on the right to free movement for non-economically active citizens and the corollary right to a family life. The case concerned the right to family reunification of a German national living in Liechtenstein.

8.2.2 The Facts

Arnulf Clauder, a German national, had resided in Liechtenstein since 1992. His first wife, also of German nationality, had taken up residence in Liechtenstein, and Mr Clauder was first granted a right of residence as a family member of a worker. In 2002, Mr Clauder received a permanent residence permit. In 2009, Mr Clauder and his wife divorced. In 2010, Mr Clauder married a German national. On 1 February 2010, he applied to the Liechtenstein Immigration Office for a family reunification permit for his new wife.

At the time of this application, Mr Clauder was a pensioner in receipt of old-age pensions from both Germany and Liechtenstein. As the old-age pensions, even in combination, were relatively modest, he received supplementary benefits in Liechtenstein pursuant to national legislation on supplementary benefits to old-age, survivors' and invalidity insurance.

On 12 February 2010, the application for family reunification was rejected on the grounds that Mr Clauder could not prove that he had sufficient financial resources for himself and his wife. Given that Mrs Clauder was not working either, it was undisputed in the case that if Mrs Clauder were allowed to reside with her husband in Liechtenstein, the amount of the supplementary benefits received by Mr Clauder would increase. Hence, the national condition of having sufficient resources to not become a burden on the social assistance system of the host EEA state was not satisfied either by Mrs Clauder as a family member or by Mr Clauder as a national of an EEA state whom Mrs Clauder wished to join in the host EEA state. The case concerned only the derivative right of residence of a family member of an EEA citizen. Mrs Clauder's possible independent right to reside in Liechtenstein as a German citizen was, according to the reference outside the scope of the case.

8.2.3 The Legal Question

The Administrative Court in Liechtenstein asked three questions in the case distinguishing between the rights of the economically active and those of the non-economically active. The formulation of the questions by the Administrative Court serves to indicate how the EFTA Court could have solved the question in the EEA context. Hence, one alternative for the EFTA Court would have been to uphold the distinction between the economically active and the non-economically active in EEA law in accordance with the formulations of the questions in the preliminary reference. For the latter group, a possible outcome could have been a literal reading of the rights spelt out in the text of the Citizens Directive. This was, however, not the path chosen by the EFTA Court. Before going more into the details of the decision, the legal question raised by the national court will be explained in more detail.[7]

According to the wording of the Citizens Directive, it is possible to separate between the three types of residence status for family members with a derivative right of entry and residence. It follows from Article 6 that a family member may have a derivative right of residence for up to 3 months.[8] This may be termed an informal residence status.[9] The conditions of a residence status for more than 3 months are regulated in Article 7(1), see subparagraph (d) with further references, in particular the requirement of being a family member of a worker or a self-employed person, see subparagraph (a), or a person with sufficient means for himself and his family members not to become a burden on the social assistance system of the host state, see subparagraph (b). This second status may be termed a temporary residence status.[10] Finally, the conditions for having a permanent residence status are enshrined in Article 16(2).

Hence, a family member may be entitled to acquire any of the three residence statuses (informal, temporary or permanent) if he or she fulfils all the relevant conditions attached to the respective status.[11]

In contrast to Articles 6 and 7 of the Directive, Article 16 does not explicitly regulate the right to family reunification. Regarding family members, the wording of the provision only provides the conditions for a permanent residence permit. A literal reading would support the argument that the legislator did not intend to grant further rights to family reunification to EEA nationals holding a permanent residence status than those mentioned in Articles 6 and 7.

A frequent limitation in national migration law is the requirement of a form of self-sufficiency test before family reunification is granted.[12] The existence of this habitual limitation in national law may explain the careful drafting of the wording in the Citizens Directive. Limiting the right to family reunification for moving citizens to persons with sufficient means would guarantee states the freedom to apply the same financial test regardless of whether the potential right holder is a national

---

[7] See also the Report for the hearing, http://www.eftacourt.int/uploads/tx_nvcases/4_11_RH_EN.pdf.

[8] For job-seekers the time period is extended to 6 months.

[9] See written observations from the Government of Liechtenstein, paragraphs 8 and 24 and 25.

[10] See written observations from the Government of Liechtenstein, paragraphs 8 and 24 and 25.

[11] See this distinction into three categories in the reference from the national court.

[12] See also the argumentation in the Reasoned opinion 8 July 2015, case No 73930, page 22 on the Norwegian subsistence requirement, a requirement of previous income for the right to family reunification.

of the state or a migrant citizen (or a returning own national). In other words, the literal reading supports the possibility of upholding domestic legislation where family reunification may always be conditioned on sufficient resources. Hence, the choice of wording in the provisions of the Directive may well be explained by the political sensitivity in migration law of allowing for family reunification without conditions of financial means.

Conversely, a different reading of the Directive would create inconsistency in the domestic legislation given the paradoxical result of conditioning family reunification on a requirement of sufficient means for own nationals (static citizens) but the same condition violating EU law for moving citizens (including returning own nationals). This interpretation of obligations under EU law would therefore arguably lead to reverse discrimination, insofar as nationals of the host state who have never exercised their right of freedom of movement would not derive rights of entry and residence from EU law for their family members.[13] In the following section, the analysis will focus on the impact of EU law on national migration law limiting the right to family reunification in these identified situations.[14]

From the wording of the Citizens Directive, it seems as if not only the moving EEA nationals themselves but also every single family member must go through the integration process individually in order to acquire rights under Article 16(1) and (2).

Family members who do not fulfil the requirements for permanent residence pursuant to Article 16(2) of the Directive (which Mrs Clauder did not) because they have not been residing in the host state for 5 years may thus, according to the wording and structure of the provisions, arguably only be granted a right of residence pursuant to Article 7(l)(d) in conjunction with Article 7(1)(b).

It follows from the directive:

> **Article 7**
> (1) All Union citizens shall have the right of residence on the territory of another Member State for a period of longer than three months if they: (a) are workers or self-employed persons in the host Member State; or (b) have sufficient resources for themselves and their family members not to become a burden on the social assistance system of the host Member State during their period of residence and have comprehensive sickness insurance cover in the host Member State; or ... (d) are family members accompanying or joining a Union citizen who satisfies the conditions referred to in points (a), (b) [...].

It follows from Article 7(1)(b) that the acquisition of a temporary residence status for more than 3 months depends on the fulfilment of the condition that the family member must not become a burden on the social assistance system of the host EEA state during his/her period of residence and must have comprehensive sickness

[13] Consequently, national requirements of sufficient means apply unconditionally.

[14] The same question arises for returning nationals who have not been economically active while exercising their free movement rights, confer Reasoned opinion 8 July 2015 from the EFTA Surveillance Authority regarding the limitations in Norwegian migration law.

insurance cover in the host EEA state. Mr Clauder did not comply with the conditions in Article 7(1)(b), since he depended on social welfare benefits himself.

As mentioned above, it was undisputed in the case that if Mrs Clauder joined her husband, their claims for social assistance would increase and they would, in that sense, become a burden on the welfare system in Liechtenstein. The submissions of the Governments (Liechtenstein, the Netherlands and Denmark) all concluded that the Citizens Directive did not give a derived right of residence for Mrs Clauder in the current situation.[15]

The question in the case concerned the conditions subject to which a family member can derive a residence right in order to stay in a host state with an EEA national holding a right of permanent residence. In particular, the question was whether a host state requirement of sufficient resources for the right to family reunification was compatible with EEA law.

8.2.4 The Advisory Opinion by the EFTA Court

In its decision, the EFTA Court recognised that Article 16 is silent in terms of providing a right of family reunification.[16] This silence in Article 16 is further contrasted in the decision with other provisions in the Directive that explicitly provide a right of family reunification and the conditions thereof.[17] As demonstrated above, however, the application of Article 7 would not have led to the result of finding the national requirements incompatible with EEA law obligations. On the contrary, the requirement of self-sufficiency in Liechtenstein was seemingly compatible with the requirements in the harmonised legislation.[18] Despite the recognition of the lack of a provision in the Directive as a legal basis for the right of family reunification in the case of Mr Clauder, the Court nevertheless found the national requirement to be incompatible with EEA law. It is this finding by the Court that makes the case important in taking an innovative step towards free movement rights for non-economically active citizens in the EEA Agreement comparable to the Union citizenship case law in the EU legal order. In the following sections, the justification by the EFTA Court in reaching this interpretative outcome will be discussed.

The EFTA Court stated that the Directive, in light of its objective of 'promoting the right of nationals of EC Member States and EFTA States and their family members to move and reside freely within the territory of the EEA states', cannot be

[15] Report for the hearing, paragraphs 31–51.

[16] See paragraph 42.

[17] In particular Article 7, see above.

[18] The situation can be compared with the situation in the UK in the Baumbast case, Case C-413/99 Baumbast v Secretary of State, [2002] ECR I-7091 In Baumbast the national condition requiring full medical insurance before having the right to a residence permit was fully compliant with Article 1(1) of Directive 90/364/EEC.

'interpreted restrictively'.[19] Furthermore, the Court insisted that the provisions of the Directive 'must not in any event be deprived of their effectiveness'.[20]

This terminology is similar to the terminology applied in the case law of the CJEU, in particular in the Metock case,[21] which is referred to extensively throughout the decision by the EFTA Court. We find the first reference to Metock already in paragraph 33 of the Clauder decision, which introduces the findings of the Court. In the Metock case, the CJEU refers to recital 3 in the preamble to the Directive on the general aim to 'strengthen the right of free movement and residence' of nationals from an EU Member State.[22] The EFTA Court adds nationals from an EFTA State to the CJEU's statement. Second, the case is cited as authority for the provisions of the Directive not to be interpreted restrictively.[23] Third, it is referred to as a source for the general importance of ensuring the protection of family life of nationals of the EEA.[24] In this context, the EFTA Court also refers to respecting the freedom and dignity of EEA nationals.[25] Finally, in paragraph 46, the Metock case is referred to when the EFTA Court assesses the impact on Mr Clauder's residence right if he is not able to be joined by his wife in his country of residence.

Even if this case concerned family reunification with another EEA citizen, there is no reason to believe that the reasoning of the EFTA Court does not apply equally to family reunification with a TCN.[26] The general application of the decision by the EFTA Court to include family reunification regardless of the nationality of the family member also seems to be the understanding of the decision by several administrative authorities dealing with immigration law in various EU Member States and EFTA States.[27]

---

[19] Paragraph 34.

[20] Paragraph 34.

[21] Case C-127/08 Metock [2008] ECR I-6241.

[22] Case C-127/08 Metock [2008] ECR I-6241, paragraph 59, referred to in Clauder paragraph 33.

[23] Paragraphs 34 and 48.

[24] Paragraph 35.

[25] Paragraph 36.

[26] This understanding is also supported by the wording of the decision where the EFTA Court refers to the right as being irrespective of nationality of the family member, see paragraph 36.

[27] See reference to Danish practices and the practice of Dutch administrative agencies in the country studies of the Report; Legal study on Norway's obligations under the EU Citizenship Directive 2004/38/EC, Advokatfirmaet Simonsen Vogt Wiig AS, 4 January 2016 to the Udi, https://www.udi.no/statistikk-og-analyse/forsknings-og-utviklingsrapporter/norways-obligations-under-the-eu-citizenship-directive-2016/, see also Case E-28/15 Yankuba Jabbi v. Staten v/Utlendingsnemnda concerning family reunification with a TCN.

8.2.5 The Right to Family Reunification in the EU Legal Order

In contrast to the general right to respect for family life as enshrined in Article 8 ECHR,[28] the right to family reunification in EU law is in principle only a corollary right to other free movement rights. Ensuring the protection of the family life of citizens is seen as eliminating obstacles to the exercise of freedom of movement. In other words, rather than being a right based on the value of family life itself, the right is functionally based to safeguard other rights.[29] Hence, the right to family life for a moving citizen includes a derived right for family members to move to another Member State to which the citizen is migrating or has migrated. For example, a husband or wife of a moving worker has the right under EU law to move to and reside in the state where the moving worker is employed.[30] Another example is the right to family life in order to ensure the freedom to provide services.[31]

To this end, EU law has an impact on limitations in Member States' national law on the right of EU citizens to be joined by family members, regardless of their nationality, both in the host state and in the home state upon return.[32] The potential of these derived rights to have an impact on Member States' sovereign right to regulate in the field of immigration law has given rise to case law on the extent of the EU-protected right, in particular for family members who are TCNs.

Before the Metock decision, these derived rights for TCNs could be limited by national migration law to TCNs who already had the legal right to stay in the territory of the Union.[33] In the case of Akrich,[34] which concerned the rights of an economically active person, the CJEU found that national limitations on the derived rights for TCN family members, such as a requirement of the TCN to be a lawful resident in another Member State as a condition, were compatible with free movement rights for Union citizens.[35]

The CJEU's stand in Akrich (before the situation was reversed through the Metock decision) meant that the impact of EU law on national immigration law was

[28] Now included also in EU law in Article 7 of the Charter of Fundamental Rights.

[29] This was the original idea behind the right to family reunification in the EU legal order, see the comparison of the right to family life in the case law from the Court of Human Rights in Strasbourg and the CJEU in Berneri (2014), pp. 254–260.

[30] Article 10 in the former Regulation 1612/68.

[31] Case C-60/00 Carpenter [2002] ECR I-6279, later confirmed in Case C-457/12 S. and G. EU:C:2014:136.

[32] Cases C-370/90 Singh [1992] ECR I-04265, C-291/05 Eind [2007] ECR I-10719 and C-456/12 O and B EU:C:2014:135.

[33] This was made clear in the Akrich, Case C-109/01 Akrich [2003] ECR I-9607.

[34] Case C-109/01 Akrich [2003] ECR I-9607.

[35] See also the analysis of the later case C-1/05 Jia in CML Rev (44) 2007, pp. 787–801 by M. Elsmore and P. Starup, Case C-1/05, Yunying Jia v. Migrationsverket, Judgment of the Court (Grand Chamber), 9. January 2007 in which the authors claim that the exercise of free movement included entitlement of being accompanied or joined by family members irrespective of nationality.

limited. The Metock decision fundamentally changed this. The case clarified that national immigration law could no longer require a legal right to stay in the territory of the Union as a precondition for granting the right to family reunification for a moving citizen.

The political sensitivity of the issues at stake in the Metock case was formulated by Advocate General Maduro:

> The issue is a sensitive one because it involves drawing a dividing line between what is covered by the provisions on Union citizens' freedom of movement and residence and what comes under immigration control, a matter over which the Member States retain competence in so far as and to the extent that the European Community has not brought about complete harmonisation. The constitutional significance of the subject explains the liveliness of the debate, with no less than 10 Member States intervening in support of the respondent in the main proceedings to challenge the interpretation put forward by the applicants in the main proceedings and the Commission of the European Communities.[36]

The right to family life for a citizen is, in Metock, presented as necessary to avoid obstruction of the exercise of the freedoms guaranteed by the Treaty.[37] The link between the right to family life and the fundamental freedoms guaranteed by the Treaty is the recognition that the lack of family reunification has an impact on the rights holder's own right to move and reside freely.[38] A Member State's legislation that required the spouse to have had legal residence in another Member State would discourage the right of freedom of movement laid down by the Treaty.[39] The CJEU consequently found the national requirement to be incompatible with EU law. The importance of the decision for the fundamental right to move and reside freely for all Union citizens has been highlighted in the literature:

> The importance of the Metock decision cannot be underestimated in terms of its constitutional re-enforcement of the centrality of free movement and the individual. Thus in Metock, Art.18 EC formed the epicentre of the decision and results in a most favourable determination for the litigant; matters of state interest are not at the forefront in the decision.[40]

The consequence of the decision in Metock was a fundamental shift away from national immigration law alone regulating the conditions for first entry to and residence in the territory of the Union. The legal basis was an interpretation of the Citizens Directive with a reference to the fundamental status of Union citizenship. The extent to which EU law grants derived entry and residence rights for TCNs and the subsequent impact on national migration policy therefore ultimately depends on the extent to which the Union citizen has free movement rights.

---

[36] Opinion from Advocate General Maduro in Case C-127/08 Metock and Others [2008] ECR I-6241, paragraph 1.

[37] Case C-127/08 Metock and Others [2008] ECR I-6241, paragraph 62.

[38] Confer Case C-200/02 Zhu and Chen [2004] ECR I-9925 and Case C-127/08 Metock and Others [2008] ECR I-6241.

[39] See Case C-127/08 Metock and Others [2008] ECR I-6241, paragraph 82 and the reference to Union citizens' rights in the Treaty.

[40] Fahey (2009), p. 948.

The Metock decision also falls in with various other initiatives in the EU legal order regarding rights of family reunification for TCNs and rights of intra-mobility of TCNs, including the revised primary law provision in the field of asylum and immigration in Chap. 2, in particular Article 79 TFEU and secondary legislation.[41] The CJEU also refers to the rights of family reunification for TCNs in the Metock decision, arguing that Union citizens cannot have more limited rights to family reunification as compared to TCNs.[42]

This legal framework is not part of the EEA Agreement, meaning that not only is there no parallel to Chap. 2 TFEU (and Article 79 TFEU) in the main part of the EEA Agreement but there are no parallels to the pieces of secondary legislation on rights of TCNs included in the annexes. To this end, the EEA Agreement differs from the EU legal order, making the unconditional application of the principles of the Metock decision in the EEA problematic and unexpected. Put differently, there is no parallel legal basis for EEA law to have similar impact on national immigration law as compared to EU law. On the contrary, in the Joint Declaration when the Citizens Directive was included in the EEA Agreement the Contracting Parties reiterated that immigration policy is outside the scope of the Agreement.[43] Based on this legal situation, the argument of reverse discrimination arguably stands in a different light and has considerably more legal weight as an argument in the EEA. Asylum, immigration and the rights of TCNs are all, in principle, outside the scope of the EEA Agreement, and this puts limits on the extent to which EEA law can create legal differences between static citizens and migrants (including returning nationals) in the field of migration law a point further elaborated on here.

8.2.6 The Situation of Reverse Discrimination and the Existence of a General Fundamental Right

It is common ground in EU law that interpretations of the law may result in discrimination against the nationals who have not availed themselves of free movement rights (internal situations), often referred to as reverse discrimination.[44]

[41] Relevant pieces of secondary legislation include Directive 2003/86/EC on the right of family reunification for TCN, Directive 2003/109/EC on rights of long term TCN residents, Directive 2009/50/EC, Directive 2005/71/EC, Directive 2011/98/EU.

[42] See paragraph 69; 'Furthermore, the interpretation mentioned in paragraph 66 above would lead to the paradoxical outcome that a Member State would be obliged, under Council Directive 2003/86/EC of 22 September 2003 on the right to family reunification (OJ 2003 L 251, p. 12), to authorise the entry and residence of the spouse of a national of a non-member country lawfully resident in its territory where the spouse is not already lawfully resident in another Member State, but would be free to refuse the entry and residence of the spouse of a Union citizen in the same circumstances.'

[43] See Sect. 6.3.2.

[44] See, inter alia, with regard to freedom of establishment and freedom of movement for workers, respectively, Case 20/87 Gauchard [1987] ECR 4879, paragraphs 12 and 13, and Case C-18/95

Discrimination is characterised as reverse when an unexpected group of people is treated less favourably. The discrimination suffered by people in internal situations is defined as reverse since it is the norm for states to favour their own nationals whereas with reverse discrimination it is exactly this group that is treated less favourably.[45] In cases concerning Union citizens and TCN family members reverse discrimination occurs when some EU citizens are granted family reunification with their TCN family member just because they can claim a link with EU law while other static citizens that cannot claim this link but find themselves in similar circumstances simply see the very same right being denied.

This is commonly viewed as an unavoidable consequence of the scope of EU law. In other words, EU law cannot impose obligations on EU Member States in wholly internal situations.[46] As stated by the CJEU in Metock to refute the Governments' argument on reverse discrimination, '[I]t is settled case law that the treaty rules governing freedom of movement for persons and the measures adopted to implement them cannot be applied to activities which have no factor linking them with any of the situations governed by Community law and which are confined in all relevant respects within a single Member State (Case C-212/06 Government of the French Community and Walloon Government [2008] ECR I-0000, paragraph 33)'.[47]

Thus, the CJEU addressed the Governments' concerns regarding reverse discrimination in Metock as a question of EU competence. In the name of strengthening and reinforcing the internal market, domestic legislation that operates counter to this overall goal is not compatible with EU law. The logic seems to be that the validity of the argument is not changed by the lack of reach of EU law into purely internal situations. In that sense, the Governments' concerns for reverse discrimination in Metock are simply refuted by a reference to the scope of EU law.

Within the economic rationale, the same logic applies in an EEA context. Hence, whenever the internal market is operating, EEA law has embarked on a journey to set aside obstacles to free movement to improve market conditions. This 'breakdown' of national rules applies equally in the EU and in the EEA. However, outside the market rationale, the same type of reasoning on the situation of reverse discrimination presupposes an already-defined general right to be relied upon to set aside domestic legislation based on the national political priorities. In the EU, the status of Union citizenship has become the important individual right that the EU guarantees to its citizens.[48] Hence, the right to move and reside freely for all Union citizens

---

Terhoeve [1999] ECR I-345, paragraph 26, and the decisions there cited. The same holds good in respect of the provisions of Regulation No 1408/71 (see, to that effect, Case C-153/91 Petit [1992] ECR I-4973, paragraph 10, and joined Cases C-95/99 to C-98/99 and C-180/99 Khalil and Others [2001] ECR I-7413, paragraph 70).

[45] Berneri (2014), p. 260.

[46] See for example the reasoning in Case C-127/08 Metock and Others [2008] ECR I-6241, paragraphs 76–78 where difference of treatment was regarded as a consequence of the scope of EU law.

[47] Case C-127/08 Metock and Others [2008] ECR I-6241, paragraph 77.

[48] Communication from the Commission COM(2010)373 final p. 2 and numerous cases from the CJEU referred to in the Communication.

enshrined in the Treaty is based on a higher principle of law. In the EU, this fundamental right may justify setting aside domestic legislation based on national political priorities in order to protect this free movement right for the non-economically active. In continuation, the fact that the EU obligation may lead to reverse discrimination can, as shown above, be refuted by a reference to the scope of EU law. Hence, in EU law, own nationals can be subject to financial means testing before family reunification is granted, but the same legislation may not apply to migrating citizens.

In the Clauder case, the EFTA Court seems to build on the existence of a parallel general right to free movement in the EEA regardless of economic activity. This understanding explains the reference to 'the right of EEA nationals to move and reside freely within the EEA'.[49] A national obstacle requiring sufficient resources is seen as impairing this right.

The reference by the Court to this general right of free movement in the EEA makes it easier to understand that national law requiring sufficient means to obtain family reunification can violate EEA law for moving non-economically active EEA nationals (even if the same requirement applies to static citizens).

In Metock, the CJEU rebutted the intervening Governments' submission regarding the lack of EU competence in matters of migration by referring to the right to family life as part of eliminating obstacles to the exercise of the fundamental freedoms guaranteed by the Treaty, stating in paragraph 56:

> Even before the adoption of Directive 2004/38, the Community legislature recognised the importance of ensuring the protection of the family life of nationals of the Member States in order to eliminate obstacles to the exercise of the fundamental freedoms guaranteed by the EC Treaty (Case C-60/00 Carpenter [2002] ECR I-6279, paragraph 38; Case C-459/99 MRAX [2002] ECR I-6591, paragraph 53; Case C-157/03 Commission v Spain [2005] ECR I-2911, paragraph 26; Case C-503/03 Commission v Spain [2006] ECR I-1097, paragraph 41; Case C-441/02 Commission v Germany [2006] ECR I-3449, paragraph 109; and Case C-291/05 Eind [2007] ECR I-0000, paragraph 44).

In parallel with this approach, the EFTA Court notes the following in Clauder:

> that even before the adoption of Directive 2004/38, the legislature recognised the importance of ensuring the protection of the family life of nationals of the EEA States in order to eliminate obstacles to the exercise of the fundamental freedoms guaranteed by EEA law.[50]

This statement shows that the EFTA Court also adheres to the need to legitimise intervention in national immigration/welfare law by referring to the fundamental freedoms. The EFTA Court seems to be building its interpretation of Article 16 of the Directive precisely on the fact that if EEA nationals were, indirectly, not allowed to lead a normal family life in the host EEA state, the exercise of the right of residence granted to EEA nationals could be seriously obstructed and could become ineffective.

---

[49] Paragraph 46.

[50] Paragraph 35.

The EFTA Court's heavy reliance on and references to the Metock case imported the methodology of interpretation in cases regarding Union citizenship rights in the EU (interpreted in the context of EU policies on immigration) into the EEA Agreement. The CJEU's general statements on the interpretation of the Directive are clearly based on the Court's interpretation of the rights conferred on Union citizens laid down by the Treaty. The right to respect for family life and the respect of the freedom and dignity of EEA nationals are all worthy values. The difficulty lies, however, with balancing these individual rights against the well-recognised right of the state (on behalf of the national community of interest) to protect the borders of its national welfare system. This balancing act is arguably one in need of a political decision where all relevant factors can be taken into account and decisions can be legitimately made. Courts are limited in many ways and provide a forum dominated by individual claims and an agenda of furthering integration, which perhaps is not suitable for these difficult balancing acts.[51] Similar criticism has been made against the CJEU and its case law on the rights based on Union citizenship,[52] but in the context of the EEA, there is additionally no legal basis comparable to either the Union citizenship provisions or immigration law.

8.2.7 *The Citizens Directive Upholds the Distinction Between Economically Active and Non-Economically Active Persons*

In the Clauder case, the EFTA Court also relies on an argument based on the direction of the changes made in the Citizens Directive as compared to earlier secondary legislation. The EFTA Court points to the fact that, in its opinion, the Directive no longer contains a general requirement of sufficient resources.[53] This is a legally valid point, but it is not accurately presented by the Court in paragraph 38:

> In this regard, the Court notes that, in contrast to Article 1 of Directive 90/364/EEC and Article 1 of Directive 90/365/EEC, Directive 2004/38 does not contain a general requirement of sufficient resources. Such a requirement exists neither with regard to workers and self-employed persons nor with regard to persons who have acquired a permanent right of residence pursuant to the Directive.[54]

A first comment relates to the reference by the Court to the lack of a general requirement of sufficient resources regarding economically active persons. For persons who are already economically active, the requirement of having sufficient resources is relevant to a lesser degree. The early case law from the CJEU setting aside similar national requirements that were determined to be obstacles to the free

[51] See also the analysis of the Clauder case in Burri and Pirker (2013), pp. 217–219.

[52] Dougan (2009), chapter 7, Spaventa (2008), pp. 13–45.

[53] Paragraph 38.

[54] Paragraph 38.

movement of workers and the self-employed, in other words for the purpose of the functioning of the internal market, may therefore be considered less intrusive on Member States' freedom compared to setting aside similar requirements for the non-economically active.[55]

Furthermore, the EFTA Court is not being accurate when it seems to indicate that the Citizens Directive changed the requirements for the economically active in the direction of not requiring a condition of sufficient resources for family reunification for this category (i.e. workers and self-employed persons).

A requirement of a self-sufficiency test was part of the former residence directives that all concerned the non-economically active. The Citizens Directive joined the Regulation of the economically active and the non-economically active but did not change the legal requirements for economically active persons on this point.

As already demonstrated, the former Residence Directives on the free movement of non-economically active citizens[56] merely provided residence rights for those who could support themselves. The purpose was to exclude risks for the social systems in the Member States stemming from the immigration of persons who might become a burden on the social assistance systems.[57] Article 1 in each of the three Residence Directives stated that the granting of a residence right was only required for nationals of Member States provided that they themselves and the members of their families avoided 'becoming a burden on the social assistance system of the host Member States during their period of residence'.[58]

In principle, the Citizens Directive continued the requirement for non-economically active citizens to have sufficient resources and insurance fully covering the risk of illness for themselves and their family members not to become a burden on the social welfare system of the host state.[59] Thus, the EFTA Court seems to not pay sufficient attention to the fact that Article 1 of the previous residence directives has been continued, albeit in a different form, by, for example, Article 8(4) of the Directive with the exceptions provided in Article 16. The claim that the requirement of sufficient resources in general (and not only in Article 16) has been discontinued (contrary to the wording of Article 8(4)) is then relied on in the Court's reasoning in two central paragraphs.[60]

It is correct that a new group of migrants was created who had the right to a permanent residence permit after 5 years. Beyond the creation of this group, however, there is no support for the general statement made by the EFTA Court. The

---

[55] See Cases C-370/90 Singh [1992] ECR I-04265, C-291/05 Eind [2007] ECR I-10719 (Eind had been previously (before returning to the Netherlands) economically active).

[56] The string of Directives enacted in the early 1990s; Article 1 of Directive 90/364, Directive 90/365, Directive 93/96 (now recast as Article 8 (4) of Directive 2004/38).

[57] The scope of Directive 90/364 was general, whereas Directive 90/365 concerned retired people and Directive 93/96 concerned students.

[58] Directive 90/365 on retired Union citizens refers to social security instead of social assistance system presumably without any intentional legal difference.

[59] See Articles 7, 14 (1) and (2) and 24.

[60] Paragraphs 38 and 48.

temporary stay category (of persons staying up to 3 months (or 6 months for job-seekers)) has no right to social assistance from the host state. This group must, in other words, support themselves financially. The category of residents between 3 (or 6) months and 5 years is also required to have sufficient resources for a right of residence in line with the previous legislation. Thus, from the point of view of the secondary legislation, no general right to free movement and residence exists for non-economically active persons. The only exception was the category created in Article 16, which, according to the wording, did not include rights to family reunification.

8.2.8 Concluding Observations

It has been demonstrated that the right to family reunification is only a corollary right in the EU/EEA legal order. Hence, the right to family reunification depends on another EU/EEA-based right being present. In the EU, the impact on national immigration law and welfare law is based on the gradual expansion of the general right to free movement for all regardless of economic activity. In this context, the advisory opinion of the EFTA Court in Clauder can be viewed as effectively paralleling EU free movement rights for the non-economically active persons in the EEA. The Clauder case clearly laid the substantive foundation for the EEA integration process to include a parallel right to free movement, residence and equal treatment to all EEA citizens.[61]

8.2.9 The Clauder Case in the EU Legal Order

EU Law (Without an EEA Law Dimension) in the EU Legal Order

A case with facts similar to those of the Clauder case as an EU law case would undoubtedly have included in the assessment the right to move and reside freely based on Union citizenship. The reasoning of the EFTA Court is closely linked with making this general right to free movement and residence efficient.[62] Efficiency arguments support the stance that family reunification is needed to ensure the citizen's own right to freely move to and reside in the host state. Absent the right to family reunification, the citizen may be forced to choose between not having a family member joining or giving up integration and moving to the family member abroad.

---

[61] See also the analyses of the case by Burri and Pirker (2013), pp. 207–229 stating on p. 220 that 'there is EEA citizenship'.

[62] See in particular paragraph 46.

The CJEU has reiterated on a number of occasions that if Union citizens were not allowed to lead a normal family life in the host state, the exercise of the freedoms they are guaranteed by the Treaty would be seriously obstructed and the right of residence could even become ineffective. In addition to Metock-like situations, the CJEU has focused on the right to family reunification as part of the fundamental freedom involving also the rights of minors to be joined by family members being caretakers of the child.[63]

In the written observations from the Commission in the Clauder case, the right of family reunification as part of the Union citizen's own right to move and reside freely as enshrined in the Treaty is relied upon in several paragraphs.[64] The Commission argues extensively with references to case law involving Union citizenship.[65] The fact that citizenship forms no part of the EEA Agreement did not in any way deter the Commission from these arguments effectively demonstrating the view on EEA law as seen from the Commission.

EEA Law in the EU Legal Order

Even if the outcome of the Clauder case interpreted in an EU context would lead to the same result based on the status of being a Union citizen, it is not a given that the EU Member States would approve of the outcome being extended to the EEA. Provided the EFTA Court case is accepted as representative of EEA law, the extension represents a potential increased burden on Member States' social security systems stemming from free movement rights of non-economically active EFTA State citizens in the EU Member States. The reciprocity aspect of the extension of what may be termed Union citizenship rights in the EU into the EEA, nevertheless, makes this interpretation less controversial compared to other EFTA Court cases. As will be demonstrated when analysing the Gunnarsson case below, paralleling free movement rights in the EEA for non-economically active moving citizens in the situation of rights against the home state has a wider potential for causing tension in the EU Member States. This is the matter of analysis in the next section on rights against the home state.

---

[63] See Cases C-200/02 Zhu and Chen [2004] ECR I-9925, paragraph 45, C-310/08 Ibrahim [2010] ECR I-1065 and C-480/08 Teixeira [2010] ECR I-1107.

[64] Written observations from the Commission, 2 May 2011, see in particular paragraphs 54–64.

[65] Written observations from the Commission, 2 May 2011, see paragraphs 44–64 with further references.

8.3 Rights Against the Home State: Cases E-26/13 Gunnarsson, E-28/15 Jabbi

8.3.1 Introduction

The Gunnarsson case raised a novel question of EEA law. The question in the case was whether non-economically active persons who had made use of their free movement rights could claim rights against their home state (state of origin) based on EEA law. The later Jabbi case raised similar issues directly challenging the EEA dimension of national immigration law.

8.3.2 Union Citizens' Rights Against the Home State in the EU Legal Order

The Citizens Directive distinguishes between Chapter II, Regulating the Right of Exit and Entry, and Chapter III, Regulating the Right of Residence on the Territory of Another Member State. The provisions in Chapter II, for example, give the national certain rights against the home state. The home state is prohibited from requiring exit visas or equivalent formalities and is obliged to issue identity cards or passports for nationals leaving its territory.[66] Corresponding obligations on the host state are laid down in Article 5 of the Citizens Directive.

Regulating both home and host state obligations are, however, limited in the Directive to Chapter II on exit and entry. Chapter III has a different structure and establishes only the right of residence on the territory of another Member State. This is clear from the wording in Article 3(1) of the Citizens Directive, which only applies to Union citizens (and their family members) who move to or reside in a Member State *other than* the Union citizen's home state. This wording has led the CJEU[67] to conclude that the Directive does not regulate the Union citizen's and his/her family members' right of residence in the Union citizen's own Member State. This has been confirmed by the CJEU also in relation to the prior legislation that the Directive amends or repeals.[68] Union citizens' right to reside in their own Member State is ascribed to them by principles of international law. A state cannot refuse its own nationals to enter and reside on its territory.[69] The purpose of the Directive is to strengthen the right of freedom of movement to other Member States. Hence, the

---

[66] The Citizens Directive Article 4.

[67] And Advocate General Sharpston, see the opinion in joined Cases C-523/11 and C-585/11 Prinz and Seeberger, paragraph 35 and Sect. 7.3.3 above.

[68] See i.a. Cases C-60/00 Carpenter [2002] ECR I-6279, paragraphs 35–36, C-457/12 S. and G. EU:C:2014:136, paragraphs 34–35 and C-456/12 O and B EU:C:2014:135, paragraphs 37–43.

[69] European Convention on Human Rights Protocol No 4 Article 3.

Union citizens and the family members may only invoke the Directive for the purpose of rights in Member States other than the Union citizen's home state.[70]

Nevertheless, the CJEU has found that, under certain circumstances, a Union citizen and his or her family members may have rights against their home state based on provisions in the Treaties.[71] The derived right for family members to enter and reside in the home state of the Union citizen is based on the consideration that a refusal to allow a right of entry and residence for the family members could interfere with the Union citizen's right of freedom of movement. Similarly, obstacles from the home state may interfere with the Union citizen's personal right to free movement.

According to the CJEU, a granting of a derived right of residence on the TCN family member upon return to the Union citizen's home Member State:

> seeks to remove the [...] obstacle on leaving the Member State of origin [...] by guaranteeing that the citizen will be able, in his Member State of origin, to continue the family life which he created or strengthened in the host Member State.[72]

The CJEU has ruled that the conditions for granting such a right of residence 'should not, in principle, be stricter than those provided for by the Citizens Directive'.[73]

The O and B case, C-456/12, concerned a TCN family member's right of residence in the Union citizen's state of origin. O, a Nigerian national, lived in Spain. His spouse, a Dutch national, resided with him there for 2 months without pursuing economic activity. She moved back to the Netherlands when she could not find a job in Spain. B, a Moroccan national, was resident in Belgium. His partner, a Dutch national, was resident in the Netherlands, but she was visiting B regularly in Belgium for a period of one and a half years. Both the TCNs applied for a right to reside in the Netherlands with their respective wife and partner. The applications were refused. The question before the CJEU was whether the TCNs were entitled to a derived right of residence in the Netherlands on the basis of Article 21(1) TFEU. The CJEU had ruled in previous cases that such a right should be granted to TCN family members of returning Union citizens who had engaged in economic activity in the host Member State.

The first of these previous economic cases was Case C-370/90 Singh, which concerned a UK national who had resided in Germany for 2 years as a worker together with her Chinese spouse. They returned to the UK as self-employed. The CJEU ruled that the rights of movement and establishment conferred upon EU

---

[70] See also the wording in Article 7(1)(b) referring to the need to have sufficient resources not to become a burden on the social assistance system of the *host* Member State. Furthermore, Article 24(1) refers to discrimination carried out by the *host* Member State, hence the right to equal treatment is with the nationals of that Member State (emphasis added).

[71] For the Union citizen own rights, see as an example Case C-224/02 Pusa v Osuuspankkien [2004] ECR I-5763, for family members' derived rights, see Cases C-370/90 Singh [1992] ECR I-04265, C-291/05 Eind [2007] ECR I-10719 and C-456/12 O and B EU:C:2014:135.

[72] Case C-456/12 O and B EU:C:2014:135, paragraph 49.

[73] Case C-456/12 O and B EU:C:2014:135, paragraph 50.

nationals by virtue of Articles 48 and 52 EEC (now Articles 45 and 49 TFEU) 'cannot be fully effective if such a person may be deterred from exercising them by obstacles raised in his or her country of origin to the entry and residence of his or her spouse'.[74]

In Case C-291/05 Eind, the question raised was whether a TCN daughter of a Dutch national who had resided in the UK, on the basis of Regulation 1612/68 Article 10, was entitled to a derived right of residence in the Netherlands when the father moved back to the home state. According to the CJEU, the right of a migrant worker to return to his home Member State 'after being gainfully employed in another Member State is conferred by Community law, to the extent necessary to ensure the useful effect of the right to free movement for workers under Article 39 EC (now Article 45 TFEU) and the provisions adopted to give effect to that right'.[75] The CJEU stated the following:

> [a] national of a Member State could be deterred from leaving that Member State in order to pursue gainful employment in the territory of another Member State if he does not have the certainty of being able to return to his Member State of origin, irrespective of whether he is going to engage in economic activity in the latter State.[76]

The CJEU found that a worker's right to return to his/her home Member State could not be considered a purely internal situation and that

> [b]arriers to family reunification are therefore liable to undermine the right to free movement which the nationals of the Member States have under Community law.[77]

It is clear from the two cases that the TCN family members' right of residence in the Union citizen's home Member State situations is based on the prohibition on restrictions on free movement pursuant to the Treaty provisions.

In the case of O and B, the question was whether the case law resulting from Singh and Eind could be applied generally in situations covered by Article 21(1) TFEU. The CJEU's answer to a similar application of primary law in the situation of a non-economically active Union citizen was in the affirmative. However, the scope of application of Article 21(1) TFEU was limited to circumstances where the 'residence of the Union citizen in the host Member State (by virtue of Article 21(1) TFEU) has been sufficiently genuine so as to enable that citizen to create or strengthen family life in that Member State'.[78]

It was firmly established in the O and B case that Article 7 of the Citizens Directive did not place any obligations on the home state regarding rights of own nationals who have exercised their free movement rights. The Court was unusually clear, stating that this interpretation of the limits of the application of the Directive follows from a 'literal, systematic and teleological interpretation' of the Citizens

---

[74] Case C-370/90 Singh [1992] ECR I-04265, paragraph 23.

[75] Case C-291/05 Eind [2007] ECR I-10719, paragraph 32.

[76] Case C-291/05 Eind [2007] ECR I-10719, paragraph 35.

[77] Case C-291/05 Eind [2007] ECR I-10719, paragraph 37.

[78] Case C-456/12 O and B EU:C:2014:135, paragraph 51.

Directive.[79] Thus, it follows that a Union citizen may not rely upon Article 7 of the Directive against his or her home state under EU law.

Home state obligations for Union citizens have also been particularly relevant in cases on student mobility analysed in Part I in particular Chap. 4. The Court has made it clear that students can rely on neither the Citizens Directive nor the coordination regime for social security benefits for the right to export of student financing.[80] In cases C-523/11 and 585/11, Prinz and Seeberger, Advocate General Sharpston made it clear that the national court had made the right decision when formulating the questions for the preliminary reference procedure. The referring court had asked the CJEU solely to interpret the Treaty provisions on Union citizenship, and Sharpston made the following comment in paragraph 35 in her opinion:

> They were clearly right not to ask the Court to examine Article 24 of Directive 2004/38. That provision governs when a host Member State is required to give EU citizens who reside in its territory on the basis of the directive equal treatment with its own nationals, including in relation to maintenance aid for studies. However, there is no indication that Miss Prinz and Mr Seeberger have applied for funding in, respectively, the Netherlands and Spain. Rather, they have applied for funding to their Member State of origin.

The statement is consistent with the CJEU's earlier ruling, making it clear that the Citizens Directive does not provide rights in this situation. Hence, rights against the home state in specific situations are based on the Treaty provisions on Union citizenship.

Having regard to the first paragraph of its preamble, the Citizens Directive clearly promotes free movement in the context of economic activity (workers, services and establishments) as well as free movement in the context of Union citizens regardless of economic activity. Articles 45, 49 and 56 TFEU constitute the legal bases for rights in the sphere of economic activity. Articles 20 and 21 TFEU constitute the legal bases for rights beyond the sphere of economic activity. The changed legal environment introduced with the provisions on Union citizenship was spelt out by the CJEU in Baumbast in the following manner:

> Although, before the Treaty on European Union entered into force, the Court had held that that right of residence, conferred directly by the EC Treaty, was subject to the condition that the person concerned was carrying on an economic activity within the meaning of Articles 48, 52 or 59 of the EC Treaty (now, after amendment, Articles 39 EC, 43 EC and 49 EC) (see Case C-363/89 Roux [1991] ECR I-273, paragraph 9), it is none the less the case that, since then, Union citizenship has been introduced into the EC Treaty and Article 18(1) EC has conferred a right, for every citizen, to move and reside freely within the territory of the Member States.[81]

This is the legal context when the EFTA Court decided its first case regarding the possibility of invoking the Citizens Directive as incorporated in the EEA Agreement for rights against the home state for the non-economically active moving citizen.

---

[79] Case C-456/12 O and B EU:C:2014:135, paragraph 37.

[80] See the analysis in the previous chapters in Part I.

[81] Case C-413/99 Baumbast v Secretary of State [2002] ECR I-7091, paragraph 81.

8.3.3 *The Gunnarsson Case*

The Facts

The Gunnarsson case concerned two Icelandic citizens, Mr and Mrs Gunnarsson. They were both resident in Denmark from 24 January 2004 to 3 September 2009. During that period, they lived on Mr Gunnarsson's disability pension from the Icelandic social insurance administration together with benefit payments received from two Icelandic pension funds. Mr Gunnarsson paid tax in Iceland. Under the Icelandic tax legislation applicable at the time, there was an inter-spousal personal tax credit where husband and wife could pool their tax credits if this was to their financial advantage.

Mr Gunnarsson and his wife's application for tax pooling in Iceland was turned down on the grounds that such pooling was only possible between taxpayers with unlimited tax liability in Iceland (essentially resident taxpayers) or where both spouses were in receipt of an Icelandic pension. As Mr Gunnarsson and his wife were neither resident in Iceland nor both in receipt of a pension pursuant to Icelandic law during the relevant period, the administrative decision concluded that the conditions authorising the transfer of unused personal tax credits between spouses were not fulfilled. Essentially, the national legislation precluded pensioners who were resident in another EEA state to utilise the same tax credit that they would have been able to use if they had been resident in Iceland.

Mr Gunnarsson claimed repayment of the excess taxes paid. The Supreme Court of Iceland decided to seek an advisory opinion from the EFTA Court on the compatibility of the national rule with EEA law. The national court specifically asked the EFTA Court whether it made any difference that the Treaty provisions on Union citizenship in EU law were not paralleled in the EEA.[82] The EFTA Court issued a ruling favourable to Mr Gunnarsson, adjudicating that the national rule was incompatible with the previous Directive 90/365 and subsequently the Citizens Directive.

The Advisory Opinion of the EFTA Court

The EFTA Court concluded in Gunnarsson that Article 7(1)(b) of the Directive must be interpreted as granting the moving person not merely a right of residence in relation to the host state but also a right to move freely away from the state of nationality:

> [t]he latter right prohibits the home State from hindering such a person from moving to another EEA State.[83]

This represents a significant divergence from the CJEU's position regarding rights stemming from the Directive. The EFTA Court observed that less favourable

[82] See question 2 from the Supreme Court, cited in decision by the EFTA Court paragraph 29.

[83] Case E-26/13 Gunnarsson, paragraph 82.

treatment in the state of nationality of persons who have moved compared to those who have remained would constitute a hindrance on the right to move freely. This is familiar terminology from the CJEU's case law on the right to move freely, which, under the Union citizenship provisions, includes, as already demonstrated, the non-economically active person.[84]

Arguably, the EFTA Court's diverging interpretation of the Directive maintained substantive parity with EU law, ensuring equal levels of protection for individual rights throughout the EEA.[85] The applied methodology is highly unusual. This is the first time the EFTA Court has applied secondary legislation to grant rights under the EEA legal order that did not accrue by virtue of an identical provision within the EU legal order. Divergence compared to the EU legal order on an identical point of law has materialised previously under the EEA Agreement. This has, however, led to a more narrow range of available rights. The Gunnarsson case is the first case where the EFTA Court has interpreted EEA law to entail more extensive rights than what follows from a settled interpretation of an identical provision by the CJEU. This has a range of implications, which will be returned to in the following sections. The same approach was taken in the later Jabbi case.

8.3.4 *The Jabbi Case*

The Facts

The Jabbi case concerned a Gambian national who married a Norwegian national in Spain and lived with her in Spain almost a year. The Norwegian sponsor did not engage in economic activity during her stay in Spain and it was undisputed that she was entitled to receive a disability pension. Mr. Jabbi's application for residence in Norway, as the spouse of an EEA national, was rejected by the immigration authorities. Proceedings were therefore instigated before Oslo District Court with the claim

---

[84] See for instance the Cases C-224/02 Pusa [2004] ECR I-5763 and Case C-520/04 Turpeinen [2002] ECR I-70070. Both cases involved retired Finnish nationals who moved to Spain and who incurred greater tax liability in Finland than would have applied had they remained resident there. In neither case did the CJEU consider the provisions of Directive 90/365 EEC (which preceded Directive 2004/38). The CJEU decided that the rights of Union citizens stemming from the Treaty were violated when the national rules had the effect of placing some of its nationals at a disadvantage 'simply because they [had] exercised their freedom to move and to reside in another Member State', see Cases C-224/02 Pusa [2004] ECR I-5763, paragraph 20 and C-520/04 Turpeinen [2002] ECR I-70070, paragraph 22.

[85] Supporting this interpretation of the decision, see Burke and Hannesson (2015), pp. 1–24. The authors seem to embrace so-called effect-related homogeneity and refers to one of three aspects of homogeneity identified by Carl Baudenbacher, see Baudenbacher (2013), p. 183. For a different view on effect-related homogeneity, see the comments from the editors in Arnesen et al. (2018), pp. 1–12, on p. 6.

that Mr. Jabbi had a derived right of residence in Norway as a result of his wife's stay in Spain and subsequent return to Norway.[86]

The principal question in the case was whether an economically inactive EEA citizen seeking family reunification with a TCN national has EEA-based rights upon the return to his/her home state based on EEA law. In other words, the question was whether the described situation is governed exclusively by national domestic (immigration) law or whether rights in this regard can be derived from EEA law. The Court noted that a gap between the two EEA pillars had emerged since the signing of the EEA Agreement in 1992. This development creating certain discrepancies could, depending on the circumstances, have an impact on the interpretation of EEA law.

The Advisory Opinion of the EFTA Court

Regarding the right to free movement of persons, the EFTA Court seemed, however, determined to avoid an unequal level of protection between the EEA and the EU. The Court relied on both Eind and Gunnarsson to reach the following conclusion: Where an EEA national has created or strengthened a family life with a third country national, during genuine residence in an EEA State other than that of which he or she is a national, Articles 7(1)(b) and 7(2) of the Directive apply by analogy where that EEA national returns with the family member to his or her home state. Through the advisory opinion in Jabbi the EFTA Court took yet another step to ensure substantial similarity of rights of free movement of persons in the EEA legal order corresponding to the EU legal order.

Paragraphs 78 and 82 of the EFTA Court's advisory opinion subscribes that Article 7(1)(b) applies by analogy to a returning national's situation. The Court made this reference stating that a derived right depends on the conditions in this article to be fulfilled (in addition to other conditions familiar from CJEU Union citizenship case law regarding 'genuine stay' and length of stay for the Union citizen to find him/herself in a cross-border situation). The Court's statements can be interpreted as a means to maintain national requirements for family reunification in terms of financial means available for the sponsor. However, the decision is consistent with the Gunnarson case in paralleling the EEA right to free movement for persons independent of their economic activity.[87]

[86] The national case was in the Court of first instance ultimately decided based on national law, see decision 23 March 2017, Case nr 15-052864TVI-OTIR/0.

[87] See for an analysis of the Jabbi case in a different context by Olafur Einarsson comments on Art. 30–39 EEA in Arnesen et al. (2018), pp. 391–433.

8.3.5 *Implications of the Gunnarsson and Jabbi Cases in the EEA Legal Order*

It is the nature of adjudication that cases that reach the higher levels of any court system are rarely straightforward. Only genuine legal questions will be admitted to the preliminary reference procedure. Without discussing the details of the 'acte clair' doctrine,[88] it follows from the decision in CIBA[89] that if the same question were to be referred to the EFTA Court again without any new arguments being put forward, it would be dismissed. Hence, national courts in the EFTA States are not supposed to refer questions to the EFTA Court unless there is a genuine question regarding the interpretation of EEA law.

Given that the Icelandic Court decided to refer the Gunnarsson case and the Norwegian Court decided to refer the Jabbi case to the EFTA Court, there is a clear presumption that the national courts considered that the case could not simply be resolved on the basis of an interpretation of the already-existing law as interpreted in the EU legal order by the CJEU, including the clear statement by the CJEU on the interpretation of the Citizens Directive. Upon looking carefully at the questions asked by the national courts, it is clear that the concern of the national courts centres around the possible effects of the Treaty provisions on Union citizenship in the EEA Agreement. This is the crux of the matter even if the EFTA Court, seemingly in one sentence both in Gunnarsson and in Jabbi, clarifies that these unparalleled provisions of Union citizenship do not apply in the EEA.[90]

The EFTA Court in Gunnarsson formulated its reasoning by referring to rights against the home state for moving individuals being already inherent in Directive 90/365 and stated that

> individuals cannot be deprived of rights that they have already acquired under the EEA Agreement before the introduction of Union Citizenship in the EU.[91]

The logic of the Court seems to be that given that (in the Court's view) rights for individuals against their home state already existed before the introduction of Union citizenship, this additional legal basis was not necessary in an EEA context in order to arrive to an in-substance parallel end result.

The reasoning of the Court cannot be reconciled with the case law from the CJEU interpreting the relevant secondary legislation. Directive 90/365 was about prescribing conditions governing the exercise of the right to move to and reside in the host state. The Residence Directives, much like the Citizens Directive, were never set out to prevent obstacles to free movement and were never interpreted in that way. Rather, the Residence Directives ensured the right to move to and reside in the host state for pensioners, students and persons with sufficient means.

---

[88] Established by the CJEU in the CILFIT case, Case C-283/81CILFIT [1982] ECR 3415.

[89] Case E-6/01 CIBA, paragraphs 21–23.

[90] Paragraph 34.

[91] Paragraph 80.

A general right for all to move and reside freely interpreted to include also the right not to meet obstacles when exercising this freedom from the home state has always been a *Treaty-based right* in EU law whether for the economically active (Articles 45, 49 and 56 TFEU) or for the non-economically active (Article 21(1) TFEU).

In D'Hoop[92] and later in Pusa,[93] the CJEU referred to the status of being a Union citizen in order to justify a general right to free movement regardless of economic activity. Furthermore, this general right to free movement could only be fully effective if obstacles raised by legislation of the home state penalising the exercise of free movement also had to be compatible with EU law. In other words, the protection of free movement for Union citizens depended on the scope of national legislation to be reviewed under EU law extending to all obstacles to free movement including that of the home state. However, for the non-economically active, this general right was based on the existence of the provisions on Citizenship of the Union when adjudicated on by the CJEU.

To this end, the EFTA Court's reasoning in Gunnarsson and Jabbi hardly seems limited to the restriction at stake, namely a residence requirement for the application of a tax advantage and the right to family reunification. Rather, the Court's reasoning in the cases indicates that any obstacle on the part of the home state may potentially be incompatible with EEA law in parallel with EU Union citizenship law. Arguably, through its legal reasoning, the EFTA Court has effectively paralleled the free movement right of Union citizens regardless of economic activity also in the EEA Agreement. In other words, with the Gunnarsson and Jabbi cases, the EEA Agreement includes free movement rights for the non-economically active persons in parallel with the right granted in EU law through the status of Union citizenship.

Gunnarsson and Jabbi are the clearest examples of cases decided by the EFTA Court on how to apply the concept of Union citizenship in EEA law. The cases are criticised for their lack of justification and explanation of the result but embraced for securing equal legal protection for moving citizens in the EEA parallel to the EU.[94] A question remains for further comment, namely whether the CJEU will follow the lead of the EFTA Court and embrace this application of the homogeneity principle in its own interpretation of EEA law. The assessment of this question requires an analysis of a Gunnarsson/Jabbi-like case in the EU legal order.

---

[92] Case C-224/98, D'Hoop [2002] ECR I-06191.

[93] Case C-224/02 Pusa [2004] ECR I-5763.

[94] Burke and Hannesson (2015), pp. 1–24.

8.3.6 Implications of the Gunnarsson and Jabbi Cases in the EU Legal Order

Introduction

Gunnarsson was an EFTA State national, and the case concerned obligations on an EFTA State for an own national having exercised his right to free movement in the territory of the EEA. Jabbi was married to an EFTA State national and the case concerned obligations on an EFTA State for family reunification for an own national having exercised her right to free movement in the territory of the EEA. Pusa and Turpeinen[95] concerned Union citizens, and the cases concerned obligations on an EU Member State for own nationals having exercised their free movement rights in the territory of the EU. This next section will analyse the potential obligations on EU Member States for own nationals who have exercised free movement to the territory of the EFTA States.

The decisions in Gunnarsson and Jabbi have sparked a new debate in EEA law on the possibility of a foreign (to the EU and its Member States) court deciding on EU Member States' legal obligations. This possibility is not limited to Gunnarsson-type cases but can also arise from decisions by the EFTA Court in other areas of law, in particular regarding the application of the Charter of Fundamental Rights in the EEA.[96] The final word on whether the EFTA Court decision will in the end limit EU Member States' sovereignty beyond EU law obligations will always be finally adjudicated in the CJEU. Until the CJEU decides on this question, the EFTA Court's decision is, however, a valid legal source on how to interpret EEA law generally (including obligations under EEA law on the EU Member States) and as such may impose legal limits on Member States' sovereignty in areas such as the right to welfare benefits and family reunification with TCNs extending to movements not only in the territory of the EU but including also EEA territory. Furthermore, it can also be argued that once the EFTA Court has decided upon the right interpretation (formally limited to the EFTA pillar), there is a threshold inherent in the legal architecture of the EEA Agreement for the CJEU to reach a different conclusion in the EU pillar. This more general point will be illustrated with similar facts to the Gunnarsson case but involving an EU national (a Union citizen) claiming rights against the home state (the EU Member State) based on movement to EFTA States territory (territory of the EEA).

Traditionally, the EEA Agreement has not been the source of additional obligations on the Member States of the EU beyond the very aim of the agreement to

[95] Case C 224/02 Pusa [2004] ECR I 5763 and C-520/04 Turpeinen [2002] ECR I-70070.

[96] Whenever there is an opt-out by Member States in the EU legal order there is a potential problem when the same provisions are applied in the EEA context, see the previous discussion of Case C-431/11 United Kingdom v Council EU:C:2013:589. The question is whether the opt-out also applies in the EEA. For example, in the area of fundamental rights and the UK and Polish opt-outs of the Charter, see Protocol No. 30 on the application of the Charter of Fundamental Rights of the EU to the UK and Poland similar legal questions may arise.

increase the geographical area of the internal market and apply parallel rules to facilitate the free movement of goods, services, economic actors and capital. To this end, the agreement has ensured economic participation of the EFTA States in the internal market with mutual benefits for all parties to the Agreement. In the sector of welfare services increasing the territory of the application of the rules may not be perceived as equally mutually beneficial as the extended application regarding economic activity. The recent cases of Gunnarsson and Jabbi have challenged this traditional functioning of the EEA Agreement to be in principal limited to economic activity. It will be explained how the EFTA Court with its decisions in Gunnarsson and Jabbi has potentially widened the scope of the Agreement and created rights for individuals with corresponding obligations for states beyond rights and obligations relevant for the function of the market. Directly, the cases concern the EFTA States. Given that all EU Member States are also party to the EEA Agreement, any obligation on states under the agreement (if not challenged and later reversed) is, however, also a possible obligation on the EU Member States.

Reciprocity: The Same Legal Rights and Obligations in the Whole of the EEA

EEA law is binding upon the EU and its Member States through the EEA Agreement. It is not foreseen that EEA law will be different in the EFTA and in the EU legal order. Hence, if the case law from the EFTA Court represents a valid interpretation of EEA law in the EFTA pillar, it will potentially also be a valid interpretation in the EU pillar. This view is based on the reflection of the universal assumption that an international agreement is intended to have the same legal content regardless of where and by whom it is interpreted and applied. International agreements are generally regarded as having one correct interpretation regardless of where they apply.

Hence, even if the EFTA Court only has jurisdiction in the EFTA States and Gunnarsson and Jabbi are about EFTA States' obligations towards own non-economically active nationals who have exercised free movement to a state party to the EEA Agreement, the decision from the EFTA Court carries substantial legal weight when interpreting EEA law in general, including EEA law obligations on EU Member States.

Up until now, case law from the EFTA Court, which in a similar manner has widened the scope of the EEA Agreement through interpretation, has merely ensured parallel obligations on EFTA States as compared to EU Member States.[97] The obligations stemming from the EEA Agreement have already existed as obligations on the EU Member States through EU law. The case law from the EFTA Court has therefore had the more welcoming effect seen from the perspective of the EU Member States of increasing the obligations of the EFTA States and to this end

[97] Cases like E-9/97 Sveinbjörnsdottir on state liability and Case E-8/97 TV1000 on the application of fundamental rights in practice only increased the EFTA State legal obligations towards citizens.

ensuring reciprocity.[98] From the perspective of the EFTA States, the EFTA Court case law has, however, raised controversies and disputes.[99] By and large, the EFTA States nevertheless seem to have accepted and adjusted to the EFTA Court case law, including the interpretations that have been based on a rather vague reference to general principles going beyond a literal understanding of the provisions.[100] However, unexpectedly, the effects of the recent EFTA Court case law on the EU Member States' obligations go beyond the market rationale and move into the welfare sector creating unprecedented effects of EEA law. The final word on the correct interpretation of EEA law in the EU legal order lies with the CJEU, and its opinion is awaited with great interest. Absent an opinion from the CJEU, the case law from the EFTA Court is legally significant also in establishing the EU Member States' obligations under the EEA Agreement elaborated on in the next section.

The Right to Move and Reside Freely Within 'the Territory of the Member States': The Cross-Border Element

The right to move and reside freely for Union citizens, including all the additional rights that the Treaty provisions has been interpreted to include, presupposes that the Treaty provisions are applicable. If Union law is not applicable, a specific question will be exclusively dealt with under national law. For instance, the rights to welfare benefits and the rights to family reunification for own nationals who have not availed themselves of any free movement rights will be decided according to national law, and the substantive rights vary from Member State to Member State. The national law in these internal situations (own national against home state) cannot, save in exceptional circumstances, be challenged under EU law on the grounds that the provisions violate the rights of a Union citizen. Thus, national laws restricting rights to welfare benefits or the right to family reunification for own nationals are generally not in violation of EU law obligations and cannot be challenged under these provisions.[101] For such rights to potentially be anchored in EU law and consequently for the national law to be assessed as potentially incompatible, there must be an element of cross-border free movement rights involved.

This demonstrates the importance of the criteria of cross-border free movement being involved. Only then will the citizens be able to potentially deduce any rights from EU law.

[98] Fredriksen has demonstrated how EEA law is part of EU law and therefore already has included state liability, Fredriksen (2013).

[99] One example being the Karlsson case, Case E-4/01 case trying to revise the Sveinbjörnsdottir case, E-9/97.

[100] The STX case, E-2/11 and the national decision in RT 2012 p 1447 which may be an exception, see the speech by Justice Skoghøy in the Norwegian Supreme Court with further references, EFTA seminar 7–8 October 2014.

[101] This situation of reverse discrimination has been criticised by a number of academics, see one contribution from Groenendijk (2014), pp. 169–189.

Hence, the Treaty provisions (the Union citizenship provisions included) are generally understood to require a cross-border element, i.e. purely internal situations are outside the scope of the provisions.[102] It is well known that this cross-border element need not be physical movements in order for the provisions to apply. In fact, the Court has been lenient in its interpretation of what may constitute a cross-border element. It is sufficient to refer to cases like Alokpa,[103] Chen[104] and McCarthy[105] where dual citizenship in two Member States was sufficient for the condition to be met. However, there is no doubt that the cross-border element needs to include a situation involving two or more Member States. Hence, a situation involving a Member State and a third country (a non-EU Member State) will be considered equal to a purely internal situation and thus covered only by national legislation. In other words, for example, dual citizenship in an EU Member State and a third country will not fulfil the criteria of a cross-border element that is needed to potentially give individual rights under the Treaty provisions on Union citizenship. Equally, movement between an EU Member State and a third country (a non-EU Member State) will not fulfil the criteria of a cross-border element under the same provisions. In conclusion, Union citizenship rights according to the Treaty provisions are limited to situations involving two or more Member States of the Union and not only one Member State and a third country (a non-EU Member State).

The right to move and reside freely under the Union citizenship provisions is limited to the territory of the Member States.[106] The EFTA States are not Member States of the EU. The EFTA States are linked to the EU through an association agreement. Even if the association agreement connects the EFTA States closer to the EU than any other association agreement and indeed has a number of supranational elements in parallel with the EU and contrary to international agreements in general, it is still only an association agreement. Thus, the EFTA States remain outside the EU as non-members, and their territory is outside the territory of the Union. Furthermore, the citizens of the EFTA States party to the agreement are not Union citizens.[107]

The expression ‘the territory of the Member States’ therefore does not include the territory of the EFTA States party to the EEA Agreement, and these states must

[102] The Zambrano case, Case C-34/09 Gerardo Ruiz Zambrano v. Office national de l’emploi [2011] ECR I-01177 is an exception but the legal significance of the case has later been modified. The decision is now interpreted to only give rights to a Union citizen when the essence of this citizenship is threatened referring essentially to situations when a Union citizen risks being expelled from the territory of the Union. Given that states cannot expel their own nationals is it difficult to see when this situation can occur outside the Zambrano-type cases, namely in the case of a child and the need for a caretaker in order to stay in the territory of the Union.

[103] Case C-86/12 Alokpa, EU:C:2013:645.

[104] Case C-200/02 Zhu and Chen [2004] ECR I-9925.

[105] Case C-202/13 McCarthy EU:C:2014:2450.

[106] See formulation in Article 21(1) TFEU.

[107] As made abundantly clear by all Contracting Parties to the EEA Agreement in the Joint Declaration incorporating the Citizens Directive into the EEA Agreement, see above Sect. 6.3.2.

in principle be considered as third countries in this relation. As an illustration of this point, it may be useful to have regard to the formulations in the adaptation text whenever secondary legislation is included in the EEA Agreement. The adaptation texts always make it clear that the territory of the Union should be changed to the territory of the EEA in the context of the legislation being made part of the EEA Agreement. Hence, it is clear that the legislation applies to a different territory geographically. The Treaty provisions on Union citizenship have never been transposed to the EEA Agreement, and hence, there is no adaptation text making these provisions geographically applicable in the territory of the EEA.

Thus, Union citizenship rights cannot in principle be rooted in cross-border elements limited to the territory of one Member State and an EFTA State, neither in the form of dual citizenship in an EU Member State and an EFTA State nor in the form of movements between the territory of an EU Member State and an EFTA State. Thus, before moving to the next step of the analysis, a provisional conclusion is that the Union citizenship rights according to the wording in Article 21 TFEU are limited to situations involving a cross-border element between two or more Member States of the Union.

With the Gunnarsson and Jabbi caselaw this limitation on the extent to which Member States' obligations fall to be assessed for compatibility with EU law may have come to an end. A logical consequence of the decision is that movement in the EEA, hence movement between any state being a Contracting Party to the EEA Agreement, even by non-economically active persons, is sufficient to trigger an assessment of Member States' obligations under EEA law and possibly extend them beyond national limitations. Continuing this line of reasoning, the case law may therefore have extended the territory upon which movement by individuals may trigger scrutiny of Member States' national law to include an area outside the scope of economic activity.

Already limited to the EU legal order, the case law on Union citizenship rights is controversial and contested. Recent cases in the field of territorial protection of social assistance benefits are illustrative.[108] Even if the CJEU may be perceived as slowing down the pace of integration in terms of free movement rights for the non-economically active, it would no doubt create controversies if the EEA Agreement suddenly extended Member States' obligations in a sensitive area such as rights to welfare benefits (and family reunification/immigration law).

Beyond this territorial extension of the relevant area for own nationals to move in order to enjoy protection from home state obstacles, the EFTA Court case law may also be interpreted as incorporating 'Union citizen-like protection' for all EEA nationals, including citizens of EFTA States, in the protection already enjoyed by citizens of the Union. This has potential consequences in terms of affording protection for a wider category of people as well as for affording a wider scope of rights than what follows from the current secondary legislation, which undoubtedly has been made part of the EEA Agreement. As demonstrated, the CJEU case law on

[108] See previous analysis of the Cases C- 333/13 Dano EU:C:2014:2358 and C 67/14 Alimanovic EU:C:2015:5 and C-308/14 UK v Commission EU:C:2016:436.

rights of Union citizens based on primary law has gone beyond rights stemming from the secondary legislation and to some extent ignored the negotiated limits therein.

Applying this interpretation of EEA law may therefore be problematic from the point of view of the EU Member States in the EU legal order. The principal objection to this understanding of EEA law is the fact that the rights stemming from Union citizenship, which include free movement rights of non-economically active citizens, are part of the widening and deepening EU integration process. Building a Union as well as building a nation depends on a range of factors, including creating a common identity and developing solidarities. Free movement rights for individuals detached from market objectives substantiate this Union building. An important part of building a Union, however, is also to define the insiders and the outsiders—us and them.[109] Only by this notion can common identities and mutual solidarities develop. On the inside, the citizens should ideally move freely, and therefore, the states have obligations not to create barriers to movement. This mutual obligation between the states is motivated by the creation of a Union but logically cannot extend beyond the territory of this very same Union. The EFTA States have chosen not to be part of the Union. They are associated to the Union, but they are not Member States. Their citizens are not Union citizens by the very definition of the fundamental condition for having Union citizenship, namely to be a citizen of a Member State.[110] Including the same free movement rights to the nationals of EFTA States and applying welfare provisions in EFTA State territory would therefore arguably go against and not support the very precondition of constructing the status of Union citizenship in the EU integration process.

8.3.7 Concluding Observations

A number of arguments must be assessed more closely in order to determine the correct interpretation of EEA law obligations for the Contracting Parties to the EEA Agreement regarding free movement rights for the non-economically active citizens in the EEA. Notwithstanding this observation, the decisions in Gunnarsson and Jabbi have contributed significantly to answering the question of how the institutions applying EEA law approach the lack of parallel provisions in the EEA Agreement and the objective of a dynamic and homogenous legal order. The EFTA Court has, in its decisions, taken the step of interpreting parallel provisions in the secondary legislation differently from the interpretation by the CJEU in order to mitigate the lack of a parallel provision of Union citizenship. To this end, the EFTA Court has created parallel free movement rights for all citizens in the EEA integration process comparable to the free movement rights as Union citizens in the EU

[109] In the literature this is often referred to as inclusionary ideologies, see C. Barnard, The substantive law of the EU, 2013, chapter 12 on Union citizenship p. 433 with further references.

[110] Article 20(1) TFEU, Union citizenship is condition on being a national of a Member State.

integration process. The next section will focus on adjacent case law from the EFTA Court regarding the coordination regime for social security. This field also influences the right to free movement for the non-economically active and therefore sheds light on the overall question addressed. First, however, the next section will include also the perspective of the EFTA Surveillance Authority demonstrating how the case law from the EFTA Court is subsequently built upon by the Authority in its decisional practice.

8.4 Decisional Practice of the EFTA Surveillance Authority: Case No 73930

The EFTA Surveillance Authority delivered a Reasoned opinion against Norway for breach of Directive 2004/38 by not fully ensuring the derived rights of family members of EEA nationals and Norwegian nationals who had exercised their free movement rights under EEA law 8 July 2015.[111] For the purpose of this book, the alleged rights of returning non-economically active Norwegian nationals are of particular interest.[112] The Authority claims that the rights of returning nationals are the same regardless of economic activity. Hence, the Authority concludes that national requirements of economic activity and subsistence requirements for the rights to family reunification are incompatible with EEA law.[113]

The Authority's interpretation of the EEA Agreement in this field and the lack of provisions equivalent to the Union citizenship provisions in Article 20–21 TFEU are expressed in the following manner:

> 61. The Authority notes that according to the case law of the Court of Justice, Articles 7(1) and 7(2) of Directive 2004/38/EC refer to the right of residence of a Union citizen and to the derived right of residence conferred on the family members of that citizen in "another Member State" or in "the host Member State" and thus confirm that a third-country national who is a family member of a Union citizen cannot invoke, on the basis of that directive, a derived right of residence in the Member State of which that citizen is a national.[114]

This statement makes it clear that the Authority is aware that the harmonised secondary legislation does not require Norway to ensure rights of family reunification under the Directive for non-economically active returning own nationals. The Authority continues:

[111] Reasoned opinion 8 July 2015, case No 73930.

[112] Reasoned opinion 8 July 2015, case No 73930, pp. 10–11, the means testing criteria for a right to family reunification is substantiated by the protection of public funds, a requirement based on EEA law to disapply the criteria for certain groups will increase the financial burden on welfare states.

[113] Reasoned opinion 8 July 2015, case No 73930, pp. 16–17 and 22.

[114] Reasoned opinion 8 July 2015, case No 73930, pp. 11–12. A reference is made to the Case C-456/12 O and B EU:C:2014:135, see Sect. 8.3.2 above.

62. However, an EEA national, returning to his own EEA State, should enjoy "conditions of his entry and residence […] *at least equivalent* to those which he would enjoy under the Treaty or secondary law in the territory of another Member State".[115]

63. That means that in the case of returning nationals the Directive should be applied by analogy and, within the EU, the nationals at issue derive their rights, which are "at least equivalent" to those enshrined in the Directive, against their own State of nationality, from the free movement provisions in the Treaty on the Functioning of the European Union ("TFEU"), i.e. Articles 45 TFEU and 49 TFEU, as regards economically active Union citizens, and Article 21 TFEU, as regards non economically active EU citizens.

64. The EEA Agreement does not contain a provision corresponding to Article 21(l) TFEU.

65. However, as was established by the EFTA Court in Case E-26/13 Gunnarsson, within the EEA, Article 7(1)(b) of Directive 2004/38/EC can be invoked by non-economically active EEA nationals who have used their free movement rights against their own EEA State.

66. The EFTA Court did not expressly address whether, in the EEA, Article 7(1) of Directive 2004/38/EC is applicable only to non-economically active EEA nationals invoking their rights against their own EEA State whereas economically active EEA nationals should derive their rights under Articles 28, 31 and 36 EEA or whether Article 7(1) of Directive 20041381EC is applicable both to economically active and non-economically active EEA nationals.

67. In any case, it is the Authority's understanding that the substance of the rights at issue should be the same as regards economically active and non-economically active EEA nationals.

68. Therefore, the Authority will proceed further to examining the substance of the derived rights of TCN family members of returning Norwegian nationals under EEA law, on the premise that non-economically active EEA nationals can invoke Article 7(1)(b) of Directive 2004/38/EC against their own EEA State and economically active EEA nationals derive their corresponding rights under Articles 28 and 31 EEA.[116]

Through this Reasoned opinion, the EFTA Surveillance Authority demonstrates its view that the EEA Agreement ensures parallel free movement rights for both the economically and the non-economically active persons as compared to the EU legal order. The Authority is also clear in pointing out that the EEA Agreement has not paralleled the primary law provisions providing the legal basis for these rights in the EU legal order. However, the Authority finds the necessary legal basis in interpreting the harmonised secondary legislation differently in the EEA legal order than in the EU legal order.[117] This is a powerful demonstration of the view of the Authority on the position of the EEA Agreement in a revised constitutional framework in the EU legal order.

---

[115] Reference is made here to Cases C-370/90 Singh [1992] ECR I-04265 and C-291/05 Eind [2007] ECR I-10719, see Sect. 8.3.2 above.

[116] Reasoned opinion 8 July 2015, case No 73930, p. 11.

[117] See also the response from the Norwegian Ministry of Labour and Social affairs 8 October 2015 and the follow up letter from the Authority 16 March 2016.

References

Arnesen F, Fredriksen HH, Graver HP, Mestad O, Vedder C (eds) (2018) Agreement on the European Economic Area, a commentary. C.H. Beck, Hart, Nomos, Universitetsforlaget, pp 1–12

Baudenbacher C (2013) The EFTA Court and the ECJ – coming in parts but winning together. In: The Court of Justice and the construction of Europe: analysis and perspectives on sixty years of case law. Springer/Asser Press, p 183

Berneri C (2014) Protection of families composed by EU citizens and third-country nationals: some suggestions to tackle reverse discrimination. Eur J Migr Law 16:249–275

Burke C, Hannesson OI (2015) Citizenship by the back door? Gunnarsson. Common Mark Law Rev 52:1–24

Burri T, Pirker B (2013) Constitutionalization by Association? The doubtful case of the European Economic Area. Yearb Eur Law 32:207–229

Dougan M (2009) Expanding the frontiers of EU citizenship. In: Barnard C, Odudu O (eds) The outer limits of European Union law. Hart

Fahey E (2009) Interpretive legitimacy and the distinction between "social assistance" and "work seekers allowance": comment on cases C-22/08 and C-23/08 Vatsouras and Koupatantze. Eur Law Rev 34(6):933–949

Fredriksen HH (2013) Offentligrettslig erstatningsansvar ved brudd på EØS-avtalen. PhD ved Universitet i Bergen

Groenendijk K (2014) Reverse discrimination, family reunification and Union Citizens of immigrant origin. In: Guild E, Gortazar Rotaeche CJ, Kostakopoulou D (eds) The reconceptualization of European Union, citizenship. Brill/Nijhoff, pp 169–189

Reding V (2013) Free movement of people and the European Economic Area. In: EFTA Court (ed) The EEA and the EFTA Court – decentred integration. Hart, pp 193–202

Spaventa E (2008) Seeing the wood despite the trees? On the scope of Union citizenship and its constitutional effects. Common Mark Law Rev 45:13–45

Tobler C (2013) Bikers Are(n't) Welcome, Jan Anfinn Wahl v The Icelandic State, EFTA Court Judgment of 22 July 2013, E-15/12. Eur Law Rep 9:246–256

Miscellaneous

Legal study on Norway's obligations under the EU Citizenship Directive 2004/38/EC, Advokatfirmaet Simonsen Vogt Wiig AS, 4 January 2016

Chapter 9
Case Law from the EFTA Court and Decisional Practice of the EFTA Surveillance Authority on the Right to Free Movement, Residence and Equal Treatment Under the Coordination Regime for Social Security Benefits

9.1 Introduction

This section will analyse case law from the EFTA Court and decisional practice of the EFTA Surveillance Authority outside the field of the Citizens Directive. The case law analysed concerns rights under the coordination of social security schemes where Union citizenship has been a decisive factor for the development of the law in the EU legal order.

The case law from the EFTA Court regarding the coordination of social security schemes is more extensive than the case law regarding the Citizens Directive. The EFTA Court has, in a number of cases, been asked to interpret 'residence-like' requirements and the refusal to export social benefits. The cases reviewed all concern refusals from EFTA States in situations of minor or no economic activity on the part of the beneficiary. The cases concern the situation of claims being made by the moving individual against both the host state and the home state, and they include both preliminary references and infringement proceedings. All three EFTA States have been involved in cases regarding the coordination of social security schemes. Furthermore, the CJEU has decided in one case regarding the coordination regime for social security and the EEA Agreement in a situation involving non-economically active moving nationals.[1] All the cases decided thus far point in the same direction, namely to the free movement rights being paralleled regardless of economic activity and regardless of whether claims are made against the home or against the host state.

In summary, the EFTA Court and the CJEU have moved the EEA Agreement beyond the economically active, and the case law may be summarised as rather 'Union citizenship friendly', developing the EEA integration process in parallel with the EU integration process also under the coordination regime.

---

[1] Case C-431/11 United Kingdom v Council EU:C:2013:589, see above Sect. 6.3.3.

K. Fløistad, *The EEA Agreement in a Revised EU Framework for Welfare Services*, Studies in European Economic Law and Regulation 13,
https://doi.org/10.1007/978-3-319-95043-3_9

The analysis will distinguish between rights against the host state, Case E-4/07 Þorkelsson (Sect. 9.3), and rights against the home state, Cases E-3/12 Jonsson (Sect. 9.4) and E-6/12 Childcare benefit (Sect. 9.5). The first case analysed included, however, rights against both the home and host states. Case E-5/06 (Sect. 9.2) marks the first step taken by the EFTA Court to develop the EEA Agreement beyond the economically active in the field of the coordination regime for social security benefits. The case law analysis is followed by a concluding section (Chap. 10).

9.2 Case E-5/06 EFTA Surveillance Authority v. the Principality of Liechtenstein

9.2.1 The Coordination of Social Security Schemes

The first step to develop the EEA Agreement in the direction of encompassing social rights beyond the rights afforded to the economically active citizen was taken in Case E-5/06 regarding the understanding of the coordination regime in Regulations 1408/71 and 574/72.[2] The coordination of social security schemes in Regulations 1408/71 and 574/72 was made part of the EEA Agreement through the inclusion in Point 1 of annex VI at the adoption of the Agreement. The main reason for adopting a coordination system was based on the fact that national social welfare systems in large remain built on the principle of territoriality and nationality.[3] Territoriality of the national welfare systems means that the states in principle confine payments to residents and for consumption within the state borders. Not being able to export a social security benefit would seriously deter the beneficiary from using his or her right of free movement. The EEA Agreement, therefore, guarantees, subject to the coordination, that a person who has been covered for a certain period under an EEA state's social welfare system does not lose entitlement to a benefit as a consequence of settling in another EEA state. However, in this lie also the limits of the Regulation. Regulation 1408/71[4] only aims to overrule the 'principle of territoriality' as far as this is necessary to prevent people who cross national frontiers from being disadvantaged in the field of social security benefits.

It is essential to understand that rather than being harmonised, social security schemes are coordinated. Coordination in the EU means that the individual will not lose his or her social security rights as a consequence of exercising the right to freedom of movement. Social security coordination aims to secure access to social security in the new host state and to prevent the loss of acquired social security rights in the former state of residence or employment (home state). Coordination is

[2] The Regulations are later replaced by Regulations 883/2004 and 987/2009, see Sect. 7.2.2.

[3] See generally on the coordination of social security schemes in Van der Mei (2003) which also includes an analysis of the EEA dimension to the coordination.

[4] And the successor, Regulation 883/2004.

a method that leaves the competence to legislate on social security matters in the hands of the states and secures the possibility of maintaining a variety of different national social security schemes. 'It is based on the understanding that disparities would and should exist, but ought not to create an obstacle to free movement'.[5]

The coordination regime includes social welfare-type benefits, which typically cover social security schemes as opposed to social assistance schemes. Social security-type schemes are characterised by legally defined rights and an element of contribution by the beneficiary, typically through previous work engagement. This payment of social charges by the worker and/or his/her employer entitles the worker to sickness, unemployment or pension benefits. The level of the benefit is fixed, and it generally does not depend on other sources of income. Normally, payments are funded out of collectively paid contributions.

The coordination regime does not cover social assistance-type benefits, which are not legally defined rights and which are generally means tested. Social assistance is subsidiary in nature. These benefit schemes are usually offered to all members of a society and serve as a financial safety net for those in need. Normally, they are paid out of general tax revenues, and enjoyment does not depend on previous contribution.

The legal question in Case E-5/06 concerned a benefit that was 'half way' between traditional social security and social assistance. The so-called special non-contributory benefits of a mixed kind are based on a legally defined right, but they do not depend on periods of work or contribution, and they are intended to relieve a clear financial need. Other examples than the benefit in the case would be supplements to pension and special benefits for disabled persons.

There are three main reasons why social assistance-type benefits are not covered by the coordination regime and thus why enjoyment is normally limited by the territoriality/nationality principle. Such benefits are perceived as being connected to an understanding of solidarity and thus the responsibility of the state, which normally does not extend beyond the borders. Furthermore, such benefits are determined by the cost of living in each state and in a way presuppose consumption within the state territory. A third obstacle concerns the administrative difficulties of checking the fulfilment of conditions for eligibility and other more technical obstacles involved for export of benefits. The question for the EFTA Court was how to balance these considerations for 'special non-contributory benefits of a mixed kind' with free movement rights.[6]

[5] Sakslien (2000), pp. 157–183.

[6] See paragraphs 65–69 in particular.

9.2.2 The Non-contributory Benefit in the Form of a Helplessness Allowance

The non-contributory benefit in Case E-5/06 was in the form of a helplessness allowance. According to Liechtenstein law, a person was considered to be helpless if he permanently required a degree of help from third persons or personal surveillance in order to carry out daily tasks such as getting up, getting dressed and undressed, preparing meals, maintaining personal hygiene and engaging in social interaction. The allowance was part of a system that provided specific protection for the disabled who were unfortunate enough not to be able to accomplish daily tasks on their own. It was obvious that the majority of beneficiaries would not have sufficient means of subsistence without the benefit. The award of the helplessness allowance was not conditional upon the completion of periods of insurance but depended only on the degree of helplessness. Thus, there was a link between the helplessness allowance and social assistance.[7]

The question in the case was whether the requirement of residence in Liechtenstein for entitlement to the helplessness allowance was in accordance with EEA law.

The justification for limiting the export of this benefit was mainly that it was meant to guarantee a level of subsistence taking into account the cost of such help and integration in Liechtenstein as well as the fact that the benefit was not based on the payment of contribution but on the needs of the persons. Given that a comparable benefit would not (most likely did not) exist in a new host state, the loss of the benefit would, however, evidently create an obstacle to the right of free movement.

9.2.3 The Parties to the Case: The Principal Question

At the time, the relevance of the case seemed to have been perceived as limited. The case was regarded as a question of interpretation limited to a specific benefit in Liechtenstein and thus of little general significance. Neither Norway nor Iceland participated in the case. Thus, the voices of the other EFTA States were not heard in the case. On the EU side, the UK chose to participate both in the written and in the oral procedure in addition to the European Commission.

Even though the case concerned a specific social benefit exclusive to the social welfare system in Liechtenstein, the principal question of the case was one of the boundaries of the basic systems of solidarity guaranteeing a minimum level of subsistence for non-economically active persons. Here, the very boundaries of the national solidarity mechanisms were at stake. For economically active persons, participation in national solidarity is to a large extent taken for granted in the context of the internal market of the EEA. The direct contribution to the economic life of the

[7] See a reference to the relevant national law in paragraphs 20–29.

host state secures the right to participate in national social systems. This fits the traditional paradigm of solidarity in the EEA based on economic integration.

For non-economically active persons, the link to the participation of these persons in the economic internal market is mostly lacking. Consequently, the question is directly related to the definition of the scope of the solidarity mechanisms set up at the national level by the EEA state. A balance needs to be struck between the free movement rights also for non-economically active persons and the interest of the EEA states to limit access to their solidarity systems.

9.2.4 The Background for the Case: The Case Law of the CJEU

The EFTA Court case can only be properly understood by taking account of a development in the EU legal order where the CJEU in 2001 changed its opinion on the discretion of the Member States to refuse the export of certain benefits.

In this regard, the case is also interesting in relation to the limitation inherent in SCA Article 3(2)[8] on the relevance of later case law from the CJEU.

The story of the 'special non-contributory benefits of a mixed kind' began with the CJEU developing a broad definition of social security benefits. This subjected several national 'special non-contributory benefits' to the export provisions.[9] As a reaction to this case law, a separate coordination regime was created for these benefits by introducing Articles 4(2)(a) and 10(a) and annex IIa in Regulation 1408/71 whereby Member States could apply a residence condition preventing the export of such benefits.[10]

In Snares[11] and Partridge,[12] the ECJ was confronted with the question of whether the limitation of export of annex IIa benefits was compatible with the fundamental freedom of movement. The Court concluded that the Member States were entitled to limit the exportability of the mixed-type non-contributory benefits insofar as they are closely linked to the social environment of the Member State. The Court did not, however, examine in detail whether the benefits in these cases were to be considered as 'special non-contributory benefits of a mixed kind'. In other words, the Court left a considerable margin of discretion to the national systems.

---

[8] As well as Article 6 EEA.

[9] The first case was Case 1/72 Frilli [1972] ECR 667.

[10] Council Regulation (EEC) No 1247/92 of 30 April 1992 amending Regulation (EEC) No 1408/71 on the application of social security schemes to employed persons, to self- employed persons and to members of their families moving within the Community.

[11] Case C-20/96 Snares [1997] ECR I-6057.

[12] Case C-297/96 Partridge [1998] ECR I-3467.

In Jauch[13] and Leclere,[14] however, the Court did examine this question. It considered the two benefits at stake—the Austrian 'care allowance' and the Luxembourg maternity allowance, respectively—as not corresponding to the criteria of being 'special' and of a 'mixed kind' in order to justify their non-exportation. Hence, the listing in annex IIa was declared invalid. The Court motivated its position by stating that derogations from the principle of the exportability of social security benefits must be interpreted strictly. For the purpose of this book, it is not necessary to go into further detail of later case law where the CJEU has both confirmed and invalidated the Member States' position that the benefit should be listed in annex IIa.[15] The main point in this context is that the CJEU changed its approach from leaving the choice to the discretion of the Member States to engaging itself in judicial review of the benefit and substituting if necessary the Member States' view on the listing with that of the Court.

9.2.5 The Listing of the Helpless Allowance by Liechtenstein

When it acceded to the EEA Agreement, Liechtenstein classified the helplessness allowance within the system of Regulation 1408/71 as a 'special non-contributory benefit' in accordance with Article 4(2a) of the Regulation. All the Contracting Parties to the EEA Agreement had, in principle, assessed the benefit against the conditions for listing it in annex IIa. Liechtenstein had adapted its scheme in order to fit the conditions. Therefore, arguably, Liechtenstein could, in good faith, rely on the consensus and the result reached by the Contracting Parties when adopting the EEA Agreement.

The substantial reasons for the listing were also clearly explained by the Government in the case, demonstrating why exporting the benefit would go beyond the solidarity objective in the national system.[16] The Government stressed that there are two systems in place in Liechtenstein that cover the need for domiciliary care. The basic system, on the one hand, of which the helplessness allowance is a part, provides specific protection for the disabled and has a strong emphasis on improving or maintaining quality of life. The sickness insurance system, on the other hand, of which domiciliary healthcare is a part, has as its aim to improve or maintain the state of health. It was argued that these two benefits should be distinguished and that only the latter benefit is a sickness insurance benefit in accordance with Article 4(1)

---

[13] Case C-215/99 Jauch [2001] ECR I-1901.

[14] Case C-43/99 Leclere [2001] ECR I-4265.

[15] See as an example of confirming the listing in Case C-160/02 Skalka [2004] ECR I-5613, on the Austrian Compensatory supplement to pensions. See also Case C-299/05 on the Finnish childcare allowance, the Swedish 'Disability allowance and care allowance for disabled children' and the UK 'Disability Living Allowance, Attendance Allowance and Carer's Allowance.

[16] See the Report for the Hearing paragraphs 65–80 and the decision of the Court paragraphs 45–55.

of Regulation 1408/71 (thus exportable). The helplessness allowance was a 'mixed-type benefit', which had characteristics of both social security and social assistance, thereby in the view of the Government rightfully belonging in annex IIa to Regulation 1408/71 (thus not exportable). Moreover, it was argued that the helplessness allowance differed from the benefits at issue in Jauch[17] on the Austrian care allowance, in that this case concerned a contribution-based scheme, the purpose of which was more closely linked to healthcare than the Liechtenstein benefit. It was argued that the helplessness allowance was more similar to the UK systems at issue in Snares[18] (on the UK disability care allowance) and Partridge[19] (on the UK attendance allowance).

9.2.6 The View of the EFTA Court

Of central importance for the EFTA Court decision was whether the case law of the CJEU that stated that the listing itself does not have constitutive effect was relevant in the EEA. There were at least two main lines of argument against applying the same understanding in an EEA context, taking into account the sensitive substantive issue at stake, namely that national boundaries of solidarity would be expanded.

The first was the complete turnaround by the CJEU in its understanding of Member States' competence over their own benefits. In striking contrast to earlier case law, the CJEU has since 2001 begun to assess, independently of a listing in the annex, whether the benefit in question fulfils the conditions in Article 4(2)(a) or rather should be classified as a benefit under either Article 4(1) or 4(4). Until 2001, the CJEU had accepted the Member States' choice of classification without scrutinising in detail whether the conditions were fulfilled. Thus, as long as there was in a sense a political agreement between the Member States, there was no reason to believe that such benefits would be exportable.

The principle of homogeneity clearly spoke in favour of the EFTA Court adopting the most recent view of the CJEU. Indeed, the most efficient way of ensuring the homogeneity principle is to always take note of the present stage of law as perceived by the CJEU. However, the fact that the CJEU had completely changed and reversed its position on a legal question meant that there is little predictability and possibility for affected parties to adapt to the situation. Nevertheless, in concurrence with the EFTA Court's earlier position, when confronted with new and/or changed law through the jurisprudence of the CJEU, the latter's most recent view prevailed.[20] The EFTA Court chose to follow the CJEU despite the concerns about expanding the territorial limits of the national welfare benefits.

---

[17] Case C-215/99 Jauch [2001] ECR I-1901.

[18] Case C-20/96 Snares [1997] ECR I-6057.

[19] Case C-297/96 Partridge [1998] ECR I-3467.

[20] Reference is made to the L'Oréal case E-9/07 and 10/07 and to the Waterfall case E-2/06.

However, the EFTA Court was confronted with a second obstacle created by the particular structure of the EEA. The entry of the benefit in annex IIa with the result that the Liechtenstein helplessness allowance did not have to be exported to residents in other EEA states was the result of the accession negotiations. Arguably, this listing had to be considered as the result of consent amongst the Contracting Parties of the EEA Agreement. The fact that the Liechtenstein entry into annex IIa formed part of EEA Council Decision 1/95 could therefore be interpreted as meaning that the relevant rules for interpretation followed the rules of public international law. Hence, the question was whether the listing should be interpreted as part of the EEA Council decision, which was to be interpreted in accordance with Article 26 of the Vienna Convention on the Law of Treaties.[21] To this end, the argument would be that every Treaty in force is binding upon the parties to it and must be performed by them in good faith in the sense of *pacta sunt servanda.*

Furthermore, as stated by Liechtenstein in no uncertain terms, at the time, the entry into annex IIa was considered as having constitutive effect, meaning that benefits listed therein were recognised as being non-exportable. Until the year 2001, the CJEU did not question whether the listing of a benefit in annex IIa was compatible with EU law. When applying a residence requirement, Liechtenstein was thus relying in good faith on this understanding at the time of the conclusion of the EEA Agreement.

The EFTA Court, confronted with this second obstacle, again made use of the homogeneity principle and this time in an unprecedented manner.[22] According to the Court, the line of reasoning by the Liechtenstein Government even in a sensitive area such as expanding the national boundaries of solidarity could not succeed.

The EFTA Court decided that Liechtenstein was obliged to grant the benefit to applicants residing in an EEA state other than Liechtenstein, including its own nationals who had availed themselves of the right to free movement. According to Article 19(1)(b) of the Regulation, persons employed or self-employed in Liechtenstein but residing outside the state should therefore receive the helplessness allowance. Article 25(1)(b) of the Regulation stipulated that the same was the case for unemployed persons residing outside Liechtenstein that were formerly employed or self-employed in the state, provided they fulfilled the other conditions in Regulation 1408/71 for being subject to Liechtenstein social security law. As for pensioners receiving a pension from Liechtenstein without residing in that state, the same principle followed from Article 28(1)(b) of the Regulation. Hence, the entitlement to the helplessness allowance is not, as regards the circle of persons covered by these provisions, subject to the condition that the person be resident in the territory of Liechtenstein.

---

[21] See the Report to the Hearing, paragraph 40.

[22] See the decision paragraph 63 where the EFTA Court frames the question as if it is a matter of Liechtenstein having other obligations than the other Contracting Parties to the Agreement.

9.2.7 Concluding Observations

The reason why this decision can be seen as the first step towards creating transnational solidarity with non-economic contributors is that Liechtenstein was forced to give up its territorial principle for a benefit closely resembling social assistance schemes. This decision meant that Liechtenstein had to pay this benefit to categories of people not residing in its territory and not contributing to the finances of the state. The main objective of the coordination regime is to ensure the free movement of primarily economically active persons while at the same time respecting the special characteristics of national social security legislation. Regulation 1408/71 has, nevertheless, always been applicable to non-economically active persons, such as pensioners, unemployed persons and the family members of workers and self-employed persons. Even students can be covered by the legislation provided that they are or have been subject to the legislation of one or more EEA states.[23] Despite the primary objective of the Regulation, which concerns the free movement of economically active persons, the relevant parameter for being covered by the coordination system is not the exercise of an economic activity as such, but the fact of being covered or having been covered as an employed or self-employed person by the social security system of an EEA state (or being a family member of these persons).[24]

Consequently, a large number of the non-economically active persons in the EEA are covered by this coordination of social security schemes, making any extension of the regimes to social assistance-like benefits inevitably also an expansion of the solidarity previously limited by territorial boundaries. This is the case even more so in Regulation 883/2004, which refers in the definition of its personal scope to all nationals of a Member State (in the adapted EEA text, this is a reference to all nationals of an EEA state) who are or have been subject to the legislation of one or more Member States (EEA states),[25] without referring any longer to the status of employed or self-employed persons. The personal scope of the coordination system is defined in such a broad manner that almost all citizens of the EEA states will be covered by it.[26]

Taking this into account, it is not surprising that the UK decided to try to apply its reservations regarding TCNs in the process of incorporating the coordination regime into the EEA Agreement.[27] What is perhaps quite surprising is that the adoption does not seem to have initiated any controversy in the EFTA States.

---

[23] Students were introduced in the scope of Regulation 1408/71 by Regulation 307/1999 of 8 February 1999, later replaced by Directive 2004/38, see Chap. 4. See also Article 2 on persons covered in the present Regulation 883/2004, see Sect. 6.3.3.

[24] On the implied solidarity with non-economic actors through the coordination regime of social security, see Verschueren (2007), pp. 307–346.

[25] Article 2.

[26] For a discussion of personal scope in the EU see Pennings (2005), pp. 245–246.

[27] Case C-431/11 United Kingdom v Council EU:C:2013:589, see point 6.3.3 above.

Through its decision, the EFTA Court demonstrated how the EEA Agreement affects the boundaries of the national solidarity systems and laid the ground for future cases.[28] When Regulation 1408/71 was adopted into the EEA Agreement, one may safely assume that the EFTA States believed that the ceiling for how much of the welfare systems the states were expected to export was established. The application of the homogeneity principle in later case law, however, proved that it was no longer a ceiling but a floor.

9.3 Case E-4/07 Jon Gunnar Þorkelsson v Gildi Pension Fund

9.3.1 The Facts of the Case and the Legal Dispute

In a preliminary reference from a national court in Iceland, the EFTA Court was, in Case E-4/07,[29] asked about the exportability of a not yet acquired invalidity benefit from an Icelandic pension fund. The dispute arose in a situation where the accident that triggered the payment of the benefit happened after the claimant had found employment, set up a new residence in another EEA state (Denmark) and was paying contributions for sickness insurance in his new place of residence. In essence, the question was whether the national rule that only allowed the export of acquired rights, thereby confining the solidarity of the national system accordingly, violated the freedom of movement of workers and/or export provisions in the former Regulation 1408/71.

The claimant was an Icelandic mariner who in September 1995 left his job in Iceland to move to Denmark, where he continued to work as a mariner. He paid contributions to a Danish pension fund. On 16 September 1996, while at work on board a Danish fishing vessel, he suffered an accident that left him an invalid. At the time of the accident, the claimant had accrued rights to pension payments from several Icelandic pension funds. The export of these existing rights was not the subject of the case. These rights were not in any way reduced, modified, suspended, withdrawn or confiscated; cf. Article 10 of Regulation 1408/71.[30] For his accident, he was also awarded a lump-sum payment from his Danish pension fund as well as receiving a monthly pension from the Danish municipality where he lived. In accordance with the principle in Regulation 1408/71, the state where the claimant worked and lived had assumed responsibility under its existing social welfare system for the Icelandic mariner (*lex loci laboris*).

[28] Later case law which expands this solidarity dimension further makes references to case E-5/06, see as an example paragraphs 36 and 47 in case E-4/07 Þorkelsson.

[29] See also the later case E-11/16 Tryg Forsikring on institutions responsible for benefits against liable third parties.

[30] This was undisputed in the case, see paragraph 67.

The subject of the case was whether the claimant under EEA law had a right to have his invalidity pension (from Iceland) calculated on the basis of projected points, i.e. pension points that he would have been able to accrue with the Icelandic pension fund, had he remained a member of that pension fund and continued working until reaching the age of retirement. The reason he did not fulfil this requirement was that he failed to pay contributions to the fund for at least 6 of the 12 months preceding the accident.[31] The reason he had not paid the contribution was that he had moved to Denmark and taken up employment there. The dispute was concerned with whether the 'six-out-of-the-last-twelve-months' rule infringed the right to freedom of movement of workers and/or provisions on export in Regulation 1408/71.[32]

It was not disputed in the case that the same lack of calculation based on projected pension points would occur if a national worker moving within Iceland started to pay premiums to another national pension fund not party to the same agreement as the Gildi Pension Fund.[33] This distinction in Icelandic law was based on a premise that the right to disability benefits based on projection did not constitute an acquired right in a legal sense. Basically, a member in an Icelandic pension fund is entitled to specific benefits in the event of disability, in proportion to the member's contribution to the fund. Given that the right to projection depended on ongoing payments to his pension fund, this claim was rejected by the fund.

9.3.2 No Obstacle to the Free Movement of Workers: Article 28 EEA

Social security coordination is limited to securing access to social security in the new host country and preventing losses of acquired social security rights in the former country of residence or employment. The fact that social rights in one EEA state are better than those in another is not in itself contrary to the coordination regime.[34] Coordination is a method that leaves the competence to legislate on social security matters in the hands of the EEA states and secures the possibility of maintaining a variety of different national social security systems. In fact, the Regulation does not detract from the power of the EEA states to organise their social security schemes.[35]

---

[31] The national rules are described in paragraphs 7–14.

[32] One of the questions in the case was whether this was a national rule or simply part of an industrial Agreement. For the purpose of this analysis it is not necessary to investigate this question further.

[33] See paragraph 71.

[34] See for a general analysis of the coordination regime which includes the EEA in Van der Mei (2003).

[35] See for instance the reference to this by the EFTA Court in Case E-3/12 Jonsson paragraph 55, Sect. 9.4.

The starting point for the claimant was, however, that the national rule violated the free movement of workers in Article 28.[36] The general provisions of free movement preclude all provisions, which, although applicable without discrimination on the grounds of nationality, are nevertheless liable to hinder or make less attractive the exercise of the fundamental freedoms guaranteed by the EEA Agreement.[37] The added value of the prohibition of non-discriminatory rules for the free movement of persons concerns primarily the possibility to challenge rules imposed by the state of origin that hamper the right to work in another EEA state.[38] The judgment in Graf demonstrates, nevertheless, that there are limits to the prohibition for the Member State of origin to apply rules that may hamper the right to move to another Member State.[39] The Graf case involved a German national who voluntarily terminated his employment in Austria in order to take up a new job in Germany. Mr. Graf claimed that he was entitled to compensation from his former employer under Austrian law. The employer argued that the law only gave right to compensation if the contract was terminated by the employer. The CJEU made it clear that in order for a national rule to be an obstacle to free movement of workers, the rule must affect access of workers to labour markets in other EEA states.[40] The Austrian rule depended on a future and hypothetical event that was too uncertain and indirect a possibility for the legislation to be capable of being regarded as liable to hinder the free movement of workers.

Similarly, the events in Case E-4/07 leading up to the claimant not being entitled to a calculation of projected points seemed too uncertain and indirect a possibility for the national legislation to be regarded as liable to hinder the free movement of workers. First of all, the issue of calculation based on projected points would only arise in the case of a future hypothetical event such as an accident. Furthermore, the stopping of payment into Icelandic pension funds occurred simultaneously with the starting of payments into the Danish system. There is interplay between the public social security system and the independent funds in Iceland, which aims at preventing citizens from being compensated several times for the same loss.[41] There was no such coordination between the rights accrued under the Danish payments and the rights accrued under the Icelandic system. If the claimant wanted full protection

---

[36] See paragraph 5.

[37] Case C-19/92 Kraus [1993] ECR I-1663, paragraph 32 and Case C-55/94 Gebhard [1995] ECR I-4165, paragraph 37.

[38] See Case C-18/95 Terhoeve [1999] ECR I-345.

[39] Case C-190/98 Graf [2000] ECR I-493.

[40] See Case C-190/98 Graf [2000] ECR I-493 on the limit of what constitutes an obstacle to free movement, paras 23- See Case C-18/95 Terhoeve [1999] ECR I-345.

Case C-190/98 Graf [2000] ECR I-493.

See Case C-190/98 Graf [2000] ECR I-493 on the limit of what constitutes an obstacle to free movement, paragraphs 23–25.

[41] See paragraph 70 where Iceland draws attention to the possibility that the if the former mariner would receive payments in line with his projected entitlements from the pension funds, he should receive less from the public social security systems concerned.

under both sets of rules, he could also have chosen voluntarily to continue paying contributions to the Icelandic fund. Thus, the national rule was difficult to perceive as an obstacle.

In Hartmann, the German Government argued successfully that it should not be overlooked that by transferring residence to another Member State, other forms of entitlement may be opened.

> It should not be overlooked that by transferring his residence to another Member State other forms of entitlement may be opened in the host Member State. To paraphrase the German Government at the hearing, where Member States are obliged not to impose any restrictions on their nationals wishing to move to another Member State, neither are they required to give them a bonus for leaving.[42]

Having protection under both sets of rules, both Danish and Icelandic, without the same coordination as nationals would seem like a bonus. Finally, the national rule applied equally to internal and external situations, in that moving to another job within Iceland could also trigger the same risk. The national rule consequently did not hinder access to employment markets in other EEA states. Thus, the facts of the case did not support the claimant's principal objection that the national rule was an obstacle to the free movement of workers as laid down in Article 28 EEA.

The EFTA Court seemed to be of a similar opinion regarding the application of the free movement of workers provision in the decision, although the Court did not give any reasons for its position. In the decision paragraph 54, the Court rejected the claimant's principal submission and stated that it did not find reasons to rely on the freedom of movement of workers as the legal basis in the case. The Court therefore spelt out rather clearly that it did not find any of the fundamental freedoms applicable to the case. It seems clear that the case did not concern the freedom of movement of economically active persons. In other words, the Court did not think that the free movement of workers was obstructed by a national rule requiring payments to the pension fund in the last 6 out of 12 months in order to have the calculation based on projected points.

This view of the EFTA Court meant that the Court did not follow the line of reasoning established by the EFTA Surveillance Authority in its written submission in the case. The Authority based its argumentation on the premise that the national rule violated the free movement of workers.[43] The Authority saw the principle of free movement of workers as underlying Regulation 1408/71.[44] The Authority therefore suggested that the answer on the application of the Regulation 'would follow equally' if Articles 28 and 29 EEA were applied directly. Regulation 1408/71 simply laid down detailed rules implementing the principles set out in those provisions

---

[42] Case C-212/05 Opinion of Advocate General Geelhoed in Hartmann v Freistaat [2007] ECR I-06303, paragraph 86.

[43] See in particular paragraphs 67–80 of the written intervention by the Authority 18 June 2007, made public after decision 19 March 2014.

[44] Written intervention by the Authority 18 June 2007, paragraph 79.

and was not meant to ‘create any additional rights for the individual which went beyond what already followed from the main provisions of the agreement’.[45]

Having established that the case was not about the free movement of economically active persons, the next question was whether the claimant had a right based on the EEA Agreement also protecting the free movement of non-economically active persons. For this right to exist, the EFTA Court had to build on its previous understanding from Case E-5/06 whereby the agreement also contained a principle of solidarity beyond the factors of production, i.e. the economically active.[46]

9.3.3 *Exporting Benefits to a Non-economically Active Person*

Thus, the case of Porkelsson is really about exporting welfare benefits to a non-economically active person. The starting point for the concept of exporting welfare benefits is that it violates the territoriality of the welfare state and its public benefit scheme. Territoriality means that public benefits are preserved for persons residing or working within the state territory. Conversely, public benefits are not intended for those living or working outside the state border, including the state’s own citizens. Territoriality also implies that welfare state benefits must be consumed within the state borders. Public benefits, such as education, housing or healthcare, often can only be effectively provided and consumed in the state territory, and in principle, territoriality for cash benefits implies that they cannot be transferred abroad. Thus, moving to other states is interpreted as giving up membership and hence entitlement to social welfare benefits. An important reasoning underlying non-exportability is that governments lack sufficient powers to effectively control and enforce conditions of eligibility in other states. In summary, citizens who choose to go abroad and no longer participate in the national community, or pay taxes to the national community or yield themselves to administrative control by the national authorities, in principle lose the expectation of welfare support from their home state.

Objectively, the situation was that the claimant had voluntarily given up his job in Iceland and had found new employment in another EEA state where he had set up residence. Thus, by his own choice, he had left his country of origin and he was no longer an economic contributor to the finances of his home country. This was perhaps even more evident in the case at hand given that the problem arose precisely from the fact that the claimant had ceased to pay contributions to the pension fund. Thus, the claimant had given up membership in the social welfare community in his home state and had become a member in the social welfare community in his new country of employment and residence (host state).

The principal question was whether EEA law requires the home state in such a situation to still take social responsibility for one of its citizens even after the citizen

[45] Written intervention by the Authority 18 June 2007, paragraph 80.

[46] And indeed several references are made to this case in the decision, see i.a. paragraph 47.

has given up membership of the social welfare community. In EU law, this issue has been subject to an extensive review of national rules in light of the provisions of Union citizenship.[47] There is a strong policy objective in the EU of a general right to free movement and residence to be enjoyed by all citizens regardless of their financial and economic status. Union citizenship thus provides the legal basis in the EU to require the country of origin to continue, at least temporarily, to take social responsibility even after the citizen has given up his/her membership in the national community of solidarity.

The conceptual underpinning seems to be that any national rule that places those who have moved (or have returned after having exercised a right to move) at a disadvantage compared to those who have not moved may involve an element of discrimination or an obstacle that must undergo scrutiny by the Court for compliance with the principle of proportionality. Territoriality limitations place citizens at a disadvantage 'simply' because they have exercised their right of movement.

Thus, in D'Hoop,[48] the CJEU made it clear that Member States cannot impose rules that have the effect of placing at a disadvantage their own citizens who have exercised the right to move. This is stated quite clearly by the Court:

> In that a citizen of the Union must be granted in all Member States the same treatment in law as that accorded to the nationals of those Member States who find themselves in the same situation, it would be incompatible with the right to freedom of movement were a citizen, in the Member State of which he is a national, to receive treatment less favourable than he would enjoy if he had not availed himself of the opportunities offered by the Treaty in relation of freedom of movement.[49]

In De Cuyper,[50] a similar reasoning was applied in relation to a residence requirement to receive unemployment benefits.[51] Belgian rules requiring that those in receipt of such benefits had to reside within the national territory were found to fall within the scope of Article 18(1) EC (now Article 21(1) TFEU). The ruling in De Cuyper is a good example of the far-reaching consequences of the case law. Pre-Union citizenship, the residence requirement would not have been subject to the proportionality/necessity scrutiny, since it was compatible with the coordination regime.[52] With Union citizenship, the residence requirement must undergo scrutiny by the Court. The latest perhaps most far-reaching case in this line of thinking by the CJEU on social security benefits is the Stewart case on obligations on Member States to export an incapacity benefit in youth.[53] The home state requirements

---

[47] See more generally on this in Sect. 7.3.

[48] Case C-224/98 D'Hoop [2002] ECR I-06191.

[49] Case C-224/98 D'Hoop [2002] ECR I-06191, paragraph 30.

[50] Case C-406/04 De Cuyper [2006] ECR I-06947.

[51] See for a more thorough analysis of this case in Sect. 9.4 on unemployment benefits.

[52] Regulation 1408/71 Article 10(1) conferred the limited access to export the benefit in Article 69(1), see more on this in the next section.

[53] Case C-503/09 Lucy Stewart v Secretary of State for Work and Pensions [2011] ECR I-6497. The more recent cases on student rights against their home state are also illustrative, see Chap. 4.

towards Union citizens thus aim not only to prevent discrimination but also to have potential obstacles to movement removed.

The right to mobility gives rise to two claims: first, the right to non-discrimination on the grounds of mobility and, second, the right to have potential obstacles to mobility removed, regardless of whether they are discriminatory or not.[54]

9.3.4 The View of the EFTA Court

The Court chose to rely on an interpretation of Regulation 1408/71 to some extent against both the structure of the regime and against a literal interpretation of the requirements to export welfare benefits under the coordination regime. First of all, the main objective of the coordination regime is to protect the free movement of workers including their families. The EFTA Surveillance Authority saw this as an essential component of the application of the Regulation.[55] The Court disagreed with the Authority as to whether the national rule in the case was an obstacle to the free movement of workers as laid down in Article 28 EEA.

Furthermore, the Regulation established a structure for the right to export of acquired welfare benefits to prevent the loss of such benefits from being an obstacle to free movement.[56] In Case E-4/07, there was no existing welfare benefit to export when the claimant decided to seek work in another EEA state and settle there. Given that the possible right arose only after the claimant had left the solidarity community of which he used to be part, the case was really about the continued social responsibility of the state of origin for their own citizens.[57]

In addition, the coordination regime does not provide for the harmonisation of national social security laws. The Regulation is thus not intended to give individuals substantive rights that go beyond their rights under the national legislation concerned. In other words, the individual has to fulfil all the national requirements to be eligible for the support. The Regulation only aims for what can be termed a procedural right, namely that of exportability of the benefit. Thus, substantively, the conditions for the right to the benefit are determined by national law. Procedurally, national law cannot hinder the export of an already-existing substantive right in the situations covered by the Regulation.

The rules on projection applied equally to everyone working in Iceland, and there were various reasons why a worker might lose the right to projected points. The national substantive requirement for eligibility was membership of the pension

---

[54] Somek (2007), p. 793.

[55] Written observations by the Authority 18 June 2007, paragraphs 79 and 80.

[56] The projection of entitlements did not constitute acquired social security rights within the meaning of the Regulation, see Article 29 EEA and the decision paragraph 35 and the intervention by the Icelandic Government.

[57] For this argument it is also referred to the structure of the pension funds in Iceland and the interplay with the basic social security system as discussed above.

fund. When this national condition was not satisfied regardless of the reason being movement within or outside Iceland, no right existed under national law. Given that the Regulation did not create new rights substantively but aimed at ensuring exportability of existing rights, the Icelandic mariner arguably did not have a right to projected points under the Regulation. There was simply no substantive right under national law to export. In citizenship cases, this last point is to a large extent disregarded by the CJEU building on an understanding that the person who moves requires special protection even of non-discriminatory rules in his or her country of origin.

> Citizenship not only protects the national from one Member State against discrimination by another but also the Member States own national against being worse off than fellow nationals who do not avail themselves of the opportunities offered by Art.18. The national plays the role of an "honorary foreigner" inasmuch as he or she shares with foreigners the essential characteristic of being mobile or having moved.[58]

The coordination regime is about the right to export benefits to not deter freedom of movement. To this end, the regime sets a limit on the principle of territoriality, but only as far as the EEA states have been willing to do so in the agreed coordinated regime.[59] This limit may, however, not comply with the requirements under the provisions on Union citizenship, as has been illustrated by numerous cases from the CJEU. In fact, it is apparent that the prohibition to export benefits always entails a potential infringement of an individual's right to freely move throughout the EU, an infringement that might be justified in practical cases by applying national law in conformity with the principles of proportionality.

The provisions on Union citizenship have accordingly prompted the CJEU to go beyond the agreed legislative limits of the Regulation.[60]

The EFTA Court has no such legal sources available as an interpretative tool of EEA law beyond the fundamental freedoms, and in this case, as we have seen, the latter was not applicable. Interestingly, the homogeneity principle seemed nevertheless to trump any objection to such expansion of the rights of individuals under the EEA Agreement even at the expense of private parties with competing interests.[61] Thus, the EFTA Court ruled in favour of the Icelandic claimant and gave him the right under EEA law to have his pension points calculated based on projected points.

Through this case law, it has become evident that the EFTA Court is also ready to protect the non-economically active free movers under EEA law. The next section analyses two cases concerning Norway where the Court has ruled on the compatibility of national territorial boundaries of welfare solidarity enshrined in national

---

[58] Somek (2007), p. 793.

[59] For a more complete account of the view of the Icelandic Government of how far the coordination regime required export of benefits, see the Report for the Hearing, paragraphs 63–76.

[60] Dougan (2006), pp. 613–641.

[61] In the literature, this has been suggested as an absolute limit on the homogeneity principle. Thus, in cases involving duties on private parties, the EFTA Court cannot rely on the homogeneity principle in the same way as in cases involving duties on states. The rule of law constitutes an obstacle to such interpretation, see Fenger (2006) , pp. 131–154.

provisions limiting the export of unemployment benefits and child benefits, respectively.

9.4 Case E-3/12 Jonsson: The Special Character of Unemployment Benefits

9.4.1 Introduction

Benefits relating to involuntary unemployment aim to offer a guarantee of support in the event of temporary and involuntary unemployment. Those entitled to such benefits are thus people forming part of the regular labour market. Normally, the benefits have the character of a payment that, up to a certain maximum, is related to the last salary earned.

These characteristics imply that those receiving unemployment benefits must remain available on the labour market. National requirements for the eligibility of the benefit vary, but generally, the unemployed must be resident in the state responsible for the benefit and registered with a body in said state, which facilitates finding a new position. In general, an unemployed person has the greatest chance of finding work in the last state of employment.[62]

Generally, those entitled to benefits must, in addition, accept any offer of suitable employment and may not undertake any activities whereby they receive income simultaneously with receiving an unemployment benefit. In the absence of cooperation between authorities in the different EEA states, a residence requirement may also be appropriate in order to ensure that effective checks on an unemployed person's remunerated activity and family situation are carried out.

As described by Advocate General Geelhoed in his opinion in the De Cuyper case, '[T]he aim of these requirements—which in principle must be strictly applied—is to prevent improper use or abuse of unemployment benefits, and to prevent unfair competition on the labour market by those receiving unemployment benefits'.[63]

In general, unemployment benefits are related to the rights of the economically active citizen, and therefore, Articles 45, 49 and/or 56 TFEU are applicable when interpreting the coordination regime. However, in the case law from the CJEU, the Union citizenship provisions are applied to interpret or displace the coordination regime in some cases regarding the residence requirement and the right to unemployment benefit.[64] Given that the EFTA Court similarly had to

---

[62] See also the factual material relied upon by the CJEU in the case C-406/04 Gérald De Cuyper v Office national de l'emploi [2006] ECR I-6947.

[63] Opinion of Advocate General Geelhoed in case C-406/04 Gérald De Cuyper v Office national de l'emploi [2006] ECR I-6947, paragraph 59.

[64] Examples include Cases C-406/04, Gérald De Cuyper v Office national de l'emploi [2006] ECR I-6947 and C-228/07 Jørn Petersen v Arbeitsmarktservice [2008] ECR I-6989.

interpret the residence requirement in Norway regarding unemployment benefits in the Jonsson case, the decisions are of interest regarding the overall question analysed here.

9.4.2 Export of Unemployment Benefits, the Coordination Regime

The general context of unemployment benefits explains the rationale behind not including unemployment benefits in the general prohibition of residence requirements in the former Regulation No 1408/71.[65] Article 10(1) of Regulation No 1408/71 concerned the waiving of residence clauses included in national legislation on social security benefits. It contained a prohibition on all forms of modification of certain social security benefits on the grounds that the recipient resided in a Member State other than the state responsible for payment. The social security benefits listed in Article 10(1) to which that prohibition applied did not, however, include unemployment benefits. Therefore, in general, the Regulation did not prohibit a residence requirement in the case of national rules governing unemployment benefits.[66]

In relation to the general proposition that restrictions on exporting entitlement to unemployment benefits are not prohibited, Regulation No 1408/71 provided two exceptions. Article 69[67] provided for entitlement to unemployment benefits where an unemployed person moved to another Member State for no more than 3 months as a registered jobseeker in order to look for work. Article 71(1)[68] provided for entitlement to unemployment benefits for unemployed persons who, during their last employment, resided in a Member State other than the state in which they were insured for social security purposes. Mr. Jonsson's case related to the interpretation of this last article.

Article 71(1) must be interpreted and understood in its entirety. The objective of the article in line with the general objective of the Regulation was to prevent the *simultaneous* application of a number of national legislative systems and the complications that might ensue. Furthermore, the objective was to ensure that the persons covered were not left *without* social security cover because there was no legislation applicable to them.

Article 71(1) distinguishes between frontier workers (governed by a) and non-frontier workers (governed by b). Furthermore, in each category, there is a distinction between the partially and the wholly unemployed. The wholly unemployed

---

[65] Now replaced by Regulation 883/2004 Article 7.

[66] The same result is now achieved in Regulation 883/2004, see Articles 3(1)h, 11(3)c and Chapter 6 in particular Article 63 on the waiving of residence rules in Article 7 only in the cases provided for by Articles 64 and 65.

[67] Regulation 883/2004 Article 64.

[68] Regulation 883/2004 Article 65.

genuine frontier worker does not have any choice under the system of subparagraph (a): He is subject to the state of residence. This is the case even if the frontier worker only fulfils the conditions for unemployment benefits in the state of last employment or would have received considerably higher benefits if subject to the employment state. Genuine frontier workers may only exceptionally, based on case law, remain under the jurisdiction of the state of last employment if they are atypical or 'false' genuine frontier workers.[69]

According to Article 71(1)(b)(i), a wholly unemployed worker other than a frontier worker (which is the category Mr. Jonsson fell into) is given a choice between being subject to the legislation of the state of last employment (the competent state) and the state of residence. The choice is made by the unemployed person based on where he/she makes himself/herself available for the employment service.[70] A natural interpretation from the wording of the Article is that by returning to the territory of the residence state, the unemployed has chosen this country for the unemployment benefit.

This was, however, not the way the Regulation was interpreted by the EFTA Court. Before looking more closely into this decision, interesting observations can be made on the case law of the CJEU on the export of unemployment benefits and the right to move and reside freely as a Union citizen.

9.4.3 *Case Law from the CJEU on Exporting Unemployment Benefits and Union Citizenship*

The CJEU considered the limits of the obligation to export unemployment benefits in Regulation 1408/71 and the provisions on Union citizenship both in De Cuyper[71] and in Petersen.[72] The CJEU subjected the national residence requirement in the state of last employment to a proportionality test in both cases, even though the national requirement was in compliance with the right to refuse export of such benefits in Regulation 1408/17.[73]

Mr. De Cuyper was a Belgian national who had been employed in Belgium and was subsequently granted unemployment benefit. Some months later, he turned 50, at which age he was exempted from various national control procedures. He then moved to France. On becoming aware of De Cuyper's change of residence, the Belgian authority terminated his entitlement on the basis of the national requirement

[69] It is not necessary to go more into detail regarding the coordination regime for the point made here, for a more detailed explanation, see Van der Mei (2003) .

[70] This understanding is in line with the understanding expressed by the observations by the EFTA Surveillance Authority 16 August 2012, see paragraphs 23 and 24.

[71] C-406/04 Gérald De Cuyper v Office national de l'emploi [2006] ECR I-6947.

[72] Case C-228/07 Jørn Petersen v Arbeitsmarktservice [2008] ECR I-6989.

[73] Confer Regulation 1408/71 Article 10, Articles 69 and 71 were not applicable in the cases.

that he must be actually resident in Belgium. The case concerned whether the national requirement violated the right to move and reside freely as a Union citizen. The case was exceptional in the sense that it subjected a national rule compatible with provisions in the secondary legislation to a proportionality review.[74] However, the CJEU was quite receptive to the motivation behind the national rule. In particular, the Court held that a residence clause reflected 'the need to monitor the employment and family situation of unemployed persons'.[75] The Court also accepted that the effectiveness of monitoring arrangements was dependent to a large extent on the fact that it was unexpected and carried out on the spot and, for that reason, accepted that less restrictive measures would mean that monitoring would be less effective.[76] Close contact with the employment services is normally essential as part of a job-search and monitoring requirement.[77]

In the Petersen case, the Court reached the opposite conclusion, ruling that the national residence clause in Austria regarding payments of unemployment benefits was in violation of Article 39 EC (now Article 45 TFEU) of free movement of workers. Mr. Petersen was a German national who had worked in Austria. The case concerned a benefit that was given based on a reduced capacity or incapacity to work in anticipation of an invalidity pension. A main question in the case was whether the benefit was an unemployment benefit or an invalidity benefit. Unemployment benefits were generally not subject to requirements of export by Regulation 1408/71, whereas invalidity benefits were. The Court concluded that the benefit was indeed an unemployment benefit.

An interesting aspect of the case is that the Court sees the worker as a category of Union citizen and applies case law relevant for the interpretation of the legal question without distinguishing between case law regarding economically and non-economically active citizens. There are numerous examples of the same phenomenon in the Union citizenship case law.[78] In addition, the opinion of the Advocate General in the case makes it clear that EU law is moving in the direction of not

---

[74] See the comparison with Tas Hagen, Case C-192/05 [2006] ECR I-10451 by Cousins (2007), pp. 386–395.

[75] Case C-406/04 Gérald De Cuyper v Office national de l'emploi [2006] ECR I-10451, paragraph 41.

[76] The outcome of the case has been characterised as slightly surprising (compared to other cases on export of benefits and Union Citizenship like the Tas-Hagen case C-192/05) given that a core social security benefit which is subject for coordination and (albeit limited) export was unaffected by the concept of Union citizenship, see Cousins (2007), p. 393.

[77] In the De Cuyper case many of the normal components of the 'unemployment' benefit payable had been removed because of the choice of the Belgian legislature to exempt unemployed above a certain age from the requirements of being available for work and actually look for work.

[78] See C-406/04 Gérald De Cuyper v Office national de l'emploi [2006] ECR I-6947, paragraphs 38 and 39, C-135/99 Elsen [2000] ECR I-10409, paragraph 42, Case C-456/02 Trojani v Centre Public [2004] ECR I-7573, paragraph 45, Case C-85/96 Martinez Sala [1998] ECR I-2691, paragraph 48, Case C-138/02 Collins v. Secretary of State for Work and Pensions [2004] ECR I-2703, Case C-413/01 Ninni-Orasch [2003] ECR I-13187, Case C-212/05 Hartmann v Freistaat [2007] ECR I-06303, see Chap. 7.

differentiating between the scope of the articles on Union citizenship and the articles on the freedom of movement of workers. It follows from paragraph 23 of the opinion that

> [t]he Court is advancing steadily towards achieving a uniform level of protection in the field of the free movement of persons, using the provisions on citizenship as a helpful tool.

The Court refers to this paragraph of the opinion in paragraph 23 of the judgment. The Advocate General's conclusion is that

> [a]ccordingly, in the light of Articles 39 EC and 18 EC (now Articles 45 and 21 TFEU), a measure such as the one at issue, which provides for different treatment based on the place of residence of the recipient of a social security benefit, is incompatible with Community law.[79]

Thus, no distinction is made between these two legal bases in the Treaty. Consequently, it follows from the general right to free movement and residence regardless of economic activity that national residence requirements prohibiting export will undergo a proportionality scrutiny by the Court increasingly amounting to the same test.

Furthermore, in Petersen, the proportionality test seems to have been applied quite strictly, for instance by denying that protecting the integrity of the national boundaries of social security systems is an important concern. The Court argued that given that the Austrian Government was ready to accept Mr. Petersen as eligible had he remained in Austria the Government has thus demonstrated the economic capacity to bear the burden of the benefit.[80] It is difficult to see in which individual cases the state can demonstrate that it does not have the economic capacity to bear the burden of the one individual receiving support.

Unlike the Advocate General, the Court did not refer to Article 18 EC (Article 21 TFEU) in its conclusion. The Court nevertheless adopted the same approach as the Advocate General and also protected movement of Union citizens in the case of a non-economic actor as Mr. Petersen was at the time.

9.4.4 The Facts of the Jonsson Case

The case E-3/12[81] concerned a Swedish national living in Sweden who frequently (starting from 1983) worked in Norway. His last job before becoming unemployed in 2008 was in Norway. Mr. Jonsson returned to his home in Sweden after becoming unemployed. Mr. Jonsson applied for and received an unemployment benefit from Sweden subsequent to Norway's rejection of his claim. The claim was rejected in

---

[79] The opinion of the Advocate General Geelhoed in Case C-228/07 Jørn Petersen v Arbeitsmarktservice [2008] ECR I-6989, paragraph 77.

[80] See Case C-228/07 Jørn Petersen v Arbeitsmarktservice [2008] ECR I-6989, paragraph 59.

[81] Decided 20 March 2013.

Norway on the grounds that Mr. Jonsson did not reside there and therefore failed to meet the conditions for entitlement to unemployment benefit. The requirement of residence in Norway is also related to the requirement of being a genuine jobseeker available for work, which requires that the individual in question must register with and report regularly to the Norwegian Labour and Welfare Administration.[82] The question in the case was the compatibility with EEA law of the requirement of residence in Norway to be eligible for an unemployment benefit.

9.4.5 National Law

The general requirement of actual stay in Norway applies equally to both Norwegian and foreign nationals. It simply means that unemployment benefits are only awarded for the periods in which the unemployed person is actually present in Norway. A Norwegian is not entitled to receive unemployment benefits while abroad, whether on holiday or for other reasons. Such information must be given in detail every 14 days on the employment status form. There are certain exemptions from the residence requirement enshrined in the Regulation regarding frontier workers and non-genuine frontier workers who become fully unemployed and can choose between registering as unemployed in the competent state or in the resident state. The exemptions represent groups that could otherwise easily have been excluded from the right to unemployment benefit in both of the states involved. This applies, for example, to daily commuters who work in Norway but live in another country. If such daily commuters become partially unemployed, they must apply for benefits in Norway.[83] However, they often have no place to live/stay in Norway, and a requirement for stay in Norway is therefore not applied in relation to this group. These considerations did not apply in the situation of Mr. Jonsson. They demonstrate clearly, however, that the national Regulation takes account of the special situation of certain categories of migrant workers.

The requirement of actual stay in Norway is substantiated by several reasons. First, it establishes a connection between the state in which the right to unemployment benefits is acquired and the obligation to pay these benefits. The benefits are calculated on the basis of previous income, usually in Norway, and the level of compensation of previous income is based on the premise that the unemployed person is actually living in Norway.

Norway has a substantially higher wage level than most other EEA states and also a higher rate of compensation than most states. The calculation of unemployment benefits should seek to balance two interests in particular: that of ensuring a reasonable income for the unemployed but at the same time that of providing sufficient incentives for him or her to resume work as soon as possible. If the unemployed

[82] National Insurance Act of 28 February 1997 No 19, sections 4-2 and 4-5.

[83] In line with the requirements in former Regulation 1408/71 Article 71(1)(a)(i).

person lives in a state with a substantially lower cost level than Norway, this balance will be disturbed. In addition, there will be a disturbance of competition on the job market in the state of residence.[84]

It was precisely these national concerns that the CJEU accepted when it accepted the denial of export of an unemployment benefit in the De Cuyper case. The administrative concerns were less visible in that case given that the applicant was receiving an unemployment benefit but, as a result of his age, was exempted from the requirement of being available for a new job. However, there were administrative concerns regarding monitoring his family situation and whether he had actually taken up a new job. In fact, the Advocate General and the CJEU relied precisely on the general interest of the state and of the job market in general when they accepted denial of export. In Petersen, however, the CJEU relied heavily on the right to free movement in its assessment of the national residence requirement.

In the Jonsson case, the obligation to live or be present in Norway related strongly to other conditions for unemployment benefits. The unemployed must actively search for employment, and several of the requirements are more easily complied with if the person stays in the country. The jobseeker must, in other words, be a 'genuine jobseeker' with a duty to report and appear in person.

The control of unemployment benefits is primarily based on controlling different registers to which the Norwegian Labour and Welfare Administration has access. A comparable control is not possible for persons living abroad. The control unit does not have the competence to access foreign registers. There are no international agreements on the control of unemployment benefits.

9.4.6 The Advisory Opinion of the EFTA Court

The EFTA Court decided that the national requirement of stay in Norway for entitlement to an unemployment benefit for a person in Mr. Jonsson's situation violated EEA law.[85] The Court seemed to recognise the compatibility of a requirement regarding requiring availability to the employment services but does not extend this to encompassing presence or actual stay on the territory or even presence on territory geographically nearby.[86] The EFTA Court does not really address the question of whether returning to the home state after becoming unemployed actually is a decision on where to be available on the job market. Undoubtedly, Mr. Jonsson was entitled to unemployment benefit and did not fall into a category of not having rights under any legal regimes. By this decision, the EFTA Court seemed to deviate from the coordination regime's main concern, namely that of guaranteeing the migrant

[84] From an economic point of view an argument can be made to the effect that jobseekers should have comparable conditions (i.a. social benefits) in order to compete for jobs on equal terms.

[85] Case E-3/12 Jonsson, paragraphs 72 and 82.

[86] Case E-3/12, Jonsson, paragraphs 68–70, 75.

worker an unemployment benefit. It is difficult to see how the free movement of workers is facilitated by the (previous) worker being able to select this favourable position vis-a-vis other national unemployed workers, namely receiving unemployment benefits from the state most advantageous in terms of benefits. The rationale behind the Court's interpretation does not accommodate the migrant worker's special situation but seems to privilege him to some extent contrary to the objectives of the Regulation. This kind of privileging of moving individuals coincides with the emphasis on free movement rights under the Union citizenship provisions.[87] As demonstrated, the CJEU is not concerned with the possibility of creating reverse discrimination under its citizenship jurisprudence. Rather, the moving individual is considered to be in a somewhat privileged position. With this decision, the EFTA Court continues to ensure the paralleling of free movement rights beyond the economically active in the EEA integration process.

9.5 Case E-6/12 Exporting Child Benefits

9.5.1 Introduction

Case E-6/12[88] concerned the Norwegian administrative practice for entitlement to child support in cases where the parents are separated and one parent is a migrant worker residing in Norway and the other parent lives with the child in their respective state of residence. The other parent living with the child would be eligible for child support in their respective state of residence, and the Norwegian administrative practice only involved the denial of exporting the Norwegian child benefits as a so-called topping-up of the first benefit. The main concern regarding the Norwegian administrative practice in this situation was the lack of an individual evaluation of whether the child living together with the parent outside Norway was mainly dependent on the parent who was living in Norway.

This case will be analysed against the backdrop of the changed methodology stemming largely from the CJEU citizenship case law.[89] In essence, the changed methodology entails that national authorities are required to consider the personal situation of the claimant so that even when the national rule in theory is compatible with EU law, its application to that particular claimant might be contrary to the requirements of proportionality.[90] In order to illustrate the changed methodology in

[87] See for instance the reasoning in the Petersen case emphasising the right to move freely for all citizens.

[88] Decided 11 September 2013.

[89] See Sect. 7.3 above.

[90] See Case C-140/12 Brey EU:C:2013:565, see also the alleged modifications to this general rule in the string of cases commented upon above Cases C-333/13, EU:C:2014:2358 Dano, C-67/14, EU:C:2015:5 Alimanovic and C-308/14 EU:C:2016:436 on the export of childcare benefits from the UK and Ireland.

the field of the coordination regime, a case concerning the requirement of the UK to export an incapacity benefit in youth is presented.[91] In this case, there is an interesting difference between the opinion of the Advocate General and that of the CJEU. The Advocate General bases the opinion solely on the coordination regime and accepts that residence requirements can be a legitimate connecting factor to the national welfare system. In contrast, the CJEU applies the provisions of Union citizenship and conducts a proportionality review to require of the UK system to be open to other connecting factors. Thus, the residence requirement in question is found to be incompatible with the rights of Union citizens even if it is seemingly in compliance with the coordination regime.

The changed methodology in the sense of a personalised approach seems to have influenced the EFTA Court when it assessed the Norwegian administrative practice in the child support case.

9.5.2 Case Law from the CJEU on Exporting Youth Benefits and Union Citizenship

In Stewart,[92] the CJEU adopted the reasoning from the Petersen case[93] more explicitly and interpreted the right to export of benefits under Regulation 1408/71[94] in light of the right of movement of Union citizens. The case concerned an incapacity benefit in youth limited by UK legislation to persons with ordinary residence, past and present, in Great Britain. The condition of residence, reinforced by a condition requiring actual presence, on which entitlement to the benefit was dependent, was in fact a substitution for the condition of having contributed to the general social welfare system.[95]

Ms. Stewart was a British national with Down's syndrome who was born in November of 1989. In August 2000, she moved with her parents to Spain. She had been awarded a disability living allowance from the UK. Ms. Stewart had never worked and probably would never be able to due to her disability. On her behalf, her mother made a claim for short-term incapacity benefit in youth for her 16th birthday. The claim was refused by the Secretary of State for Work and Pensions on the grounds that Ms. Stewart did not satisfy the condition of presence in Great Britain.

To understand the case, it is necessary to understand the residence condition required by national law. Often, conditions for entitlement to social benefits are

---

[91] Case C-503/09 Lucy Stewart v Secretary of State for Work and Pensions [2011] ECR I-6497.

[92] Case C-503/09 Lucy Stewart v Secretary of State for Work and Pensions [2011] ECR I-6497, paragraphs 77–104.

[93] Case C-228/07 Jørn Petersen v Arbeitsmarktservice [2008] ECR I-6989, The Petersen case is dealt with more generally in Sect. 9.4.

[94] Now revised by Regulation 883/2004, see Sect. 6.3.3.

[95] The opinion of the Advocate General Cruz Villalón is built on this understanding of the UK system, see Opinion of Advocate General Cruz Villalón in Case C-503/09 Lucy Stewart v Secretary of State for Work and Pensions [2011] ECR I-6497, especially paragraphs 8–18 on national law, see also paragraph 64.

based on some sort of contribution to the social security scheme. Generally, this requirement is considered to constitute an objective consideration of public interest, which is capable of justifying a restriction on the freedom of movement of persons.[96] Conditions of residence are, however, generally held to be incompatible with the requirements of EU law when they apply as 'additional' or complementary conditions to this often general condition for entitlement to social benefits.[97] Residence conditions in these cases essentially serve to exclude beneficiaries exercising their right of freedom of movement. However, the residence condition in the Stewart case arose in a different context as a condition of entitlement to short-term incapacity benefit in youth that, in the interests of beneficiaries, replaced the ordinary condition of contribution.

In this connection, the Advocate General refers to the Court's case law that has repeatedly held that the Member States retain their powers to organise their social security systems provided that they comply with EU law when exercising those powers.[98] This retention of powers means that it is for the Member States to define both the extent of their social security systems and the conditions of entitlement to social benefits paid out under them provided that such conditions comply with EU law and, most importantly, provided that they are not discriminatory. It is for the Member States alone to define their degree of national solidarity and the conditions under which it is to be given expression. In paragraph 54, the Advocate General further refers to the fact that Regulation 1408/71 only pursues the objective of coordinating the social security laws of the Member States, not their harmonisation. Hence, the national court is advised to examine the present condition of residence to which entitlement to short-term incapacity benefit in youth is subject, in that it replaces the ordinary condition of contribution.

The CJEU takes a different approach. First, it does not accept the UK Government's first line of arguments, namely that the Regulation permits a distinction to be drawn between the acquisition of a benefit, on the one hand, and its retention, once acquired, on the other. In a broad interpretation of the purpose of Article 10 of Regulation 1408/71[99] as protecting persons from any adverse effects that might arise from the transfer of their residence from one Member State to another, the Court stated the following:

> It follows from that principle not only that the person concerned retains the right to receive benefits referred to in that provision acquired under the legislation of one or more Member States even after taking up residence in another Member State, but also that the acquisition of such entitlement may not be refused on the sole ground that he or she does not reside in the Member State in which the institution responsible for payment is situated.[100]

---

[96] Opinion of the Advocate General in Case C-503/09 Lucy Stewart v Secretary of State for Work and Pensions [2011] ECR I-6497, paragraphs 52 and 55.

[97] Opinion of the Advocate General Cruz Villalón in Case C-503/09 Lucy Stewart v Secretary of State for Work and Pensions [2011] ECR I-6497, paragraphs 36 and 51.

[98] Opinion of the Advocate General Cruz Villalón in Case C-503/09 Lucy Stewart v Secretary of State for Work and Pensions [2011] ECR I-6497, paragraph 53.

[99] Replaced by Regulation 883/2004.

[100] Case C-503/09 Lucy Stewart v Secretary of State for Work and Pensions [2011] ECR I-6497, paragraph 61.

Through this statement, the Court made it clear that the state of origin retains its social responsibility even after a claimant has settled in another Member State. In this regard, it may be observed that the Regulation does not harmonise social welfare benefits and may therefore allow the claimant to receive benefits both from the new state of residence and from the home state.

Even though the national court did not ask for guidance regarding the consequences of citizenship of the Union in order to resolve the case, the CJEU bases all its following reasoning in paragraphs 77–89 on this line of case law. This is particularly striking, because there are no references to Union citizenship in the opinion of the Advocate General. The status of citizens of the Union is repeated by the Court to be the fundamental status of nationals of the Member States.[101] Referring to cases like D'Hoop[102] and Pusa,[103] the Court finds that it would be incompatible with the right to freedom of movement were citizens to receive, in the Member State of which they are nationals, treatment less favourable than that which they would enjoy if they had not availed themselves of the opportunities offered by the Treaty in relation to freedom of movement. The national requirement is then held by the Court not to satisfy the proportionality test.[104]

The motivation inherent in national law of limiting the boundaries of its solidarity system replacing the requirement of contribution with a requirement of past and present residence in the UK, consequently, does not resonate with the Court. Instead, the Court substitutes the national limit of who is entitled to the benefit with its own criteria. The person's connection to the society can be fulfilled by any number of factors.

This line of thinking does not correspond well with the fact that contribution is one factor that is also recognised in the coordination regime. In fact, the former Regulation 1408/71 did not absolutely prohibit residence from constituting, under certain conditions, a criterion of connection to the social welfare system of a Member State in the same way as might a period of employment. This is demonstrated, in particular, by the former Article 18 of the Regulation, which contemplates the possibility of national legislatures making 'the acquisition, retention or recovery of the right to benefits conditional upon the completion of periods of insurance, employment or residence'.

In essence, the opinion of the Advocate General seems to give a wider margin of discretion to the Member States' organisation of their social welfare system, leaving the door open for residence requirements as a legal connecting factor to the national systems provided that the residence requirement is not an additional requirement that only works to exclude possible beneficiaries who would otherwise comply with

[101] Case C-503/09 Lucy Stewart v Secretary of State for Work and Pensions [2011] ECR I-6497, paragraph 80.

[102] Case C-224/98 D'Hoop [2002] ECR I-06191.

[103] Case C-224/02 Pusa [2004] ECR I-5763.

[104] Case C-503/09 Lucy Stewart v Secretary of State for Work and Pensions [2011] ECR I-6497 paragraphs 87–110.

the conditions and be eligible for the benefit in question. However, the CJEU's reasoning based on the provisions on Union citizenship seems to deny the possibility of 'residence-like requirements', because the connecting factor to the national welfare system can always be fulfilled with less restrictive means and thereby respect the right to free movement and residence. The proportionality assessment appears to require that connecting factors in national law do not unconditionally require residence. This backdrop may explain the reasoning of the EFTA Court in the case on child support.

9.5.3 The Facts of the Child Support Case

In the child support case, the EFTA Court apparently interpreted rights of migrant workers to national welfare benefits in the host state. In reality, however, it applied EEA law to broaden the scope of rights holders beyond those who satisfy the national condition of eligibility arguably even beyond the broadening of the scope required by the coordination regime.

The case, which concerned the Norwegian administrative practice for entitlement to child support, was initiated by two unresolved cases. These cases were recorded in the SOLVIT database, an online problem-solving network in which EEA states work together to solve problems caused in the application of internal market law by public authorities. The two cases concerned a Lithuanian mother and a Slovakian mother working and residing with their children in Lithuania and in Slovakia, respectively. In both cases, the parents of the children were separated, and the fathers were residing and working in Norway. The mothers were entitled to child support in their respective states of residence, and the cases only involved a so-called topping-up of the first benefit. The Norwegian administrative practice in question concerned the lack of evaluation of whether a child living together with another parent outside Norway was mainly dependent on the parent who is living in Norway and separated from the other parent.

9.5.4 The Legal Question in the Case: National Law and EEA Law

In Norway, the public contribution of a child benefit is paid to the parent with whom the child lives. According to national law, the benefit is a right for the parent and not for the child. The beneficiary is thus the parent. In a situation where the parents are married, the parents can decide to whom this support is paid. In the case where the parents are divorced, the benefit is paid to the parent with whom the child lives if this person is eligible for the benefit. The parent who does not live with the child has no right to the child benefit regardless of this parent's general rights and obligations as a parent. This means that under national law, the parent (in the two cases above, the mother) must have a sufficient link to the Norwegian welfare system that entitles this person to be a beneficiary and thus eligible for payments.

There is an absolute condition for payment that the child lives with the parent who qualifies for the benefit. In addition, there is a geographical requirement that the child lives with the parent in Norway. For the understanding of the case, it is fundamental to keep these two conditions apart and evaluate them separately.

The second condition of geographical residence in Norway for the right to payment of social security benefits stems from the obvious need to limit rights to benefits to persons who are members of the Norwegian welfare system. The social security system is national in the absence of a harmonised European social security system. Consequently, in every system, a link is required between the beneficiary and the national system responsible for the support. As will be demonstrated, the geographical requirement is, however, modified to accommodate the situation of a migrant worker. The national requirement to have one's habitual abode with the child in the home state was the subject of the case.

In the case of the child support benefit, the adaptation to the coordination regime has caused some changes in the geographical residence requirement. It is important to note, however, that the change concerns the conditions of the parent living with the child in Norway (the second condition) but not a change in terms of the condition whereby only the parent with whom the child lives has the right to general child support (the first condition). In the situation where one of the parents is a worker, is employed in Norway and has his or her habitual abode in the country where the other parent lives with the child, the family will be eligible for the benefit. This modification ensures that a cross-border situation is not deterred. Thus, a worker who has exercised his or her right to take up employment in another EEA state will have rights equal to those of other workers in the state of employment who have not exercised this right. In other words, the requirement of geographical residence with the child in Norway does not apply in a cross-border situation.

In terms of the first and second examples above where the wives and children lived in Lithuania and Slovakia, respectively, the child support was paid to the fathers working in Norway so long as the fathers' habitual abode was with the rest of the family when in Lithuania and Slovakia, respectively. When the parents divorced, custody of the child was given to the mother, and the father no longer lived with the child. Consequently, the father no longer had the right to child support under the Norwegian welfare system. This was a consequence not of any cross-border event but simply of the change in the family situation.

It should be noted that this condition applies equally to national workers. Thus, both national and migrant workers will lose their right to a child benefit if they no longer live with their child.

Comparing the situation of the migrant worker with the situation of a national worker demonstrates that there is no disadvantage to the former category. In the same situation, the national worker who does not live with the child will also be denied the right to child support. Consequently, there was no real argument in the case related to the national practice having the effect of deterring free movement as a consequence of discriminatory treatment. The question is rather whether the other parent has a sufficient link to the Norwegian welfare system that makes this person eligible for benefits. In the two cases from Lithuania and Slovakia, the mothers had no connection to the Norwegian welfare system and were therefore denied the benefit.

The EFTA Court did not approach the case based on an evaluation of whether the parent who was refused the right to the welfare benefit had a sufficient link to the national social welfare system.

9.5.5 The Decision of the EFTA Court

The EFTA Court based its decision on an interpretation of Article 1(f)(i) of the Regulation in combination with Article 73. Article 1(f)(i) lays down the basic requirement for the definition of family members.[105] The purpose of the article is to ensure that a national residence requirement does not deprive a worker in a cross-border situation of the same child benefits as a national worker. To this end, the provision requires that when national legislation regards as a 'member of the family' only a person living under the same roof as the employed person (requiring, for example, regular residence with the child), this condition shall be considered satisfied if the person in question is mainly dependent on that person. The objective is to modify national residence requirements that deter free movement of workers.

The objective of Article 1(f)(i) of the Regulation is to ensure the proper application of a residence requirement in a cross-border situation. Thus, the aim is to make sure that a condition of residence in Norway does not put a migrant worker at a disadvantage compared to fellow workers. The application of the residence requirement in a cross-border situation is ensured by the administrative practice of regular abode as described above.

The other condition for being eligible for child support in the national legislation—namely the right only for the parent who lives with the child to receive child support—has no cross-border implications. Not being able to claim a benefit that fellow workers cannot claim can hardly disadvantage the migrant worker or deter free movement.

This understanding in national law does not mean, however, that Article 1(f)(i) is not applied in Norway, which seemed to be the argument of the EFTA Court. The child falls within the scope of being a family member of the migrant worker. Being a family member is, however, not the only national condition. In order to be eligible for the child benefit, the parent has to live with the child either in Norway or in the home country of the migrant worker. This requirement is independent from the rights and obligations the parent has towards his/her child both for national and for migrant workers. By not respecting this national condition for the eligibility of a

[105] See Regulation 883/2004 Article 1(i)(3).

right to child support, the EFTA Court effectively broadened EEA law to encompass rights holders who were not eligible for the benefit in the national system in question.

In its reasoning, the Court makes a reference to the Slanina case.[106] The Slanina case concerned a different factual and legal situation from the Norwegian administrative practice concerning child support. Ms. Slanina was a divorced Austrian national who had always been the parent having the right to the child benefit. The question in this case was whether her decision to transfer her residence to another Member State (Greece) was a sufficient reason for denying her continued support. It was, in other words, a classical free movement question, namely whether the fact that a person exercises his or her right to move to another Member State means that the state of origin can deny child benefits justified by the lack of fulfilment of the condition that the child's centre of interest and permanent residence must be in Austria. This differs from the child support case, in which the mothers had never been considered eligible for the support. Thus, the child benefit case, unlike the Slanina case, was not about a transfer of geographical residence leading to the denial of the welfare benefit.

Another argument being put forward in the case was that in a purely internal situation, the other parent would normally be eligible for the child support, because this parent would often be residing in Norway. The argument is not especially persuasive given that there is a relevant factual difference between the two situations. Discrimination does not occur when different situations are treated differently. In relation to the entitlement to national welfare benefits, distinguishing between mothers living in Norway and mothers living outside of Norway seems highly relevant. The most relevant comparator to the mothers living with their children in Lithuania and Slovakia and receiving the national child support in these states would be the next-door mothers also living with their child in these states. An underlying justification for the right to a welfare benefit of child support is the cost of raising a child. Residing with your child in Norway entails a completely different level of costs than residing in either Lithuania or Slovakia. As long as the welfare states are still national in nature, residing inside or outside the state is a legitimate distinguishing factor given the need for each state to establish the criteria for membership of and exclusion from its welfare society. Thus, the comparison with a divorced mother living in Norway is neither convincing nor legally accurate.

In the child support case, the EFTA Court had to decide whether an administrative practice of always denying the right to export child benefits in situations where the migrant worker divorced the parent living with the child was compatible with EEA law. In theory, the national rule or the general practice did not violate any specific provisions of Regulation 1408/71.

The administrative practice did not, however, comply with EEA law according to the EFTA Court largely based on its failure to take into account individual circumstances on the part of the claimant. This line of thinking in the decision fits well with

[106] Case C-363/08 Slanina, ECR [2009] I-11111.

the described requirements of Member States imposed by the CJEU in its case law on citizenship rights. The national legislation with the administrative practice failed to consider the individuals in each case and excluded from the right to child benefit those claimants who after divorce no longer lived with the child. The EFTA Court's refusal to accept this national administrative practice and its requirement that the Norwegian administrative authority take individuals into consideration provides another example of ensuring free movement rights being paralleled in the EEA Agreement with developments of EU law.

9.6 Decisional Practice of the EFTA Surveillance Authority: Cases No 65876 and No 65875

The EFTA Surveillance Authority delivered two separate reasoned opinions against both Iceland and Norway for breach of Regulation 1408/71 in relation to national conditions for eligibility for unemployment benefits. Case No 65876 concerned the Icelandic national requirements for eligibility of unemployment benefits. In particular, the condition of having worked on the Icelandic labour market at least 3 months of the 12-month period (later changed to 1 month) was considered incompatible with EEA law.[107] The Icelandic Government argued that the requirement was necessary to prevent 'benefit tourism' and to ascertain that the EEA national had established a genuine link to the labour market.[108]

Case No 65875 concerned the Norwegian national requirements for eligibility of unemployment benefits. In particular, the condition of having worked full time in Norway at least 8 weeks within a period of 12 weeks to aggregate periods of insurance or work accumulated in other EEA states was considered incompatible with EEA law.[109] The Norwegian Government argued that the main condition for transferring periods of insurance or employment is work of a certain length in the state where the person concerned is entitled to unemployment benefit. Furthermore, it must be allowed to require immigrants to establish a minimum relation with the Norwegian working life to obtain the same rights.[110] Furthermore, the Norwegian Government argued that the national requirement was justified as a means to avoid benefit migration.[111]

The EFTA Surveillance Authority argued in both cases that the EEA Agreement ensures free movement rights, including rights in the field of access to national unemployment benefits requiring both EFTA States to change their national requirements. Both cases ended with the Icelandic and the Norwegian Governments adapt-

[107] Reasoned opinion 29 June 2011, Case No 65876.

[108] Reasoned opinion 29 June 2011, Case No 65876, pp. 5 and 8.

[109] Reasoned opinion 29 June 2011, Case No 65875.

[110] Reasoned opinion 29 June 2011, Case No 65875, pp. 7 and 8.

[111] Reasoned opinion 29 June 2011, Case No 65875, p. 9.

ing national legislation in line with the requirements of the Authority. The cases were consequently closed.[112] Along with the EFTA Surveillance Authority's oral and written submission in the case law the decisions demonstrate the view of the Authority on the EEA Agreement and free movement rights for the non-economically active movers.

References

Cousins M (2007) Citizenship, residence and social security. Eur Law Rev 32(3):386–395

Dougan M (2006) The constitutional dimension to the case law on Union citizenship. Eur Law Rev 31(5):613–641

Fenger N (2006) Limits to a dynamic homogeneity between EC law and EEA law. In: Fenger N, Sørensen H, Vesterdorf (eds) Festskrift Claus Gulman. Karnov Group, Copenhagen, pp 131–154

Pennings F (2005) Inclusion and exclusion of persons and benefits in the new co-ordination regulation. In: Spaventa E, Dougan M (eds) Social welfare and EU law. Hart, Oxford, pp 241–260

Sakslien M (2000) The concept of residence and social security: reflections on Finnish, Swedish and community legislation. Eur J Migr Law 2:157–183

Somek A (2007) Solidarity decomposed. Eur Law Rev 32:787–818

Van der Mei AP (2003) Free movement of persons within the European Community cross-border access to public benefits. Hart, Oxford

Verschueren H (2007) European (internal) migration law as an instrument for defining the boundaries of national solidarity systems. Eur J Migr Law 9:307–346

[112] Decisions by the EFTA Surveillance Authority 6 February 2013 in Case No 65876 and 18 January 2012 in Case No 65875.

Chapter 10
Some Reflections on the EEA Integration Process Extending into the System of Social Welfare Benefits for Non-economically Active Moving EEA Citizens

This chapter has analysed the EEA integration process in the field of freedom of movement, residence and equal treatment for non-economically active EEA citizens. The overall question was the extent to which the EU/EFTA institutions applying EEA law have paralleled the increased welfare protection for Union citizens in the EU legal order. In other words, the question was whether the EEA Agreement also requires the Contracting Parties to demonstrate a certain degree of financial solidarity characteristic of the Union citizenship jurisprudence.

The chapter began with a rough outline of the case law from the CJEU supplementing or replacing the secondary legislation with the Treaty provisions on Union citizenship including the changed methodology by the CJEU in cases of Union citizens' rights. The analysis of the case law in the EU legal order demonstrated the requirement on Member States to exercise a certain degree of financial solidarity with citizens of other Member States. Union citizenship creates a supranational notion of citizenship that influences the delicate political and social compromises made when allocating limited resources to non-economically active migrants.[1]

For the EEA analysis, the incorporation of the secondary legislation needed to be addressed. Regarding the incorporation of the Citizens Directive in the EEA Agreement, Decision No 158/2007 by the EEA Committee and in particular the Joint Declaration stating essentially that Union citizenship and immigration law are not part of the EEA Agreement were first analysed. Regarding the incorporation of the revised coordination regime for social security benefits in the EEA, the starting point for the analysis was the case of UK v. Council by the CJEU addressing the question of whether the EEA included a homogenous application of free movement rights for non-economically active persons. The Contracting Parties' view, as stated generally in the Joint Declaration and specifically by the UK and Ireland, seems to

[1] De Witte (2012), p. 699.

K. Fløistad, *The EEA Agreement in a Revised EU Framework for Welfare Services*, Studies in European Economic Law and Regulation 13,
https://doi.org/10.1007/978-3-319-95043-3_10

be opposed to the free movement rights for non-economically active persons being applied homogenously in the EEA.

The analysis of the case law and the administrative practices by the EU/EFTA institutions applying EEA law clearly indicate a different view from that of the Contracting Parties.

The analysis of the case law from the EFTA Court and the administrative practice from the EFTA Surveillance Authority was separated into two sections to distinguish between the rights for non-economically active citizens within the scope of the Citizens Directive and within the scope of rights under the coordination regime. The EFTA Court has interpreted the Citizens Directive on four occasions.[2] In the Clauder, the Gunnarsson and the Jabbi cases, the Directive was interpreted to ensure free movement rights in parallel with the Union citizenship case law in the EU legal order.[3] The EFTA Court has interpreted the coordination regime for social security on several occasions. The cases analysed in more detail here reveal a clear tendency to reach an interpretative outcome in each case to ensure free movement rights for non-economically active citizens in parallel with Union citizenship rights. The EFTA Court ensures a parallel development in the EEA integration process with the corresponding EU law including the same right to free movement, residence and equal treatment for non-economically active citizens. The analysis of the decisional practice of the EFTA Surveillance Authority both in the field of the Citizens Directive and in the field of the coordination regime demonstrates the same tendency. A rather strong statement in the same direction can be seen from the CJEU in the case of UK v. Council.

The material is limited, but some provisional conclusions may be drawn. The right to freedom of movement in the EEA includes not only the explicit rights laid down by the Citizens Directive regarding rights against the host state (such as avoiding exit barriers and the obligation to issue the necessary identity cards in Chapter II of the Citizens Directive) but also the right for the moving individual not to meet certain obstacles to movement from the home state in parallel with the rights for Union citizens in the EU legal order (such as the enjoyment of certain tax benefits/ the right to family reunification). In essence, existing case law and decisional practice support an interpretation of the same degree of financial solidarity for EEA nationals under the EEA Agreement as required for Union citizens in the territory of the EU. To this end, there is no support in the institutional practice analysed to interpret the social welfare rights for moving non-economically active citizens differently even if EEA law does not include the Treaty provisions on Union citizenship.

In conclusion, the case law from the CJEU and the EFTA Court and the decisional practice of the EFTA Surveillance Authority have broadened the scope of EEA law to encompass more rights holders and consequently to limit the states' legislative freedom also outside the area of economically active persons. In other words, the EEA Agreement requires the opening of national social welfare systems beyond economically active persons. This has consequences both for the EU Member States and for the EFTA States as Contracting Parties to the Agreement. From the perspective

[2] Cases E-15/12, E-4/11, E-26/13, E-28/15.

[3] The Wahl case did not concern a question of welfare services.

of the conceptualisation of welfare systems, this paralleling of the Union citizenship rights in the EU legal order in the EEA represents a significant change. Prior to the Union citizenship concept entitlement to welfare provision was a matter of national policymaking and could legitimately be limited to those who either belonged to the welfare community through the link of nationality or had established entitlement through economic contribution. In other words, it was compatible with the EEA Agreement to uphold the traditional link of belonging that justified subsidisation of the less fortunate through welfare benefits. Post Union citizenship, the Contracting Parties have obligations under EEA law to include also those who are neither nationals nor active economic contributors, and the legislative freedom to require consumption of social welfare benefits on the national territory has been limited.

There is a lot to say in favour of extending access to social welfare benefits to non-economically active moving EEA citizens. A higher degree of mobility, as an aim that is recognised by all Contracting Parties, would certainly be promoted by inclusion into the social systems of the EEA states. The same can be said with respect to the integration of non-economically active EEA citizens into the social assistance systems of their host EEA state. Yet, it may be argued that equal access to social benefits is of primary importance for the EEA Contracting Parties and therefore legitimately part of their (political) decision making. Expanding the EEA Agreement and deciding about a sensitive and complicated issue of financial solidarity arising from the free movement of non-economically active EEA citizens arguably must be decided by the Contracting Parties. When the Contracting Parties make the decision, national constitutional requirements regarding the involvement of parliaments will also be appropriately respected.

It is claimed here that the development of a type of social citizenship under the EEA Agreement is a legislative matter rather than part of the EU/EFTA institutions judicial and administrative competence. Although Article 4 EEA contains a general prohibition of discrimination on grounds of nationality, the issue of social rights, including right to family reunification of non-economically active moving EEA citizens and the scope of application of the equal treatment clause is based on the competence of the Contracting Parties to include access to social welfare and related systems. There is a lack of a sufficient theoretical basis in the legislative provisions of the EEA Agreement for the institutions to apply the homogeneity principle to parallel Union citizenship in the EEA. Union citizenship is based on a vision of the EU that has never been paralleled in the EEA Agreement. The homogeneity principle seems as a weak legal basis for a fundamental expansion of social welfare rights of EEA citizens with the corresponding limitations on the Contracting Parties' legislative powers in the field of access to social welfare benefits.

Reference

De Witte F (2012) Transnational solidarity and the mediation of conflicts of justice. Eur Law J 18(5):694–710

Part III
The EEA Integration Process and the Financing of Public Services: Applying State Aid Rules to Welfare Services

Chapter 11
State Aid Law and Articles 14, 106 and 107 TFEU and Articles 59 and 61 EEA

11.1 Aim and Background

From the very start, the EEA Agreement has included the task of controlling state aid. The control of state aid is an important means of ensuring that equal conditions of competition within the EEA are not distorted by the actions of states. With the adoption of the EEA Agreement, similar state aid rules to those existing in the EU legal order became applicable to the EFTA States.

A basic feature of the EEA Agreement is the creation of a two-pillar system. This system implies, in the field of state aid, that the EFTA Surveillance Authority is responsible for the control of the EEA state aid rules when aid is granted by the EFTA States, whereas the Commission is responsible for the application of state aid rules in the TFEU when aid is granted by EU Member States.[1]

In the EU legal order, the substantive primary law provisions in the chapter on competition and state aid have remained largely untouched by the process of Treaty revisions in Maastricht, Amsterdam, Nice and Lisbon. However, the position in the EU's constitutional framework of competition and state aid law and policy has shifted significantly as a result of the revision processes in the amending treaties.[2] The revised constitutional framework in the EU is now more favourable to public services,[3] but that does not mean that they are freely governed at the national level

---

[1]The power of the Authority is characterised as symmetrical with the Commission powers in the EU pillar, see Karlsson (2014), p. 470.

[2]An analysis of the constitutional implications of state aid law can be found in de Cecco (2013), see also de Cecco (2012). On the need for a legal framework in the EU for the provision of SGEI, see Krajewski (2008), pp. 377–398, for a general and updated state aid analysis, see Hancher et al. (2016).

[3]The term public services usually includes both utilities and welfare services, see Cremona (2011), chapter 1, pp. 3–4 and Sauter (2014), chapter 1.3, pp. 9–10. The focus here is on welfare services.

K. Fløistad, *The EEA Agreement in a Revised EU Framework for Welfare Services*, Studies in European Economic Law and Regulation 13,
https://doi.org/10.1007/978-3-319-95043-3_11

without EU law having an impact. Perhaps paradoxically, by securing guarantees for public services at the EU level in the constitutional texts, the Member States have also outlined and legitimised the increased application of EU law to public services, including the state aid scrutiny, by the Commission to be applied to largely non-economic welfare services.[4] No parallel revised constitutional framework to secure guarantees for public services exists in the EEA Agreement.

In this Part III, the nature of the changing role for the provision of public services and their financing in the EU legal order provides the basis for the subsequent EEA analysis. The financing of public services through subsidies is one of the tools for the state to pursue national policy objectives. Yet, the presence of EU/EEA rules on state aid control determines the shape and limits the availability of this tool. State aid law places significant constraints on Governmental decision making and may be in itself at times the expression of a fundamental political choice.

The previous Part I and Part II demonstrate the EEA integration process breaking with the traditional requirement of an economic activity for rights and obligations under EEA law to apply. The paralleling in the EEA legal order of free movement rights supports the argument that the EEA integration process has moved beyond economic efficiency and market integration even without paralleling the revised constitutional framework of the EU legal order. Hence, through the homogenous development of the law, the EEA integration process now to some extent protects EEA citizens in their capacity as citizens regardless of their economic contributions.

Citizens' protection can also be observed in the evolving EU law concerning the provision of public services and the EU concept of an economic activity. The EU integration process now includes welfare concerns (social values) as part of the law that interacts with and influences upon the application of not only free movement rules but also the provisions of competition and state aid. This chapter sets out to explore whether the EEA integrations process also includes parallel welfare concerns and, in so far as there is evidence, how these interact with and influence upon the application of EEA state aid law. In other words, the analysis centres around the significance of a lack of a parallel revised constitutional framework in the EEA and the exercise of state aid scrutiny to potentially extend to largely non-economic public services in the EFTA States.

The same concern is raised in this Part III as in the two foregoing Parts I and II, namely whether the EEA Agreement provides a sufficient legal framework for quite far-reaching intervention in the domestic social order of the EFTA States. Obviously, a single EEA market will not be realised if each EEA state is free to support its national business, including in the field of welfare services operating in the market. Articles 59 and 61 EEA intend to address this. However, there are sectors of society in which very few foreign competitors are eager to enter and in which it is national private businesses that want to supplement the public sector. These sectors include social housing, healthcare, local media, culture and education. Such services are

---

[4] See also Damjanovic (2013), p. 1691 stating that the Commission has gradually shifted the Member States' welfare regimes from the category of non-economic to economic SGI.

often local and sensitive to the needs of the immediate population with a historical and cultural bias. To what extent has the EEA integration process evolved in parallel with the EU legal order and entrusted the EFTA institutions with the parallel discretionary state aid powers in these sensitive sectors? What is crucial in Part III as well as in Parts I and II is the scope for national policies that remains available within the constraints of EEA law.

The chapter is divided into two sections. The first section concerns the legal tools to protect state welfare services from EU/EEA competition and state aid law. This section deals with the concepts of economic activity, undertaking and the Altmark-doctrine and discusses limits on the Commission's and the EFTA Surveillance Authority's state aid competences. The analysis in Chap. 12 demonstrates that the EEA integration process has developed in parallel with the EU integration process in delimiting the competence of the Authority in areas of state welfare activities from competition and state aid rules.

However, these concepts and doctrines do not exclude welfare services from the scope of EU law. There is a range of public services, including social services, which operate in a market and which are subject to state aid scrutiny to ensure a level playing field. What is argued here is that the state aid scrutiny in the EU legal order has moved to go beyond controlling the efficiency and functionality of markets and now reaches quite far into the domestic social order of the state, in particular in largely non-economic sectors. This phenomenon has increased the institutional powers significantly, and in Chap. 13, the EEA integration process regarding state aid and welfare services is analysed based on this perspective.

EU policy with regard to financing public services is largely dominated by the Commission. The institution combines a number of different roles.[5] The Commission tends to prepare its policies by issuing Communications.[6] These soft law instruments are also often accompanied with binding instruments. A good example regarding welfare services is provided by the 2005 and 2012 Altmark frameworks analysed throughout Part III and in particular in Sect. 12.5.[7] Illustrative is also the regime governing the financing of public service broadcasting adopted by the Commission first in 2001 and later in the current guidelines from 2009 analysed extensively in Chap. 13.[8]

[5] The role of the Commission to have exclusive responsibility for initiating proposals for EU legislation is not shared by the EFTA Surveillance Authority given that there is no independent legislative process in the EFTA pillar. The role of guardianship of the Treaties/EEA Agreement, i.a. through the opening of infringements proceedings against Member States/EFTA States and the role of a competition authority in the areas of state aid, antitrust and mergers are both paralleled in the EEA.

[6] The EFTA Surveillance Authority issue parallel Communications applicable to EFTA States.

[7] The first Communication relevant for public services was issued in 1996 and pioneered the concept of services of general interest (SGI). Article 4(2) TFEU add SGI to the activities of the Union (previous Article 3 EC).

[8] The reasons for exempting state aid for public service broadcasting is set out in current Protocol 29 TFEU on the system of public broadcasting which was first added to primary law by the Amsterdam Treaty.

Hence, the next sections set out to explore whether the EEA Agreement has developed in parallel in the field of scrutinising the financing of welfare services. The case study examined in detail is the media field, concentrating on public service broadcasting. This case study includes an analysis of the significance of the lack of the Amsterdam Protocol and the revised Article 107(3)(d) in the EEA in this sector. Outside the field of public service broadcasting, other potential areas for case studies to illuminate these questions would be in the sectors of social housing, healthcare, local media, culture and education.[9] Public service broadcasting is therefore not the only area to illuminate the extent to which the state aid competence of the EFTA Surveillance Authority has reached into the domestic social orders of the EFTA States. The area of public service broadcasting provides, however, an illuminating example.

11.2 Organisational Choices: Public Services and the Economic/Non-Economic Divide

Public services lie in the interplay between public and private. They challenge the roles of state and market and raise questions of the space remaining for the states' policy choices.[10] For the purpose of EU/EEA as opposed to Member States'/EFTA States' competence to regulate/freely finance public services, a line has to be drawn between economic activities and non-economic activities.[11] The state activity of organising and providing a public service of a non-economic nature in principle escapes the reach of EU/EEA law. However, the definition of what constitutes economic activity is considered to be an EU/EEA concept and hence not left to each state to decide. To this end, the EU/EFTA institutions applying EU/EEA law have significant definitional powers on the reach of EU/EEA state aid law into state activity.

Apparent from the revision processes in the amending Treaties, in particular the Amsterdam and the Lisbon Treaties, there is a move in the EU legal order towards the inclusion of an increasing number of public services to fall within the scope of EU law. The Commission has referred to a 'joint responsibility' of the EU and the Member States recognised by Article 14 TFEU and Protocol No 26 on Services of General Interest.[12] According to the Commission, public services can be divided

---

[9] Social housing and education is examined more briefly in Sect. 11.5.

[10] On public services and market integration in the EU legal order, see Cremona (2011), see also the analysis of the relationship between the state and the market in Weiler (2008), pp. 5–41.

[11] This divide also applies for the free movement of services provisions. A service is economic if it is normally provided for remuneration, although it is not necessarily the recipient that pays for the service, see Part I.

[12] See Commission Communication, Services of General Interest, including social services of general interest: a new European commitment, COM (2007) 725 final 1 and 3.

between SGEI and non-economic SGI.[13] The latter involve, according to the Commission, 'traditional state prerogatives such as police, justice and statutory social security schemes' and 'air-navigation safety or anti-pollution surveillance'. The Commission has concluded that, in practice, 'almost all services offered within the social field can be considered economic activities'.[14] Considering almost all services offered within the social field as economic activities means subjecting them to competition and state aid law with the inherent powers of the EU institutions.[15] In the words of Ulla Neergaard, the Commission claims regulatory power in the grey zone.[16] The concept of social services of general economic interest (SSGEI) has entered EU terminology and has been extensively analysed also in terms of legal consequences in the field of state aid.[17]

According to Baquero Cruz, he does not believe applying state aid rules on social services damages 'the provision of social services or puts economic interests over social policy objectives'.[18] Other academics argue that the EU is inherently biased in the direction of favouring economic objectives producing a liberal bias and a social deficit.[19] Clearly, there are differences of opinion on whether the EU institutions are well equipped to find the appropriate balance between economic and social objectives for the provision of public services and whether the balance struck has been appropriate. This is, however, not the object of concern in this analysis of the EEA integration process. The matter of interest here is a point not really addressed by Baquero Cruz,[20] namely that in the balancing act, it matters where or by whom the decision is taken. Therefore, it matters whether the EU institutions have been given the competence to conduct a state aid review of a national measure or whether the measure is considered to remain within national competences. In other words, the delimitation itself, including the question of which institution can make the delimitation decision, is one of the topics discussed in the context of the EEA integration process, state aid and welfare services.[21]

---

[13] Services of General Interest, including social services of general interest: a new European commitment, COM (2007) 725 final 4 and 5, see also the division in Protocol 26 TFEU.

[14] COM 2007(725), p. 5, see also Commission's Communication on Social services of general interest, COM(2006) 177.

[15] An academic analysis of the developments in EU law for public services in general and for social services specifically can be found in Szyszczak et al. (2011).

[16] Neergaard (2008), p. 95.

[17] The term was first mentioned in the Commission Report to the Laeken European Council, COM(2001) 598, and continuous to be used in soft law measures, see for a comprehensive academic study of the concept in EU law in Neergaard et al. (2013).

[18] Cruz (2013), p. 296.

[19] Baquero Cruz refers to Fritz Scharpf as a foremost advocate of this thesis, Cruz (2013), p. 288.

[20] Except to some extent at the end of the paper where doubts are expressed as to the Member States being the right level to find the optimal regulatory mechanism for social policies based on the understanding that in the national, regional or local context, social policies are captured by the entrenched position of various groups, see Cruz (2013), pp. 312–313.

[21] As noted by Damjanovic, the state aid rules have a potentially broader scope of application than the competition rules given that they also apply to state advantages principally granted for the

The Commission has interpreted the prohibition of state aid in Article 107 TFEU as granting wide discretionary powers to the Commission. Arguably, the Commission, when applying this power, has taken on a policymaker role. In the literature, the Commission's discretionary powers is said to have grown beyond controlling the efficiency and functionality of markets to also include safeguarding necessary national interests (including welfare concerns).[22] In the EU legal order, the growing policymaker role played by the Commission through the exercise of its state aid competence has been characterised as 'a total devolution of powers from the Council to the Commission'.[23] This role played by the Commission arguably exceeds the preventive control system targeted at addressing distortions of competition that had originally been envisioned in the prohibition of state aid in the Treaty of Rome.

In the EU legal order, this increasing policymaker role of the Commission has been officially sanctioned through various primary law amendments. The most recent amendment is paragraph 4 within the wording of Article 108 TFEU introduced by the Treaty of Lisbon. This provision has promoted to a primary source of legislation the power of the Commission to adopt block exemption regulations meant to set out the categories of aid and the conditions under which Member States can be exempted from prior notification under Article 108(3) TFEU. Inherent in appropriately reconciling the interests involved—both market and non-market concerns—is the legal recognition of the Commission as the institution vested with such wide legislative powers.

No parallel legal recognition of the EFTA Surveillance Authority has been made in the EEA Agreement. Protocol 26 EEA[24] lays down the agreed powers and functions of the EFTA Surveillance Authority in the field of state aid as follows:

> **Article 1**
> The EFTA Surveillance Authority shall, in an agreement between the EFTA States, be entrusted with equivalent powers and similar functions to those of the EC Commission, at the time of the signature of the Agreement, for the application of the competition rules applicable to State aid of the Treaty establishing the European Economic Community, enabling the EFTA Surveillance Authority to give effect to the principles expressed in Articles 1(2)(e), 49 and 61 to 63 of the Agreement.

In the later Agreement between the EFTA States—the Surveillance and Court Agreement (SCA)—Article 5(1) states that

provision of non-economic activities if the entity also provides economic activities and these two operating areas are not properly separated so that there is a threat of cross-subsidisation. An example of where this issue is relevant is public hospitals, Damjanovic (2013), p. 1698.

[22] Santa Maria (2015), p. 2, confer also the study made by Piernas Lòpez (2015).

[23] Santa Maria (2015), p. 2.

[24] Protocol 3 to the SCA lays down in more detail the Authority's powers and functions.

> The EFTA Surveillance Authority shall, in accordance with the provisions of this Agreement and the provisions of the EEA Agreement and in order to ensure the proper functioning of the EEA Agreement:
>
> (a) ensure the fulfilment by the EFTA States of their obligations under the EEA Agreement and this Agreement;
>
> (b) ensure the application of the rules of the EEA Agreement on competition;
>
> [...].

The competence is limited in scope to the provisions of the EEA Agreement or the SCA Agreement. The same limitation is clear in Article 5(2) when the Authority may

> (b) formulate recommendations, deliver opinions and issue notices or guidelines on matters dealt with in the EEA Agreement, if that Agreement or the present Agreement expressly so provides or if the EFTA Surveillance Authority considers it necessary;

The same limitation is reiterated in Article 24 SCA providing that

> The EFTA Surveillance Authority shall, in accordance with Articles 49, 61 to 64 and 109 of, and Protocols 14, 26, 27, and Annexes XIII, section I(iv), and XV to, the EEA Agreement, as well as subject to the provisions contained in Protocol 3 to the present Agreement, give effect to the provisions of the EEA Agreement concerning State aid as well as ensure that those provisions are applied by the EFTA States.
>
> In application of Article 5(2)(b), the EFTA Surveillance Authority shall, in particular, upon the entry into force of this Agreement, adopt acts corresponding to those listed in Annex I.

Accordingly, the state aid competence of the Authority is limited according to Article 1 in Protocol 26 EEA to the Authority being entrusted with 'equivalent powers and similar functions to those of the EC Commission, *at the time of the signature of the Agreement*' (emphasis added) and substantively limited by the SCA Article 5(1) to the scope of the SCA and the EEA Agreement.

Annex XV to the EEA Agreement contains relevant EU legislation applicable to the EFTA States in the field of state aid. Included here of relevance for public services is the Commission Decision No. 2012/21/EU of 20 December 2011 on the application of Article 106(2) TFEU to state aid in the form of public service compensation granted to certain undertakings entrusted with the operation of SGEI.

In addition, annex XV EEA lists various frameworks, letters from the Commission to the Member States, Commission Communications and references to Commission Annual Reports on competition policy.

The field of publicly financed welfare services therefore provides another suitable case study to illuminate the overall objective of this book for the following reasons. First, if the EFTA Surveillance Authority's discretionary power in state aid review has grown beyond controlling efficiency and functionality of markets to also include safeguarding necessary national interests (including welfare concerns), this adds to the understanding of the EEA integration process to move beyond the original objective of economic activity and market integration. Second, the role of the Commission as a policymaker in state aid cases corresponds with the changed constitutional framework for the EU legal order. Reference is made to the new aims and values recognised through primary law changes beginning with the Maastricht Treaty as outlined in Sect. 1.5 in the introduction. Regarding public services and public broadcasting in particular, the impact of primary law changes gathered headway with the Amsterdam Treaty, which included both Article 16 EC (now Article 14 TFEU) and the Amsterdam Protocol. Furthermore, the legislative role of the Commission has been officially sanctioned through various primary law amendments.[25] There is no corresponding revised constitutional framework in the EEA Agreement. Third, the institutions applying EEA law have rendered decisions that, in various ways, have had to reconcile the lack of equivalent primary law provisions in this field with the principles of dynamism and homogeneity in the EEA Agreement.[26]

11.3 Public Services in the EU Legal Order: Models of Welfare Integration

The drafters of the original Treaty of Rome had seen the need to include provisions for public undertakings and state monopolies, but the delivery of public services was for many years largely left unscrutinised by EU institutions. In fact, the Member States' traditional structures of welfare provision through typically state monopolies remained untouched by EU law virtually until the late 1980s.[27] The dismantling of national monopolies, referred to as a 'marketisation' process, in particular for utilities like electronic communications, energy and transport, was the beginning of a new era whereby the EU no longer existed alongside national governments but began to touch fundamental national policy choices in the provision of public services. This new era did not stop with the mentioned sectors but evolved later to include the application of EU law in the provision of public services, such as welfare services touching healthcare,[28] educational services,[29] social services[30] and cultural services.[31]

[25] For an informative analysis of the revised constitutional framework for public services in the EU legal order see Bauby (2011), pp. 19–35.

[26] This is particularly clear regarding the issuing of parallel Guidelines in the field of state aid by the EFTA Surveillance Authority, http://www.eftasurv.int/state-aid/legal-framework/state-aid-guidelines/.

[27] Napolitano (2005), pp. 565–581.

[28] The increased right to patient mobility is an example, see Chap. 3.

[29] The increased right to student financing in cross-border situations is an example, see Chap. 4.

[30] An example in the field of social housing is widely discussed for the so-called Dutch case, see Gruis and Elsinga (2014), pp. 463–469. Rights to welfare benefits in general as well the protection of cross-border patients' rights health services provide other examples.

[31] This can be illustrated by the effect of the liberalisation of the broadcasting market on the provision of public broadcasting by many considered of essential value for democratic, social and cultural concerns, The Authority's practice in the cultural area (film support) Decisions No. 32/02/COL and No. 169/02/COL approving aid schemes for film production and film-related activities, see also Decision No 430/08/COL on support schemes to audiovisual production.

The vehicles to initiate the liberalisation processes were primarily the primary law provisions on competition laying down the prohibition of an abuse of a dominant position (now Article 102 TFEU), the incompatibility with the Treaty of providing state aid (now Article 107 TFEU) and the public undertaking provision (now Article 106 TFEU). All of these articles are paralleled in the EEA through Articles 54, 61 and 59 EEA, respectively. In the following, the focus is on the application of state aid competence in shaping the provision of public services.

In the wake of the single market programme and therefore at the time of the adoption of the EEA Agreement, liberalisation of key public services was high on the agenda. Controversies arose over the application of the free movement rules, the role of state aid in relation to public services obligations and the use of competition policy.[32] There was general agreement on the principle of liberalisation but concerns over how to preserve specificities of public services. The EU action was criticised for leaving little room for broader social and political considerations[33] Applying competition and state aid law to public services threatened, in some instances, to bring a close to the public service tradition.[34] Partly reconsidering this approach, several initiatives were introduced to emphasise the necessity to strike a balance between marketisation and the general interest objectives entrusted to public services.[35] This process has been characterised as the EU engaging in welfare integration.[36] There is no 'one-size-fits-all' approach, and a plurality of models for EU welfare integration has been identified in the literature.[37]

It is beyond the scope of this book to analyse EU welfare integration in the field of public services in general.[38] Utilities (electronic communications, gas, electricity, post and transport) are now generally subject to liberalisation and the harmonised secondary law framework.[39] The discussion here is limited to the welfare services that have only more recently come under the influence of EU/EEA law and with no comparable uniform pattern of liberalisation and reregulation. Furthermore, it suffices here to identify certain elements of EU welfare integration in the field of welfare services with limited, if any, economic or market elements. The purpose is to identify a legal development upon which to compare and contrast the EEA integration process.

32 Cases in the healthcare sector serve as useful illustrations, see Chap. 3.

33 Ross (2000), pp. 22–38, Cruz (2005), pp. 169–212.

34 Napolitano (2005), p. 566 with further references in Chap. 1 and footnote 3.

35 And this process is ongoing, see the Report 9 May 2010, A New Strategy for the Single Market: At the Service of Europe's Economy and Society, President of the Commission Mario Monti, see also the SGEI packages from 2005 and 2011.

36 Damjanovic and de Witte (2009), pp. 53–96, see also Dougan and Spaventa (2005) and De Búrca (2005).

37 See extensive references to the literature above.

38 A significant body of literature analyses public services in the EU, see for fairly recent contributions, i.a. Sauter (2014), see also Cremona (2011).

39 Sauter (2014), p. 3 and chapter 4.

Heike Schweitzer has identified three typical patterns of welfare integration models in the EU in the field of public services, and the last model is of particular interest here.[40] The three models are as follows:

Welfare integration in the field of public services began with the universal service model in liberated sectors like communications, energy and transport. This model was created by first liberalising the particular sectors and then later by reregulating them through secondary legislation. The model transformed the system of welfare provision traditionally used by the Member States in these areas. The model changed from provision by public monopoly undertakings to provision by primarily an open competitive market accompanied by a regulatory safety net. Both the liberalisation process and including the adopted secondary legislation in these sectors were largely paralleled in the EEA Agreement.[41]

The universal service model essentially just guaranteed the universal coverage of certain services at affordable prices, that is, against an adequate remuneration. The universal service model typical for telecommunications, postal services and, to some extent, energy is based on a presumption that the protection of consumer interests and full competition can be made compatible by an adequate set of framework rules. A different approach has been chosen for public passenger transport where Schweitzer has identified the model termed regulated competition. This model acknowledges that a political choice to ensure a level of services that significantly exceeds the level the market would provide may imply a need to uphold exclusive rights, but it introduces competition for the markets at regular intervals. This model of consecutive monopolies has also been paralleled in the EEA Agreement in the relevant sectors.[42]

The third model identified by Heike Schweitzer, which is the one analysed in Chap. 13, concerns a public service of such a kind that it completely defies 'marketisation'. For this service, even competition for the market is not viable. This is true for a public service task that is inherently tied to some form of 'public ethos or value rationality'[43] and would thus change in character were it provided privately and according to market rationality. This last category includes public service broadcasting, which is examined in detail in the case study.

---

[40] Schweitzer (2011), p. 43.

[41] Like in the sectors of network industries and energy.

[42] Like in the sector of transport as demonstrated below i.a. in the case of Hurtigruten.

[43] The terms are taken by Schweitzer from Max Weber, see Schweitzer (2011), p. 43, see Chap. 3 in footnote 25.

11.4 The Changed Constitutional Framework for Public Services in the EU Integration Process

11.4.1 Setting the Scene: Articles 106 and 107 TFEU (Articles 59 and 61 EEA)

Before going into the changes of primary law in the EU legal order, it is necessary to recall the basic provisions concerning public services (in the EU Treaties regulated as SGEI).[44] This is Articles 106 and 107 TFEU, which were both part of the original Treaty of Rome (then Articles 90(2) and 92 EEC). Both articles are paralleled in the EEA with Articles 59 and 61 EEA.

Article 107 TFEU states that any aid granted by a Member State in any form that distorts or threatens to distort competition by favouring certain undertakings is incompatible with the internal market.[45] In short, this provision limits Member States' ability to fund public services (delivered outside the public sphere) in line with the overall objective of creating a market of equal conditions of competition. Article 106(1) makes it clear that this ban on state aid also applies in the case of public undertakings and on undertakings to which Member States grant special or exclusive rights. An exception to this general ban can be found in Article 106(2). According to this article, undertakings entrusted with the operation of SGEI are only subject to the application of the rules in the Treaty insofar as such rules do not obstruct the performance in law or in fact of the particular task assigned to them.

Article 106(2) TFEU became especially important in the early 1990s when the CJEU referred to it more often and began intensively to interpret its rather complicated wording and structure.[46] The context for this case law concerned the transformation of the public sector in the Member States (largely paralleled in the EFTA States). Services that used to be (before the late 80s and 90s) provided by the state or by public enterprises were increasingly liberalised and privatised. The vehicles in the EU for this transformation were internal market, competition and state aid law. However, the requirements of EU law through the rules on internal market, competition and state aid were often in conflict with traditional models of organising and financing SGEI in the Member States. The modification to the full application of

---

[44] As pointed out by Sauter the term public service is fundamentally wider than SGEI because it refers to the service as a whole not just to that element of the service that is part of or required to ensure a public service obligation or USO that will constitute an SGEI, Sauter (2014), p. 10.

[45] A measure must satisfy the following five cumulative conditions for Article 107 (1)TFEU (Article 61(1)EEA) to apply: (i) aid must be granted through state resources, (ii) it must confer an economic advantage which is not received in the normal course of business, (iii) the advantage must favour undertakings, (iv) be selective by favouring certain undertakings or the production of certain goods, and (v) it must distort competition and affect trade between Member States (EEA states), see also Chap. 12 in footnote 3.

[46] Leading cases include Case C-41/90 Höfner and Elser [1991] ECR I-1979, Case C-320/91 Corbeau [1993] ECR I-2533, Case C-393/92, Almelo [1994] ECR I-1477 and Case C-475/99 Ambulanz Glöckner [2001] ECR I-8089.

internal market, competition and state aid law for SGEI is Article 106(2). It contains an exception ground for undertakings entrusted with the operation of SGEI. In general, Article 106(2) TFEU serves to reconcile internal market and competition requirements (including the prohibition of state aid) with Member States' desire to deliver SGEI.

Even if a provision such as Article 106(2) TFEU illustrates that economic- and market-oriented objectives might be surpassed in the EU, two aspects of Article 106(2) is commented upon in order to better understand the later changes in primary law providing the revised constitutional framework for public services in the EU. First, as a derogation from the Treaty, the CJEU interpreted the provision narrowly to coincide with the Court's general understanding of exceptions.[47] The wording in the first part of the paragraph is also clear, in that the Treaty rules and in particular the competition rules do apply to undertakings entrusted with the operation of SGEI. Second, there is no express mention in the provision itself of SGEI as a value to be promoted. On the contrary, the provision emphasises competition as the value in its introductory statement. Furthermore, the notion of 'obstructing performance' as a condition for an exception to applying Treaty rules indicates an economic analysis based on the risk of harm to the market as the starting point for the analysis.[48]

The proportionality test enshrined in Article 106(2) consists of an evaluation to determine whether there can be exemption from the internal market/state aid/competition rules. In other words, is an exemption necessary to prevent hindrance to the general interest tasks assigned to the undertaking? A strict approach to the test was developed by the Commission in the early stages of application of the Article. In addition, the CJEU tended to adopt a narrow view of the scope of Article 106(2) exception given the importance of completing the internal market. Thus, both the Commission and the EU Courts considered in effect that it had to be practically impossible for the general interest task to be achieved if the internal market/state aid/competition rules were applied in order to rely on the exception.[49] Moreover, if an alternative means of fulfilling the task that was more compatible with the internal market/state aid/competition rules could be found, that in itself meant that Article 106(2) could not be relied on to provide an exemption.[50]

The approach of adopting a narrow view of the scope of Article 106(2) can be seen for example in the case of Sacchi where the Court set a high threshold for the application of the exception and furthermore in the RTT case in 1991.[51] It was even present as late as 1997 in Air Inter.[52]

---

[47] For instance Case C-174/97 FFSA [1998] ECR I-1303, paragraph 173.

[48] Ross (2000), p. 24.

[49] See the in-depth analysis of this early approach in Prosser (2005).

[50] See i.a. Cases like Case 155/73 Giuseppe Sacchi [1974] ECR 40, paragraph 15, Case 18/88 RTT [1991] ECR I-05941 paragraph 22, T-260/94 Air Inter EU:T:1994:265, paragraph 138.

[51] Case 18/88 RTT [1991] ECR I-05941.

[52] T-260/94 Air Inter EU:T:1994:265, paragraph 138.

To illuminate how strict the approach was, a decision from the Commission is illustrative:

> It is not sufficient in this regard that compliance with the provisions of the Treaty makes the performance of the particular task more complicated. A possible limitation of the application of the rules on competition can be envisaged only in the event that the undertaking concerned has no other technically and economically feasible means of performing its particular task.[53]

Since then, there has been a development away from the early approach of seeing SGEI as an obstruction to the creation of an internal market. Instead, SGEI are gradually seen as commendable and positive and as recognition of citizenship rights.[54] In this context, the concern moved away from trying to limit the scope of such services and instead towards ameliorating and facilitating their delivery. This development is reflected also in the changes of primary law in the EU, which is the subject for the next section.

11.4.2 Changing the Recognition of the Value and Special Role of SGEI and SGI: Article 14 TFEU, Article 36 Charter of Fundamental Rights, Protocol 26 TFEU

In light of the earlier described interpretation by the EU institutions of Article 106(2) as a limited exception, there were general demands to recognise the value and special role of SGEI. In other words, the limitation on the full application of internal market/state aid/competition law was not seen as sufficient to protect the provision of public services. As a reaction to these calls, namely to further limit the application of law based on economic considerations on the provision of public services, the Treaty of Amsterdam introduced a new provision to the EU Treaty, namely Article 16 EC (now Article 14 TFEU).

The wording of this provision in its present form is as follows:

> Without prejudice to Article 4 of the Treaty on European Union or to Articles 93, 106 and 107 of this Treaty, and given the place occupied by services of general economic interest in the shared values of the Union as well as their role in promoting social and territorial cohesion, the Union and the Member States, each within their respective powers and within the scope of application of the Treaties, shall take care that such services operate on the basis of principles and conditions, particularly economic and financial conditions, which enable them to fulfil their missions. The European Parliament and the Council, acting by means of regulations in accordance with the ordinary legislative procedure, shall establish

[53] Commission decision (EEC) 82/371 IV/29.995 Navewa-Anseau [1982] paragraph 66, see Prosser (2005).

[54] See Report 9 May 2010, A New Strategy for the Single Market: At the Service of Europe's Economy and Society, President of the Commission Mario Monti.

these principles and set these conditions without prejudice to the competence of Member States, in compliance with the Treaties, to provide, to commission and to fund such services.

There is academic discussion as to the interpretation of this added provision in primary law. On the one side, it is pointed out that the wording of the provision states clearly that the Article is '*without prejudice*' to Articles 93, 106 and 107 TFEU and that the provision therefore has limited influence on the interpretation of these articles.[55] Furthermore, a separate declaration stated that (then) Article 16 EC shall be implemented with full respect for the jurisprudence of the CJEU.[56] Both these elements therefore suggest a limited substantial change of EU law with the introduction of this provision.

There is, however, no doubt that the provision signalled a broad endorsement of the value of SGEI. The provisions regulating SGEI were originally only located in the chapter concerning rules on competition. Rules on competition will often be interpreted in view of a more market economic approach. It is therefore particularly striking how the general aims have developed to recognise that SGEI in themselves are located in the 'shared values of the Union' and they have a role to play in 'promoting social and territorial cohesion'.

Malcolm Ross has characterised the provision as having an interpretative capacity to shape a European policy space for the development and regulation of competition and public services.[57] Prosser has argued convincingly on the new legal environment for the provision of SGEI after the changes made by the Amsterdam Treaty. Instead of seeing SGEI as hindering the creation of a single market, the concern is instead towards improving their delivery.

In the following, the literature demonstrating that Article 14 TFEU together with other primary law changes indeed have made a difference for the provision of SGEI in EU law will be presented. In line with other general tendencies, Article 14 TFEU is undoubtedly evidence of a reorientation of Treaty goals and priorities. Rather than focusing only on market efficiency, the provision fits with the language of shared values, cohesion and cultural diversity discussed in the introduction in Sect. 1.5. In fact, the increasing importance being attached to non-economic values is sometimes said to be the new model of EU competition law.[58] The provision makes clear that the availability of the derogation is to be measured by a balancing test based upon competing priorities rather than constraining that choice by requiring a limited economic test to be satisfied before the normal market rules can be

[55] Krajewski claims that the provision did not change the law substantially, see Krajewski (2008), p. 377, 379 whereas Baquero Cruz claimed there was a substantial change in Cruz (2005), pp. 172–198. See also Prosser (2005).

[56] Declaration 13 on Article 7d (now Article 14 TFEU) of the Treaty establishing the European Community, OJ 1997, C 340/133.

[57] Ross (2007), p. 1059.

[58] Ross (2007), p. 1057, see also H. Schweitzer [2007] Competition Law and Public Policy: Reconsidering an Uneasy Relationship. The Example of Art. 81, EUI Working Paper LAW No. 2007/30.

disapplied.[59] In other words, the provision underlines and demands an emphasis on the value of SGEI independent of the economic viability of such services.[60]

Malcolm Ross demonstrates, in his analysis of case law after the insertion of Article 16 EC (now Article 14 TFEU), that in the 1990s, the CJEU (although not always consistently) changed its approach to the interpretation of Article 86(2) EC (now Article 106(2) TFEU).[61] After a period in which 'obstructing the performance' was analysed in terms of economic viability of an entrusted undertaking, it appeared that the CJEU favoured a looser assessment of how the undertaking is placed in its specific environment.[62] Article 14 TFEU is part of the Court's reorientation to adopt interpretative approaches with the objective of securing essential elements in the European social order including its understanding of growing citizenship rights.

The revised test, as demonstrated in the case law, appeared to concentrate on the justifications for protecting the service. Ross concludes that the crucial methodological switch is from economic measurement to value judgment in the application of the derogation.[63] In his analysis, he combines the legal authority and moral force of solidarity as a foundational value with the interpretative capacity of Article 14 TFEU to shape a European policy space for the development and regulation of SGEI.

Later case law on the application of the solidarity principle enshrined in Article 14 TFEU has supported a legal mandate for effective SGEI. Advocate General Jacobs for example noted that the provision emphasises the 'special importance' of SGEI.[64] Advocate General Alber has similarly stressed Article 14's wider significance in connection with the Charter of Fundamental Rights: 'The newly promulgated Article 16 (now Article 14 TFEU) and Article 36 of the Charter of Fundamental Rights of the European Union underline the importance of [Article 86(2)] as an expression of a fundamental value judgment of Community law.'[65]

This statement from Advocate General Alber was made before the Charter of Fundamental Rights had become legally binding. The function of Article 14 TFEU to safeguard public services is now supported by the legally binding Article 36 of the Charter of Fundamental Rights—placed in the title IV on Solidarity—which holds:

---

[59] Prosser (2005).

[60] Generally on promoting solidarity and public services, see Ross (2007), pp. 1057–1080.

[61] Ross (2000), pp. 22–38.

[62] Case C-320/91 Corbeau [1993] ECR I-2523, Case C-393/92 Almelo [1994] ECR I-1477 and the clutch of cases involving the energy utilities in the Netherlands, Italy, France and Spain in 1997, Ross also demonstrates that there are exceptions and that no uniform picture emerges. The general tendency seems however well documented and in line with the objective of Article 14 TFEU.

[63] Ross (2000), p. 26.

[64] Opinion of Advocate General Jacob in Case C-475/99 Ambulanz Glöckner [2001] ECR I-8089.

[65] Opinion of Advocate General Alber in Case C-340/99 TNT Traco [2001] ECR I-4109.

> The Union recognises and respects access to services of general economic interest as provided for in national laws and practices, in accordance with the Treaty establishing the European Community, in order to promote the social and territorial cohesion of the Union.[66]

Together with Article 14 TFEU, this underlines the importance of SGEI as a fundamental value protected by EU law.[67] This perspective is reinforced and specified by the Protocol on Services of General Interest (SGI), which the Treaty of Lisbon adds to the European Treaties. According to this Protocol, the shared values of the Union in respect of SGEI include

> the essential role and the wide discretion of national, regional and local authorities in providing, commissioning and organizing services of general economic interest as closely as possible to the needs of the users; the diversity between various services of general economic interest and the differences in the needs and preferences of users that may result from different geographical, social or cultural situations' and 'a high level of quality, safety and affordability, equal treatment and the promotion of universal access and of user rights.[68]

Reference should also be made to the new Article 4 paragraph 2 TEU on the respect for national identities.

Articles 14 and 106(2) TFEU, Article 4(2) TEU and Article 36 of the Charter of Fundamental Rights and Protocol 26 TFEU lay out the constitutional framework for public services in EU law. To this end, Article 14 TFEU, Article 36 of the Charter and Protocol 26 influence the interpretation of Article 106(2), and thereby, the balancing of Member States interference with the internal market, the state aid prohibition and competition rules and the supply of SGEI, or, in other words, in the choice between market values and other values, in particular how to balance them.

The main part of the EEA Agreement still reflects the primary law of the EU prior to this revised constitutional framework for the provision of public services. The analysis going forward seeks to compare the evolving European approach of including an increasing number of social sectors in the state aid scrutiny as well the inclusion of welfare concerns in the assessments with the EEA integration process. The aim is to illuminate the role played by the homogeneity principle through analysing both case law from the EFTA Court and decisional practice of the EFTA Surveillance Authority related to EU/EEA state aid law and the financing of public services. The first section will focus on the paralleling in the EEA of the legal tools to protect state welfare activities from EU free movement, competition and state aid

[66] Pursuant to Article 6 of the TEU the Union recognises the rights, freedoms and principles set out in the Charter of Fundamental Rights of the EU of 7 December 2000 as adapted at Strasbourg on 12 December 2007, which shall have the same legal value as the Treaties—placed in the Title IV on Solidarity—thereof should be mentioned.

[67] Opinion of Advocate General Alber in Case C-340/99 TNT Traco [2001] ECR I-4109, paragraph 94.

[68] Protocol on Services of General Interest, OJ 2007, C 306/158 Note that Article 2 has the following wording; 'The provisions of the Treaties do not affect in any way the competence of Member States to provide, commission and organise non-economic services of general interest.' See also the Communication from the Commission on the Notion of State Aid (2016). The term non-economic service is far from a clear concept, see further in Sect. 12.2 below.

law (Chap. 12). Next, the case study of the provision of a specific public service in the periphery of market activities will be analysed (Chap. 13).

The findings indicate that the homogeneity principle ensures that the EEA integration process parallels the European legal approach towards the role of the market and the role of the state in the financing of public services including the application of the rules to largely non-economic welfare services.

11.5 Structure

This chapter needs to take into account the more complex evolution of EU law based on the interpretation of the Treaty revisions by the CJEU compared to the two previous parts. Part I and Part II on the free movement provisions have demonstrated the evolving EU law as interpreted by the CJEU to move in the direction of broadening the scope of EU law and increasing the powers of the institutions. The Treaty revisions in the field of financing public services have been interpreted by the CJEU also as limitations on the scope of EU law for the Commission's state aid scrutiny. This chapter will examine the EEA integration process and the financing of public services first, in terms of the CJEU case law protecting state welfare activities from the Commission's state aid scrutiny (Chap. 12) and second, the expansion of the scope of EU law both generally through the Commission's Communications defining almost all social services as economic activity and specifically regarding the state aid scrutiny in the field of a largely non-economic service of public service broadcasting (Chap. 13).

Section 11.2 will address key concepts like the definition of an undertaking and what constitutes an economic activity to illustrate limitations on the Commission's state aid competence as interpreted by the CJEU. The EFTA Court's response to this case law is illustrated by key cases like E-8/00, E-14/15 and E-5/07 (Sect. 12.3). The Altmark doctrine considered in the literature to be heavily influenced by Article 14 TFEU provides another limitation on the competences of the Commission (see Sect. 12.4). The paralleling of this doctrine is particularly clear in the case law under the EEA Agreement given that the EFTA Court prior to the Altmark case did not adopt the 'compensation approach' in its case law but rather the so-called state aid approach. After the rendering of the Altmark decision by the CJEU, the case law review in Sect. 12.5 patently demonstrates an EFTA Court changing its approach to comply with the Altmark doctrine.

After having demonstrated how limitations on the competence of state aid scrutiny evolved in the EU legal order (and was paralleled in the EEA), a different consequence of the changed constitutional framework of the EU legal order in state aid cases is analysed in Chap. 13. Through general guidelines and decisional practice, the Commission's application of its state aid competence on public services has turned the Commission into a significant policymaking institution weighing interests of both an economic and a non-economic character and safeguarding previous national concerns in increasingly expanding fields. State aid scrutiny by the

Authority in areas like social housing,[69] educational funding[70] and health provision[71] are illustrative of the EEA integration process. A more detailed case study is conducted regarding the service of public broadcasting exemplifying a service falling into the third model described above.[72] The issuing of guidelines and the decisional practice of the EFTA Surveillance Authority paralleling those of the Commission in the field of public service broadcasting are analysed taking a particularly close look at the Amsterdam Protocol.[73] This chapter demonstrates the paralleling in the EEA of the state aid competence of the EFTA Surveillance Authority issuing identical general guidelines and decisional practice also in the field of public services in the periphery of economic activity. Consequently, the powers of the Authority now include the balancing of welfare concerns for an increasing number of public services. The analysis of the Authority's policymaking role illuminates the EEA integration process in the interface between economic and social policy always evolving homogenously with EU law even without the revised constitutional framework.

Hence, the way forward is organised in two rather different steps. The first step concerns the legal tools to protect welfare activities from EU/EEA free movement and competition/state aid law. This first part demonstrates how the EFTA Court has

---

[69] The 'Husbanken' decision involved an assessment of whether the framework conditions for the Norwegian State Housing Bank (Husbanken) were in conformity with the EEA Agreement. Husbanken provided subsidised loans for housing purposes and was shielded against competition from banks and mortgage companies. The framework conditions enjoyed by Husbanken were regarded as going beyond what was acceptable under Article 59(2) of the EEA Agreement, see Case E-4/97. The Court required the Authority to conduct a proportionality test which involved an assessment of whether Husbanken's cost to render the SGEI were not overcompensated, were limited to what was necessary for Husbanken to perform the specific service in question and would not affect trade to an extent contrary to the interests of the Contracting Parties. The decision by the EFTA Court prompts the question whether the state aid review was to be conducted in a manner where the Authority was entitled to prescribe the least distortive solution for the achievement of the Norwegian housing policy goals. In doing so, the rights of Norway to regulate its housing policy according to political goals would be limited. The Authority concluded, however, in its final decision that the Husbanken system did not appear inappropriate for the realisation of housing policy objectives; see Decision No. 121/00/COL, 28 June 2000. For other cases on social housing measures, see also the Icelandic saga of the Housing Financing Fund (HFF). The decision to close the investigation by the Authority on the grounds that the measure was compatible with the EEA Agreement under Article 59(2) in Decision No. COL 213/04 was challenged by competitors in commercial banks. The EFTA Court annulled the Authority's Decision in Case E-9/04, The Bankers' and Securities Dealers' Association of Iceland. The aid was later considered as existing aid and appropriate measures were proposed, See Decisions No COL 406/08, COL 247/11 and COL 364/11. For an analysis of tensions between the provision of social housing in several Member States and EU market regulations see Gruis and Elsinga (2014), pp. 463–469.

[70] The Authority's decision regarding safety training in high schools, 267/13/COL on 26 June 2013.

[71] The Authority's decision on hospital pharmacies, 460/13/COL on 20 November 2013.

[72] Another potential area for a case study to illuminate these questions would be social housing. This has already been analysed for Iceland by Karlsson (2014), pp. 470–490.

[73] Significant for public service broadcasting is the extent of primary law regulation of this particular service, see the Amsterdam Protocol on the Systems of Public Broadcasting in the Member States, now Protocol 29 annexed to the TFEU, last sentence.

applied the homogeneity principle to parallel legal developments by the CJEU delimiting the state aid competence of the EFTA Surveillance Authority. In this part, central concepts such as economic activity and undertaking as well as the Altmark doctrine[74] are analysed. The second step concerns the impact of the Commission's and, in parallel, the Authority's state aid scrutiny on the financing of public services of a largely non-economic character. This second part demonstrates how the homogeneity principle is applied to increase the policymaking role of an EFTA institution to parallel the role of the Commission for a public service considered to be largely beyond 'marketisation'.[75]

References

Bauby P (2011) From Rome to Lisbon: SGIs in primary law. In: Szyszczak E, Davies J, Andenæs M, Bekkedal T (eds) Developments in services of general interest. Springer, pp 19–35

Cremona M (ed) (2011) Public services and market integration. Oxford University Press, pp 3–4

Cruz JB (2005) Beyond competition: services of general interest and European Community law. In: de Búrca G (ed) EU law and the welfare state – in search of solidarity. Oxford University Press, Oxford, pp 169–212

Cruz JB (2013) Social services of general interest and the State aid rules. In: Neergaard U, Szyszczak E, van de Gronden JW, Krajewski M (eds) Social services of general interest in the EU. Asser Press, pp 287–313

Damjanovic D (2013) The EU market rules as social market rules: why the EU can be a social market economy. Common Mark Law Rev 50:1685–1718

Damjanovic D, de Witte B (2009) Welfare integration through EU law: the overall picture in the light of the Lisbon treaty. In: Neergaard U, Nielsen R, Roseberry LM (eds) Integrating welfare functions into EU law – from Rome to Lisbon. DJØF Publishing, pp 53–96

De Búrca G (2005) EU law and the welfare state – in search of solidarity. Oxford University Press

de Cecco F (2012) State aid and self-government: regional taxation and the shifting spaces of constitutional autonomy. In: Shuibhne N, Gormley L (eds) From single market of Economic Union. Oxford University Press, Oxford

de Cecco F (2013) State aid and the European economic constitution. Hart, Oxford

Dougan M, Spaventa E (eds) (2005) Social welfare and EU law. Hart, Oxford

Gruis V, Elsinga M (2014) Tensions between social housing and EU market regulations. Eur State Aid Law 3:463–469

Hancher L, Ottervanger T, Slot PJ (2016) EU State aids. Sweet & Maxwell

Karlsson HL (2014) Twenty years of Icelandic State aid enforcement. Eur State Aid Law 3:470–490

Krajewski M (2008) Providing legal clarity and securing policy space for public services through a legal framework for services of general economic interest: squaring the circle? Eur Public Law 14:377–398

[74] Named after the Altmark decision, Case C-280/00 Altmark [2003] ECR I-7747.

[75] Some explanation of the use of terminology is required. In EU primary law, the concept of services of general economic interest (SGEI) is used to refer to the public services that fall under the exception in Article 106(2). Other important concepts are services of general interest (SGI), introduced in EU primary law for the first time with the Lisbon Treaty and also the concept of social services of general interest (SSGI). The concepts and their significance in the EEA context will be returned to.

Napolitano G (2005) Towards a European legal order for services of general economic interest. Eur Public Law 11(4):565–581

Neergaard U (2008) Services of general (Economic) interests and the services directive – what is left out, why and where to go? In: Neergaard U, Nielsen R, Roseberry LM (eds) The services directive: consequences for the welfare state and the European social model. DJØF Publishing, Copenhagen, pp 65–120

Neergaard U, Szyszczak E, van de Gronden JW, Krajewski M (eds) (2013) Social services of general interest in the EU. Asser Press

Piernas Lòpez JJ (2015) The concept of State aid under EU law, from internal market to competition and beyond. Oxford University Press, Oxford

Prosser T (2005) The limits of competition law: markets and public services. Oxford University Press

Ross M (2000) Article 16 E.C. and services of general interest: from derogation to obligation. Eur Law Rev 25(1):22–38

Ross M (2007) Promoting solidarity: from public services to a European model of competition. Common Mark Law Rev 44:1057–1080

Santa Maria A (2015) Competition and State aid, an analysis of the EU practice, 2nd edn. Wolters Kluwer, p 2

Sauter W (2014) Public services in EU law. Cambridge University Press, pp 9–10

Schweitzer H (2011) Services of general economic interest: European law's impact of the role of markets and of member states. In: Cremona M (ed) Market integration and public services in the European Union. Oxford University Press, Oxford, pp 11–62

Szyszczak E, Davies J, Andenæs M, Bekkedal T (2011) Developments in services of general interest. Springer

Weiler J (2008) The state of international economic law: re-thinking sovereignty in Europe. J Int Econ Law 11(1):5–41

Chapter 12
Legal Tools to Protect State Welfare Services from EU/EEA Competition and State Aid Law

12.1 Introduction

The state aid competence of the Commission (and the EFTA Surveillance Authority) to assess states' financing of public services for compatibility with EU/EEA law is limited by the notion of state aid. State aid is not defined in Article 107(1) TFEU (Article 61(1) EEA), but the provision limits its own application.[1] Hence, if the financing of the public service does not meet the requirements for state aid to have materialised, the state measure escapes entirely the scrutiny by the Commission (and the Authority). For EU or EEA law to apply, it is decisive whether the service concerned is economic in nature (and therefore qualifies as an SGEI). Social services may frequently constitute non-economic SGI, which in principle remain outside the scope of EU/EEA law.[2]

In this section, the analysis of the case law is focused on the requirement for state aid to have materialised inherent in the limitation of a gratuitous advantage to the recipient.[3] A gratuitous advantage to the recipient is discussed both regarding the limitation to the aid recipient of the notion of undertaking and the limitation inherent in the requirement of an economic activity (Sects. 12.2 and 12.3) as well as the

[1] The list of requirements must all be met for state aid to be deemed to have materialised;

(1) It must be an intervention imputable to the State or carried out through State resources
(2) It must give a gratuitous advantage to the recipient
(3) It must be of a 'selective' character, i.e. intended to favour just certain undertakings or certain business sectors
(4) It must have an impact on trade between Member States
(5) And it must distort competition in the internal market. See also Chap. 11 in footnote 47.

[2] SGIs may be subject to the application of some principles like non-discrimination, a point which will be addressed.

[3] This is where the case law has dealt with the distinction between public services of an economic/non-economic character.

K. Fløistad, *The EEA Agreement in a Revised EU Framework for Welfare Services*, Studies in European Economic Law and Regulation 13,
https://doi.org/10.1007/978-3-319-95043-3_12

compensation approach (the Altmark-doctrine) (Sect. 12.4). Neither the term undertaking nor the term economic activity is defined in the EU Treaties, and the Altmark-doctrine was developed by the CJEU. In the following, the case law from the CJEU, which provides further guidance on the understanding of the limitation of the state aid competence of the Commission, is described. Then, case law from the EFTA Court developing EEA law in parallel with EU law regarding the limitations of the state aid competence of the EFTA Surveillance Authority is analysed.

12.2 Case Law from the CJEU on the Non-Applicability of EU Rules: Undertaking/Economic Activity

It is crucial for the applicability of competition and state aid law to first define the concept of undertaking. The definition of an undertaking is considered to be an EU concept and hence not left to each Member State to decide. An undertaking is an entity engaged in economic activity.[4] The functional character of the concept of undertaking implies that the type of activity performed rather than the characteristics of the actors that perform it is relevant. Furthermore, the social objectives associated with the activity or the regulatory or funding arrangements to which it is subject in a particular Member State do not exclude the activity from being characterised as economic. The functional approach entails that all sorts of public interests can be brought within the ambit of the competition and state aid rules.[5]

Public services delivered outside market mechanisms are generally not held to be economic. This means that the same public service can be economic in one Member State and non-economic in another.[6] Furthermore, the characterisation of the service may vary over time.

The EU Member States may decide on the extent to which public services should be publicly owned,[7] but the degree of public ownership does not determine the application of EU rules. In other words, the choice of public entities, the state or regional communes, to deliver a public service in-house is not in itself decisive in

[4] The leading case is C-41/90 Höfner and Elser [1991] ECR I-1979, paragraph 21, see also the most recent Communication from the Commission on economic/non-economic activity, The Notion on State Aid [2016], section 2.

[5] Advocate General Jacobs Opinion in Joined Cases C-246/01, C-306/01, 354/01 and C-355/01 AOK [2004] ECR I-2493, paragraphs 25–43 provides a very useful discussion of the relevant criteria on the basis of which the CJEU decides whether or not the activity is carried out by an undertaking.

[6] In the Netherlands the marketisation of health services implies that a wider range of health services are considered economic than in a Member State where the health system is largely organised, financed and delivered by the state itself without the sector having been liberalised and privatised, see also the BUPA-decision, Case T-289/03 BUPA v Commission [2008] ECR II-81.

[7] Article 345 TFEU is paralleled in the EEA Agreement in Article 125; 'This Agreement shall in no way prejudice the rules of the Contracting Parties governing the system of property ownership'.

terms of the economic/non-economic characterisation.[8] Relevant for the assessment of a public service's economic dimension is, in addition to ownership, whether the service is rendered against remuneration.[9] The objective of the activity, i.e. to deliver a service, need not be to generate surplus in order for the activity to be economic and the entity to be considered an undertaking.[10] The main objective of this functional definition of an undertaking in EU law is to ensure that all entities, whether public or private, which operate on the market should compete on a level playing field. However, the functional approach has been modified in certain sectors, in particular where national solidarities have prevailed. For social security, the definition of an undertaking depends on whether it is the solidarity principle or instead an economic motive that is decisive for the purposes of a particular scheme.[11]

The approach of exempting the application of competition and state aid provisions for reasons of national solidarity was first adopted in the case of Poucet and Pistre,[12] where the CJEU held that certain French bodies administering sickness and maternity insurance schemes and a basic pension scheme were not classified as undertakings for the purpose of competition and state aid law The judgment of the Court in FFSA,[13] however, modified the understanding of non-applicability of internal market rules for social funds. The case concerned a pension fund supplementing the basic and compulsory pension fund for self-employed farmers. Significantly, affiliation was optional, and while some rules reflected an idea of solidarity, these were of limited importance in the overall scheme. The Court found that the pension fund constituted an undertaking engaged in economic activity. In Sodemar,[14] the CJEU, however, again accepted that the right to freedom of establishment did not preclude the Member State from allowing only non-profit-making private operators to participate in the running of its social welfare system.

After the entering into force of the Amsterdam Treaty, the CJEU, sitting in plenary in three joined cases and after having a detailed common opinion by Advocate General Jacobs, handed down its principal decision regarding the non-economic character of activities of entities entrusted with the management of social welfare funds. In Albany, Brentjens and Drijvende,[15] the CJEU recognised that the solidarity elements of a pension fund charged with the management of supplementary pensions schemes set up by collective agreements justified the exclusive right of the fund to manage the scheme. Consequently, there was no breach of antitrust provisions (including the prohibition of state aid).

---

[8] Case C-343/95 Diego Figli Srl v Porto di Genova ECR-1997 I-1547, paragraphs 16–18.

[9] See the Commission Communication on The Notion of State Aid [2016], section 2.1 nr 12.

[10] Case C-70/95 Sodemare v Regione Lombardia [1997] ECR I-3395.

[11] See the analysis of public services in Sauter (2014), pp. 120–122.

[12] Joined Cases C-159/91 and 160/91 Poucet and Pistre v AGF and Cancava [1993] ECR I-637.

[13] Case C-244/94 FFSA [1995] ECR I-4013.

[14] Case C-70/95 Sodemare v Regione Lombardia [1997] ECR I-3395.

[15] Case C-67/96 Albany [1999] ECR I-5751 Joined Cases C-115/97 to C-117/97 Brentjens' and Case C-219/97 Drijvende Bokken [1999] ECR I-5751.

In FENIN v Commission,[16] the General Court held that an organisation that purchases goods solely for its use in the context of an activity that is qualified as non-economic, due to the exclusively social objective pursued and its functioning according to the principle of solidarity, cannot be considered an 'undertaking' even in its purchasing activity. The finding was approved by the CJEU.[17] The interpretation by the Courts in this decision has been criticised from a competition policy perspective in the literature.[18] Solidarity arguments are crucial to determine whether entities that fulfil a social function are outside the scope of competition and state aid rules. An assessment depends on the degree of solidarity or competition built in the arrangement. The more competition is being brought into a sector, the greater the economic associations will be, and hence, the higher the chance that the activity is within the scope of the competition and state aid rules. This brief review shows that the CJEU has used the solidarity principle to ensure that EU law, to some extent, respects national choices.[19] To this end, it is possible for Member States to lay down national regulations for the provision of a public service that escapes the concept of an undertaking. Hence, in principle, it is up to the Member States to decide whether or not to provide certain goods or services through undertakings, i.e. the market, or through public institutions.[20]

However, the exercise of this choice and, maybe more importantly, the consequences of the choice must be in compliance with EU law.[21] As pointed out by Malcolm Ross,

> European law does not as such say anything about the size of public budgets allocated by Member States to public services. Nor does it predetermine choices as to how such services are to be delivered. However, EU law is not neutral towards the way public services are organized and operated within those choices.[22]

The case law from the CJEU on the distinction between economic and non-economic activities has been characterised as biased in the sense that there is a presumption in favour of finding an economic activity.[23] The notion of economic activity (offering goods or services in the market) is wide and flexible, and the notion of non-economic activity is seen as a residual notion. Baquero Cruz thinks this is the right legal approach given that finding a non-economic activity means not subjecting the activity to the balancing act between economic and other policy

[16] Case T-319/99 FENIN [2003] ECR II-357.

[17] Case C-205/03 FENIN [2006] ECR I-6295.

[18] See one commentary on the difficulty of excluding potential abuses of buyer power from the scope of the EU competition rules, Schweitzer (2011), p. 24.

[19] In Wouters, Case C-309/99 [2002] ECR I-1577 the CJEU made clear in paragraph 57 that certain activities cannot be classified as economic. The rules on competition do not apply to an activity (i) which is connected with the exercise of the powers of public authority; or (ii) which by its nature, its aim and the rules to which it is subject does not belong to the sphere of economic activity.

[20] See the analysis of this in Slot (2013), p. 251.

[21] Tryfonidou (2013), p. 163.

[22] Ross (2000), pp. 22–38.

[23] Cruz (2013), p. 293.

objectives.[24] It is argued that, in economic terms, activities completely devoid of economic activities are rare. This understanding in the literature demonstrates the extent to which there is flexibility in the EU concepts to include activities previously understood to be exclusively within national competences, including in sectors such as publicly financed social housing, healthcare, local media, culture and education, as economic activities. The consequence of this for the EEA integration process is the topic of Chap. 13, but first, the case law from the EFTA Court on the economic/non-economic distinction as well as the Altmark doctrine in both the EU and the EEA legal order will be presented.

12.3 Case Law from the EFTA Court on the Distinction Between Economic and Non-Economic Activities and the Concept of an Undertaking

12.3.1 Case E-8/00 LO

The EFTA Court was confronted with a case on the distinction between economic and non-economic activities for bodies with a social function in Case E-8/00 LO.[25] The question was if and how to apply competition rules in regard of a transfer of an occupational pension scheme.[26] Pension and other welfare schemes, often privately organised but on a not-for-profit basis, need a constant flow of members to keep them solvent, often to facilitate that those still in employment pay for those who are retired.

The case concerned a dispute between the local public authorities (the municipalities) acting as an employer and the employees represented by trade unions. The question raised concerned the compatibility of making changes in the pension schemes for the employees with clauses in the collective agreements. The restrictions posed by the collective agreements limiting the employer's possibility of making changes to the pension schemes were challenged as incompatible with the

[24] Cruz (2013), p. 293.

[25] Decided 22 March 2002.

[26] The exclusion of collective agreements from the reach of competition law was also part of the questions submitted to the EFTA Court in the fairly recent Case E-14/15 Holship Norge AS decided by the Court 19 April 2016. The questions arose in a case concerning a boycott act regarding protection of labour rights of dockworkers in Drammen havn. The Court refers to the LO case regarding the conditions for exempting collective agreements from the reach of competition law in Case E-14/15, paragraphs 40–53 and regarding the notion of an undertaking in paragraphs 67–73. The EFTA Court concurs with its own decision in the LO case regarding the conditions for an exemption but concludes based on a concrete assessment of the Holship case that the competition rules are applicable in the case. Furthermore, for the concept of an undertaking the EFTA Court refers to its earlier decision in the LO case as well as to the CJEU decision in Albany C-67/96. The decision in the Holship case does not alter the analysis above regarding the paralleling in the EEA of the legal tools to protect state welfare activity from competition and state aid rules.

antitrust provisions of the EEA Agreement. In essence, the employers wanted to have the freedom to substitute the provider of the pension schemes from one supplier (the joint municipal pension scheme organised in KLP[27] that had a dispensation from certain provisions of the Insurance Activity Act) to other suppliers (including private life insurance companies). One of the arguments of the trade unions was that such freedom would threaten the solidarity principle involved. By keeping the traditional provider of the pension scheme (KLP), including a joint scheme for the municipalities, the submitted argument was that a gender- and age-neutral financing system could be achieved. By spreading the premium out over a large group of municipalities, the financing system under the pension scheme was the expression of weighty human resource policy considerations. The overall social purpose of this part of the collective agreement was to prevent employers from having economic motives for recruiting men ahead of women and younger employees ahead of older ones. It was argued that the solidarity-oriented nature of the pension scheme would be jeopardised if the municipalities were free to enter into separate pension agreements with private life insurance companies.

It is interesting to note that several of the employers in their interventions relied substantially on the argument that a collective agreement was not necessary to achieve the solidarity goal in question.[28] This viewpoint presupposes that the employers were ready to accept that EEA law will protect social values.[29]

The arguments in the case presented the EFTA Court with a dilemma: While keen to remove barriers to the creation of a single EEA market, the Court was also conscious of the social policy dimension and did not want to jeopardise the viability of the schemes, fearing that if they did so, it would undermine social welfare protection in the EFTA States.

This dilemma led the EFTA Court to develop a principle of protection of national solidarity referring to the same principle already established by the CJEU in cases such as Albany International.[30] When a sufficient degree of solidarity is involved, there is justification for finding that the activity is not economic and thus falls outside the scope of the antitrust provisions. In other words, the case demonstrates that the EEA Agreement (in parallel with EU law) is not just about unrestricted access for all economic operators to the market but recognises the need for protection for bodies that fulfil a social function.

The introductory remarks by the Court starting from paragraph 33 in the LO decision illustrate the Court's reasoning. Here, the EFTA Court emphasises the lack of harmonisation within the EEA of the law governing agreements concluded in the

[27] Kommunal Landspensjonskasse.

[28] Report for the hearing in Case E-8/00, paragraphs 119 and 120, interventions from Hidra and Steigen kommune.

[29] The case ended in the national specialised court of labour law (Arbeidsretten) where all submissions by the employers claiming that the collective agreements violated the antitrust provisions of the EEA Agreement were dismissed, see Case ARD-2002-90.

[30] See section above analysing Case C-67/96 Albany [1999] ECR I-5751.

process of collective bargaining between management and labour. This leads the Court to conclude that

> [t]he legal foundation for dealing with a collective agreement is therefore to be found in national law.

In the following paragraphs,[31] the EFTA Court refers to the case law of the CJEU with special emphasis on the statement in Albany paragraph 59 where the CJEU recognises the restriction of competition inherent in collective agreements and the need to shield such social policy objectives from the application of the antitrust provisions.

The EFTA Court confirms in the introduction that there are fundamental differences that distinguish the labour market from the goods, service and capital markets and consequently that there is a need to enact labour laws (albeit at the national level) to authorise unions of workers to negotiate collective agreements with employers. Based on this understanding, the EFTA Court sets out to explore if there is sufficient basis in the EEA Agreement to limit the applicability of the antitrust provisions corresponding to the limits already recognised by the CJEU in EU law.

The judgment then provides a textbook example of the application of the homogeneity principle in practice. After verifying in a preliminary point the identical wording of Article 53 EEA and the then Article 81 EC (now Article 101 TFEU) and the relevance of the case law from the CJEU according to Articles 6 EEA and 3(2) SCA, the EFTA Court concludes that the test identified by the CJEU for defining the scope of the antitrust provisions must likewise be applied with respect to the scope of Article 53 EEA.[32]

The Court states in accordance with statements made by the CJEU that

> [a]greements entered into in the framework of collective bargaining between employers and employees and intended to improve conditions of work and employment must, by virtue of their nature and purpose, be regarded as falling outside the scope of the prohibition contained in Article 53(1) EEA.[33]

The language in the case confirms that the EFTA Court's objective is to establish the same national flexibility to achieve social welfare objectives under the EEA Agreement as that which has been given to the Member States by virtue of EU law.[34]

It has, however, been pointed out that the EFTA Court has limited the social objectives to that of improving work and employment conditions, whereas other social objectives may also legitimise an exception.[35]

Given that the EFTA Court itself states that the term *'conditions of work and employment'* must be interpreted broadly, the choice of wording does not seem to

---

[31] Paragraphs 34–36.

[32] Paragraphs 33–44.

[33] Paragraph 44.

[34] The EFTA Court makes the reservation in paragraph 55 that the national court must verify that the collective agreement actually pursues the objective of improving work and employment conditions.

[35] Sørum (2003), pp. 251–270, MARIUS-2003-309-251.

imply a difference in substance. A more likely explanation seems to be that the EFTA Court has chosen its wording on the basis of the subject matter of the case. Since the case concerned collective agreements regarding work and employment conditions, the Court did not need to address the question of whether other social objectives regulated in collective agreements were immune to the antitrust provisions.

The EFTA Court has been accused of being 'more Catholic than the pope,' an expression intended to illustrate that the EFTA Court is more internal market friendly than even the CJEU.[36] Under this line of reasoning, the LO case has been criticised for creating a higher threshold for the test of immunity of collective agreements than for the test articulated by the CJEU.[37]

The reference in the decision to Advocate General Jacob's opinion in Albany, in which he argued that collective agreements cannot deprive the prohibition of cartels of all its meaning,[38] has also been taken as an indication of a difference between the EFTA Court and CJEU. The CJEU does not refer to Advocate General Jacob's opinion, and this has led commentators to categorise the EFTA Court as more competition friendly than the CJEU, thus modifying the extent to which the decision achieved the aim of homogeneity.[39]

In the national court, which ultimately decided the case, there are, however, no traces of any difference in the test required. Quite the contrary, the national court makes constant references to the test, mentioning both the CJEU and the EFTA Court and without any distinction between EEA and EU law.[40]

Undoubtedly, the EFTA Court relied on a principle of national solidarity when it decided that collective agreements improving work and employment conditions enjoyed immunity from antitrust provisions also under EEA law. The academic discussion referred to has been on whether the principle of national solidarity is protected to the same extent under EEA law as under EU law. Formulated differently, one could ask the question of whether the competition rules in the EEA Agreement cover more collective agreements than in the EU. There is no evidence in the case law from the courts of such a difference. The national court in the LO case applied the test in the same manner as prescribed by the CJEU. In addition, perhaps most importantly, if we take the EFTA Court at its word, it stated in paragraph 44 of the decision that the test should be applied equally under EEA law as in EU law.

As Advocate General Jacobs pointed out in his opinion in Albany, both Article 81 EC (now Article 101 TFEU) and the rules assuming the right to collective bargaining are Treaty provisions of the same rank, and one set of rules should not take

[36] Fredriksen (2009), pp. 507–576.

[37] Fredriksen (2009), pp. 539–540.

[38] Opinion of Advocate General Jacobs in Case C-67/96 Albany [1999] ECR I-5751, paragraph 186.

[39] Fredriksen (2010), p. 748.

[40] See in particular the national Decision paragraphs 658 and 659, ARD-2002-90.

absolute precedence over another set but must be harmonised.[41] In later cases, the scrutiny of collective agreements has increased significantly.[42] If there was any difference between the EFTA Court in the LO case and the CJEU in the Albany case, this did not pose a threat to the aim of homogeneity but rather showed the importance of the principle given that the CJEU was developing in the same direction as the EFTA Court had taken in the LO case. Given that the legal orders are constantly developing, the aim of the homogeneity objective is to ensure parallel development.

For the present purposes, it suffices to show that the EFTA Court has used the solidarity principle (in parallel with the case law from the CJEU) to ensure that entities fulfilling a social function and operating based on the principle of solidarity are preserved from the reach of EEA antitrust law (including also state aid scrutiny) and hence ensured the paralleling of the legal protection in the EEA of state welfare activities. If it were otherwise, the very legitimacy of EEA law would arguably be undermined.

The LO case concerns the distinction between economic and non-economic activity. Another key concept central to this discussion is the concept of what constitutes an undertaking. Before shifting the attention away from how to protect states' welfare activities from EU/EEA law to how welfare concerns are integrated in EU/EEA law, the key EFTA Court case on the concept of an undertaking will be analysed with a view to determine whether EEA law continues to parallel EU law in the field of protecting state welfare activity from competition and state aid rules.

12.3.2 Case E-5/07 Private Barnehagers Landsforbund (PBL)

The concept of an undertaking was the object of evaluation for the EFTA Court in Case E-5/07[43] concerning a complaint on the EFTA Surveillance Authority's refusal to consider funding given to kindergarten facilities in Norway as state aid.[44] The

[41] Opinion of Advocate General Jacobs in C-67/96 Albany [1999] ECR I-5751, Joined Cases C-115/97 to C-117/97 Brentjens' and Case C-219/97 Drijvende Bokken [1999] ECRI-5751, paragraph 179.

[42] In both Viking Line, Case C-438/05 ECR [2007] I-10779 and Laval, Case C-341/05 ECR [2007] I-11767 the CJEU firmly rejected the notion that collective bargaining and thus collective agreements are outside the scope of EU law per se. The principles from these important cases in EU law have been largely accepted also in an EEA context, illustrated by the EFTA Court's decision in Case E-2/11, STX Norway Offshore AS m.fl. v Staten v/ Tariffnemnda and more recently in Case E-14/15 Holship.

[43] Decided 21 February 2008.

[44] Prior to the Decision by the Authority challenged in Case E-5/07 the Authority had indeed concluded that day-care providers of kindergarten services were conducting an economic activity, see Decision 291/03/COL, 18 December 2003. However, in a later letter to the Norwegian state regarding financing of private day-care facilities for children the Authority considers kindergarten services as non-economic, letter 3 February 2012, Case No 68577.

refusal by the Authority meant that the question of overcompensation was never addressed in relation to the Norwegian system for funding of kindergartens. Moreover, the right to equal treatment between private and public kindergartens was not assessed given that the Authority and later the EFTA Court decided that public kindergartens were not undertakings for the purpose of EEA law and therefore not subject to limitations as regards funding from the state.

The case concerned a reform of the financing of the kindergarten sector with a maximum price ceiling on parental fees in Norway from 2003.

Kindergartens for children under compulsory school have been available in Norway for decades. Public kindergartens are normally run by the municipalities. Private kindergartens are run by companies or organisations or as family day-care institutions. At the relevant time, out of 235,000 children enrolled in kindergartens in Norway, 108,000 attended private kindergartens. Since the start of funding of the kindergarten sector by the state in 1963, there had been three sources of finance for kindergartens in Norway: the state, the municipalities and the parents. Activity-based state subsidies were granted equally to the municipalities and to private kindergartens. The scale of these grants was set by the Norwegian Parliament (Storting) annually, with a present target of an average of 50% coverage of the operational costs of day-care centres. With regard to parental fees, there were no limitations on municipal and private kindergartens before 2003.

Municipal kindergartens in general had been and still are organised like other municipal activities. As such, the financing of the municipal kindergartens is a part of the general budget of the municipality. It is subject to the general rules of public budgeting, which means that the municipal budget has to be complete, meaning that all expected costs connected with an activity have to be budgeted in full.

In 2003, a reform of the financing of the kindergarten sector took place. It originated from an agreement between political parties in June 2002, the so-called Kindergarten Agreement. From the outset, it was recognised that a system where the majority of the costs should be borne by the central state budget had to take into account the important cost deviations with regard to kindergartens amongst the different municipalities. It became furthermore clear in the legislative procedure that the municipalities had much higher costs than the private kindergartens. In 2003, the costs per child per hour of the private kindergartens were on average 85% of the costs of the municipal kindergartens, and this was central to the case.

The major change introduced by the abovementioned reform was the introduction of a maximum price ceiling on parental fees to obtain the goal of capping parents' fees at 20% of the costs of the services. As of 1 January 2006, the applicable rate was fixed at NOK 2250 (approx. 240 Euro) per month with an intention of reducing it to approximately NOK 1800 (approx. 190 Euro). The parental fee is disconnected from the actual costs of the service; cost differences stemming from the age of the child (for instance, given that costs for children aged 0–2 years are substantially higher than those for children aged 3–6 years) or from special needs are not accounted for. Furthermore, parents with more than one child benefit from a fee reduction. Another main change was the introduction of a new obligation of the municipalities to cover operational costs of non-municipal kindergartens.

In order to compensate for the new obligations of the municipalities (i.e. the loss of revenue of both municipal and non-municipal kindergartens through the introduction of the price ceiling that had to be covered by the municipalities), so-called discretionary funds were introduced. These earmarked subsidies were paid to the municipalities from the state budget and could be used to compensate for the loss of revenue of existing kindergartens (non-municipal or municipal) or for running costs of new kindergarten places. The system came into effect on 1 May 2004, and for the year 2004, NOK 485 million was allocated in the state budget for this purpose.

The organisation for private kindergartens (PBL) submitted a formal complaint alleging that the system for public contributions to the operation of municipally owned day-care centres contained elements of state aid. PBL alleged that the system was incompatible with state aid rules, as it favoured municipal kindergartens over non-municipal kindergartens, in particular private kindergartens.

In its description of the facts, the PBL elaborated on how the regulation distorted the competition between municipal and private kindergartens. First, the financing system perpetuated the cost differences between municipal and private kindergartens as existing in 2003 to the detriment of the latter. Second, the municipalities were free to change the cost levels of their kindergartens, whereas the private kindergartens were limited to the general rise of municipal costs. This especially impaired the private kindergartens in the competition for qualified workforce if the salaries offered by the municipalities rose faster than the general cost level in the municipalities, as was the case in 2006. Taken all together, these factors would, according to the PBL, lead to a lower service level offered by the private kindergartens compared to the municipal kindergartens and accordingly damage their ability to take on more children.[45]

The PBL relied on the fact that most municipal kindergartens received a higher nominal amount in public funding than non-municipal kindergartens. The general allegation was therefore that the Norwegian rules entailed a systematic discrimination to the detriment of private kindergartens. The reason why municipal kindergartens received a higher nominal amount in public funding was due to the fact that municipal kindergartens in general had a higher cost level than non-municipal kindergartens and that the financing was organised as a system of cost coverage rather than according to a unit cost principle.

The allegation was i.a. that a unit cost model would neutralise the established fact demonstrated by several studies, namely that the average level of cost per child per hour is substantially lower in a non-municipal kindergarten than in a municipal kindergarten. A unit cost model would imply a system where all received the same amount per child regardless of their actual costs.[46]

[45] Report for the hearing in Case E-5/07, p. 17 Chap. 1 in footnote 40.

[46] Se studies referred to on page 14 of the Statement of Defence from the EFTA Surveillance Authority 13 June 2007 with further reference in Chap. 1 in footnotes 36–40.

In the contested decision from the EFTA Surveillance Authority, the Authority concluded that

> the system of financing municipal day-care institutions in Norway does not constitute State aid within the meaning of Article 61 (1) of the EEA Agreement.[47]

The Authority had based its conclusion on three separate grounds. The first was that municipal kindergartens are not undertakings in the meaning of Article 61(1) EEA. Second, the Authority held that the measure did not affect trade between EEA states as required by Article 61(1) EEA. Third, and finally, the Authority concluded that even if the measure would be considered state aid, the activity concerned constituted a SGEI, and the contested measure constituted an appropriate and not manifestly discriminatory compensation thereof. This means that the Authority found the measure justified on the grounds of Article 59(2) EEA.

The procedural questions including the question of *locus standi* will not be dealt with here.[48] Of interest is the substantive discussion whereby the EFTA Court made several interesting remarks on the nature of an activity being a service of economic activity as opposed to where powers are exercised to fulfil duties towards the population.[49] The general observation is that the Court, instead of engaging in a detailed economic analysis, took a wider and more flexible view on other values at stake, such as educational, cultural and societal concerns. It is argued that this methodological approach was a necessary precondition to arrive at the conclusion that public kindergartens did not qualify as undertakings under EEA law.

The starting point under EEA competition/state aid law is that the concept of an undertaking encompasses every entity engaged in economic activity, regardless of the legal status of the entity and the way in which it is financed.[50] However, only entities engaged in 'economic activity' are undertakings.[51] According to settled case law, 'economic activity' is any activity consisting in offering goods or services on a given market'.[52] An economic activity presupposes the assumption of risk for the purpose of remuneration.[53] Undoubtedly, the public kindergartens were offering a service to assist parents in their upbringing of children. This service was offered in exchange for the parents' payment of a fee. The question was whether elements such as an entity's public-law status, its non-profit character and its pursuit of social objectives could be taken into account when assessing whether it pursued an economic activity.[54]

---

[47] Decision 39/07/COL, 27 February 2007.

[48] The findings of the Court on the procedural questions are in paragraphs 45–53, second, third and fourth plea.

[49] See the formulation in Humbel.

[50] Article 1 of Protocol 22 to the EEA Agreement and Case E-8/00 LO, paragraph 62.

[51] Case C-41/90 Höfner [1991] ECR I-1979, paragraph 21, see above in Sect. 11.2 on the economic/non-economic divide.

[52] Case C-36/96 Commission v Italy [1998] ECR I-3851, paragraph 36.

[53] Case C-184/98 Pavlov and Others [2000] ECR I-6451, paragraphs 76–77.

[54] Cases C-41/90 Höfner and Elser [1991] ECR I-1979, paragraph 21, C-82/01 P Aéroports de Paris v Commission [2002] ECR I-9297, C-67/96 Albany [1999] ECR I-5751, paragraphs 77–86.

The first question was whether the municipalities, when providing kindergarten services, were acting as a public authority. The PBL purported that the Authority should have distinguished between the municipality's roles as authority and as operator. Some of the duties referred to by the Authority apply to any operator of a kindergarten, while the duties the municipalities had in their role as kindergarten authority did not require them to actually operate any kindergarten themselves. It is recalled that under the relevant case law, an entity's exercise of regulatory functions does not impede a finding that the entity is engaged in economic activity.[55] Furthermore, in terms of the cultural, educational and social aspects, there were no differences between the obligations put on the public and on the private kindergartens. It was all regulated by law, and no particular feature was part of the public but not the private operations. Thus, all the obligations arising under Articles 1 and 2 of the National Kindergarten Act, which laid down the purpose and contents of kindergartens, were incumbent upon all operators. The kindergarten sector is indeed a sector under heavy regulation, but the operation of the task was conducted by both private and public entities.

The question of whether it is decisive for a service that is regulated with a view to promote social values for an understanding of the service to be of a non-economic character has been commented upon by the CJEU. In Hofner and Elser, the activity of the German Employment Service was also highly regulated; that did not, however, prevent the CJEU from finding that one was in the presence of an entity engaged in economic activity.[56] Advocate General Jacobs summarises the Court's case law as follows in his opinion in Cisal[57]:

> It follows in my view from the Court's case-law and in particular from the cases set out above that the INAIL's public-law status, its non-profit-making character and the pursuit of social objectives cannot be taken into account for its classification. It is a separate question whether those features might help to justify the grant to the INAIL of exclusive or special rights under Article 86(2). They cannot however as such have a bearing on the question whether the INAIL's insurance activities should or should not be regarded as economic activities.[58]

The relevant question required, according to the PBL, to assess the notion of undertaking is whether the municipalities are providing services on a given market that could, at least in principle, be carried out by a private actor in order to make a profit. In that regard, it was pointed out that childcare services have traditionally been provided on the market by private actors, that the Norwegian State never attempted to establish an entirely public system and that notwithstanding the limitations to pricing competition introduced by the reform of 2003, there was competition amongst the providers of the service.

---

[55] Reference is made to Case C-69/91 Decoster [1993] ECR I-5335, at paragraph 15 and the Opinion of Advocate General Jacobs in Case C-218/00 Cisal [2002] ECR I-691.

[56] Case C-41/90 [1991] ECR I-1979, paragraph 21.

[57] Case C-218/00 [2002] ECR I-691.

[58] Opinion of Advocate General Jacobs in Case C-218/00 Cisal [2002] ECR I-691, paragraph 46.

Although it was admitted that the aid granted to operational costs was very important,[59] the PBL explained that the aid increases had largely become necessary due to the caps on parental payments and new requirements imposed by regulation. It was argued quite persuasively that, nonetheless, private kindergartens were operating according to market principles with regard to investment, capital costs, return on invested capital and risks related to loss and bankruptcy. The existence of certain socially motivated graduated fees, it was argued, is common in many sectors and cannot lead to the conclusion that the entity would not be engaged in an economic activity. Heavy public regulation of a sector does not mean that the remaining competition is not protected and that this parameter has never been included in the CJEU's test of what qualifies as an undertaking.

The Norwegian Government took the view that the municipal kindergartens were based on the principle of solidarity.[60] In particular, the Government emphasised that the purpose of the system is to enable all parents to afford kindergarten places. It explained that the public grants should be seen rather as financial contributions to parents in order to promote social equality than as a financial support to kindergartens as such. The Government further pointed to the existence of graduated fees for social reasons. It refuted the argument of the PBL that graduated fees are also common in other sectors such as transportation, as in these sectors, even the graduated fee was never below marginal costs, thus having a different rationale than the discounts in the kindergarten system.

However, the Government never seemed to answer or address the question of the market that undoubtedly existed in the kindergarten sector in Norway. The PBL represented private kindergartens that were undertakings operating in a market even if the competing factors were limited. The relationship between this fact and the question of state aid to municipal kindergartens seems to have been left out of the Government's intervention. Even more interesting is the Court's approach. The EFTA Court chose not to engage in an economic analysis of the kindergarten market or in particular in an evaluation of the possible distortion of the market stemming from the reform. One possible question that was never answered would have to be if Article 59(2) EEA only permits a system of public funding by which the state is required to base the compensation of public services on the cost level of a real or hypothetical efficient service provider.

First of all, the EFTA Court, instead of engaging in an economic analysis and taking account of the entire market situation, chose a more value judgment approach. First, it dismissed the idea that an activity that could, at least in principle, be carried out by a private operator is thereby economic in nature.[61] The reason why the Court

[59] See the Report for the hearing, p. 21, paragraph 81.

[60] The observation is partly cited in the Report for the hearing paragraphs 115–128, see also the Statement of observation by the Norwegian Government 8 October 2007.

[61] Case E-5/07, paragraph 79. It is unclear to what extent this applies generally in all areas. The fact that the activity can be provided by private parties is a clear indication of the activity being economic, see the discussion in alt advokatfirma [2013] Kommunal virksomhet i lys av EØS-avtalens statstøtteregler, pp. 46–47.

did not agree with the PBL on this point was a rather loose reference to the fact that such an interpretation would bring almost any activity of the state not consisting in an exercise of public authority under the notion of economic activity. This reasoning is not entirely convincing given the distinction in the case law of the CJEU between exercising regulatory functions and actually operating kindergartens themselves in a market where private actors offer the same service. Rather, the Court insisted that 'the specific circumstances under which the activity is performed have to be taken into account'.[62] In reaching this conclusion, the Court perhaps also relied on the view that public educational institutions that, when viewed in isolation, do not perform an economic activity cannot be held to do so simply because other entities perform similar educational activities in a way that qualifies them as economic activities for the purposes of EU/EEA law. Indeed, as expressed by the CJEU i.a. in Wirth, the existence of educational courses financed essentially out of private funds with the aim of making an economic profit does not lead to the conclusion that also educational institutions financed primarily from the public purse, with no gainful motive, can be said to perform a service.[63] However, this being true in the sector of compulsory education does not mean that the same holds true outside this area, which is often regulated separately.[64] First, kindergartens are not part of the compulsory education system, and second, for many years, in particular when the children are small, they have more in common with childcare than with education. The provision of childcare is a service that has traditionally been provided on the market.

However, the Court agreed with the Authority that kindergartens in Norway have important social, cultural, educational and pedagogical purposes.

The reasoning of the Court in relation to education and training is very much in line with a Commission Communication entitled 'Implementing the Community Lisbon programme: Social services of general interest in the European Union'.[65] It follows from the Communication itself that '[t]his communication should be seen in the context of the shared responsibility of the Community and of the Member States for services of general economic interest, established by Article 16 of the EC Treaty' (now Article 14 TFEU). The Communication is thus linked precisely to the Treaty Article, which has no corresponding provision in the EEA. The Commission's

[62] Case E-5/07, paragraph 80.

[63] Case C-109/92 Wirth [1993] ECR I-6447, paragraphs 16–19, see also Case C-263/86 Humbel [1998] ECR 5365. The reasoning in both these cases are confirmed in the Case C-76/05 Schwarz [2007] I-6849, see in particular paragraphs 38–40, paragraph 39; 'The Court thus held that, by establishing and maintaining such a system of public education, financed as a general rule by the public budget and not by pupils or their parents, the State did not intend to involve itself in remunerated activities, but was carrying out its task in the social, cultural and educational fields towards its population.' See Part I Chap. 4 on students and educational activity.

[64] See the Services Directive, and Commission Communication on SGEI 2007, COM/2006/0177 final, The Communication can be found at: http://ec.europa.eu/employment_social/social_protection/docs/com_2006_177_en.pdf.

[65] COM/2006/0177 final, The Communication can be found at: http://ec.europa.eu/employment_social/social_protection/docs/com_2006_177_en.pdf.

Communication is referred to both by the PBL and the Authority as well as in the Report for the Hearing.[66]

The PBL stated that the Communication provided guidance as to such social services' standing under the internal market rules and quoted from the communication that 'almost all services offered within the social field can be considered economic activities'. In Chap. 1 footnote 7 of the Communication, however, it is stated that '[e]ducation and training, although they are SGI with a clear social function, are not covered by this Communication'. Thus, the EFTA Court's reasoning when it has defined kindergartens as educational institutions seems to coincide with the Communication's definition of what constitutes an economic activity as spelt out by the Commission relying on Article 14 TFEU (previous Article 16 EC).

Following from the foregoing elements of the specific circumstances of the performance of the activity, the Court found that the element of remuneration was absent in the activity of municipal kindergartens in Norway.[67]

Furthermore, it was pointed out by the Court that when the Norwegian state established and maintained a system where every child increased the costs incurred, the state was not seeking to engage in gainful activity but was in fact fulfilling its duties towards its own population in the social, cultural and educational fields. This finding of the activity not being of an economic character was of course sufficient to exclude the existence of state aid in the measure at stake, and thus, the application was dismissed.

The EFTA Court relied on jurisprudence from the CJEU, which did not expressly concern the concept of undertaking.[68] Humbel, Wirth and Schwarz all concern the question of whether services provided by certain public educational institutions could be considered services 'normally provided for remuneration'. The logic of the EFTA Court was built on the notion that whether the entity is an undertaking turns on whether that entity is engaged in 'economic activity'. Reference is made to paragraph 80 of the decision where the EFTA Court refers to the reasoning concerning the notion of a service and transposes this reasoning to a state aid case.

> In this respect, the reasoning of the ECJ in Humbel, which concerned the notion of "service" within the meaning of the fundamental freedoms, can be transposed to a State aid case such as the one at hand.

Economic activity is usually defined as any activity consisting in offering goods and services on a given market. The essential characteristic of goods and services offered on a market is that they are normally provided for remuneration. The EFTA Court refers in paragraph 81 to Humbel and Schwarz to assess whether the kindergarten sector in Norway is a service rendered with the essential characteristic of remuneration.

---

[66] Confer paragraph 62 of the application from PBL, paragraph 84 of the Statement of Defence from the Authority and the Report for the Hearing, paragraph 97.

[67] Paragraph 82.

[68] See Chap. 4 on educational services.

From the judgments in Humbel and Schwarz, it can be concluded that institutions, of whichever level, which form part of the national education system and which are essentially funded by the state are not to be regarded as providers of a service. In running these establishments, the state is not pursuing gainful activity. It is thus not providing a service on a market. Rather, the CJEU found that the state in establishing and maintaining these systems was 'fulfilling its duties towards its own population in the social, cultural and educational fields'.[69]

The maximum price ceiling on kindergarten services in Norway implied that there was no possibility for the parental fee to be anywhere near the actual value of the service. The principle of solidarity was demonstrated *inter alia* by the way the parental fee was fixed. The purpose of the reform with a constant lowering of parental fees was to enable all families to afford kindergarten places. If the parents had been made to pay for the actual value of the service, only a small portion of the population would be able to afford kindergarten services, even more so considering that several parents have more than one child. Reserving kindergarten only for the rich would be inconsistent with the authorities' aim to make kindergarten available to all. The public grants in place, the purpose of which is to render kindergarten services accessible, promote social equality, and one of the main purposes of the current regime was to promote solidarity. Reference in this context is also made to the graduated fees applying to families with more than one child and the fact that children with special needs do not pay higher fees, illustrating the application of the solidarity principle within the kindergarten sector. In line with the decisions in Humbel and Schwarz, the EFTA Court concluded that the system was instrumental for the fulfilment of the authorities' obligation towards the population in the social, cultural and educational fields.[70]

Hence, the EFTA Court concluded that the provision of the day-care service of municipal kindergartens was not an economic activity. The decision therefore supports the claim that the EEA integration process has evolved homogenously with the EU legal order in the field of protecting state welfare activities from EU/EEA competition and state aid rules. In the process, both the EFTA Court and the EFTA Surveillance Authority rely on a combination of sources, not paying attention to whether the legal provisions relied on in the EU legal order have been made part of the EEA Agreement. The next section will address the same question in relation to the Altmark-doctrine, which delimits the Commission's state aid competence in cases where the compensation approach applies.

[69] Case 263/86 Humbel [1988] ECR 5365, paragraph 18 and Case C-76/05 Schwarz [2007] I-6849, paragraph 39, the Court thus held that, 'by establishing and maintaining such a system of public education, financed as a general rule by the public budget and not by pupils or their parents, the State did not intend to involve itself in remunerated activities, but was carrying out its task in the social, cultural and educational fields towards its population.' See Part I Chap. 4 on students and educational activity.

[70] Paragraph 83 of the Decision.

12.4 Case Law from the CJEU Delimiting the Commission's State Aid Competence in Case of Compensation: The Altmark Doctrine

In light of the lack of a clear methodology to delimit competence between the EU and the Member States in the binary divide between economic and non-economic dimensions, other devices are applied, such as the criteria of impact on trade between the Member States and *de minimis* rules.[71] In addition, another delimitation of the application of the Commission's state aid competence was developed by the CJEU in the so-called Altmark-doctrine.

The Altmark Trans decision marked the ending of a debate on the question of whether the financial transfer of resources by the state that are meant to merely compensate an entrusted undertaking for the net costs incurred in providing a public service should nevertheless be qualified as state aid.[72] The Commission argued for always requiring administrative control for financial transfers by the state. This point of view would strengthen the general position of the Commission in its state aid review to also investigate compatibility of the transfer with EU state aid law as well as ensure the possibility to include conditions for the transfer to be compatible. Arguably, there is always a risk of overcompensation when the financial transfer is not determined in the marketplace. However, the procedural duty of notification[73] with the inherent possibility of the Commission to condition the transfer combined with a standstill clause raised concerns among Member States for the respect of national choices and the continuous provision of public services. The sensitivity on the part of the Member States of being subject to Commission administrative control of the financing of public services is clear from the debate.

The CJEU held in Altmark[74] that where a state measure must be regarded as a compensation for the services provided by the recipient undertaking in order to discharge public service obligations, and where the recipient undertaking thus does not enjoy a real financial advantage and is not put in a more favourable competitive position than its competitors, such measure is not caught by Article 107(1) TFEU (ex Article 87(1) EC).[75]

---

[71] See SGEI package from the Commission, first the 'Altmark package' in July 2005 and then the second package—the Alumnia package—adopted on 20 December 2011, see more details below.

[72] Case C-280/00 Altmark [2003] ECR I-7747.

[73] Article 108(3) TFEU.

[74] Case C-280/00 Altmark [2003] ECR I-7747, paragraph 31.

[75] Four cumulative conditions must be met for a public service compensation to escape classification as state aid: (1) The recipient undertaking must actually have a public service obligation to discharge, and the obligations must be clearly defined, (2) the parameters on the basis of which the compensation will be calculated must be established in advance in an objective and transparent manner, (3) the compensation must not exceed what is necessary to cover all or part of the costs incurred in the discharge of the public service obligation, taking into account the relevant receipts and a reasonable profit and (4) either the undertaking has been chosen pursuant to a public procurement procedure or the level of compensation has been determined based on the basis of an analysis

Hence, the CJEU opted for the compensation approach in Altmark. The distinction between what is referred to as 'the compensation approach' and what has been referred to as 'the state aid approach' is based on the analysis of Advocate General Jacobs in Case C-126/01 GEMO.[76] Jacobs refers in this opinion in GEMO to the ongoing Altmark Trans case and the opinion of Advocate General Léger in this case.[77] Jacobs partly disagrees with Léger and offers his own analysis on how the Court should decide in Altmark Trans. The Court in Altmark Trans is clearly influenced by the opinion by Advocate General Jacobs, choosing the same language and similar conditions as suggested in the opinion in GEMO as well as referring to the opinion directly.[78] The opinion of Advocate General Jacobs in GEMO is developed based on Article 16 EC (now in a revised form Article 14 TFEU).[79] When providing his novel solution to the disputed question, Jacobs refers to Article 16 EC in striking the right balance between the two approaches.[80] It is therefore commonly held that the CJEU, although not referring to Article 16 EC (now in a revised form Article 14 TFEU) in the Altmark Trans judgment, was strongly influenced by the provision.[81]

The Court's decision in Altmark Trans is important i.a. because it demonstrates the recognition by the Court of the concerns expressed by the Member States in the field of applying state aid rules to public services. The application of the Altmark compensation approach allowed the Member States some latitude to define an SGEI and to provide proportionate compensation for the performance of the public service.[82] Altmark has been described as an important turning point for the modernisation of state aid in the EU.[83] An analysis demonstrates, however, that the criteria set for the compensation approach provided a set of conditions that were not entirely clear or straightforward to apply. In particular, it has been difficult to meet the condition of a clear definition (referred to as the second condition) and the condition of pursuing a public procurement procedure or being compared to a typical, well-run undertaking (referred to as the fourth condition).[84] Nevertheless, the Altmark

of the costs which a typical undertaking well run and adequately provided with means would have incurred.

[76] Opinion of Advocate General Jacobs in Case C-126/01 GEMO[2003] ECR I-13769, paragraph 94 for the state aid approach and paragraph 95 for the compensation approach.

[77] Opinion of Advocate General Jacobs in Case C-126/01 GEMO [2003] ECR I-13769, paragraph 105.

[78] Case C-280/00 Altmark Trans, ECR I-7810, paragraphs 73 and 87–94.

[79] Opinion of Advocate General Jacobs in Case C-126/01 GEMO [2003] ECR I-13769, paragraph 124.

[80] Opinion of Advocate General Jacobs in Case C-126/01 GEMO [2003] ECR I-13769, paragraph 124.

[81] de Cecco (2013), p. 143, Bekkedal (2008), p. 145 with further references.

[82] Similarly the General Court indicated a flexibility regarding the application of the criteria, especially where a social, healthcare service was being provided, see Case T-289/03 BUPA v Commission [2008] ECR II-81.

[83] Szyszczak (2012), p. 333.

[84] See above on the four conditions.

decision opened the possibility for the self-assessment by Member States of financing schemes and diminished the necessity to rely upon Article 106(2) TFEU as well as the necessity to notify financing for SGEI to the Commission under Article 108(3) TFEU.

In the academic literature on Altmark and the ensuing case law, the European Courts' decisions are interpreted as revealing 'flexibility and a deference towards Member States in ring-fencing of public services away from the harsh application of the state aid rule'.[85] In contrast, the Commission has taken a tougher stance on Member States' practices.[86] There are relatively few examples of decisions in which the Altmark criteria have been held by the Commission to have been fulfilled.[87] In the later examined sector of public service broadcasting, none of the Member States' notifications on new regimes have been accepted to be caught by the exception.[88] The question of whether the Commission's interpretation of the Altmark conditions is actually compliant with the understanding of the CJEU is rarely tested. In nearly all the notified changes, for example, in the sector of public service broadcasting, the proposals are eventually justified under Article 106(2) TFEU; see below Sect. 13.5. Article 106(2) TFEU ensures the possibility for the Commission to examine the measure administratively as well as the possibility to set conditions for the compatibility of the measure with the inherent political influence on the final design of the service.[89]

The Commission adopted its first 'Altmark package' in July 2005 to clarify how it would approach the application of Article 106(2) TFEU in case of financial transfers for the provision of public services. The second package, the Alumnia package, was adopted on 20 December 2011 and is the most recent reform on the financing of SGEI.[90] The Alumnia package comprises two Communications[91] and

---

[85] Szyszczak (2011).

[86] See references to Commission decisions in chapter 13 in the field of public service broadcasting. See also the study done by Klasse (2010).

[87] See i.a. the findings by Hancher, Ottervanger, and Slot [2006] EC State Aids (3 ed), paragraphs 8-026 to 8-028. It is not entirely clear to what extent Member States themselves assess whether the Altmark criteria are fulfilled and therefore never presents the public compensation for an assessment to the Commission.

[88] An interesting case is the notification by Denmark on public service radio, see Commission case no SA.32019 (2010/N) Denmark, 23 March 2011.

[89] In the BUPA judgment, Case T-289/03 BUPA v Commission [2008] ECR II-81 the Altmark exception is somewhat extended to include also instances where the risk of overcompensation is minimal and the public service is within the health sector which falls almost exclusively within the competence of the Member State, see paragraph 167 which also refers to Article 14 TFEU (ex Article 16 EC).

[90] For a fairly recent publication on the financing of SGEI including an analysis of the Alumnia package, see Szyszczak and van de Gronden (2013).

[91] Communication from the Commission on the application of the European Union State aid rules to compensation granted for the provision of services of general economic interest, OJ 2012 C 8/4; Communication from the Commission, European Union framework for State aid in the form of public service compensation, OJ 2012 C 8/15.

a Decision.[92] A regulation on *de minimis* aid was adopted on 25 April 2012.[93] Accompanying the Alumnia package was an Impact Assessment and a Quality Framework.[94]

Corresponding Communications were subsequently made part of the EEA Agreement.[95] Furthermore, a decision to integrate into the EEA the Commission Decision 2012/21/EU of 20 December 2011 on the application of Article 106(2) of the TFEU to state aid in the form of public service compensation granted to certain undertakings entrusted with the operation of SGEI in the EEA Agreement was adopted 30 March 2012, and the subsequent changes to annex XV were made.[96]

For the purpose of the analysis here, it is of interest to point out that the adoption of the Altmark and the Alumnia packages has been viewed in the literature as the Commission to some extent seizing back control over the monitoring of the financing of SGEI.[97] The Commission's approach after the Altmark ruling has been extensively analysed[98] and also questioned.[99] It is beyond the scope of this book to enter into a general analysis of the conditions of application of state aid provisions on Member States' financing of public services including any possible differences between the European Courts and the Commission regarding this question. Undoubtedly, the application of state aid law to public services, in particular services in the social sector, has proved to be both controversial and disputed.

This observation underlines, however, the complexity and sensitive nature of applying state aid law to public services and increasingly so when the services reach far into the social orders of the state. This observation is relevant for the EEA analysis in the sense that controversial and sensitive application of the law, including instituting the power to apply the law to specific EU/EFTA institutions, generally requires a clear legal basis. In the EU legal order, there has been a constitutional change for the provision of public services increasingly including welfare concerns

[92] Commission Decision of 20 December on the application of Article 106(2) of the Treaty on the Functioning of the European Union to State aid in the form of public service compensation granted to certain undertakings entrusted with the operation of services of general economic interest, OJ 2012 L 7/3.

[93] Commission Regulation on the application of Articles 107 and 108 of the Treaty on the Functioning of the European Union to *de minimis* aid granted to undertakings providing services of general economic interest, OJ 2012 L 114/8.

[94] For a positive view of the SGEI packages from the Commission see Cruz (2013), pp. 287–313.

[95] http://www.eftasurv.int/media/state-aid-guidelines/Part-VI%2D%2D-Compensation-granted-for-the-provision-of-services-of-general-economic-interest.pdf.

http://www.eftasurv.int/media/state-aid-guidelines/Part-VI%2D%2D-Framework-for-state-aid-in-the-form-of-public-service-compensation.pdf.

[96] See Decision by the EEA Committee no 66/2012 and changes to annex XV.

[97] See the comment of Szyszczak in Szyszczak (2012), p. 333.

[98] An early analysis can be found in Rapp-Junga (2004), pp. 205–215. For a fairly recent analysis, see Szyszczak and Van de Gronden (2013) in particular chapter 2 by Max Klasse, The impact of Altmark: The European Commission Case Law Responses. See also Neergaard et al. (2013) Social Services of general Interest in the EU, Asser Press.

[99] See i.a. the early analysis of Rapp-Junga (2004), pp. 208–212.

in primary law and recognising the legislative powers of the Commission, which is lacking in the EEA legal order. This point will be returned to in the case study in Chap. 13, but first, the EFTA Court's response to the Altmark-doctrine will be briefly commented upon below.

12.5 Case Law from the EFTA Court Paralleling the Altmark-Doctrine

The EFTA Court has referred to the Altmark-doctrine and applied the compensation approach in a number of cases since the Altmark Trans decision was taken by the CJEU. For an analysis of Altmark in the EFTA Court, reference is made to Peter Dyrberg and Hulda Kristin Magnusdottir's 'Altmark in the EFTA Court with a special focus on Case E-10/11 and 11/11 Hurtigruten'.[100] Other cases include the previously analysed case of E-5/07 Private Barnehagers Landsforbund and Cases E-9/04 The Bankers' and Securities Dealers' Association of Iceland and E-14/10 and E-19/13 Konkurrenten. The case of Hurtigruten was reopened by the Authority, Decision number 490/15/COL, 9 December 2015. The Authority applied the new framework for the provision of SGEI in an EEA context in this reopening decision (see the reference to Commission Decision 2012/21/EU on the application of Article 106(2) TFEU on p 17), and it conducts a detailed assessment of the Altmark criteria on p 9–17. The case was later closed by the Authority.

For present purposes, it is not necessary to include a more detailed analysis of this case law. It is clear that the EFTA Court applies the Altmark doctrine in the EEA regardless of the reliance by the CJEU on Article 14 TFEU for developing this approach. For the purpose of analysing the homogeneity principle, it is worth referring to the fact that the EFTA Court prior to the Altmark decision laying down 'the compensation approach' had adopted the 'state aid approach' originally preferred by the Commission; see Case E-4/97 on the Norwegian State Housing Bank. After the Altmark decision, however, the EFTA Court changed its own earlier approach to align its practice with the decision of the CJEU. Hence, the EFTA Court (and the Authority) has, through the application of the Altmark doctrine, ensured the parallel protection from competition and state aid rules for the provision of public services in the EEA as compared to the EU regardless of the legal basis for this approach referred to in the EU legal order.

As already pointed to, the Altmark doctrine, however, does not provide a sufficient delimitation between the Commission's state aid competence and the Member States' competence to finance public services in the interface between social and economic policy.[101] The next section therefore sets out to analyse in more detail the

[100] Dyrberg and Magnusdottir (2013), pp. 744–751 with a special focus on Case E-10/11 and 11/11 Hurtigruten.

[101] See for a comprehensive analysis in Neergaard et al. (2013).

application of state aid competence by the Commission and the Authority in the sectors of largely non-economic welfare services, in particular of public service broadcasting.

References

Bekkedal T (2008) Frihet, likhet og fellesskap, Fagbokforlaget, p 145
Cruz JB (2013) Social services of general interest and the state aid rules. In: Neergaard U, Szyszczak E, van de Gronden JW, Krajewski M (eds) Social services of general interest in the EU. Asser Press, pp 287–313
de Cecco F (2013) State aid and the European economic constitution. Hart, Oxford, p 143
Dyrberg P, Magnusdottir HK (2013) Altmark in the EFTA court. EStAL, pp 744–751
Fredriksen HH (2009) Er EFTA-domstolen mer katolsk enn paven? Tidsskrift for rettsvitenskap, pp 507–576
Fredriksen HH (2010) The EFTA Court 15 years on. Int Comp Q 59(3):748
Klasse M (2010) Services of general economic interest. In: Heidenhain M (ed) European state aid law handbook. Hart, Oxford
Neergaard U, Szyszczak E, van de Gronden JW, Krajewski M (eds) (2013) Social services of general interest in the EU. Asser Press
Rapp-Junga B (2004) State financing of public services – the commission's new approach, is Altmark the rule or the exception? EStAL 2 2004, pp 205–215
Ross M (2000) Article 16 E.C. and services of general interest: from derogation to obligation. Eur Law Rev 25(1):22–38
Sauter W (2014) Public services in EU law. Cambridge University Press, pp 120–122
Schweitzer H (2011) Services of general economic interest: European law's impact of the role of markets and of member states. In: Cremona M (ed) Market integration and public services in the European Union. Oxford University Press, pp 11–62
Slot PJ (2013) Public distortions of competition: the importance of Article 106 TFEU and the state action doctrine. In: Neergaard U, Szyszczak E, van de Gronden JW, Krajewski M (eds) Social services of general interest in the EU. Asser Press, pp 245–262
Sørum T (2003) Collective agreements and competition law, point 3.8., SIMPLY, vol 309, pp 251–270
Szyszczak E (2011) Altmark assessed. In: Szyszczak E (ed) Research handbook on European State aid law. Edward Elgar, Cheltenham
Szyszczak E (2012) Modernising State aid and the financing of SGEI. J Eur Competition Law Pract 3(4):332–343
Szyszczak E, van de Gronden JW (eds) (2013) Financing services of general economic interest. Springer
Tryfonidou A (2013) Free movement of workers and Union citizens. In: Neergaard U, Szyszczak E, van de Gronden JW, Krajewski M (eds) Social services of general interest in the EU. Asser Press, pp 161–183

Chapter 13
The Exercise of State Aid Competence by the Commission and the EFTA Surveillance Authority in the Sectors of Largely Non-economic Welfare Services

13.1 Introduction

The constitutional framework of the EU legal order has changed from being market oriented to encompassing other aims and values. This includes protecting citizens in the field of public services. The CJEU has ensured that state welfare provision in the form of financing public services to some extent enjoys protection from EU competition and state aid law by respecting national choices to this effect. The above analysis of the two concepts of economic versus non-economic activity and the concept of an undertaking as well as the Altmark doctrine demonstrates areas where the Court has imposed limits on the competence of the Commission to conduct a state aid review of national measures. The analysis demonstrates that the EEA integration process has developed in parallel with the EU integration in delimiting the competence of the Authority in areas of state welfare activities from competition and state aid rules.

However, these concepts and doctrines do not exclude social welfare services from the scope of EU law. There are a range of public services, including social services, which operate in a market and which are subject to state aid scrutiny to ensure a level playing field. What is argued here is that the state aid scrutiny in the EU legal order has moved to go beyond controlling efficiency and functionality of markets and now reaches quite far into the domestic social order of the state. This section sets out to explore whether the EEA Agreement has developed in parallel also in these sectors, which include social housing, healthcare, local media, culture and education.

The case study examined in detail is the media field, concentrating on public service broadcasting. This case study includes an analysis of the significance of the lack of the Amsterdam Protocol and the revised Article 107(3)(d) TFEU in the EEA in this sector. Outside the field of public service broadcasting, another potential area

K. Fløistad, *The EEA Agreement in a Revised EU Framework for Welfare Services*, Studies in European Economic Law and Regulation 13,
https://doi.org/10.1007/978-3-319-95043-3_13

for a case study to illuminate these questions would be social housing.[1] The Husbanken decision involved an assessment of whether the framework conditions for the Norwegian State Housing Bank (Husbanken) were in conformity with the EEA Agreement. Husbanken provided subsidised loans for housing purposes and was shielded against competition from banks and mortgage companies. The framework conditions enjoyed by Husbanken were regarded as going beyond what was acceptable under Article 59(2) of the EEA Agreement; see Case E-4/97. The Court required the Authority to conduct a proportionality test that involved an assessment of whether Husbanken's costs to render the SGEI were not overcompensated, were limited to what was necessary for Husbanken to perform the specific service in question and would not affect trade to an extent contrary to the interests of the Contracting Parties. The decision by the EFTA Court prompts the question of whether the state aid review was to be conducted in a manner where the EFTA Surveillance Authority was entitled to prescribe the least distortive solution for the achievement of the Norwegian housing policy goals. In doing so, the freedom of Norway to regulate its housing policy according to political goals could potentially be limited. In the final decisions, the Authority concluded that the Husbanken system did not appear inappropriate for the realisation of housing policy objectives; see Decision No. 121/00/COL, 28 June 2000.

For other cases on social housing measures, see also the Icelandic saga of the Housing Financing Fund (HFF). The decision to close the investigation by the Authority on the grounds that the measure was compatible with the EEA Agreement under Article 59(2) in Decision No. COL 213/04 was challenged by competitors in commercial banks. The EFTA Court annulled the Authority's decision in Case E-9/04, The Bankers' and Securities Dealers' Association of Iceland. The aid was later considered as existing aid, and appropriate measures were proposed; see Decisions No COL 406/08, COL 247/11 and COL 364/11.[2]

In the field of education and learning materials note should also be taken of Case E-1/12[3] regarding alleged state aid granted to Nasjonal Digital Læringsarena, an inter-county cooperation body involved in the obligation of the counties to provide pupils with the necessary printed and digital learning materials. The EFTA Surveillance Authority concluded that the transfer of 30, five million Norwegian kroner to the participating counties over a 3 year period did not constitute state aid. The reasoning was based on the lack of economic activity and the solidaristic nature of the activity of the cooperation body. The Authority considered the activity of purchasing, developing and supplying digital learning materials for free to fall within the scope of activities that fulfils the duties towards the population in the educational field.[4] The EFTA Court on the other hand dismissed the reasoning of the

[1] This has to some extent already been analysed by Karlsson (2014), pp. 470–490, see previous chapter.

[2] For an analysis of the tensions between the provision of social housing in several Member States and EU market regulations, see Gruis and Elsinga's article (2014), pp. 463–469.

[3] Decided 11 December 2012.

[4] Case E-1/12 Den norske forleggerforening, paragraph 31.

EFTA Surveillance Authority, annulled the decision and ordered the Authority to initiate the state aid procedure.[5]

Public broadcasting service is therefore not the only area to illuminate the extent to which the state aid competences of the EFTA Surveillance Authority have reached into the domestic social orders of the EFTA States. Public service broadcasting provides, however, an illuminating example of this tendency for several reasons.

In the public broadcasting sector, the Commission guidelines essentially set out how to balance conflicting concerns in providing this essentially non-economic service.[6] This is an example of the Commission and the Authority performing a policy-maker role, applying their discretionary powers in the interface between economic and social policy. In the public broadcasting field, additional primary law changes provide the legal basis for the Commission's guidelines and practices.[7]

To carry out the study, the analysis begins with the special character of this public service and continues with a description of how a broadcasting market was created, including the impact of the market on national public broadcasters. Subsequent steps of the analysis provide an assessment of both the Commission's and the Authority's general guidelines and decisional practice in the field of state aid to public service broadcasting. Finally, some concluding remarks are presented.

13.2 The Special Character of the Provision of Public Service Broadcasting

Public service broadcasting is not comparable to a public service in any other sector. No other service 'has access to such a wide sector of the population, provides it with so much information and content, and by doing so conveys and influences both individual and public opinion'.[8]

Public service broadcasting provides an example of the public interest being linked to a certain ethos and value orientation that is inherently foreign to any form of market rationality.[9] It is difficult to consider public service broadcasting as an economic activity given that the market is considered per se to be incapable in providing the public interest task.[10] Unlike other public services, for example, in the sectors of communication and transport, even periodic competition for the market is

[5] See also Case E-8/13 Abelia regarding state aid in the educational sector.

[6] Confer Schweitzer three models presented in the introduction, Schweitzer (2011), pp. 11–62.

[7] The Amsterdam Protocol and the revised Article 107(3)(d) TFEU.

[8] 2009 Commission Broadcasting Communication, EFTA Surveillance Authority's Broadcasting Communication.

[9] Schweitzer (2011), p. 46.

[10] Case T-442/03 SIC v Commission [2008] ECR II-1161, paragraphs 151, 153, 154.

incompatible with the values attached to a public service like public service broadcasting.[11]

In the M6/TF1 Decision, the General Court made an important statement about the special characteristics of the public service broadcasting sector by underlining that it is not so much about the commercial dimension of public service broadcasting itself but rather about its impact on the other commercial broadcasters that this service is at all qualified as a service of general economic interest rather than a non-economic activity.

> Furthermore, in the absence—as in this case—of Community rules governing the matter, the Commission is not entitled to rule on the basis of public service tasks assigned to the public operator, such as the level of costs linked to that service, or the expediency of the political choices made in this regard by the national authorities, or the economic efficiency of the public operator.[12]

In the SIC judgment regarding the Portuguese public service broadcaster RTP, the General Court pointed to the specific nature of public broadcasting, namely its direct relation to 'the democratic, social and cultural needs of society' and its 'specific status' under the Amsterdam Protocol.[13] This supported the Court in finding that a Member State cannot be required to have recourse to competitive tendering for the award of such a service.[14] It is also claimed in the literature with a reference to the case law that where a Member State determines the amount of compensation to be paid for public service broadcasting within the framework of a procedure that involves a serious economic analysis drawn up with relevant input from the competitors of the public service broadcasters, the Altmark conditions should in principle be fulfilled and the application of Article 107(1) TFEU rejected on that basis.[15]

Nevertheless, both the Commission and the Authority conduct state aid reviews in the sector of public service broadcasting through guidelines and individual decisions. This case study sets out to examine first the Commission's approach including the legal basis and next the approach of the Authority.[16] The overall aim is to examine the extent to which the homogeneity principle ensures a parallel

[11] Cremona (2011), p. 5.

[12] Joined Cases T-568/08 and T-573/08, M6 [2010] ECR 2010 II-3397, appeal rejected Case C-451/10.

[13] Case T-442/03 SIC v Commission [2008] ECR II-1161, paragraphs 151, 153, 154.

[14] At least where it has decided to ensure that public service itself through a public company, Case T-442/03 SIC v Commission [2008] ECR II-1161, paragraphs 151, 153, 154. In such circumstances the Court's concerns seems to be limited to ensuring that the competition *in* the market is distorted as little as possible.

[15] Se the view of the General Court in Joined Cases T-309/04, 317/04, 329/04 and 336/04 TV 2 Denmark A/S v Commission [2008] ECR II-2935, paragraphs 232–233 and the analysis by Schweitzer (2011), p. 47.

[16] The individual decisions by the Commission are by no means exhaustively analysed. Fairly recent articles on the Commission decisional practice can be found in Donders (2015), pp. 68–87. The decisional practice is only analysed for the purpose of the consequences for the EEA Agreement.

development of regulating public service broadcasting in the EEA integration process despite differences in the legal framework.

The section is structured in the following way. First, how the internal market contributed to the creation of a broadcasting market is explained, and second, the effect this market had on the public service broadcasters allegedly interfering with the safeguarding of democratic, social and cultural concerns at the national level is examined (Sect. 13.3). The next section addresses the means under EU law to address the conflicting interest involved for the organising and financing of this public service (Sect. 13.4). In short, the Member States at first insisted on full protection for national public service broadcasters, introducing several primary law initiatives to this effect.[17] One important initiative was the adoption of the Amsterdam Protocol. While the Protocol clearly pointed to Member States' sovereign rights in the field of public service broadcasting, the Commission has also interpreted the Amsterdam Protocol to include more powers at the EU level in line with its general understanding of an increased policymaking role through the state aid review.[18]

The identified need to protect public service broadcasters from the adverse effects resulting from the application of market rules prompted the Commission to develop a policy of public service broadcasting (Sect. 13.5). This policy has affected the Member States' competences to freely organise and finance their public service broadcasters. The Commission policy has been conducted through issuing general guidelines but also through its individual decisional practice.[19] It will be demonstrated how both the guidelines and the decisional practice involve necessarily a degree of balancing of interests by the Commission at the EU level that goes beyond controlling the efficiency and functionality of markets to also include safeguarding necessary national interests, such as democratic, social and cultural concerns. Analysing this policy has led commentators to question the detailed regulation of public service broadcasters stemming from the exercise of state aid competence by the Commission, which arguably has limited Member States' autonomy in protecting their national public service broadcasters, in particular in the delivery of new services.[20] The present analysis does not take a stance on the right level of intervention by the Commission in EU law. The discussion is merely presented as a basis upon which to analyse the EEA integration process.

Finally, the analysis is concentrated on the EFTA Surveillance Authority and the exercise of its state aid competence under the EEA Agreement in the sector of public service broadcasting (Sect. 13.6). Both the general guidelines and the individual

[17] Reference is made to now Article 14 TFEU (introduced by the Treaty of Amsterdam as Article 16) and Article 167 TFEU on culture and Article 4(2) TEU on regions.

[18] It is the following condition within the last sentence in the Protocol which has been interpreted in this manner, see also Sect. 11.1 above on the policymaking role 'and insofar as such funding does not affect trading conditions and competition in the Community to an extent which would be contrary to the common interest'.

[19] See the fairly recent analysis by Karen Donders of the Commission's decisional practice, Donders (2015), pp. 68–87.

[20] See reference above Donders (2015), pp. 68–87.

decision making are included. Despite the fact that no revised constitutional framework has been included in the EEA Agreement, the analysis demonstrates that the Authority exercises its state aid competence in full parallel with the Commission, taking on the same legislative role.

The provision of certain public services is concerns citizens' participation in a democratic society, and in the case of public broadcasting, even further considerations justify special treatment. The provision of news, comment and current affairs programmes are, for reasons of civil society, to be provided in a fact-oriented way and by numerous sources. To achieve media pluralism, there is need for the presentation of different points of view. In addition, public broadcasting raises cultural concerns. The citizens expect to receive a certain variety of programmes, to learn from them and even perhaps to discover new preferences. Furthermore, there are lingual concerns linked to culture also in need of protection.[21] This includes national/regional language considerations, national/regional cultural productions and more generally cultural identity concerns. Taking a holistic approach, the public service broadcaster appeals to the various groups that constitute a society and brings them together.[22]

Public service broadcasters safeguard a number of these concerns at the national level. They are often appreciated in their role in promoting cultural diversity, in providing educational programming, in informing public opinion and in supplying quality entertainment. The importance of public service broadcasting for social, democratic and cultural life is broadly recognised.[23]

It is well established in economic literature that the provision of programmes aimed at addressing the needs related to the democratic, social and cultural needs of each society and the need to preserve media pluralism is likely to result in market failure. Examples include public broadcasting aimed at regional even linguistic minorities, concerning niche events or allowing debate/new documentaries with equal representation of political voices. More examples could be listed of programmes which are almost by definition unlikely to attract large audiences. The advertising revenues depend on the number and age category of viewers and will be insufficient to compensate the costs incurred for the provision of these programmes. The same holds true for distribution revenue.

Since the market does not provide for sufficient incentives for providing this media pluralism, public intervention is in order, and this calls for the characterisation of public broadcasting as a public service. In addition to identifying specific programmes not provided for by the market, it is often argued that the public service

[21] A fairly recent Report to the Norwegian Parliament discusses these concerns in view of the Norwegian model for delivering public service broadcasting; see Stortingsmelding Meld. St.38 (2014–15) Åpen og opplyst—Allmennkringkasting og mediemangfald.

[22] See the development of the 'cultural model' for public service broadcasting with citizenship, universality and quality, Prosser (2005), p. 210 with further references.

[23] There are a number of academic studies in the media sector analysing these effects, see Craufurd Smith (2011), pp. 869–897 with further references.

broadcasters must be viewed in a holistic manner.[24] It is the totality of the service that ensures the broad influence and the wide penetration and deserves to be characterised as a fundamental area of traditional state activity.[25] Based on the importance of the public broadcasting service for democratic, social and cultural concerns, there is an assumption that such broadcasters should be active in different markets on different platforms with a diversity of genres and content.[26]

Within the recognition of this special character of public service broadcasting, there are two conflicting perspectives on public service broadcasting operating in a market. Following one perspective, public broadcasters have a competitive advantage over other market players. They may be viewed as too generously funded, and their activities lack sufficient transparency and control. According to this perspective, public broadcasters should be small and constrained in their activities with limited possibilities to expand their services to the internet, digital television and mobile devices. Defenders of an opposite perspective support the idea of a strong and 'all-encompassing' public broadcaster providing different genres of content (also entertainment and sports) and a public broadcaster that is active in all media markets. Regulation as well as public funding should, according to this second perspective, be flexible to guarantee the independence and secure the innovative potential of public broadcasters as holistic service providers.[27]

Cutting across these two perspectives is the dimension of competence. In other words, this refers to how to draw the line between EU competence and Member State competence to assess the conflicting interests. The classical approach for SGEI in general is that the Member States have definitional powers over what constitutes a SGEI, the level or quality of the service provided nationally and, in essence, the amount of public spending that should be attributed to providing the service. The EU will in general have competence to assess that the financing complies with state aid principles, such as avoiding overcompensation and cross-subsidies into possible market activities of the public service provider. This assessment requires transparency and openness to be effective. In the public broadcasting sector, this means that it is for the Member State to define the public service remit, including the level or quality of the service, to ensure democratic, social and cultural concerns at the national level. Only in cases of manifest errors will this definitional freedom be limited. The EU will generally scrutinise the financing of the

[24] See the case TV2 A/S Denmark and the wide margin of discretion regarding the definition of the remit, Case C-660/15 P Viasat, see also the approach taken by the General Court in Joined Cases T-309/04, 317/04, 329/04 and 336/04 TV 2 Denmark A/S v Commission [2008] ECR II-2935.

[25] With the technological changes, linear television is for at least some groups of the population replaced by streaming. The argument of the totality of the service is somewhat different when programmes are streamed. Surveys demonstrate however that for large parts of the population linear television is still the preferred option.

[26] A number of decisions from the EU Courts recognise the special character of this service, see the referred decisions in this chapter.

[27] More on these perspectives in Stortingsmelding Meld. St.38 (2014–15) Åpen og opplyst—Allmennkringkasting og mediemangfald, and Innstilling frå familie. Og kulturkomiteen om Open og opplyst. Allmennkringkasting og mediemangfald.

public service provider for possible overcompensation and incidents of cross-subsidisation. It is argued here that, increasingly in the EU, this division of competence is being blurred to the detriment of Member States' definitional freedom. Before exploring the consequences of this perspective for the EEA integration process, the creation of a broadcasting market will be presented.

13.3 Creating a Broadcasting Market: The Non-profit Provision of Public Service Broadcasting

Until the early 1980s, very little market integration had been achieved in the broadcasting sector. The 1984 Green Paper on Television Without Frontiers (TWF Green Paper)[28] revealed the existence of ten different national broadcasting markets dominated by and large by public undertakings. The segmentation of the market along national boundaries was furthermore ensured by the CJEU in its early rulings accepting wide discretion on each Member State in the absence of any harmonisation.[29] Illustrative is the Sacchi case where the Italian statutory broadcasting monopoly was brought before the Court.[30] It was understood that nothing in EU law prevented the Member States from removing radio and television transmissions from the field of competition by conferring on an undertaking an exclusive right to carry out such activities.[31] Thus, the EU institutions at the time in principle did not interfere with these public undertakings enjoying special and exclusive rights, since public broadcasters under the Sacchi doctrine were legitimately sheltered from competition at the national level.[32,33]

The TWF Green Paper paved the way for the Television Without Frontiers Directive (TWF Directive) adopted 5 years later. The TWF Green Paper is of interest here given that it laid down some key principles governing the application of EU law to public service broadcasting. In particular, the paper clarified the interpretation of three primary law provisions, which are all paralleled in the EEA Agreement

[28] Green paper on the establishment of the common market for broadcasting, especially by satellite and cable, COM (1984) 300 final (TWF Green Paper), pp. 63–105.

[29] See i.a. Case 52/79 Debauve [1980] ECR 833.

[30] Case 155/73 Sacchi [1974] ECR 40.

[31] Provided the principle of non-discrimination was not violated.

[32] The ruling in ERT provided further guidance as to the scope of statutory monopolies, Case C-260/89 Elliniki Radiophonia [1991] ECR I-2925. In regard to monopolies the Court stated that 'Article 90(1) of the Treaty (now Article 106 (1) TFEU prohibits the granting of an exclusive right to transmit and an exclusive right to retransmit television broadcasts to a single undertaking, where those rights are liable to create a situation in which that undertaking is led to infringe Article 86 (now Article 102) by virtue of a discriminatory broadcasting policy which favours its own programmes, unless the application of Article 86 (now article 102) obstructs the performance of the particular tasks entrusted to it'.

[33] Regarding the question of establishing state monopolies in certain sectors reference should be made to the EFTA Court Cases E-1/06 Norsk Tipping and the subsequent E-3/06 Ladbrokes.

and which could have brought public service broadcasting outside the scope of EU law. The Green Paper is thus important to understand the Commission's interpretation of the following provisions: Articles 54 (2), 51(1), 106(2) TFEU paralleled in the EEA by Articles 34(2), 32 and 59(2).

Given that several of the important undertakings entrusted with the operation of public service broadcasting at the time were non-profit making,[34] it could be argued that those undertakings fell outside the scope of EU law. The Commission specified, however, that non-profit making in Article 54(2) TFEU (Article 34(2) EEA) should not be interpreted literally but was rather a Union concept applying to companies that took part in commercial life, namely carried out 'an economic activity'. Even if the objective had to do with information, culture or sport, once this was linked to a commercially relevant activity, the company was within the scope of EU law.[35]

Furthermore, the Commission refused to recognise public service broadcasting as an activity even occasionally connected to the exercise of official authority, which is outside the scope by virtue of Article 51 (Article 32 EEA).[36] The national broadcasters are 'not placed over the people they deal with' but rather at the same level, and thus, the broadcasters did not issue binding legal acts or exercise compulsion.[37]

In terms of Article 106(2) (Article 59(2) EEA), see more details on these provisions in previous Chap. 11, the Commission dealt with the concept of an undertaking and the concept of an entrustment act. The national broadcasters were considered as undertakings, and conditions were put in place for the entrustment act to ensure that the particular task assigned to it was to be recognised under EU law as being in the general economic interest. In broader terms, the provision was referred to as a 'conditional exception', i.e. an exception dependent on a prior examination of the consequences of the application of the individual Treaty rules to the undertaking concerned. It was thus for the Commission on a case-by-case basis to determine whether the application of those rules would obstruct the performance of the general interest task assigned to that undertaking. The Commission also seems to have established a presumption that the application of the rules on free movement in principle did not obstruct the performance by public service broadcasters of their own task.[38]

Thus, the articles that could have brought public service broadcasting outside the scope of EU law did not do so according to the Commission, and this understanding

---

[34] According to the TWF Green Paper, this included the RAI in Italy, DR in Denmark, ERT in Greece, RTE in Ireland and the BBC and IBA in the UK, p 205. Although not included in the Green paper the Norwegian NRK and the Icelandic RÚV could have been listed as a non-profit undertaking.

[35] Green paper on the establishment of the common market for broadcasting, especially by satellite and cable, COM (1984) 300 final (TWF Green paper), p. 206.

[36] This approach was based on case law from the CJEU, see i.a. Case C-149/79 Commission v Belgium [1982] ECR 1845.

[37] TWF Green paper, p. 203.

[38] See the interpretation by Mastroianni (2011), p. 157.

was later adopted as EU law and as EEA law through the adoption of harmonised legislation and later through the adoption of general guidelines for public service broadcasting and decisional practice.

In the broadcasting sector, the TWF Directive approximated the legislation of Member States in certain sensitive sectors of the broadcasting activity.[39] However, most importantly, in terms of opening up for competition is the system set up by the Directive of home state control for the subject matters that fall within its scope. It is for the transmitting state to ensure compliance by the rules applicable to the broadcaster. The receiving state cannot restrict retransmission on its territory of audiovisual media services from other Member States for reasons that fall within the fields covered by the Directive. The exceptions from this obligation not to restrict retransmission are narrow and presuppose that a broadcast 'manifestly, seriously and gravely' infringes specific Directive provisions.[40] Thus, effectively, the TWF Directive and its successor the AVMS Directive are market integration instruments.[41]

The home state control principle opened up to foreign competition on formerly closed national broadcasting markets. The decoupling of national boundaries threatened to undermine the financial position of the public broadcasters. The question arose as to the possibility of keeping the privileges the public broadcasters enjoyed in terms of preferential access to broadcasting frequencies, financial assistance by way of subventions or licence fees revenues etc. In other words, the adoption of the harmonising measure called for a new approach to justify these privileges, which in the language of market efficiency placed commercial broadcasters at a competitive disadvantage.

As already pointed to above, EU action was critisised by some for not leaving enough room for broader social and political considerations, and more specifically, for the EU action not to sufficiently take account of local or national concerns. The focus on economic efficiency highlighted tensions in relation to other concerns, in particular concerns over social and cultural matters. Applying competition and state aid law to public services threatened, in some instances, to bring a close to the public service tradition. An identified need to combine open markets with public interest in this sector as well as in other sectors gradually became more evident.

Several initiatives were introduced to emphasise the necessity to strike a better balance between liberalisation and market integration and the general interest objectives entrusted to these services. The necessity stems from the perceived threat of liberalisation measures to services which include distinct social and cultural concerns. This recognition led to new strategies for the internal market to properly take account of the need to reconcile market objectives with social aspects.[42]

---

[39] Sectors such as television advertising (now Articles 19–26 AVMS), the protection of minors (Article 27 AVMS), the right of reply (Article 28 AVMS).

[40] See Articles 3(2), 3(4).

[41] The EFTA Court case law on the Directive includes the Mattel/Lego Decision, Joined Cases 8/94 and 9/94 and the TV1000 case, E-8/97.

[42] See i.a. Report to the President of the European Commission published 9 May 2010, A New Strategy for the Single market: At the Service of Europe's Economy and Society.

The shift in focus is brought about by a combination of legal sources including changes in primary law, which will be the focus in the next sections.

13.4 The Legal Framework for the Provision of Public Service Broadcasting

As already demonstrated, the opening up of markets for broadcasting in the EU Member States including the EFTA States in the 1980s and 1990s had an effect on the traditional national monopolies of public service broadcasting. Over the years, beginning in the late 1990s, the Commission received a number of complaints from private broadcasters and other market actors regarding the mandate, the operation and the financing of the different public service broadcasters. A growing concern for a level playing field emerged with calls for strict state aid control from new entrants and private competitors. The Commission communicated its policies in the public broadcasting sector first in the Communication from 2001[43] and then in its revised Communication from 2009.[44] Both Communications were largely reproduced in the EEA and are of particular interest here.

Due to the conflicting perspectives regarding the role of public service broadcasters in the liberalised broadcasting market, the need for an EU policy became increasingly important. The question for the EU was how to reconcile the different interests (economic efficiency and market integration in the broadcasting sector with democratic, social and cultural values provided by the public service broadcasters) when developing an EU policy for intervention to scrutinise the national actors providing public service broadcasting.

The legal framework upon which to base the EU broadcasting policy included several primary law provisions. First, it was the Treaty provisions stemming from the Treaty of Rome regarding SGEI in general: the prohibition of state aid in Article 107 TFEU and the exception for the application of the Treaty rules under specific conditions (including the state aid provision) in Article 106(2) TFEU. Second, the revised primary law of the EU such as Article 14 TFEU and the Amsterdam Protocol on public service broadcasting (both introduced by the Amsterdam Treaty), as well as Article 167 TFEU on respecting national cultures (introduced as Article 151 EEC by the Maastricht Treaty), were all part of the legal framework to develop an EU policy in the field of public service broadcasting.

Of particular importance is the introduction of the Protocol on public broadcasters in the Amsterdam Treaty.[45] The Amsterdam Protocol is binding in nature and ranks at primary law level in the hierarchy of legal sources. According to Article 51

[43] Commission Broadcasting Communication 2001, 2001/C 320/04.

[44] Commission Broadcasting Communication 2009, 2009/C 257/01.

[45] Treaty of Amsterdam, Protocol on the Systems of Public Broadcasting in the Member States (1997), now Protocol 29 annexed to the TFEU.

TEU, protocols have the same legal status as Treaty provisions. The protocols are thus considered as primary law in the EU.

The Protocol recites that

> the system of public broadcasting in the Member States is directly related to the democratic, social and cultural needs of each society and to the need to preserve media pluralism'. It states further that the provisions of the Treaty 'shall be without prejudice to the competence of Member States to provide for the funding of public service broadcasting insofar as such funding is granted to broadcasting organisations for the fulfilment of the public service remit as conferred, defined and organised by each Member State, and insofar as such funding does not affect trading conditions and competition in the Community to an extent which would be contrary to the common interest, while the realisation of the remit of that public service shall be taken into account.

The Amsterdam Treaty entered into force in 1999, and the Commission published its first Communication on public service broadcasting in 2001. More than 20 cases were later assessed individually based on this Communication, including the role of national public service broadcasters in Member States such as the UK, the Netherlands, Belgium, Denmark, Germany, Ireland, Spain and Italy.[46] The Communication has a dual nature. On the one hand, its goal is to stress the recognition in EU law of the important public interest objectives that public service broadcasting serves, and on the other, it articulates the importance of limitations on the funding of public service broadcasters by EU state aid rules. The Communication gives three criteria for the Commission's assessment of the compatibility of public service broadcasters with the primary law. These criteria are (i) definition and entrustment, (ii) control and monitoring and (iii) proportionality. All three criteria are important for the assessment of Member States' definitional freedom.

The 2001 Communication was later revised in 2009 i.a. introducing the so-called Amsterdam test to assess new media activity of public service broadcasters. In the revised Communication, the Commission increases the pressure on Member States when defining and entrusting the public service remit, especially concerning digital services; see criteria (i) above. This runs the risk of limiting further the definitional freedom of the Member States, making it difficult for the national actors to experiment with new business models according to market developments. Furthermore, the monitoring and control mechanisms (see criteria ii), which are closely linked to the remit, are more scrupulously assessed. Regarding the third criteria on proportionality, the question of overcompensation becomes more detailed regarding the digital expansion of the remit. Overcompensation, which in turn assumes a high degree of transparency, also has an impact on Member States' definitional freedom, since the calculation is by no means a straightforward mathematical exercise.

The 'Amsterdam test' is based on an understanding of the Amsterdam Protocol to grant citizens and market participants the opportunity to give their views on the value and potential impact of planned new media offers based on public spending.

[46] http://ec.europa.eu/competition/sectors/media/decisions_psb.pdf.

The pros and cons stemming from the public consultation complying with the Amsterdam test should then be taken into account at the national level in a balancing exercise of how public money for new media offers should be spent. Arguably, the Amsterdam test integrates the balancing of economic efficiency and market integration with public policy concerns of a broader nature into an EU framework.

The 2009 broadcasting Communication is rooted in a wider policy of the EU revolving around the SGEI package[47] and the reconciliation of economic efficiency and market integration with other values of public services in general. The Amsterdam test does not change fundamentally the division of competences between the EU and its Member States regarding defining the remit of public service broadcasters and the financing of these services, but it does demonstrate an ever more active EU engaging with uniform standards and procedures to influence essentially (previously) national decisions. The Communication underlines the role of the Commission being a policymaker with significant discretionary powers.

13.5 The European Commission's Decisional Practice

The Commission has decided several cases affecting the funding schemes of public broadcasters in EU Member States. The main principles upon which the Commission has reached its decisions are the following: (1) a well-defined public task, (2) the formal entrustment and independent control thereof and (3) proportionality of state aid. Karen Donders has reviewed the Commission's decisional practice.[48] Her findings indicate that not only has the Commission forced Member States to introduce basic principles of good governance into their aid schemes for public service broadcasting, but the Commission seems to be moving towards a kind of 'micro-management' of public service media.

This 'micro-management' is especially striking regarding new online and mobile services of public broadcasters. In a decision regarding the Austrian public service broadcaster ORF,[49] the Commission required a clearer definition of the public service remit and set quite detailed conditions for new media services to be included in the remit in the form of an *ex ante* test. For example, in case ORF operates an online web platform for seniors and it decides to do something similar for youngsters, the initiative would generally amount to a new service having to undergo the *ex ante* test. The same requirement of undergoing a test would be needed, for example, if Austria wanted ORF to launch a new channel for documentaries and investigative journalism.[50]

In the decision regarding Dutch public broadcasting organisations, a number of issues were addressed regarding the definition of the remit, the control mechanisms

---

[47] Commission Broadcasting Communication 2001, 2001/C 320/04, Commission Broadcasting Communication 2009, 2009/C 257/01.

[48] Donders (2015), pp. 68–87.

[49] Commission decision E2/2008, 28 October 2009.

[50] Commission decision E2/2008, 28 October 2009, paragraph 177.

and the proportionality of the funding.[51] The Commission set detailed requirements concerning scope and duration of pilot projects, taking a more rigid stance compared to earlier practices.[52] Finally, in the recent decision on the Walloon public broadcaster concerning the funding for RTBF, an impressive list of appropriate measures is included.[53] The Commission included specific time limits for the offer of non-linear and online services and made specific requirements of links to be included as well as specifying that the RTBF needed to limit its digital development in some ways to ensure that the pluralism in the written press would remain and possible distortions of competition remained limited.[54] In setting this condition for compatibility, the Commission is effectively applying its state aid competence to force Member States to limit the digital development of its public service broadcasters. The requirements to conduct an ex ante test were also detailed and specific limiting the operation of the public service broadcaster.[55]

The link between this micro-management by the Commission and market concerns has been questioned, and Donders discusses whether the various requirements set by the Commission in the decisional practice in the field of public service broadcasters really can be based on state aid control.[56] Moreover, it has been questioned whether the Commission is actually pushing for regulating and harmonising public service broadcasting across Europe through the application of its state aid powers.[57] All of this is of course controversial also within the EU integration process. The task here is, however, limited to assessing whether the homogeneity principle has ensured the same intervention in the field of public service broadcasting in the EEA integration process, which leads to the next section on the EFTA Surveillance Authority's decisional practice.

13.6 The EFTA Surveillance Authority's Decisional Practice

13.6.1 General Guidelines

The EFTA Surveillance Authority issued a Communication on the application of state aid to public service broadcasters in substance parallel to the Commission's Communication issued late 2001.[58] In the EEA, the new chapter in the state aid

[51] Commission decision E5/2005, 26 January 2010.

[52] Donders (2015), pp. 68–87, in section IV, 2 with further references.

[53] Commission decision 2012/E paragraph 273–279, 7 May 2014.

[54] Commission decision 2012/E paragraph 273–279, 7 May 2014, paragraph 266.

[55] Commission decision 2012/E paragraph 273–279, 7 May 2014, paragraph 258.

[56] Donders (2015), pp. 80–81.

[57] Donders (2015), pp. 80–81.

[58] Communication from the Commission on the Application of State Aid rules to Public Service Broadcasting, 2001/C 320/4, [2001] OJ C320/05.

guidelines related to public broadcasting was adopted 24 April 2004. The 2001 Communication was later revised by the Commission in its 2009 Communication,[59] which was also paralleled in the EEA through a decision by the Authority.[60] This Communication specifically on public service broadcasting must also be seen in relation to the 2011 package on the Commission's general policy support for SGEI.[61] In addition, the 2011 package on SGEI was paralleled in the EEA in the State Aid Guidelines in Part VI: Rules on Public Service Compensation, State Ownership of Enterprises and Aid to Public Enterprises, as already commented upon.[62]

The Communication on the application of state aid rules to public service broadcasting in the EEA mainly copies word by word the Communication from the Commission. This correspondence between the two is also referred to in the Communication.[63] Interestingly, some words are, however, omitted in the Surveillance Authority's Communication. The first example can be found in paragraph 2 where the following reference in the Communication from the Commission to the Amsterdam Protocol is not included:

> This was confirmed in the interpretative protocol on the system of public broadcasting in the Member States, annexed to the EC Treaty (hereinafter referred to as the Amsterdam Protocol).

In the Commission Communication, the word 'this' in the citation refers back to the common understanding of Member States on how the public service broadcasting ought to be maintained.

The description on how the EFTA States consider that public service broadcasting ought to be maintained can be found in the Authority's Communication and is formulated in the following manner, namely as a way to ensure 'the coverage of a number of areas and the satisfaction of needs and public policy objectives that would otherwise not necessarily be fulfilled to the optimal extent'. This is, however, substantively word for word a parallel to the Commission Communication. The reference to the source for the common view, which in the EU is the Amsterdam Protocol, is, however, omitted in the EEA version. There is consequently no source for the shared view of the EFTA States. Given that the shared view referred to is identical to the shared view by the Member States, the formulation in the guidelines seems to be a technique for including primary law of the EU into the EEA Agreement, albeit in a subtle manner.

---

[59] Communication from the Commission on the application of State aid rules to public service broadcasting, OJ C 257, 27.10.2009, p. 1.

[60] http://www.eftasurv.int/media/state-aid-guidelines/Part-IV%2D%2D-The-application-of-the-state-aid-rules-to-public-service-broadcasting.pdf.

[61] The 2011 package replaced the 2005 package from the Commission on SGEI.

[62] http://www.eftasurv.int/media/state-aid-guidelines/Part-VI%2D%2D-Compensation-granted-for-the-provision-of-services-of-general-economic-interest.pdf.

[63] See Chap. 1 in note 1, p. 1.

In paragraph 10, the reference to the freedom of expression in Article 11 in the Charter for fundamental rights is omitted in the Authority's Communication given that the Charter has not been made part of the EEA Agreement.

In paragraph 11 in the Communication from the Commission, there is a reference to Article 16 EC (present Article 14 TFEU) in addition to Article 86(2) EC (present Article 106(2). In the Communication from the Authority, the reference is limited to Article 59(2) EEA, which parallels Article 106(2) TFEU. Furthermore, in the Communication from the Commission, it is stated clearly that the interpretation of these Treaty provisions is outlined in the Amsterdam Protocol, which is then cited. The Amsterdam Protocol focuses on the fact that the system of public broadcasting in the Member States is directly related to the democratic, social and cultural needs of each society and to the need to preserve media pluralism. This same terminology is used by the Authority in its examination of the national public broadcasters in Norway and Iceland, adopting the same interpretation substantively as declared in the Protocol.[64] These decisions will be examined in more detail below. In paragraph 12 of the Authority's Communication, the words social, democratic and cultural life taken from the Amsterdam Protocol are referred to, but no reference is made to the Protocol given that it has not been made part of the EEA Agreement.

In paragraph 16 of the Commission Communication, the role of private broadcasters is underlined again with a reference to the Amsterdam Protocol. In the Authority's Communication, this reference is substituted with a reference to the Resolution of the Council and of the Representatives of the Governments of the Member States, meeting with the Council of 25 January 1999 concerning public service broadcasting.[65] The Council's Resolution, however, refers to the Amsterdam Protocol and copies essentially the content of the Protocol.[66] The legal basis for the reference to the Council's Resolution in the Authority's Communication is a reference in annex XI to the EEA Agreement.[67] The Council Resolution concerning public service broadcasting is referred to in the EEA Agreement as an act that the Contracting Parties shall take note of by decision No 118/1999.[68]

Again, this reference technique seems to be a way of incorporating primary law changes into the EEA Agreement and creating a legal basis for the application of the in-substance equal rules in the EEA legal order as in the EU legal order.

Further differences in the legal context are made clear in paragraph 17 in the Communication from the Commission stating the following:

---

[64] See for example Dec No 306/09/COL paragraphs 3.2.1, 3.2.2.3.2 several references, 3.3.1, and Dec No: 36/10/COL, p. 3.

[65] OJ C 30, 5.2.1999, p. 1.

[66] See letter d) and the reference in paragraph 1–7.

[67] Resolution of the Council and of the Representatives of the Governments of the Member States, meeting with the Council of 25 January 1999 concerning public service broadcasting, OJ C 30, 5.2.1999, p. 1.

[68] OJ No L 325, 21.12.2000, p. 33 and EEA Supplement No 60, 21.12.2000, p. 423 (Icelandic) and p. 424 (Norwegian), entry into force on 1 October 1999.

> The application of State aid rules to public service broadcasting has to take into account a wide number of different elements. The State aid assessment is based on Articles 87 and 88 on State aid and Article 86(2) on the application of the rules of the Treaty and the competition rules, in particular, to services of general economic interest. The Treaty of Maastricht introduced Article 151 concerning culture and Article 87(3)(d) on aid to promote culture. The Treaty of Amsterdam introduced a specific provision (Article 16) on services of general economic interest and the Amsterdam Protocol on the system of public broadcasting in the Member States.

Again, the Communication from the Commission underlines its dedication to interpret the Treaty provisions in compliance with Article 14 TFEU (former Article 16 EC) and the Amsterdam Protocol. A number of references to primary law not paralleled in the EEA are relied on in this reference to the legal context. Still excluding any reference to Article 14 TFEU and the Amsterdam Protocol, the Communication from the Authority nevertheless makes it clear that even if Article 151 EC (now Article 167 TFEU) on the promotion of culture and Article 87(3)(d) (now Article 107(3)(d)) on aid are not paralleled in the EEA, the Authority will provide similar exceptions based on Article 61(3)(c) EEA (Article 107(3)(c)).

Paragraph 17 in the communication by the Authority states the following:

> The EEA Agreement does not contain a provision similar to Article 167 of the Treaty on the Functioning of the European Union (hereinafter referred to as TFEU) (ex Article 151 of the EC Treaty) concerning culture or a "cultural exemption" for aid to promote culture similar to that contained in Article 107(3)(d) TFEU (ex Article 87(3)(d) of the EC Treaty). However, this does not mean that an exemption for such measures is excluded. As accepted by the Authority in previous cases, such support measures might be approved on cultural grounds on the basis of Article 61(3)(c) of the EEA Agreement.

As demonstrated by the quote, the Communication from the Authority does not repeat the same wording as the Commission's Communication but makes it explicit that the Authority in its practice will reach the same substantial result in the EEA based on the interpretation of a different provision. This seems then to be yet another way of including primary law changes in the EU into the EEA if only through ensuring equal consequences or effects. The understanding by the Authority that an existing legal basis can be interpreted to include the same legal result as a newly introduced Treaty article in the EU is quite novel. It implies that the introduction in the EU legal order of another legal basis for making an exception to the otherwise incompatible state aid measure is actually superfluous.

The Treaty provision on the respect for culture means that the compatibility assessment of aid under Article 107(3) TFEU must take cultural considerations into account. In the Communication by the Commission, there are references to a number of primary law provisions concerning culture that are not paralleled in the EEA. Accordingly, paragraph 33 states the following:

> In accordance with Article 151(4) of the Treaty, the Community is to take cultural aspects into account in its action under other provisions of the Treaty, in particular in order to respect and to promote the diversity of its cultures. Article 87(3)(d) of the Treaty allows the Commission to regard aid to promote culture as compatible with the common market where such aid does not affect trading conditions and competition in the Community to an extent that is contrary to the common interest.

In the Communication from the Authority, this lack of legal provisions on culture is dealt with in a similar manner as already cited. Accordingly, paragraph 32 states the following:

> The EEA Agreement does not contain a provision corresponding to Article 167(4) TFEU, which obliges the Commission to take cultural aspects into account in its actions under other provisions of the Treaty on the Functioning of the European Union, in particular in order to respect and to promote the diversity of its cultures. Nor does it contain a cultural exemption similar to Article 107(3)(d) TFEU, which allows the Commission to regard aid to promote culture as compatible with the common market where such aid does not affect trading conditions and competition in the Community to an extent that is contrary to the common interest. This does not, however, mean that the application of the state aid rules does not leave any room for the consideration of cultural aspects. The EEA Agreement recognises the need for strengthening cultural cooperation in Article 13 of Protocol 31. In this respect, it should be recalled that the Authority established in a decision-making practice regarding state aid for film production and film related activities that measures in favour of cinematographic and audiovisual production might be approved on cultural grounds under the application of Article 61(3)(c) of the EEA Agreement, provided that this approach takes the criteria developed by the Commission sufficiently into account and that the approach does not deviate from the Commission's practice prior to the adoption of Article 107(3)(d) TFEU.

The Amsterdam Protocol is again referred to in the Communication by the Commission as an important point of reference for the Member States' competence to have a wide definition of what constitutes public service broadcasting, including a definition that reflects the development and diversification of activities in the digital age and includes audiovisual services on all distribution platforms.[69] This discretion on the part of the Member States limits the role of the Commission to only check for manifest errors as regards the definition of public service broadcasting.[70] Only activities that could not reasonably be considered to meet—in the wording of the Amsterdam Protocol—the 'democratic, social and cultural needs of each society' would constitute a manifest error. That would normally be the case of '*advertising, e-commerce, teleshopping, the use of premium rate numbers in prize games, sponsoring or merchandising*'.[71] Moreover, a manifest error could occur where state aid is used to finance activities that do not bring added value in terms of serving the social, democratic and cultural needs of society. In other words, the Amsterdam Protocol primarily ensures a wide margin of discretion for Member States in defining, organising and financing their public service broadcasting.

As demonstrated from the decisional practice of the Commission, the Amsterdam Protocol is in the EU legal order also used to enhance the powers of the EU institutions. The Commission has subsequently applied this power in proposing measures when exercising its state aid competence to review the organisation and financing of national public service broadcasters.

---

[69] See paragraph 47 in the Communication.

[70] See paragraph 48 in the Communication.

[71] See paragraph 48 in the Communication.

The same wording and the same concerns—but without the reference to the Amsterdam Protocol—are repeated in the Communication from the Authority in paragraphs 47 and 48. Replacing the reference to the Amsterdam Protocol is a reference to Article 59(2) EEA. Thus, where the Member States decided that there was a need to supplement Article 106(2) TFEU (which equals Article 59(2) EEA) with Article 14 TFEU and the Amsterdam Protocol to ensure the Member States' competence in the public broadcasting field, the EEA Agreement relies on the same substantial outcome, referring only to Article 59(2) EEA as the legal basis.

The same occurs in paragraph 54 of the Communication from the Commission regarding the surveillance mechanism.[72] Furthermore, concerning the acceptance of dual funding, the Commission's reference to the Amsterdam Protocol is substituted by a reference to the Council resolution, which refers back to the Amsterdam Protocol, as already demonstrated. On the duty to keep a separation of accounts and avoid cross-subsidisation, the reference to the Amsterdam Protocol is omitted in the Authority's Communication. On the issues of diversification of the public broadcaster and of proportionality and market behaviour, the Authority refers only to Article 59(2) EEA.[73] Regarding anti-competitive behaviour such as price undercutting, the Commission refers to such conduct as infringing the Amsterdam Protocol.[74] In the Authority's Communication, this behaviour infringes Article 59(2) EEA.[75]

13.6.2 *Individual Decisions*

The EFTA Surveillance Authority has opened cases both against Norway and against Iceland on the application of state aid rules to public service broadcasting.[76] In both cases, the Authority proposed a set of appropriate measures to eliminate any incompatible aid; see Decision 306/09/COL[77] on the Norwegian Broadcasting Corporation (NRK) and Decision 38/11/COL[78] on the Icelandic National Broadcasting Service Ríkisútvarpið (RÚV). Dating back to the time before the broadcasting guidelines is also a decision from the Authority regarding a financial contribution to Radio Liechtenstein. In the absence of specific state aid rules for the media sector at the time, the Authority assessed the aid measure under Article 61(3)(c). In the case of Liechtenstein the Authority verified that the aid was necessary to reach objectives not achieved by market forces and recognised the national

[72] Confer paragraph 54 in the Authority's Communication.

[73] Confer paragraphs 84 and 86 in the Authority's Communication.

[74] See paragraph 94 in the Communication.

[75] Confer paragraph 94 in the Authority's Communication.

[76] Case No 48095 (Norway) and Cases No 48094 and 55944 (Iceland).

[77] Decision 8 July 2009.

[78] Decision 9 February 2011.

objectives of promoting media pluralism and media diversity; see Decision No 331/99/COL.[79]

Regarding the case against Norway on the organisation and financing of the NRK, the Authority proposed a number of appropriate measures involving several changes to the company statutes of NRK. The Authority proposed to clarify the public service remit and to establish an *ex ante* entrustment procedure for significant amendments in the public service remit. Such procedure would, in accordance with the guidelines, be based on verifiable criteria in the form of an 'added public value' test. Relevant amendments would therefore undergo scrutiny whereby it should be possible to compare the new service to be launched to offers already existing in the market and to examine any potential restrictions of competition. A change in the remit is considered significant according to the Authority if it is likely to have an impact on the market. In addition to the establishment of a future test, the Authority proposed to the Norwegian Government to instruct the Media Authority to carry out an assessment on the existing public service activities based on the newly adopted statutes.

Furthermore, the appropriate measures included ensuring the independence of the Media Authority and preventing the Norwegian Government from being able to give instructions to the Media Authority in the process of monitoring NRK's compliance with the entrusted public policy remit. There were also proposed requirements to ensure the separation of accounts and avoid cross-subsidisation between the commercial activities of NRK and its public service task.[80]

The Norwegian Government accepted, in a letter dated 13 October 2009 and further correspondence,[81] to implement the appropriate measures to the satisfaction of the Authority. The Authority decided to close the case against Norway in Decision No 36/10/COL.[82]

The Norwegian Media Authority subsequently conducted the *ex ante* entrustment procedure as required. The conclusions were presented in a report that was sent to the Ministry of Culture.[83] Most of NRK's services were considered within the existing public service remit according to the Media Authority even if several competitors disagreed with the outcome. Some services were nevertheless considered problematic.[84] An example is the internet service called ut.no, which provides services in the field of outdoor life and hiking trips. The Media Authority considered for various reasons this service to be outside the public service remit of NRK. The Ministry of Culture nevertheless later approved the service, and it is now in a revised form part of the public broadcasting remit of NRK. Later changes to the public

---

[79] Decision 16 December 1999.

[80] The complete set of proposed measures can be found on pages 46–47 in decision 306/09/COL.

[81] In particular an e-mail dated 23 November 2009.

[82] Decision 3 February 2010.

[83] http://www.medietilsynet.no/Documents/Nyhetsdokumenter/Allmennkringkasting/300610_rapport_nrks_nettjenester.pdf.

[84] For example the planned wildlife internet service from NRK (UT.NO) and also some mobile services, see report from the Media Authority, p. 49.

service remit were also eventually approved even if, for other reasons, they are not all operating.[85]

In summary, the administrative decisions from the Authority regarding the public broadcasting service in Norway through the NRK and the follow-up procedures concurred with the procedures against the EU Member States. Both the definition of the public service remit, in particular regarding new media services, and the financing were altered pursuant to the decisions by the Authority. Furthermore, the compliance procedure was conducted nationally by the Media Authority, and changes were made to the public service remit decided by the Ministry of Culture. The review procedure and the *ex ante* test for new media services undoubtedly had an impact on the innovation mode and expansion incentives of the NRK to move on to new platforms and reach new audiences.

In Iceland, the proposed measures were similar in terms of the requirements of a precise definition of the public remit, a separation between market activities and the public service, the requirements to have an independent media authority and to establish an *ex ante* procedure for future changes to the public service remit to allow for an assessment of anti-competitive effects.[86] In addition, in Iceland, structural changes were made in the organisation and the financing of the RÚV including the abolishment of the unlimited state guarantee in favour of the RÚV. In essence, the whole system of public service broadcasting was more or less changed as a result of the state aid review conducted by the Authority. The Icelandic Authorities accepted all the proposed measures to the satisfaction of the Authority, and the case against Iceland was closed by Decision No 318/13/COL.[87]

13.7 Concluding Observations

The case study in the field of public service broadcasting has demonstrated different legal techniques to ensure the paralleling in the EEA law of EU public broadcasting policy. The paralleling includes enforcing the policies by the Authority regardless of the fact that the Commission's discretionary powers in the state aid review have grown beyond controlling efficiency and functionality of markets to also include safeguarding necessary national interests (including welfare concerns such as media pluralism) and regardless of the legal basis (partly) relied on not being paralleled in the EEA.

This finding adds to the preceding sections to demonstrate how the EEA integration process is moving beyond economic concerns to stay in parallel with the EU integration process. The EEA Agreement lacks the revised constitutional framework for the provision of public services included in EU primary law but continues

[85] One example being Trafikkportalen which was approved by the Ministry of Culture.

[86] See Decisions NO 38/11/COL and 318/13/COL.

[87] Decision 11 September 2013.

to develop in parallel also regarding public services as far as these services analysed here are concerned. This includes the rather extensive powers of the institutions to review national policy choices in the field of public services through the review of financing measures and to some extent to substitute national policies with their own policies also for largely non-economic services.

References

Cremona M (ed) (2011) Market integration and public services in the European Union. Oxford University Press, Oxford, p 5

Craufurd Smith R (2011) The evolution of cultural policy in the European Union in Craig/de Burca, the evolution of EU law. Oxford University Press, Oxford, pp 869–897

Donders K (2015) State aid to public service media: European Commission decisional practice before and after the 2009 broadcasting communication. Eur State Aid Law Q 2015(14):68–87

Gruis V, Elsinga M (2014) Tensions between social housing and EU market regulations. Eur State Aid Law Q 3:463–469

Karlsson HL (2014) Twenty years of Icelandic state aid enforcement. Eur State Aid Law Q 3(2014):470–490

Mastroianni R (2011) Public service media and market integration. In: Cremona M (ed) Market integration and public services in the European Union. Oxford University Press, Oxford, pp 149–178

Prosser T (2005) The limits of competition law: markets and public services, published to Oxford Scholarship online, p 210

Schweitzer H (2011) Services of general economic interest: European law's impact of the role of markets and of member states. In: Cremona M (ed) Market integration and public Services in the European Union. Oxford University Press, Oxford, pp 11–62

Miscellaneous

Report to the President of the European Commission published 9 May 2010, A New Strategy for the Single Market: At the Service of Europe's Economy and Society

Report from the Media Authority, Review of NRK's existing services on new media platforms, 29 June 2010

Stortingsmelding Meld. St.38 (2014-15) Open og opplyst – Allmennkringkasting og mediemangfald

Innst. 178 S (2015-2016) Open og opplyst

Chapter 14
Some Reflections on the EEA Integration Process Extending Deeper Into the Financing of Public Services and Limiting States' Legislative Freedom Through State Aid Rules

Part III has analysed the EEA integration process in the field of financing public services and the state aid provisions. The overall question was the extent to which the EU/EFTA institutions applying EEA law have paralleled the EU legal order in the field of competition and state aid despite the lack of a parallel revised constitutional framework.

Chapter 11 began with a rough outline of the development of public services and the European integration process including the privatisation and de-monopolisation of these services in states. The following chapters were then divided in two distinct sections. Chapter 12 dealt with the case law from the CJEU based on the revised constitutional framework leading to increased protection from free movement and competition law for the provision of state welfare services. The analysed case law from the EFTA Court supported the understanding of similar developments in the EEA integration process paralleling concepts of economic/non-economic activity, the concept of an undertaking as well as the Altmark doctrine.

Chapter 13 dealt with the increased scope of scrutiny through state aid provisions into the provision of state welfare services in particular including almost all social services. A case study was undertaken in the field of a largely non-economic service such as public service broadcasting. The analysed practices from the EFTA Surveillance Authority both in terms of paralleling general guidelines as well as individual cases led to the finding that the EEA integration process includes the same scope of state aid review reaching far into the social domain of the EFTA States and involving the balancing of welfare concerns.

It is demonstrated here that the EFTA Surveillance Authority has, in line with the European Commission's interpretation of Article 107 TFEU, interpreted the prohibition of state aid in the EEA Agreement (Article 61 EEA) as granting wide discretionary powers to the Authority. When applying this power, the Authority has taken on a policymaker role. This role played by the Authority in the EEA arguably exceeds the preventive control system targeted at addressing distortions of competition that had originally been envisioned in the prohibition of state aid in the EEA Agreement.

K. Fløistad, *The EEA Agreement in a Revised EU Framework for Welfare Services*, Studies in European Economic Law and Regulation 13,
https://doi.org/10.1007/978-3-319-95043-3_14

Chapter 15
Final Observations: Concluding Remarks

15.1 Introduction

Originally, in a broad sense, ensuring the optimal market conditions for economic prosperity legitimated the transfer of competences to the EU institutions in the economic field, whereas the social responsibilities were seen to be separate and still remaining as part of national sovereign policies outside the competence of the Union. Treaty revisions in the EU legal order give expression to a different and much more advanced understanding of the concept of market integration. Whereas market integration initially was viewed as separate from socially oriented objectives, the emerging understanding changed to include these concerns as part of the market integration process. The viability of the EU project came to depend on understanding the complexities involved, in particular the need to align the economic and the social dimensions. Hence, market integration simply could not be isolated from other concerns in particular in the welfare field. This considerably more advanced understanding of the market integration process in line with political preferences challenged the original separation of the economic and the social spheres.

This distinction has by no means ceased to exist, and it remains an important dividing line between EU competence and Member States' national sovereignty. However, what has changed significantly is the recognition that the economic dimension and the social protection dimension are significantly more intertwined than the original Treaty of Rome envisaged.

This recognition has led to significant primary law changes in the EU legal order to reflect the kind of market integration and value-based organisation the EU project actually is.

The primary law changes in the EU legal order include both general provisions such as provisions on new aims and values as well as more specific provisions all of which have an impact on concrete legal questions as demonstrated in the institutional

K. Fløistad, *The EEA Agreement in a Revised EU Framework for Welfare Services*, Studies in European Economic Law and Regulation 13,
https://doi.org/10.1007/978-3-319-95043-3_15

practices analysed. With this in mind, this project has sought to identify how the Contracting Parties to the EEA Agreement are affected by the revised EU constitutional framework for welfare services in particular through the EEA principles of dynamism and homogeneity.

The EEA dimension became particularly acute when the revised legal framework in the EU was analysed in terms of new powers of the EU institutions. In other words, given that the revised Treaty provisions include new competences or broader competences to the EU institutions, to what extent was this development paralleled in the EEA integration process? In addition, perhaps unexpected consequences for the EU Member States of a geographical extension of the application of welfare provisions to include the EFTA States—both the territory and the citizens—emerged. With the finding indicating that the EEA integration process includes similar or equal powers to the institutions applying EEA law as well as potential EEA specific obligations on EU Member States in the welfare field, a new dimension must be added to the legal effect of the principles of dynamism and homogeneity and indeed to the EEA integration process itself.

15.2 Findings

15.2.1 Introduction

The main finding of this study is the EEA integration process moving homogenously with the EU integration process in the field of publicly funded welfare services despite significant differences in the legal framework. This finding adds a new element to the supranational character of the EEA Agreement. The EFTA Court has stated that the institutions must remedy the lack of parallel provisions on a case-by-case basis.[1] In the field of welfare integration, this case-by-case approach has thus far favoured the homogenous approach. Significantly, this adds powers to the institutions applying the EEA Agreement in an unprecedented manner.

In the following, this concluding section will first offer observations related to explaining this overall finding based on the sequences of events. Second, the concluding section will focus on the legal techniques as they emerge from the institutional practices that led the EEA integration process in this direction. Finally, the concluding section will offer some thoughts on political implications along with areas for future research.

[1] Case E-15/12 Wahl, paragraph 75.

15.2.2 The Sequences of Events: Applying the Free Movement of Services Provision

The first category of welfare services analysed is publicly financed healthcare services. As demonstrated in Chap. 3, the reasoning of the CJEU in the healthcare cases led to the gradual emergence of a new right for citizens insured in national healthcare systems to effective and speedy medical treatment. Initially, citizens had limited rights more directly linked to free choice of healthcare services operating under market conditions. In subsequent case law, the legal question was less about the freedom to provide and receive healthcare services in a market and more about whether the individual freedom of each patient belonging to a national system of health services could extend to receiving funding from the home state for a treatment abroad instead of receiving the benefits in kind in the home state. Now, the CJEU has ensured that citizens, insured in national healthcare systems, benefit from a right to high-quality healthcare in the home state, but, and if this cannot be achieved, the patients can seek medical treatment in another Member State for which the home state will be liable.

In the case law from the CJEU, the legal basis for rights in the field of healthcare, including in the field of publicly financed healthcare, was the free movement of services provision. As demonstrated, the arguments by the CJEU were built on the primary law right to free movement of services, and the Court interpreted the provision to include rights for the service recipient as well as going beyond potential limitations in the secondary legislation. The Court's case law has, nevertheless, as demonstrated been viewed by a number of academics as based on a commitment to bring the EU closer to its citizens. Greater exportability is arguably best viewed as part of a broader process of constructing a European area of healthcare services protecting the individual patients' rights. This is not the place to engage in the debate on the EU integration process going forward in the social fields.

The point here is rather that even if the outcome of the case law led to an individual right for a non-economically active person comparable to the case law on Union citizenship, the legal basis as expressed by the Court in the case law was always primarily the Treaty provision on free movement of services. The CJEU developed this right in the EU legal order by, on the one hand, finding a 'cross-border element' when a person who is insured under a national healthcare system, but not able to receive adequate healthcare in the home state, has exercised the right under Article 56 TFEU and has sought treatment in another state and, on the other hand, applying the rules of the internal market, in particular now Article 56 to healthcare services covered by national health insurance schemes without paying particular attention to the limitations on state responsibility enshrined in the secondary legislation.

As demonstrated in Chap. 3 (and in Chap. 4 on educational rights), the EFTA Court and the EFTA Surveillance Authority have developed a parallel new right under EEA law for EEA citizens. The manner in which this new right has been created is surprising if one takes into account that, first, EEA law does not apply to purely domestic situations and, second, the EEA Agreement contains neither a parallel provision to Article 35 of the Charter of Fundamental Rights, which states that everyone has the right of access to preventive healthcare and the right to benefit from medical treatment, nor parallel provisions to Articles 20 and 21 on Union citizenship. Furthermore, the EEA Agreement does not distinguish between primary and secondary law comparable to the EU legal order arguably in principle giving more interpretative weight to the limitations in the secondary legislation.

The EFTA institutions managed, nevertheless, to create and develop this new right through relying on the EEA Agreement to develop in step with EU law. It is argued here that this was made possible primarily through the choice of the main legal basis for the CJEU in the healthcare case law to be the free movement of services provision, which is paralleled in the EEA Agreement in Article 36 EEA. This legal basis meant that there were (some) parallel provisions and there was a link to economic activity even if it was distant and somewhat inventive. In contrast, the CJEU case law in other areas of welfare services has ensured individual rights based on primary law provisions not paralleled in the EEA and more clearly moving away from any link to economic activity. However, moving the EEA integration process significantly into the field of welfare services and going beyond the requirements of economic activity or a market link in other areas was facilitated by the choice of legal basis in the EU legal order in the case law in the healthcare sector, a case law which was extensively referred to in later developments of welfare integration.

The same tendency can be identified in the early 'citizenship' case law. The expansive interpretation by the CJEU of rights to social security benefits from both the home and the host state was initially based on a form of economic activity (in the sense that the right was limited to persons with some form of economic activity, workers/self-employed) even if the concept of what constituted economic activity was stretched. Hence, the CJEU increased individual rights through a wide interpretation of what constituted economic activity and through the inclusion of ing rights to welfare benefits not linked to employment. Having already taken these steps the next step of including also the non-economically active movers in the scope of beneficiaries was facilitated. Chapters 6–10 demonstrate how the EU/EFTA institutions applying EEA law paralleled on a case-by case basis free movement, residence and equal treatment rights for the non-economically active persons in the EEA legal order.

The project further identified conflicting consequences stemming from the complex legal construction of the EEA Agreement. The limits to the EEA Joint Committee's competence to update and include changes in EU law into the EEA Agreement has led to a situation where pieces of secondary legislation like the Citizens Directive, the revised coordination regime for social security benefits, the Patient's Rights Directive and State Aid Regulation on SGEI have all been included in the annexes of the Agreement without a parallel incorporation of relevant primary law. The legal situation was made even more complex with the Joint Declaration from the EEA Joint Committee with a statement to the effect that the EEA Agreement does not include Union citizenship or immigration policy when incorporating the Citizens Directive. When the EEA Joint Committee agreed to a compromise and to incorporate all the provisions of the Citizens Directive while at the same time making the reservations in a Joint Declaration the Contracting Parties essentially left it to the EU/EFTA institutions to decide through interpretation what this meant in concrete terms. In some EFTA Court cases the Contracting Parties have relied on the revised EU constitutional framework provisions to secure the state more national legislative freedom.[2] In other EFTA Court cases the Contracting Parties have referred to the revised EU constitutional framework to be outside the scope of the EEA Agreement.[3] In CJEU case law the Member States (UK and Ireland) argued essentially that free movement rights for the non-economically active was not paralleled in the EEA Agreement.[4] The Commission has, however, consistently argued the opposite in the case law.[5] Hence, the Contracting Parties have not demonstrated a consistent approach to guide the institutions applying EEA law on how to reconcile the legal differences between the two legal orders with the principles of dynamism and homogeneity.

The project has demonstrated that the revised constitutional framework in the EU is more favourable to public services. However, by securing guarantees for public services at the EU level in the constitutional texts, the increased application of EU law to public services have also been outlined and legitimised. Hence, the position in the revised EU constitutional framework of competition and state aid law and policy has shifted significantly as a result of the revision processes in the amending treaties. The project has identified the increased political and legislative role of the EFTA Surveillance Authority paralleling that of the Commission. The state aid review is inherently complex and entails a range of political considerations as it evolves to include an increasing number of social services. The balancing of welfare concerns in state aid review requires both legal institutional legitimacy and necessary institutional resources. This new role of the EFTA Surveillance Authority seems to have developed rather unnoticed by the Contracting Parties.

Clearly, the EU/EFTA institutions applying EEA law have been left with a fragmented and unclear legal framework. Their decisions in individual cases may be open to criticism regardless of whether they emphasis a homogenous and dynamic evolvement of EEA law or a more separate and independent EEA path.

[2] See the Norwegian Government's submission in Case E-1/02 referring to the revised primary law provision on equality of sexes and the Icelandic Government's submission in Case E-12/10 referring to several provisions in the Charter of Fundamental Rights.

[3] Both the Icelandic and the Norwegian submissions in Case E-26/13 and the Norwegian Government's submission in Cases E-10/14 and E-28/15.

[4] Case C-341/11 UK v Council, EU:C:2013:589.

[5] This includes all the relevant cases analyse in the EFTA Court and the Case C-341/11 UK v Council, EU:C:2013:589 in the CJEU.

15.2.3 Identified Legal Techniques

This contribution has analysed how the revised constitutional framework of the EU in the field of welfare services has led to a shift in the EU away from being limited to the protection of market integration and economic efficiency to also include other aims and values creating a much broader identity of the Union to ensure the well-being of citizens. This revised constitutional framework has given new powers to the supranational institutions sometimes explicitly expressed[6] and other times more difficult to observe.[7] This book has analysed the question about how the Contracting Parties to the EEA Agreement are affected by the EU's revised constitutional framework in the field of welfare services. The book has engaged in this debate from the point of view of the Treaty revisions that reflect the social concerns of the market integration process. Various legal methodologies and techniques have emerged from the cases studied. The project has identified different ways the EU/EFTA institutions have approached the lack of a revised constitutional framework in the EEA. In the various chapters on different welfare services and the EEA integration process, a range of legal techniques has been identified from the decisions by the EU/EFTA institutions. The consistency lies in the emphasis of always developing the EEA integration process in a homogeneous manner.

One technique identified was to apply indirectly the revised constitutional framework of the EU in an interpretation process of already-existing provisions in the EEA. This technique coincides rather well with common features in judicial reasoning. Hence, even if the CJEU developed rights that relied partly on primary law provisions not paralleled in the EEA Agreement, the EEA institutions were able to apply EEA law provisions (albeit different provisions than the ones relied on by the CJEU) to ensure a homogenous development of the EEA legal order through the flexible judicial process of interpretation.

A more controversial legal technique was identified in situations where the CJEU developed rights that relied exclusively or mainly on primary law provisions not paralleled in the EEA. Hence, this is not the situation where the revised constitutional framework constitutes an interpretative factor for a particular legal outcome or part of the legal basis but a situation where the new legal (primary law) provision is in itself the principle legal basis for a particular legal outcome.[8]

In all the three areas of welfare services studied, it has been argued in this book that this last situation has occurred. Consequently, the institutions applying EEA law have had to render decisions in areas of EEA law where rights, obligations or competences in the EU legal order have been based on a new legal provision that in itself was the legal basis for a particular outcome. To this end, in the area of welfare services the institutions applying EEA law have been faced with the difficulty of

---

[6] An example would be the application of the state aid provisions by the Commission.

[7] An example would be the CJEU's application of the citizenship provisions in the Treaty.

[8] See on this distinction in Fredriksen (2013), pp. 371–399, see Chap. 1 Introduction Sect. 1.6, see also Bjørgvinsson (2014), pp. 263–280.

coupling the principles of dynamism and homogeneity with the lack of a parallel legal framework.

In these situations, as emerges from the project, the institutions have consistently opted for a legal outcome of achieving the same end result in the EEA as in the EU legal order even without a parallel legal framework.

One aspect of achieving this aim identified in all the three areas of welfare services was a legal technique whereby *other* EEA provisions (the word 'other' refers to different provisions than the ones relied on by the CJEU in its decision making in the parallel cases), often secondary law provisions, are applied to achieve the in-substance same legal outcome. The interpretation of these *other* provisions (in the EEA legal order) has necessarily had to be different from how their counterparts in the EU legal framework have been interpreted. In other words, the CJEU has relied on the primary law provisions, because in the Court's view, the *other* provisions, usually secondary law (later relied on by the institutions applying EEA law), have not provided the sufficient legal basis for the chosen outcome. This legal technique by the institutions applying EEA law has led to the rather extraordinary situation of equal provisions in the EEA and EU legal orders being interpreted differently. In other words, this has resulted in the opposite of what is required traditionally by the principle of homogeneity. However, the end result is parallel rights and obligations.

In the healthcare sector, the previous Article 22 in Regulation 1408/71 was in the EU legal order interpreted as not extending to include the export of public funding in the analysed cases. Hence, the CJEU based the legal outcome in the cases on the right of service recipients under primary law, which took precedence based on the primary/secondary law distinction. In the EEA, this limitation of the scope of obligations to export in Article 22 of the Regulation was largely ignored by the EFTA Court for the purpose of applying the free movement of services provision. To this end, the Court was able to develop the EEA integration process in parallel with the EU legal order even without the primary/secondary law distinction being part of the Agreement.

In the case law of social rights of non-economically active moving citizens the Citizens Directive is in the EU legal order interpreted as not applying in the situation of returning nationals, so-called home state obligations. In the EEA legal order, on the contrary, the Directive does, in some instances, apply in this situation. This can be seen in both the Gunnarsson and the Jabbi cases where the applicants could rely on the Directive for rights against their home state even if the situation did not fall within the scope of the Directive as interpreted in the EU legal order. The same legal technique is relied upon by both the EFTA Surveillance Authority and the Commission demonstrated lastly in the Jabbi case regarding the right to family reunification for a non-economically active EEA citizen upon return to her home state.[9]

[9] See written observations from the Commission and the Surveillance Authority and the Report for the Hearing.

In the field of compatible state aid for cultural reasons, Article 107(3)(c) TFEU is interpreted in the EU legal order not to include the cultural exceptions inherent in the new Article 107(3)(d) TFEU. The two provisions are complementary legal bases for finding aid compatible with the internal market. In the EEA legal order, Article 61(3)(c) EEA does not have a supplement, and the provision is therefore interpreted to cover more ground for exception including those that are covered by Article 107(3)(d) TFEU. In addition, various other legal techniques were identified in the section on public service broadcasting to ensure the parallel development for state aid scrutiny of welfare services, in particular to remedy the lack of Article 14 TFEU and the Amsterdam Protocol when adopting the broadcasting guidelines.

One aspect of the institutions having chosen to apply these legal techniques is the difficulty of upholding the interpretative result in the EEA legal order in the situation where the CJEU changes its interpretation of the primary law provisions in the EU legal order. In the opinion of many academics, this is what has happened in the field of social rights for non-economically active citizens.[10] It is argued that the CJEU has moved from a constitutional protection of citizens' rights based on Union citizenship to respecting the boundaries in the secondary legislation and limiting rights to social benefits accordingly in the recent case law.[11] This certainly entails a challenge for the institutions applying EEA law. Are they also to change their interpretation of the secondary legislation 'back' to the original interpretation of the CJEU to ensure a parallel development in the EEA? Giving such force to dynamic homogeneity must be weighed against important counterarguments such as impairment of legal certainty and the denial of legitimate expectations. This reflection illuminates the difficulty facing the EU/EFTA institutions applying EEA law when the institutions are trying to reconcile homogeneity with the lack of parallel provisions. The legal techniques applied by the institutions applying EEA law is questionable in terms of acceptable legal reasoning but also inherently vulnerable and always dependent on the actions of a different and separate entity.

15.3 Reflections: Implications—Future Research

This book is limited to the legal aspects. The book has not taken a normative stance on the way the European integration process has developed to include social concerns in the analysis of the parallel development of the EEA integration process. The book never tried to make the point that European integration, including the EEA integration process, should be limited to the economic sphere. Rather, this author concurs with the broad consensus of the interaction between the economic and the social and the need to recognise this interaction rather than trying to keep

[10] See Cases C-333/13 Dano EU:C:2014:2358 and C-67/14 Alimanovic EU:C:2015:5 and C-308/14, Commission v. UK and Ireland decided 14 June 2016, EU:C:2016:436.

[11] See the earlier referred articles in CML Rev (52) 2015.

them separate. Taking this as a starting point, the author sympathises with the EU/ EFTA institutions applying EEA law in making the various decisions analysed in this book. It is certainly not an easy task to try to ensure a dynamic and homogenous development of the EEA integration process in step with the EU process in the field of adding the social to the economic dimension of market integration without a parallel legal framework.

This author is more concerned with the demonstrated consequences of these institutional choices in terms of the actual transfer of powers to primarily the EFTA institutions in fields not covered by the Agreement. This concern is strengthened by the demonstrated development in a sensitive and highly policy-oriented domain such as the welfare sector. Within finite budgets, decisions on welfare services cannot be made without regard to the impact on different groups in society. Individual cases highlight individual circumstances, and this entails a risk of not bringing in the rights and interests of those others who may be affected by the decision. The balancing act is arguably one in need of a political decision where all relevant factors can be taken into account and decisions can be legitimately made. Courts and surveillance authorities are limited in many ways and provide forums dominated by individual claims and an agenda of furthering integration, which perhaps is not suitable for these difficult balancing acts.

Hence, transferring powers to EU/EFTA institutions in the domain of welfare allocation of limited resources is a complex decision. As a minimum, the institutions with these types of powers must be clearly mandated with the task as well as adequately equipped to make the decisions including with the necessary institutional legitimacy of actually being a policymaker. It is argued here that there has been a lack of transparency of the process as it has evolved. The work done in this project has laid out the legal aspect of the current development.

This book has demonstrated how power has transferred to the EU/EFTA institutions applying EEA law in the field of welfare services. This transfer of powers has not been endorsed by the Contracting Parties to the EEA Agreement in the same manner as in the EU legal order. On the contrary, the book points to several instances where the Contracting Parties have objected to an interpretation of the EEA Agreement whereby such powers have been transferred. It should be added that even if most of the demonstrated transfer of powers under the EEA Agreement is related to the sovereignty of the EFTA States in the field of welfare services, the analysis made in this book also points to possible consequences for EU Member States of a geographically enlarged area of application of the provisions on welfare services. Both the EU and the EFTA side may have (and indeed have had as demonstrated in the case law) significant objections to the transfer of similar powers to the EU/EFTA institutions and similar applicability of welfare rights in the EEA legal order as compared to the EU legal order.

With the extension of Union citizenship rights to include EFTA States nationals and the territory of the EFTA States a new dimension must be added on the extent to which EU Member States' obligations fall to be assessed for compatibility with EEA law. Incorporating 'Union citizen-like protection' for all EEA nationals, including citizens of EFTA States, in the protection already enjoyed by citizens of the Union has potential substantial consequences for individual rights and corresponding states' obligations under EEA law in a sensitive area such as rights to welfare benefits (and family reunification/immigration law).

The rights stemming from Union citizenship are part of increasing and deepening the EU integration process. Free movement rights for individuals detached from market objectives substantiate this Union building. Part of building a Union is also to define the insiders and the outsiders—us and them. Only by this notion can common identities and mutual solidarities develop. On the inside, the citizens should ideally move freely, and therefore, the states have obligations not to create barriers to movement. This mutual obligation between the states is motivated by the creation of a Union but logically cannot extend beyond the territory of this very same Union. Including the same free movement rights to the nationals of EFTA States and in the territory of the EFTA States would therefore arguably go against and not support the conceptual underpinning of creating the status of Union citizenship in the EU legal order.

The main purpose of the project was to make known what has happened, to analyse consequences and to point to relevant concerns. The urgent need for better transparency of the process is the recurring theme in the book. The demonstrated development into the welfare sphere of the EEA Agreement raises several questions of a more political nature, such as the role of EU/EFTA institutions, power allocation and the need for necessary political awareness and discussion at the national political level. Legally, it may be argued that the phenomenon can be easily remedied through a revision of the main part of the EEA Agreement to reflect the state of the law of the EU after the Lisbon Treaty. Thus far, this is also how the topic has been mostly dealt with both by practitioners and by academics, namely as a legal technical question involving a step-by-step approach by the institutions administering the EEA Agreement and ultimately just calling for a technical revision process.[12]

This project demonstrates some of the complexities involved in applying EEA law to welfare services. Even if the courts and the authorities administering the EEA Agreement have effectively paralleled rights and obligations in this area in the past, the political decision to include all or some of these concerns in the EEA Agreement is far from a technical legal question. It involves a range of decisions of a principle nature. Having to take a stance in these complicated questions may not be desired from any of the Contracting Parties to the EEA Agreement. However, refraining from doing so is not an option based on the urgent needs of the institutions that must address the question whenever faced with claims. The EFTA States are not only associated with the EU Member States; they are adapted and arguably almost assimilated into the internal market through the decision making of the EU/EFTA institutions applying the EEA Agreement. This calls for further action on the part of the Contracting Parties to the EEA Agreement.

[12] Fredriksen and Franklin (2015), pp. 629–684.

References

Bjørgvinsson DT (2014) EFTA Court, The EEA and the EFTA Court, chapter 22, Fundamental Rights in EEA Law, pp 263–280

Fredriksen HH (2013) Betydningen av EUs pakt om grunnleggende rettigheter for EØS-retten. Jussens Venner 48:371–399

Fredriksen HH, Franklin CNK (2015) Of pragmatism and principles: the EEA Agreement 20 years on. Common Mark Law Rev 52:629–684

Table of Case Law

EFTA Court

K. Fløistad, *The EEA Agreement in a Revised EU Framework for Welfare Services*, Studies in European Economic Law and Regulation 13,
https://doi.org/10.1007/978-3-319-95043-3

- Case E-2/06, EFTA Surveillance Authority v Kingdom of Norway (The waterfall case), EFTA Ct. Rep. [2007] p 164
- Case E-3/06, Ladbrokes v Government of Norway, EFTA Ct. Rep. [2007] p 86
- Case E-5/06, EFTA Surveillance Authority v The Principality of Liechtenstein, EFTA Ct. Rep. [2007] p 296
- Case E-4/07, Jón Gunnar Þorkelsson and Gildi-lífeyrissjóður, EFTA Ct. Rep. [2008] p 3
- Case E-5/07, Private Barnehagers Landsforbund v EFTA Surveillance Authority, EFTA Ct. Rep. [2008] p 62
- Cases E-9/07 and E-10/07, L'Oréal v Aarskog, EFTA Ct. Rep. [2008] p 258
- Joined Cases E-11/07 and E-1/08, Olga Rindal and Therese Slinning v Staten v/ Dispensasjons - og klagenemnda for bidrag til behandling i utlandet, EFTA Ct. Rep. [2008] p 320
- Case E-12/10, EFTA Surveillance Authority v Iceland, EFTA Ct. Rep. [2011] p 117
- Joined Cases E-14/10 and E-19/13, Konkurrenten v EFTA Surveillance Authority, EFTA Ct. Rep. [2011] p 266
- Case E-15/10, Posten Norge AS v EFTA Surveillance Authority, EFTA Ct. Rep. [2012] p 246
- Case E-1/11, Norwegian appeal board for health personal, Dr A., EFTA Ct. Rep. [2011] p 484
- Case E-2/11, STX Norway Offshore AS m.fl. v Staten v/ Tariffnemnda, EFTA Ct. Rep. [2012] p 4
- Case E-3/11 Sigmarsson v the Central Bank of Iceland, EFTA Ct. Rep. [2011] p 430
- Case E-4/11, Arnulf Clauder, decision 26 July 2011, EFTA Ct. Rep. [2011] p 216
- Joined Cases E-10/11 and 11/11, Hurtigruten v EFTA Surveillance Authority, EFTA Ct. Rep. [2012] p 758
- Case E-16/11, EFTA Surveillance Authority v Iceland (Icesave), EFTA Ct. Rep. [2013] p 4
- Case E-1/12 Den norske forleggerforening v EFTA Surveillance Authority, EFTA Ct. Rep. [2012] p 1040
- Case E-3/12, Staten v/Arbeidsdepartementet v Stig Arne Jonsson, EFTA Ct. Rep. [2013] p 136
- Case E-6/12, EFTA Surveillance Authority v Kingdom of Norway, EFTA Ct. Rep. [2013] p 618
- Case E-8/13, Abelia decided 29 August 2014, not yet published
- Case E-26/13, Icelandic State v Atli Gunnarsson, EFTA Ct. Rep. [2014] p 254
- Case E-10/14, Deveci v Scandinavian Airlines System, EFTA Ct. Rep. [2014] p 1364
- Case E-14/15, Holship v Norsk Transportarbeiderforbund, not yet reported, Decision 19 April 2016
- Case E-28/15, Jabbi v Staten v/Utlendingsnemnda
- Case E-1/06, Synnøve Finden v Staten v/Landbruks- og matdepartementet

Court of Justice of the European Union

- Case 1/72, Frilli, [1972] ECR 667
- Case 155/73, Giuseppe Sacchi, [1974] ECR 40
- Case 207/78, Even, [1979] ECR 2019
- Case 52/79, Debauve, [1980] ECR 833
- Case C-149/79, Commission v Belgium, [1982] ECR 1845
- Case 53/81, Levin, [1982] ECR 1035
- Joined Cases 115/81 and 116/81, Adoui, [2982] ECR 1665
- Case C-283/81, CILFIT, [1982] ECR 3415
- Joined Cases 286/82 and 26/83, Luisi & Carbone, [1984] ECR 377
- Case C-249/83, Hoeckx, [1985] ECR 973
- Case 293/83, Gravier, [1985] ECR 593
- Case 24/86, Blaizot, [1988] ECR 379
- Case 39/86, Lair, [1988] ECR 3161
- Case 197/86, Brown [1988] ECR 3205
- Case 263/86, Humbel, [1988] ECR 5365
- Case 186/87 Cowan, [1989] ECR 195
- Case 196/87, Steymann, [1988] ECR 6159
- Joined cases 389/87 and 390/87, Echternach, [1982] ECR 723
- Case 18/88, RTT, [1991] ECR I-05941
- Case C-260/89, Elliniki Radiophonia, [1991] ECR I-2925
- Case C-357/89, Raulin, [1992] ECR I-1027
- Case C-41/90, Höfner and Elser, [1991] ECR I-1979
- Case C-159/90, Society for the Protection of Unborn Children Ireland, [1991] ECR I-4685
- Case C-370/90, Singh, [1992] ECR I-04265
- Opinion 1/91, European Court Reports 1991 Page I-06079
- Case C-69/91, Decoster, [1993] ECR I-5335
- Joined Cases C-159/91 and 160/91, Poucet and Pistre, [1993] ECR I-637
- Case C-320/91, Corbeau, [1993] ECR I-2523
- Case C-19/92, Kraus, [1993] ECR I-1663
- Case C-109/92, Wirth, [1993] ECR I-6447
- Case C-393/92, Almelo, [1994] ECR I-1477
- Case C-55/94, Gebhard, [1995] ECR I-4165
- Case C-157/94, Commission v Netherlands [1997] ECR I-5699
- Case C-158/94, Commission v Italy [1997] ECR I-5789
- Case C-159/94 Commission v France [1997] ECR I-5815
- Case C-244/94, FFSA, [1995] ECR I-4013
- Case C-18/95, Terhoeve, [1999] ECR I-345
- Case C-70/95, Sodemare, [1997] ECR I-3395
- Case C-120/95, Decker, [1998] ECR I-01831
- Case C-343/95, Porto di Genova, [1997] ECR I-1547
- Case C-67/96, Albany International BV, [1999] ECR I-5751

- Case C-20/96, Snares, [1997] ECR I-6057
- Case C-85/96, Martinez Sala, [1998] ECR I-2691
- Case C-158/96, Kohll, [1998] ECR I-1931
- Case C-297/96, Partridge, [1998] ECR I-3467
- Joined Cases C-115/97 to C-117/97, Brentjens, [1999] ECR I-6025
- Case C-219/97 Drijvende Bokken, [1999] ECR I-6121
- Case C-174/97, FFSA, [1998] ECR I-1303
- Case C-190/98, Graf, [2000] ECR I-493
- Case C-224/98, d'Hoop, [2002] ECR I-06191
- Case C-368/98, Vanbraekel, [2001] ECR I-5363
- Case C-43/99, Leclere, [2001] ECR I-4265
- Case C-157/99, Geraets-Smits and Peerbooms, [2001] ECR I-5473
- Case C-184/99, Grzelczyk, [2001] ECR I-6193
- Case C-215/99, Jauch, [2001] ECR I-1901
- Case C-309/99, Wouters, [2002] ECR I-1577
- Case C-385/99, Müller-Faure, [2003] ECR I-4509
- Case C-413/99, Baumbast, [2002] ECR I-7091
- Case C-60/00, Carpenter, [2002] ECR I-6279
- Case C-218/00, Cisal, [2002] ECR I-691
- Case C-280/00, Altmark, [2003] ECR I-7747
- Case C-56/01, Inizan, [2003] ECR I-12403
- Case C-82/01 P Aéroports de Paris, [2002] ECR I-9297
- Case C-92/01, Stylianakis, [2003] ECR I-1291
- Case C-100/01, Olazabal, [2002] ECR I-10981
- Case C-109/01, Akrich, [2003] ECR I-09607
- Case C-126/01, GEMO, [2003] ECR I-13769
- Joined Cases C-246/01, C-306/01, 354/01 and C-355/01, AOK, [2004] ECR I-2493
- Case C-413/01, Ninni-Orasch, [2003] ECR I-13187
- Joined Cases C-502/01 and C-31/02, Gaumain Cerri and Barth, [2004] ECR I-6483
- Case C-138/02, Collins, [2004] ECR I-2703
- Case C-160/02, Skalka, [2004] ECR I-5613
- Case C-200/02, Zhu and Chen, [2004] ECR I-9925
- Case C-224/02, Pusa, [2004] ECR I-5763
- Case C-456/02, Trojani, [2004] ECR I-7573
- Case C-65/03, Commission v Belgium, [2004] ECR I-6427
- Case C-147/03, Commission v Republic of Austria, [2005] ECR I-5969
- Case C-205/03, FENIN, [2006] ECR-I-6295
- Case C-209/03, Bidar, [2005] ECR I-2119
- Case C-372/04, Watts, [2006] ECR I-4325
- Case C-406/04, Gérald De Cuyper, [2006] ECR I-6947
- Case 520/04, Pirkko Marjatta Turpeinen, [2002] ECR I-70070
- Case C-76/05, Schwarz, [2007] I-6849

- Case C-152/05, Germany, [2008] ECR I-39
- Case C-192/05, Tas-Hagen and Tas, [2006] ECR I-10451
- Case C-291/05, Eind, [2007] ECR I-10719
- Case C-299/05, Commission v Parliament and Council, [2007] ECR I-08695
- Case C-318/05, Commission v Germany [2007] ECR I-6957
- Case 341/05, Laval un Partneri, ECR [2007] I-11767
- Case C-392/05, Alevizos, [2007] ECR I-3505
- Case 438/05, Viking Line, [2007] ECR I-10779
- Case C-444/05, Stamatelaki, [2007] ECR I-3185
- Joined Cases C-11/06 and 12/06, Morgan and Bucher, [2007] ECR I-9161
- Case C-158/07, Förster, [2008] ECR I-08507
- Case C-208/07, von Chamier-Glisczinski, [2009] ECR I-6095
- Case C-228/07, Jørn Petersen, [2008] ECR I-6989
- Joined Cases C-22/08 and 23/08, Vatsouras and Koupatantze, [2009] ECR I-4585
- Case C-127/08, Metock and Others, [2008] ECR I-6241
- Case C-310/08, Ibrahim, [2010] ECR I-1065
- Case C-363/08, Romana Slanina, [2009] ECR I-11111
- Case C-480/08, Teixeira, [2010] ECR I-1107
- Case C-512/08, Commission v France, [2010] ECR I-8833
- Case C-34/09, Gerardo Ruiz Zambrano, [2011] ECR I-01177
- Case C-173/09, Elchinov, [2010] ECR I-8889
- Case C-255/09, Commission v Portugal, [2001] ECR I-10547
- Case C-439/09, McCarthy v Home Department, [2011] ECR I-3375
- Case C-503/09, Lucy Stewart, [2011] ECR I-6497
- Case C-542/09, Netherlands v Commission, EU:C:2012:346
- Joined Cases C-424/10 and 425/10, Zilokowski and Szeja, [2011] ECR I-14035
- Case C-426/11, Alemo-Herron, EU:C:2013:521
- Case C-431/11, UK v Council, EU:C:2013:589
- Case C-523/11 and C-585/11, Prinz and Seeberger, EU:C:2013:524
- Case C-656/11, UK v Council, EU:C:2014:9727
- Case C-46/12, L.N, EU:C:2013:97
- Case C-86/12, Alokpa, EU:C:2013:645
- Case C-140/12, Brey, EU:C:2013:565
- Case C-220/12, Thiele, EU:C:2013:683
- Case C-456/12, O. and B., EU:C:2014:135
- Case 457/12, S. and G., EU:C:2014:136
- Case C-81/13, UK v Council, EU:C:2014:2449
- Case C-202/13, McCarthy, EU:C:2014:2450
- Case C-268/13, Petru, EU:C:2014:2271
- Case C-333/13, Dano, EU:C:2014:23584
- Case C-359/13, Martens, EU:C:2015:118
- Case C-67/14, Alimanovic, EU:C:2015:597
- Case C-308/14, Commission v UK and Ireland, EU:C:2016:436

General Court

- Case T-319/99 FENIN, [2003] ECR II-357
- Case T-289/03 BUPA, [2008] ECR II-81
- Case T-442/03 SIC, [2008] ECR II-1161
- Joined Cases T-309/04, 317/04, 329/04 and 336/04 TV 2 Denmark AS, [2008] ECR II-2935
- Joined Cases T-568/08 and T-573/08, M6, [2010] ECR 2010 II-3397

Opinions of Advocate Generals

- Opinion of Advocate General Fennelly in Case C-70/95, Sodemar, [1997] ECR I-3395
- Opinion of Advocate General Jacobs in Case C-67/96, Albany, [1999] ECR I-5751
- Opinion of Advocate General Jacobs in Case C-274/96 Criminal Proceedings against Bickel and Franz, [1998] ECR I-7637
- Opinion of Advocate General Jacobs in Joined Cases C-115/97 to C- 117/97 Brentjens' and Case C-219/97 Drijvende Bokken, [1999] ECR I-5751
- Opinion of Advocate General Ruiz-Jarabo Colomer in Case C-157/99, Geraets-Smits and Peerbooms, [2001] ECR I-5473
- Opinion of Advocate General Alber in Case C-340/99, TNT Traco, [2001] ECR I-4109
- Opinion of Advocate General Jacob in Case C-475/99, Ambulanz Glöckner, [2001] ECR I-8089
- Opinion of Advocate General Jacobs in Case C-218/00, Cisal, [2002] ECR I-691
- Opinion of Advocate General Jacobs in Case C-126/01, GEMO, [2003] ECR I-13769
- Opinion of Advocate General Jacobs in Joined Cases C-246/01, C-306/01, 354/01 and C-355/01, AOK, [2004] ECR I-2493
- Opinion of Advocate General Jacobs in Case C-147/03, Commission v Austria, [2005] ECR I-5969
- Opinion of Advocate General Geelhoed in Case C-406/04, Gérald De Cuyper, [2006] ECR I-6947
- Opinion of Advocate General Geelhoed in Case C-212/05, Hartmann, [2007] ECR I-06303
- Opinion of Advocate General Maduro in Case C-127/08, Metock and Others, [2008] ECR I-6241
- Opinion of Advocate General Ruiz-Jarabo Colomer in Case C-228/07, Jørn Petersen, [2008] ECR I-6989
- Opinion of Advocate General Jacobs in Case C-218/00, Cisal, [2002] ECR I-691

- Opinion of Advocate General Cruz Villalón in Case C-503/09, Lucy Stewart, [2011] ECR I-6497
- Opinion of Advocate General Sharpston, Case C-359/13, EU:C:2014:2240

Written Observations and Court Reports EFTA Court Litigation (On File with the Author)

E-28/15

- Written observations from the European Commission, 4 February 2016, made public by request
- Report for the Hearing, http://www.eftacourt.int/uploads/tx_nvcases/21_RH_EN.pdf

E-26/13

- Written observations from the EFTA Surveillance Authority, 24 January 2014, made public by request
- Written observations from the European Commission, 28 January 2014, made public by request
- Reply to questions by the Court from the Kingdom of Norway, 9 April 2014
- Written observations from the Icelandic Government, made public only by actually looking through the document when physically at the EFTA Court's premises, 12 June 2015, no copying of document allowed
- Report for the Hearing, http://www.eftacourt.int/uploads/tx_nvcases/26_13_RH_EN.pdf

E-6/12

- Application from the EFTA Surveillance Authority, 18 June 2012
- Written observations by the Norwegian Government, 27 August 2012
- Reply from the EFTA Surveillance Authority, 2 October 2012
- Written observations from the European Commission, 5 November 2012, made public by request
- Rejoinder from the Norwegian Government, 9 November 2012
- Report for the Hearing, http://www.eftacourt.int/uploads/tx_nvcases/6_12_RH_EN.pdf

E-3/12

- Written observations from the EFTA Surveillance Authority, 16 August 2012, made public through decision 17 March 2014
- Written observations from the Norwegian Government, 16 August 2012
- Report for the Hearing, http://www.eftacourt.int/uploads/tx_nvcases/3_12_RH_EN.pdf

E-4/11

- Request for an Advisory Opinion from the Administrative Court, 14 February 2011
- Written observations from the EFTA Surveillance Authority, 29 April 2011, made public through decision 17 March 2014
- Written observations from the European Commission, 2 May 2011, made public by request
- Written observations from the Government of the Principality of Liechtenstein, 2 May 2011
- Written observations from the Dutch Government, 2 May 2011
- Report for the Hearing, http://www.eftacourt.int/uploads/tx_nvcases/4_11_RH_EN.pdf

E-11/07 and 1/08

- Written observations from the EFTA Surveillance Authority, 18 April 2008
- Written observations from the Norwegian Government, 18 April 2008, made public 14 March 2014
- Report for the Hearing, http://www.eftacourt.int/uploads/tx_nvcases/11_07_1_08_Judgment_EN.pdf

E-5/07

- Application from Private Barnehagers Landsforbund (PBL), 4 April 2007, made public 8 October 2014
- Statement of defence from the EFTA Surveillance Authority, 13 June 2007, made public by request 15 September 2014
- Written observations from the European Commission, 16 August 2007, made public by request 6 October 2014
- Reply from PBL, 20 August 2007
- Rejoinder from the EFTA Surveillance Authority, 4 October 2007, made public by request 15 September 2014

- Statement in Intervention from the Norwegian Government, 8 October 2007, made public by request 17 September 2014
- Reply from PBL, 26 October 2007
- Report for the Hearing, http://www.eftacourt.int/uploads/tx_nvcases/5_07_RH_Rev_EN.pdf

E-4/07, Documents Made Public by the EFTA Court 20 June 2014

- Written observations from the plaintiff, 19 June 2007
- Written observations from the defendant, 18 June 2007
- Written observations from the Government of Iceland, 18 June 2007
- Written observations from the EFTA Surveillance Authority, 18 June 2007, made public through decision 19 March 2014
- Written observations from the European Commission, 14 June 2007, made public by request
- Report for the Hearing, http://www.eftacourt.int/uploads/tx_nvcases/4_07_RH_EN.pdf

E-5/06, Documents Made Public by the EFTA Court 20 June 2014

- Application from the EFTA Surveillance Authority, 14 November 2006, made public through decision 4 April 2014
- Defence from the Government of Liechtenstein, 19 January 2007
- Written observations from the United Kingdom, 22 March 2007
- Written observations from the European Commission, 22 March 2007
- *Report for the Hearing,* http://www.eftacourt.int/uploads/tx_nvcases/5_06_RH_EN.pdf

ESA and Government Correspondence in Administrative Cases (On File with the Author)

Cases in the Sector of Education/Student Funding

- Letter from the Ministry of Education and Research to the EFTA Surveillance Authority, 17 August 2015
- Letter from the EFTA Surveillance Authority to the Norwegian Government, 10 July 2015, Case No 69199
- Letter from the EFTA Surveillance Authority to the Norwegian Government, 8 July 2015, Case No 69199
- Letter from the EFTA Surveillance Authority to the Norwegian Government, 17 June 2015, Case No 77396

- Letters from the EFTA Surveillance Authority to the Norwegian Government, 3 June 2015 and 8 May 2015
- Letter from the Ministry of Education and Research to the EFTA Surveillance Authority, 17 March 2015
- Letter from the Ministry of Education and Research to the EFTA Surveillance Authority, 9 October 2014
- Letter from the Ministry of Education and Research to the EFTA Surveillance Authority 2 September 2014, Case No 69199
- Reasoned Opinion, 2 July 2014, Case No 69199
- Letter from the Ministry of Education and Research to the EFTA Surveillance Authority, 1 March 2014, Case No 69199
- Letter of formal notice to the Norwegian Government from the EFTA Surveillance Authority, 6 November 2013, Case No 69199
- Letter of formal notice to the Norwegian Government from the EFTA Surveillance Authority, 15 May 2013
- Letter from the Ministry of Education and Research to the Authority, 30 March 2007
- The EFTA Surveillance Authority's decision regarding safety training in high schools, 267/13/COL on 26 June 2013
- The EFTA Surveillance Authority's decision regarding alleged aid to Nasjonal Digital Læringsarena, case No 68123, 12 October 2011

Cases in the Sector of Social Housing

- Icelandic case
- Decision No. 2013/04/COL
- COL 406/08
- COL 247/11
- COL 364/11
- Norwegian case
- Decision No. 121/00/COL

Cases in the Sector of Patient Mobility and Healthcare

- Supplementary letter from the EFTA Surveillance Authority 3 February 2016, Case No. 72376
- Response by the Norwegian Ministry of Health and Care services 15 August 2015, Case No. 72376
- Letter of formal notice to the Norwegian Government 14 May 2014, Case No. 72376
- The Authority's decision on hospital pharmacies, 460/13/COL on 20 November 2013

Cases in the Sector of Immigration Law/Family Reunification/Non-economically Active Returning Nationals

- Letter from the EFTA Surveillance Authority to the Norwegian Government, 6 February 2016, Case No 76560
- Letter from the Ministry of Labour and Social Affairs to the EFTA Surveillance Authority, 8 October 2015
- Letter from the Ministry of Justice and Public Security to the EFTA Surveillance Authority, 7 September 2015
- Reasoned Opinion 8 July 2015, Case No 73930
- Letter from the EFTA Surveillance Authority to the Norwegian Government, 30 June 2015, Case No 77287
- Letter from the Ministry of Justice and Public Security to the EFTA Surveillance Authority, 27 March 2015
- Letter from the EFTA Surveillance Authority to the Norwegian Government, 6 February 2015, Case No 76560
- Letter from the EFTA Surveillance Authority to the Norwegian Government, 3 February 2015, Case No 76561
- Letter from the Ministry of Labour and Social Affairs to the EFTA Surveillance Authority, 1 December 2014
- Letter from the EFTA Surveillance Authority to the Norwegian Government, 17 July 2014, Case No 74864
- Letter from the Ministry of Justice and Public Security to the EFTA Surveillance Authority, 2 June 2014
- Letter from the EFTA Surveillance Authority to the Norwegian Government, 1 April 2014, Case No 73930, 74207, 74690, 75109, 75136, 75148
- Letter from the Ministry of Labour and Social Affairs to the EFTA Surveillance Authority, 3 March 2014
- Letter from the EFTA Surveillance Authority to the Norwegian Government, 28 January 2014, 74864

Cases in the Broadcasting Sector

- Dec No 306/09/COL Norwegian Broadcasting Corporation (NRK)
- Dec No 36/10/COL Icelandic National Broadcasting Service Ríkisútvarpið (RÚV)
- Dec No 38/11/COL
- Dec No 318/13/COL

Case in the Transport Sector

- Decision by the EFTA Surveillance Authority, No 490/15/COL, 9 December 2015 Hurtigruten

Cases in the Childcare Sector/Export of Child Benefits

- Letter from the EFTA Surveillance Authority to the Norwegian Government, 3 February 2012, Case No 68577
- Letter from the Ministry of Children, Equality and Social Inclusion, 6 October 2011, Case No 68468
- Letter of formal notice, 8 December 2010, Case No 68468
- Reasoned Opinion, 6 July 2011, Case No 68468
- Decision by the EFTA Surveillance Authority 39/07/COL, 27 February 2007 regarding organisation of childcare services in Norway
- Letter from the Ministry of Children, Equality and Social Inclusion, 8 February 2011, Case No 68468
- Decision by the EFTA Surveillance Authority 291/03/COL, 18 December 2003

European Commission Administrative Decisions/ Communications

- Commission decision (EEC) 82/371 IV/29.995 Navewa-Anseau [1982]
- Commission decision E2/2008, 28 October 2009
- Commission decision E5/2005, 26 January 2010
- Commission decision 2012/E paragraph 273–279, 7 May 2014
- Commission Case no SA.32019 (2010/N) Denmark Radio, 23 March 2011
- Communication from the Commission – Implementing the Community Lisbon programme – Social services of general interest in the European Union, COM (2006) 177 final, 26 April 2006
- Green paper on the establishment of the common market for broadcasting, especially by satellite and cable, COM (1984) 300 final, 14 June 1984
- Communication from the Commission, Renewed Social Agenda: Opportunities, Access and Solidarity in 21st Century Europe, COM (2008) 412 final, 2 July 2008
- Report to the President of the European Commission published 9 May 2010, A New Strategy for the Single Market: At the Service of Europe's Economy and Society

Miscellaneous

- Norwegian Labour Law Court (Arbeidsretten) ARD-2002-90
- German Constitutional Court, BVerfG, 30 June 2009, 2, BvE 2/08

Bibliography

Miscellaneous

Stortingsmelding Meld. St 14 (2016–2017) Kommersiell allmennkringkasting
Innst. 178 S (2015–2016) Open og opplyst
Innst. 235 S (2016–2017) Kommersiell allmennkringkasting

K. Fløistad, *The EEA Agreement in a Revised EU Framework for Welfare Services*, Studies in European Economic Law and Regulation 13,
https://doi.org/10.1007/978-3-319-95043-3

The manufacturer's authorised representative in the EU is Springer Nature Customer Service Centre GmbH, Europaplatz 3, 69115 Heidelberg, Germany. If you have any concerns regarding our products, please contact ProductSafety@springernature.com

Printed and bound by CPI Group (UK) Ltd, Croydon, CR0 4YY
30/09/2026
02225659-0009